Salafism in Lebanon

The past two decades have seen an increasing association between Lebanese Salafism and violence, with less attention being paid to Salafis who focus on peaceful proselytization. In reality, it is these Salafis whose influence has dramatically grown since the eruption of the Syrian conflict that profoundly affected Lebanon as well.

Based on extensive fieldwork, Zoltan Pall offers insights into the dynamics of nonviolent Lebanese Salafi groups and examines the importance of transnational links in shaping the trajectory of the movement. In particular, he shows how the internal transformation of Salafism in Kuwait, Qatar, and Saudi Arabia led to the fragmentation of the Lebanese Salafi community. By analyzing Salafism as a network, this book shows how the movement creates and mobilizes material and symbolic resources, and how it contributes to reshaping the structures of authority within the country's Sunni Muslim community.

ZOLTAN PALL is a research fellow at the Middle East Institute at the National University of Singapore, and a former visiting assistant professor at the Gulf University of Science and Technology in Kuwait. He has done fieldwork in the Middle East and Southeast Asia, and taught at universities in the Netherlands, Kuwait, and Indonesia. His main research interests include Salafism, the dynamics of Muslim transnational networks, and Middle East–Southeast Asia relations. He has published academic articles, book chapters, and policy papers on these subjects. Pall's current project focuses on the activities of Kuwaiti Islamic charities in Cambodia and Indonesia.

Cambridge Middle East Studies

Editorial Board

Cambridge Middle East Studies has been established to publish books on the nineteenth- to twenty-first-century Middle East and North Africa. The series offers new and original interpretations of aspects of Middle Eastern societies and their histories. To achieve disciplinary diversity, books are solicited from authors writing in a wide range of fields including history, sociology, anthropology, political science, and political economy. The emphasis is on producing books affording an original approach along theoretical and empirical lines. The series is intended for students and academics, but the more accessible and wide-ranging studies will also appeal to the interested general reader.

A list of books in the series can be found after the index.

Salafism in Lebanon

Local and Transnational Movements

Zoltan Pall

National University of Singapore

CAMBRIDGE
UNIVERSITY PRESS

CAMBRIDGE
UNIVERSITY PRESS

University Printing House, Cambridge CB2 8BS, United Kingdom

One Liberty Plaza, 20th Floor, New York, NY 10006, USA

477 Williamstown Road, Port Melbourne, VIC 3207, Australia

314–321, 3rd Floor, Plot 3, Splendor Forum, Jasola District Centre, New Delhi – 110025, India

79 Anson Road, #06–04/06, Singapore 079906

Cambridge University Press is part of the University of Cambridge.

It furthers the University's mission by disseminating knowledge in the pursuit of education, learning, and research at the highest international levels of excellence.

www.cambridge.org
Information on this title: www.cambridge.org/9781108426886
DOI: 10.1017/9781108551366

First published 2018

Printed in the United Kingdom by Clays, St Ives plc

A catalogue record for this publication is available from the British Library.

Library of Congress Cataloging-in-Publication Data
Names: Pall, Zoltan, author.
Title: Salafism in Lebanon : local and transnational movements / Zoltan Pall, National University of Singapore.
Description: 1 [edition]. | New York : Cambridge University Press, 2018. | Includes bibliographical references and index.
Identifiers: LCCN 2017056434 | ISBN 9781108426886 (hardback : alk. paper) | ISBN 9781108446099 (pbk. : alk. paper)
Subjects: LCSH: Salafiyah–Lebanon.
Classification: LCC BP195.S18 P355 2018 | DDC 297.8/3–dc23
LC record available at https://lccn.loc.gov/2017056434

ISBN 978-1-108-42688-6 Hardback

Contents

Acknowledgments

The idea of conducting the research that led to the writing of this book came when I was working in Lebanon as the foreign correspondent of the Hungarian daily *Népszabadság* in the mid-2000s. While wandering the streets of the Northern Lebanese city of Tripoli and its surrounding areas, I discovered that many well-respected preachers and imams of mosques had adopted the Salafi creed and methodology. Their discourses and views on different religious and worldly matters were echoed by young Sunni Muslims whom I encountered in the city's coffee stands and cafes. My discussions with Salafi religious specialists and their constituency revealed a dynamic and discursively diverse movement with myriad connections to the outside world, especially to the Persian Gulf and Europe. My curiosity to observe the evolution of Salafism in Lebanon's multisectarian sociopolitical context led me to leave journalism and engage with academic research.

Many people provided support in my nine-year journey to finalize this manuscript. I am especially grateful to my former supervisor Professor Martin van Bruinessen, whose constructive suggestions and critical comments helped me tremendously during my years as a Ph.D. candidate at Utrecht University. The late Professor Peter Sluglett gave me invaluable advice and comments while turning my doctoral dissertation into a monograph as a research fellow at the Middle East Institute, National University of Singapore. I am thankful to Katayoun Shafei and Annabelle Boetcher, who commented on several draft chapters of this book. I greatly benefited from discussions with the following people: Martijn de Koning, Joas Wagemakers, Carmen Becker, Din Wahid, Nisha Mary Matthews, Roel Meijer, Noorhaidi Hasan, Engseng Ho, Mohamed-Ali Adraoui, Michael Feener, Asef Bayat, and Gwenn Okruhlik.

The generous financial support that I received from the Middle East Institute at the National University of Singapore, the Netherlands Interuniversity School for Islamic Studies (NISIS), and the International

Institute for the Study of Islam in the Modern World (ISIM) was invaluable for me to be able to conduct my research.

I cannot express enough gratitude to the hundreds of Lebanese, Kuwaiti, and Qatari Salafis and non-Salafis who assisted me during my fieldwork. Among them, I would like to mention Shaykh Muhammad 'Abd al-Ghani and Shaykh Haitham al-Sa'id, who granted me their trust and provided me with deep insight into the internal dynamics of Salafism. I would like to thank Shaykh Safwan al-Za'bi, who connected me with many Lebanese Salafis and helped me to establish my social network among the Salafi community in Kuwait. Shaykh 'Imad Mulabbas and his family hosted me in Wadi Khalid in North Lebanon many times, and made it possible for me to observe the expansion of Salafism in this unique and still secluded region. Sami al-Adwani often spent hours and sometimes days with me discussing the dynamics of Kuwait's Islamic scene and its linkages to Lebanon. His help to connect dozens of people from various segments of Kuwaiti society was tremendous.

Last but not least, I would like to thank the expert help and invaluable advice of Cambridge University Press' editors and staff including Maria Marsh, Charles Tripp, William Hammell, and Cassi Roberts.

Introduction

During the autumn of 2009, I had a discussion with a few young, long bearded Salafi preachers dressed in robes that did not reach beyond their ankles and a handful of local men in a bakery in the Mina district of the Northern Lebanese city of Tripoli. After the preachers had left, I referred to them as Salafis, representatives of a puritan Sunni Islamic movement that intends to return to the morality and belief of the first Muslims, in front of the locals. The locals expressed astonishment; one of them told me: "*Wallahi hol shabab tayyibin-tayyibin, ma 'araft annon Salafiyya!* [I swear to God, those guys are very good people, I didn't know they were Salafis]." At the time, the term "Salafism" had negative connotations.

The three preachers were well-known in the neighborhood for their personal piety and for providing religious consultation and conflict mediation to the members of the local communities. No one would ever connect them to any violent acts, and people commonly associated Salafism with violence. In the 1990s and 2000s, Salafist Jihadi groups had gained prominence in the Lebanon by causing a number of violent incidents, such as the Battle of al-Dinniya in 1999 and the Battle of Nahr al-Barid in 2007.

During the first of these battles, the Lebanese army and an armed Salafi group in the mountainous Sir al-Dinniya region near Tripoli clashed on New Year's Eve 1999. Bassam al-Kanj, a veteran Jihadi with combat experience in Afghanistan, set up a training camp to prepare and send fighters to Chechnya. The army's final besiegement of the camp left thirty people dead.[1] The three-months long fighting in Nahr al-Barid Palestinian refugee camp on the outskirts of Tripoli between May and September 2007 led to even more casualties. In the battle between the *Fath al-Islam*, an al-Qaida-inspired militant organization,

---

[1] Bernard Rougier, *Everyday Jihad*. Cambridge and London: Harvard University Press, 2007, pp. 229–266.

1

and the Lebanese army, around 600 people died and tens of thousands of people were displaced.[2]

Many press reports appeared also on '*Usbat al-Ansar*, another Jihadi group that controlled areas in 'Ayn al-Hilwa Palestinian camp near the southern city of Sidon.[3] Since the jurisdiction of the Lebanese authorities does not extend to the Palestinian refugee camps, the group could emerge in the 1990s as one of the most powerful forces of 'Ayn al-Hilwa, and they rivalled the major Palestinian factions such as Fatah and Hamas.[4] In short, due to the prominence of Jihadi Salafism in Lebanon's political events, the label "Salafism" was almost exclusively associated with Jihadi Salafism.

The majority of Salafis who carried out peaceful proselytization did not appear in the Lebanese public sphere that frequently. This is despite the fact that they made up the majority of Lebanese Salafism, constituting ideologically diverse networks with dense linkages to the Arabian Gulf and Europe. As my anecdote demonstrates, people were not aware that some of the preachers were Salafis. Many of the latter also did not use the label very often because of the negative connotation attached to it. Some Salafis argue that Salafis simply follow the original and uncorrupted form of Islam, therefore another label than Muslim is not necessary.

The situation changed radically after the 2010–2011 Arab Uprisings. Although the protest movement that emerged in Lebanon was too modest in scale to bring down the sectarian-based regime, the wave of revolutions in the region has nevertheless had a severe sociopolitical impact that contributed to the rise of nonviolent Salafi groups. During my visits in 2011 and 2012, I observed that the movement's activists were increasingly participating in managing the affairs of local communities. In Tripoli's al-Tabbana district, leading Salafi figures established a con-sultative council (*shūra* in Arabic) to discuss local issues such as social welfare, the hosting of the constantly increasing numbers of Syrian refugees, and political action to free prisoners who are being held by the Lebanese authorities without trial and accused of "terrorism."

Some prominent Salafi shaykhs, with the leadership of Salim al-Rafi'i and Zakariyya al-Masri, openly challenged the authority of Dar al-Fatwa

---

[2] See this series of reports: "The Story of Nahr al-Bared," NOW, October 10, 2007, https://now.mmedia.me/lb/en/commentaryanalysis/the_story_of_nahr_al-bared (accessed December 28, 2016).

[3] "Za'im 'Usbat al-Ansar bi-Lubnan Yatahaddath 'an al-'alaqa ma'al-Qa'ida," *al-'Arabiyya*, June 17, 2007. www.alarabiya.net/articles/2007/06/17/35582.html (accessed November 7, 2010).

[4] Rougier, *Everyday Jihad*, pp. 143–169.

when they joined and filled leading positions in *Hay'at 'Ulama'*
al-Muslimin (League of Muslim Scholars). The League was created in
2011 and included religious scholars *('ulama')* mainly from the Salafi
movement and the Lebanese Muslim Brothers *(al-Jama'a al-Islamiyya)*.
It claims to represent the majority of the Sunni *'ulama'*, and issues
statements and *fatawa* (nonbinding legal opinions) relating to many
of the most important concerns of the Sunni community. In fact, some
analysts regard it as a "counter-Dar al-Fatwa."[5] Both the international
and local media have paid significant attention to the Salafi ascend-
ancy in North Lebanon.[6] Salafi personalities are frequent guests on
Beirut-based TV channels' political programs. While previously perhaps the only publicly known Lebanese Salafi personality was Shaykh
Da'i al-Islam al-Shahhal, the head of the oldest Lebanese Salafi organization, *Jama'iyyat al-Hidaya wa-l-Ihsan* (Guidance and Charity Society –
GCS), today many Lebanese know about other leading Salafi figures
such as the Tripolitan shaykhs Salim al-Rafi'i, Zakariyya al-Masri and
Ra'id Hulayhil.

This book traces the evolution and dynamics of non-Jihadi Salafi
groups in Lebanon. Throughout the monograph I use the term Salafi
to refer to nonviolent groups unless indicated otherwise. The historical dynamics of Salafism globally have been crucial in shaping the
structure of the Lebanese Salafi scene due to its dense transnational
linkages, especially to the Arabian Gulf. Therefore, I will provide
insights into how both the global split of Salafism into a politically
quietist (which later I call purist) and activist (or in Arabic *haraki*)
faction and the internal transformation of the movement in Kuwait,
Qatar, and Saudi Arabia led to the fragmentation of the Lebanese
Salafi community. Schisms at the transnational level have led to the
emergence of the purist–*haraki* dichotomy in Lebanon as well. I will
also discuss how and why the *haraki* faction emerged as predominant
in the post–Arab Uprisings period. Transnational charities that support Lebanese Salafi groups played imperative roles in these developments. Therefore, I put special emphasis on examining the linkages of
the latter, especially the Kuwaiti *Jama'iyyat Ihya' al-Turath al-Islami*

---

[5] "Radical mosques pose challenge for Dar al-Fatwa," *The Daily Star*, February 21, 2015,
www.dailystar.com.lb/News/Lebanon-News/2015/Feb-21/288240-radical-mosques-
pose-challenge-for-dar-al-fatwa.ashx (accessed October 17, 2015).
[6] Wassim Mroueh, "Salafism gains ground in Lebanon over Syria," *The Daily Star*, August
22, 2013; Hashem Osseiran, "Lebanon's Salafists poised for parliamentary polls?"
The Arab Weekly, November 27, 2016, www.thearabweekly.com/?wrid=156 (accessed
December 20, 2016).

(Society for the Revival of Islamic Heritage – SRIH) and the Qatari Mu'assasat al-Shaykh 'Aid al-Khayriyya (Shaykh 'Aid Charity Foundation – SACF) to the Lebanese Salafi scene.

After taking a closer look at the historical trajectory of Lebanese Salafism, the second focus of this monograph is explaining how these Salafi groups establish their authority, create and mobilize symbolic and material resources, and attract their followers. I will do so by analyzing the movement's internal structure, and explain how Lebanese Salafis constitute collectivities and what their transnational ties look like. Lebanese Salafis have strong local roots and were not planted by the Gulf countries; nevertheless, charities and private donors from Kuwait, Qatar, and Saudi Arabia have been crucial in facilitating the expansion of the movement. Money that Lebanese Salafi shaykhs received from the Gulf enabled them to build religious infrastructure and provide financial assistance to their followers. Scholarships from the Gulf States made it possible for many Lebanese Salafis to pursue their studies at the Islamic University of Medina or other Saudi Islamic higher educational institutions. This is why part of the book examines the structure of Lebanese Salafism not only locally but also in a transnational context.

I.1   The Rise of Salafism

Since the Arab Spring, Salafism has increased its presence on the sociopolitical map of the Middle East. While the authoritarian regimes in Cairo and Tunis had limited their options and often repressed them, the activism of Salafis reached an unprecedented level after state control had been lifted in 2011. In Egypt, for example, besides increasing proselytization in the mosques, universities, and the media, Salafi parties formed the second largest parliamentary block. Salafism remained a relevant force in the country even after the coup on July 3, 2013 when the army overthrew President Muhammad Mursi, who had been delegated by the Muslim Brotherhood. Even in countries where the ruling system did not collapse during the Arab Spring, many people started to see Salafis as a potential alternative to their Sunni Muslim leaders. This is an important factor and is one reason, among others, why Lebanon is currently experiencing a Salafi upsurge.

The Syrian uprising and civil war have affected Lebanon severely. As its neighbor gradually sank into the abyss of civil war after the spring of 2011, the Lebanese economy suffered heavy losses, as it is largely dependent on Syrian imports and exports. As a result, tourists and investors, mainly from the Gulf countries, also tend to avoid the country, exacerbating an already severe financial crisis. The influx of more than a million Syrian refugees has also added to Lebanon's socioeconomic instability.[7]

The deepening political divisions resulting from the events in Syria, however, have posed a bigger threat to Lebanon than the worsening economic conditions. Syria, which occupied the country between 1976 and 2005 and dominated its political and economic life, has long-term allies among the country's fragmented political elite. Since the 1980s, Hizbullah, the Shi'ite Islamist militia and political party, has enjoyed the protection of the Syrian government, first that of President Hafiz al-Assad and then later his son, Bashar. Other forces, such as the Shi'ite AMAL (*Lebanese Resistance Battalions – Afwaj al-Muqawwama al-Lubnaniyya*) movement, and the secular Syrian Social Nationalist Party, all forged strong relationships with the Syrian regime. Michel 'Awn's Christian Free Patriotic Movement[8] joined this alliance, which is also called March 8 block,[9] after the 2005 Syrian withdrawal. These groups are largely dependent on Syrian patronage to maintain their local influence and ensure their long-term survival.

The hostility felt by Lebanese opponents of the government in Damascus toward the Assad clan reaches back several decades. The leading force in this camp is the predominantly Sunni Muslim Future Movement (*Tayyar al-Mustaqbal*), which is dominated by the Hariri family. Walid Jumblat's mainly Druze Progressive Socialist Party and the two Maronite Christian parties, the Phalangists and Samir Ja'ja''s Lebanese Forces, are also important elements of this coalition, which is commonly referred to as March 14 block.[10] Since 2005, when the Syrian occupation ended, the positions of the pro- and anti-Syrian camps have hardened, and have often culminated in political deadlocks and crises. Today, the various

---

[7] "UNHCR: Syrian refugees cross four million mark," *Al Jazeera English*, July 9, 2015, www.aljazeera.com/news/2015/07/unhcr-syrian-refugees-4-million-150709033023489 .html (accessed July 10, 2015).

[8] Michel 'Awn had been a long-time foe of Syria since the Lebanese Civil War. However, when he abandoned the anti-Syrian block in 2005 and allied with Hizbullah in the following year, he became closer to the Assad regime. Since the outbreak of the Syrian civil war in 2011, 'Awn has openly supported the Assad regime many times.
    "Aoun defends Hezbollah's involvement in Syria Civil War," *Ya Libnan*, May 19, 2013. www.yalibnan.com/2013/05/19/aoun-defends-hezbollahs-involvement-in-syria-civil-war/ (accessed June 28, 2013).

[9] March 8 is a reference to a demonstration on March 8, 2005 in Beirut organized by the allies of Syria to show their support to Damascus even after the announcement of the withdrawal of the Syrian army.

[10] March 14 is a reference to an anti-Syrian mass demonstration in Beirut on March 14, 2005.

Lebanese factions are providing political, material, and even armed support both to the Syrian government and to the opposition.

The opposition of these two camps has led to a political deadlock that lasted more than two years. After the end of Michel Suleiman's presidency in May 2014, Lebanese voters have been unable to elect a new president until the end of 2016, when Michel 'Awn became the new head of state due to a compromise between the two camps.[11] This political feud led to the near paralysis of many state institutions, and resulted in a dire economic crisis and social instability. The Lebanese security forces were unable to establish control in most areas along the Syrian border, which are currently dominated by militant groups such as *Jabhat Fath al-Sham* (Front for the Conquest of the Levant), formerly known as *Jabhat al-Nusra* (al-Nusra Front), and the Islamic State.

The political conflict in Syria is also reflected in the sectarian tensions within Lebanese society. The majority of the Shi'i community (approximately 30–35 percent of the population) supports the Assad regime, while most Sunnis (25–30 percent of the Lebanese) are on the side of the by now extremely fragmented opposition. In recent years, Sunni–Shi'i sectarianism has often culminated in violence and armed confrontations. In 2013–2014, suicide bombings and other attacks were carried out by Sunni militants in Shi'i neighborhoods. Militants allegedly close to Hizbullah blew up Sunni mosques in Tripoli in August 2013.[12] While Shi'i militants belonging to Hizbullah have crossed the border and joined the forces of the 'Alawi[13]-dominated Assad regime, Lebanese Sunnis are fighting alongside the predominantly Sunni opposition. Between April and June 2013, hundreds of Hizbullah fighters aided the Syrian army in the siege of al-Qusayr, a rebel stronghold. The opposition forces consisted of some Lebanese Sunnis, mostly from the North.

In the midst of this sectarian upheaval, Lebanon's Sunni community is facing an intensifying leadership crisis. The dominance of political patrons (*zu'ama*) over Sunni Muslims has waned since the Arab Uprisings. Sa'd al-Hariri – the son of the murdered ex-prime minister Rafiq

---

[11] "Michel Aoun elected president of Lebanon," *Aljazeera*, October 31, 2016. www.aljazeera.com/news/2016/10/michel-aoun-elected-president-lebanon-161031105331767.html (accessed November 1, 2016).

[12] Fernande van Tets, "Lebanon: Death toll in twin mosques bombings in Tripoli rises to 47," *Independent*, August 24, 2013, www.independent.co.uk/news/world/middle-east/lebanon-death-toll-in-twin-mosques-bombings-in-tripoli-rises-to-47-8782812.html (accessed November 13, 2016).

[13] 'Alawis are considered an offshoot of Shi'i Islam. Their proportion in the Syrian population is approximately 8–10 percent. The majority of 'Alawis originate from the northwest coastal regions.

al-Hariri and the head of the Future Movement – who was regarded as the leader of the Sunni community after the 2005 Syrian withdrawal, has lost much of his authority. As prime minister, he was unable to hold his governing coalition together after the 2009 elections. In 2011, the al-Hariri government was brought down due to a series of internal disputes. In the eyes of Lebanese Sunnis, Hariri's inability to hold on to power was proof of his weak leadership skills. His lack of charisma increased the disappointment of the community. Moreover, he proved unable to fulfill any of his key promises, namely removing the weapons of Hizbullah and reinforcing the state's dominance over the entire territory of Lebanon. Hariri's successor, the more charismatic Najib Miqati, also could not unite the Sunnis under his leadership because he agreed to form a political alliance with Hizbullah, and thus was regarded as a traitor by many. Although Miqati resigned in 2013 due to disagreements with the March 8 block, during the reign of the government of Tammam Salam, a scion of a traditional Beiruti Sunni notable family, the authority of the zu'ama' did not reemerge. Internal divisions also undermined the credibility of the Future Movement.[14] At the end of 2016, Hariri returned to power and became prime minister again, but it is not yet clear at the time of writing in December 2016 if his authority will recover to the 2005 level.

Many of those who lost faith in traditional Lebanese Sunni community leaders started looking for alternatives. Some expressed sympathy or joined the Nusra Front (*Jabhat al-Nusra*) or even the Islamic State. Others rallied behind Ahmad al-Asir, a notorious cleric from Sidon, whose fierce sectarian rhetoric attracted thousands.[15] The majority, however, especially in the northern regions of the country, where the majority of the Sunnis live, sympathized with Salafi preachers, who mostly advocated peaceful means of activism.

Salafis have thrived since the eruption of the Syrian conflict. The sermons of Salafi preachers, who disseminate harsh anti-Shi'i messages and associate Hizbullah and the Assad regime with a global Shi'i conspiracy, have become increasingly popular. Salafi scholars are becoming the most influential religious authorities in the northern Sunni community, especially in Tripoli, the region's capital, where they have become

---

[14] The most notable of these divisions emerged at the beginning of 2016 between Sa'd al-Hariri and ex-Justice Minister Ashraf Rifi, "Khilaf 'Alani bayn al-Hariri wa-Rifi … 'Asifa bi-bayt al-Mustaqbal," *al-'Arabi*, February 12, 2016. https://arabi21.com/story/887179 (accessed March 18, 2016).

[15] Nour Samaha, 'Who Is Lebanon's Ahmed al-Assir?' *Al Jazeera English*, June 26, 2013, www.aljazeera.com/indepth/features/2013/06/2013625202928536151.html (accessed June 27, 2013).

visible everywhere. Increasing numbers of young men are choosing to give up their secular lifestyles and adopt a Salafi way of life. Many of those who had previously worn fashionable clothes, enjoyed Western and Arabic popular music, and consumed alcohol, now wore proper Islamic dress and grew their beards. Also, the popularity of Salafi religious lessons in mosques has risen sharply since 2011. More and more regular or ordinary believers are seeking advice and religious services from Salafi shaykhs rather than going to the *'ulama'* (religious scholars) of Dar al-Fatwa, the official religious institution of Sunni Islam in Lebanon.[16]

I.2   Sunni Movements and Religious Actors in Lebanon

Historically, Lebanon has been at the intersection of a transnational flow of ideas, and therefore many Sunni Islamic intellectual trends and movements that appeared in the Middle East in the twentieth century took root in the country.

Since its establishment in 1931, Dar al-Fatwa, headed by the Mufti of the Republic, has served as the institutional authority and supervising body of Sunni religious life in Lebanon. The institution is a part of the state administration and issues religious rulings and supervises religious institutions, such as mosques and charity endowments. Traditionally, most of Dar al-Fatwa's officials received their education at one of the major Middle Eastern Islamic educational centers, such as al-Azhar in Cairo, and most of them adopted one of the traditional schools of jurisprudence: mainly the Shafi'i and the Hanafi.

Dar al-Fatwa has to share the Sunni religious domain with various Islamic movements. Sufi orders are the oldest of the latter that have been present in the area for hundreds of years.[17] Sufis have many orientations ranging from text-based approaches to approaches that exempt their more advanced members from following the basic rulings of Islam (such as prayer or the prohibition of alcohol). What they have in common though, are their striving for a personal engagement with and experience of the divine.[18] Sufis commonly organize in orders

---

[16] Throughout this book I will use the term "ordinary believers" to refer to regular or everyday Muslims who cannot be considered as participants of any Islamic movements.

[17] Daphne Habibis, "Change and Continuity: A Sufi Order in Contemporary Lebanon," *Social Analysis*, 31, no. 2 (1992), pp. 46–47.

[18] William C. Chittick, "Sufi Thought and Practice." In *The Oxford Encyclopedia of the Islamic World*, vol. 5., edited by John L. Esposito. Oxford: Oxford University Press, 2009.

(*tariqa*) around a shaykh who is believed to have reached considerable spiritual advancement. While Sufi orders generally have declined in Lebanon, two orders, the *Naqshbandiyya* and the *Qadiriyya* are still strong, especially in the North.

The Lebanese branch of the Muslim Brotherhood, *al-Jama'a al-Islamiyya* (Islamic group – IG) was officially established in 1964. Its founder and first leader, Fathi Yakan (1933–2009), was among the internationally most influential ideologues of the Brotherhood.[19] The Brotherhood's main goal at the time of its founding stopping the "westernization" of Lebanese Sunnis and "making Islam the center of their identity."[20] For this, IG gradually built up a network of charities and schools that expanded into many Sunni-inhabited areas of the country. After the end of the civil war, IG regularly participated in parliamentary politics, but won only a few seats.[21] After the 2005 Syrian withdrawal, IG sided with the March 14 camp, which led to the split of Fathi Yakan and dozens of his supporters. Yakan, who had close relations to the Assad regime established a new, pro-March 8 Islamic movement, *Jabhat al-'Amal al-Islami* (Islamic Action Front IAF) in 2006, which, due to the anti-Syrian popular sentiment of the time among the Sunni Lebanese, remained marginal.[22]

Another movement that had a profound impact on Lebanon's Sunni Islamic scene is *Jama'iyyat al-Mashar'i al-Khayriyya* (Association of Charitable Projects) or *al-Ahbash* (Ethiopians) as people commonly refer to it. The name is a reference to the movement's founder 'Abdullah al-Harari (1910–2008), who was of Ethiopian origin. Al-Ahbash emerged in the 1960s but appeared as an influential movement in the midst of the civil war in the 1980s, when it managed to control several neighborhoods in Beirut. Al-Ahbash refer to themselves as a Sufi-inspired movement that follows Shafi'i jurisprudence, and generally oppose the ideologies of the Muslim Brotherhood and Salafism. In the 1990s, an often violent competition erupted between al-Ahbash on one side and IG and the Salafis on the other. Until the end of the Syrian occupation, the movement enjoyed the support of the regime in Damascus and had a cordial relationship with Hizbullah. These connections were helpful to expand

---

[19] While Fathi Yakan is neglected by academics, several young and middle-aged members of the Kuwaiti and Sudanese Muslim Brotherhood told me that they grew up studying his books. Series of informal conversations, Kuwait, January 2012 and January–June 2016.

[20] Interview with Ibrahim al-Masri, Beirut, July 7, 2008.

[21] Three seats in 1992 and one in 1996.

[22] Omayma Abdel-Latif, "Lebanon's Sunni Islamists – A Growing Force," *Carnegie Papers*, January 2008, pp. 9–10.

their control over several mosques and Islamic institutions. Al-Ahbash attracted many middle-class members, who voted for the candidates of the movement during parliamentary elections.[23] After 2005, public sentiment among the Sunni community turned against those who were regarded as allies of the Assad regime. This led to the rapid decrease of al-Ahbash's popularity in Lebanon.

Jama'at al-Tabligh (or al-Tabligh as local Lebanese refer to it), a prose-lytization movement that focuses on personal piety, was founded by Muhammad Iliyas (1885–1944) in British India in the 1920s, and gained a foothold in Lebanon in the 1970s. Al-Tabligh is hierarchically organ-ized, and each member has to spend three days of the month on a proselytizing tour *(khuruj)*.[24] Perhaps the most important center of the movement is the *Tinal* mosque in Tripoli. Al-Tabligh is present almost everywhere in the Sunni-inhabited areas of Lebanon. Yet, it is difficult to estimate how many followers the movement has, and how influential it is. In some of the more traditional neighborhoods of Tripoli, such as al-Qubba, Abu Samra, and some parts of al-Mina, many inhabitants are aware of the presence of the movement and talk rather positively about them, but few actually join their activities.[25]

Among the oldest Islamic movements of Lebanon is *Hizb al-Tahrir al-Islami* (Islamic Liberation Party – ILP). ILP was founded by the Palestinian Taqi al-Din al-Nabhani (1910–1973) in 1952 in East Jerusa-lem. The party's main message is the necessity of the unification of the Muslim world through the reestablishment of the Caliphate. Unlike the previously discussed movements, ILP does not have char-ity or proselytization activities. Instead, it spreads its political message through publications, organizing conferences, reading groups, and, occasionally, demonstrations.[26] ILP has been present in Lebanon since the 1950s. The country serves as one of the most important inter-national centers of the movement since its media office is located in Beirut. Despite this, similarly to al-Tabligh, it is difficult to estimate the size of ILP. In an interview in 2009, a Lebanese Palestinian ILP member claimed that the party has 4000 active members.[27] This seems

---

[23] A. Nizar Hamzeh and R. Hrair Dekmejian, "A Sufi Response to Political Islamism: al-Ahbash of Lebanon," *International Journal of Middle East Studies*, 28, no. 2 (1996), p. 226.

[24] Abdul Ghany Imad, "A Topography of Sunni Islamic Organizations and Movements in Lebanon," *Contemporary Arab Affairs*, 2, no. 1 (2009), pp. 157–158.

[25] Personal observation during my fieldwork between 2009 and 2012.

[26] Imad, "A Topography of Sunni Islamic Organizations," pp. 152–156.

[27] Interview, al-Baddawi refugee camp, October 24, 2009.

to be an exaggeration, considering that ILP is not able to mobilize more than dozens for its public demonstrations.[28]

Finally, there is *Harakat al-Tawhid al-Islami* (Islamic Unification Movement – IUM), which appeared in wartime Tripoli in the early 1980s, after unifying a number of Islamist and secular militias. It managed to rule the city until the Syrian army defeated its fighters in 1985. As Raphael Lefevre explains, IUM's founder, Sa'id Sha'ban, was inspired by some of the chief ideologues of the Muslim Brotherhood, mainly Sayyid Qutb (1906–1966) and Sa'id Hawwa (1935–1989).[29] Today, IUM stands with the March 8 camp; it is suspected to receive financial support and arms from Hizbullah, and serves as the latter's proxy in Tripoli. Its popular support is limited though, and it has no activities beyond the city.

In this contested religious field, Salafism had to find a niche. In many respects, it became more attractive than most of the previously mentioned movements. As this book will show, several of my interviewees used to be active in one or more of the previously mentioned movements before becoming committed Salafis.

I.3   Literature on Lebanese Salafism

The literature on Salafism as a global phenomenon has been burgeoning in the past one and a half decades. Scholars have extensively focused on Salafi ideology and religious discourses.[30] There are some excellent works that discuss the historical evolution of Salafism and its development into a modern Islamic movement.[31] Anthropologists have inquired why individuals are attracted to Salafism or leave the

---

[28] In 2012 I observed a few demonstrations organized by ILP in support of the Syrian revolution.

[29] Raphael Lefevre, *The "Islamic Emirate" of North Lebanon: The Rise and Fall of the Tawheed Movement in Lebanon, 1982–1985*. Cambridge: Unpublished Ph.D. Thesis Submitted at the University of Cambridge, Department of Politics and International Studies, 2016, pp. 107–110.

[30] See, for example, Joas Wagemakers, "The Transformation of a Radical Concept: al-wala' wa-l-bara' in the Ideology of Abu Muhammad al-Maqdisi." In *Global Salafism: Islam's New Religious Movement*, edited by Roel Meijer. New York: Columbia University Press, 2009; *A Quietist Jihadi: The Ideology and Influence of Abu Muhammad al-Maqdisi*. Cambridge: Cambridge University Press, 2012; Bernard Haykel, "On the Nature of Salafi Thought and Action." In Meijer, *Global Salafism*.

[31] Henri Lauziere, *The Making of Salafism: Islamic Reform in the Twentieth Century*. New York: Columbia University Press, 2015; Frank Griffel, "What Do We Mean by 'Salafi'? Connecting Muhammad 'Abduh with Egypt's Nur Party in Islam's Contemporary Intellectual History," *Die Welt des Islams*, 55, no. 2 (2015).

movement after some time.[32] Many studies have been focusing on Salafism in various national contexts in the Arab world,[33] Africa, and Asia.[34] These publications particularly traced the historical trajectory and transformation of the movement in the framework of different nation states,[35] the evolution of their ideology and discourses and their fragmentation.[36] A number of inquiries look at how Salafi groups interacted with the political system, and how Salafis reacted to the Arab Uprisings.[37]

Sunni Islamic movements in Lebanon received much less scholarly attention than movements of the Shi'ite community, especially Hizbullah.[38] The extensive academic attention to the latter is because

---

[32] Samuli Schielke, "Being Good in Ramadan: Ambivalence, Fragmentation, and the Moral Self in the Lives of Young Egyptians," *Journal of the Royal Anthropological Institute*, 15, no. s1, (2009); *Egypt in the Future Tense: Hope, Frustration and Ambivalence before and after 2011*, Kindle Edition (Bloomington: Indiana University Press, 2015), chapter 6, locations 2843–3311; Martijn de Koning, "Changing Worldviews and Friendship: An Exploration of the Life Stories of Two Female Salafis in the Netherlands." In Meijer, *Global Salafism*; Anabel Inge, *The Making of a Salafi Muslim Women: Paths to Conversion*. Oxford: Oxford University Press, 2016.

[33] On the Arabian Gulf: Stephane Lacroix *Awakening Islam: The Politics of Religious Dissent in Contemporary Saudi Arabia*. Cambridge, MA and London: Harvard University Press, 2011; Madawi Al-Rasheed *Contesting the Saudi State: Islamic Voices from a New Generation*. Cambridge: Cambridge University Press, 2007; Zoltan Pall, "Kuwaiti Salafism after the Arab Uprisings." In *Salafism after the Arab Awakening*, edited by Francesco Cavatorta and Fabio Merone, London: Hurst, 2017. On the Middle East and North Africa: Fabio Merone, "Enduring Class Struggle in Tunisia: The Fight for Identity beyond Political Islam," *British Journal of Middle Eastern Studies*, 42, no. 1 (2015); Francesco Cavatorta, "Salafism, liberalism, and democratic learning in Tunisia," *The Journal of North African Studies*. 20, no. 5 (2015); Stefano M. Torelli, Fabio Merone and Francesco Cavatorta, "Salafism in Tunisia: Challenges and Opportunities for Democratization," *Middle East Policy*, 19, no. 4 (2012); Laurent Bonnefoy, *Salafism in Yemen: Transnationalism and Religious Identity*. London: Hurst, 2011; Richard Gauvain, *Salafi Ritual Purity: In the Presence of God*. London and New York, NY: Routledge, 2013; Jacob Hoigilt and Frida Nome, "Egyptian Salafism in Revolution," *Journal of Islamic Studies*, 25, no. 1 (2015); Joas Wagemakers, *Salafism in Jordan: Political Islam in a Quietist Community*. Cambridge: Cambridge University Press, 2016.

[34] Terje Ostebo, *Localising Salafism: Religious Change among the Oromo Muslims in Bale, Ethiopia*. Leiden: Brill, 2011; Alexander Thurston, *Salafism in Nigeria: Islam, Preaching and Politics*, Kindle Edition. Cambridge: Cambridge University Press, 2016; Noorhaidi Hasan, *Laskar Jihad: Islam, Militancy and the Quest for Identity in Post–New Order Indonesia*. Ithaca, NY: Cornell Southeast Asia Program, 2006.

[35] Bonnefoy, *Salafism in Yemen*; Wagemakers, *Salafism in Jordan*; Noorhaidi. *Laskar Jihad*.

[36] Al-Rasheed, *Contesting the Saudi State*; Lacroix, *Awakening Islam*; Wagemakers *Salafism in Jordan*; Pall, *Kuwaiti Salafism*.

[37] Lacroix, *Awakening Islam*; Torelli et al., "Salafism in Tunisia"; Hoigilt and Nome, "Egyptian Salafism in Revolution"; Merone 2015, "Enduring Class Struggle"; Cavatorta, "Salafism, Liberalism and Democratic Learning"; Francesco Cavatorta and Fabio Merone (eds.) *Salafism after the Arab Awakening*. London: Hurst, 2017.

[38] There are dozens of publications. Some of the most influential ones: Ahmad Nizar Hamzeh, *In the Path of Hizbullah*. Syracuse and New York: Syracuse University Press,

Hizbullah is an important actor in international politics and enjoys overwhelming popular support in its own community. Compared to Hizbullah, Lebanese Sunni Islamic movements have been under studied. Despite being one of the oldest and most established Sunni movements, there are very few scholarly publications on IG. The existing ones discuss its ideology in length, but only briefly explain the movement's historical evolution.[39] Studies on al-Ahbash are similarly rare, and mostly focus on the group's discourses and historical roots.[40] IUM and some of the Lebanese Sufi orders, however, have received more scrutiny from sociological perspectives.[41]

Most of the studies on Lebanese Salafism are on Jihadi groups.[42] Researchers pay particular attention to Salafi armed groups that emerged in the country's Palestinian refugee camps. Of these studies, Bernard Rougier's seminal *Everyday Jihad* provides a profound analysis of the evolution of Palestinian Jihadi Salafism in transnational and local contexts.[43] Rougier's later book concentrates on the phenomenon of armed Salafi activism within the Lebanese Sunni community.[44] He explains the emergence of Jihadi groups mainly with the crisis of the post–civil war (1990–) Sunni political leadership.

Academics have paid less attention to the vast majority of Lebanon's Salafis, whose main method of action is peaceful proselytization. Studies on Jihadi Salafism often mention the peaceful Salafi networks as part of the context in which violent movements emerged.[45] Very few have studied the evolution and dynamics of these networks.[46] Most recently,

---

2004; Augustus Richard Norton, *Hezbollah: A Short History*. Princeton, NY: Princeton University Press, 2007.

[39] Robert G. Rabil, *Religion, National Identity, and Confessional Politics in Lebanon: The Challenge of Islamism*. New York: Palgrave Macmillan, 2011; Imad "A Topography of Sunni Islamic organizations."

[40] Hamzeh and Dekmejian, "A Sufi Response"; Jakob Skovgaard-Petersen "The Sunni Religious Scene in Beirut," *Mediterranean Politics*, 3, no. 1 (1998);
      Mustafa Kabha and Haggai Erlich, "Al-Ahbash and Wahhabiyya: Interpretations of Islam," *International Journal of Middle Eastern Studies* , 38, no. 4 (2006).

[41] Habibis, "Change and Continuity"; Annabelle Böttcher, "Sunni and Shi'i Networking in the Middle East," *Mediterranean Politics*, 7, no. 3 (2002).

[42] Among the first of such publications see: Bilal Y. Saab and Magnus Ranstorp, "Securing Lebanon from the Threat of Salafist Jihadism," *Studies in Conflict & Terrorism*, 30, no. 10 (2007).

[43] Rougier, *Everyday Jihad*.

[44] Bernard Rougier, *The Sunni Tragedy in the Middle East: Northern Lebanon from al-Qaeda to ISIS*. Princeton: Princeton University Press, 2015.

[45] See, for example, Saab and Ranstorp, "Securing Lebanon," pp. 827–841; Rougier, *Everyday Jihad*, pp. 254–259; Rougier, *The Sunni Tragedy*, pp. 14–17; 126–135.

[46] In my previous monograph I tried to overcome this, but due to space constraints I focused on characterizing the different factions of Salafism. See Zoltan Pall, *Lebanese*

Robert Rabil attempted to fill this gap in research to provide a comprehensive analysis on Lebanese Salafism.[47] His main focus is the evolution of Salafism in Lebanon's sectarian political context. Rabil focuses more on describing the ideology of certain Salafi shaykhs such as Zakariyya al-Masri and Sa'ad al-Din al-Kibbi, rather than on the movement's makeup, leadership structure, and transnational extensions.

Despite its growing sociopolitical significance, our knowledge on the Salafi phenomenon of Lebanon is still limited. Yet, the complex Lebanese Salafi networks serve as an excellent case study to examine the movement's local and transnational dynamics. Rougier's two books have advanced our knowledge of the evolution and appeal of Jihadi Salafism among Lebanese Sunnis. However, we still have a gap of knowledge about how nonviolent Salafis have dealt with the transformation of Lebanon's sociopolitical context, form their local networks, attract their followers, and often represent an alternative to other Sunni movements and religious authorities. This lack of attention is despite the fact that nonviolent Salafis are increasingly influential among Lebanese Sunnis. For this reason, this book intends to add to the understanding of the sociopolitical and religious dynamics of Lebanon's Sunni community.

This book also addresses the growing transnational dimension of Salafism. While there are several studies that mention the importance of transnational linkages of Salafism, not many elaborate on how transnationalism in the case of Salafis works.[48] Several studies discuss the post–Gulf War ideological fragmentation of Salafism in Saudi Arabia in the early 1990s, and the emergence of the purist and *haraki* factions,[49] but very few show how this fragmentation shaped the face of the movement on the global level.[50] Noorhaidi's monograph on the Indonesian Salafi militia that participated in the 1999–2002 conflict in the Moluccas is a notable exception. It mentions how a particular

---

Salafism between the Gulf and Europe: Development, Fractionalization and Transnational Networks of Salafism in Lebanon. Amsterdam: Amsterdam University Press, 2013.

[47] Robert G. Rabil, *Salafism in Lebanon: From Apoliticism to Transnational Jihadism.* Washington, D C: Georgetown University Press, 2014.

[48] Among the few such studies: Michael Farquhar, *Circuits of Faith: Migration, Education and the Wahhabi Mission.* Stanford, CA: Stanford University Press, 2016; Thurston. *Salafism in Nigeria,* chapter 2.

[49] Lacroix, *Awakening Islam;* Carine Tatar-Lahoud, *Islam et politique au Koweït.* Paris: PUF, 2011.

[50] Zoltan Pall, "Between Ideology and International Politics: The Dynamics and Transformation of a Transnational Islamic Charity." In *Religion and the Politics of Development: Priests, Potentates, and "Progress,"* edited by Philip Michael Fountain, Robin Bush and Michael Feener. London: Palgrave Macmillan, 2015.

Salafi leader utilized the ideological debates in the Gulf on the status of the Muslim ruler (which I will discuss in this chapter and in Chapter 1) to cement his own authority.[51] Yet, discussing the events in the Gulf and providing details on the dynamics of transnational ties is out of the scope of Noorhaidi's book as it focuses mainly on the Indonesian national level. By elaborating on the historical evolution of the *haraki* – purist divide, and analyzing the makeup of transnational networks, this monograph will fill the gap in the literature regarding the understanding of the transnational dynamics of Salafism.

Due to Lebanon's social and political makeup and location between Israel and a major Arab power (at least until the start of the current conflict), Syria, the country has been affected by all Middle Eastern conflicts in one way or another. The capital, Beirut, has always been a center of Arab cultural and scholarly activities, and has developed into one of the financial centers of the Middle East. This book, beyond being a study on one of the most important Islamic movements also intends to add to the bulk of literature on the politics, society, and history of Lebanon. Putting together the mosaics of the historical development and social dynamics of Salafism in the country contributes to a clearer understanding of Lebanese politics, society, and history.

I.4   Defining Salafism

The term "Salafism" is derived from the Arabic expression *al-Salaf al-Salih* (the righteous ancestors), which refers to the first three generations of Islam, namely the companions of the Prophet Muhammad (*sahaba*) and the first two generations of their followers. Salafis intend to purify the religion, ridding it of foreign elements and returning to the original form of Islam, the understanding of the Prophet and the *sahaba*. Salafis are not alone in emulating the pious predecessors; in fact, all Muslims regard the *sahaba* as their primary example, but there is no consensus as to how the *sahaba* understood and practiced the religion. Since all Muslims look up to *al-Salaf al-Salih*, this would not make Salafis different from other groups. Salafis today, however, represent a stream of Islam that promotes a literal understanding of the Qur'an and the Sunna (the prophetic tradition: the collection of sayings, practices, and habits of Muhammad, recorded and transmitted by men from generation to generation). One single saying or practice is a *hadith*,

---

[51] Hasan, *Laskar Jihad*.

(pl. *ahadith*), and according to the Salafis' understanding, it leaves no room for interpretation based on human reasoning (*'aql*) and opinion (*ra'y*). Salafis try to imitate the Prophet and his companions not only in their beliefs, but also in their daily practices and habits, such as in their appearance (they grow a long beard and trim their moustache).[52]

While the historical roots of Salafism go back to the first decades of the Abbasid caliphate, and modern Salafis regard Hanbali scholars such as Ibn Taymiyya (1263–1328) and Muhammad bin 'Abd Al-Wahhab (1703–1792) as their predecessors, today's Salafism is a modern movement. Salafism originally had a narrow theological meaning. It was only in the 1920s that the definition of the term shifted to refer to those who promoted Islamic revival on the basis of dealing with legal matters unencumbered by the constraints of the four *madhabs*.[53] Among them, a group of scholars and thinkers envisioned the unification of the *umma* (global Muslim community) through the uniformity of religious belief on the basis of the literal interpretation of the scripture.[54]

In the mid-twentieth century, this uniformity of practicing Islam was supposed to create a uniform Muslim identity in order to end colonial rule and achieve sociopolitical reforms in Muslim countries. Yet, in the 1970s, with the independence of most countries in the Muslim world, the focus of Salafism increasingly turned toward doctrinal purity and framing all aspects of human life in Islamic terms.[55] A number of scholars, among them the Syrian scholar Muhammad Nasir al-Din al-Albani (1914–1999), and the Saudis 'Abd al-'Aziz bin Baz (1910–1999) and Muhammad bin Salih al-'Uthaymin (1925–1991) played a crucial role in turning Salafism into an all-encompassing ideology.

I.4.1   The Core Tenets of Salafism

The basic elements of the *'aqida* (creed) are what unite all Salafis. This creed is based on the views of *Athari* or traditionalist theological school that defines the attributes and nature of God based on the literal interpretation of the scripture.[56] The Salafi creed revolves around *tawhid*, the unity of God.[57] Of course, this is the core concept of Islam, but unlike, for example, the Ash'ari theological school that is currently

---

[52] See also Chapter 4.   [53] Lauziere, *The Making of Salafism*, pp. 27–59.
[54] Ibid., pp. 95–129.   [55] Ibid., pp. 199–230.
[56] Jeffrey R. Halverson. *Theology and Creed in Sunni Islam*. New York: Palgrave Macmillan, 2010, pp. 13–31.
[57] Wagemakers points out that despite the common basic elements of the *'aqida*, Salafis differ in certain creedal matters. The most significant of these relates to the question of

dominant among Sunni Muslims, Salafis reject any philosophical interpretation of *tawhid*. Most contemporary Salafis divide *tawhid* into three
basic components, a distinction that is based on the works of the
nineteenth-century reformer Muhammad bin 'Abd al-Wahhab.[58]

The first part is *tawhid al-rububiyya* (oneness of Lordship). It means
that God is the sole creator of the universe; he is omnipotent, and
nothing is comparable to him. The second part is *tawhid al-uluhiyya*
(oneness of Godship) or *tawhid al-'ibada* (oneness of worship). It means
that all religious practices must be directed toward God alone and
no one else can be attributed with any qualities that belong to God.
This is one of the reasons for the Salafis' hostility toward Sufism and
the Shi'ites, particularly because of the latter's practice of seeking
mediation (*tawassul*) and aid (*istighatha*) from saints and the family
of the Prophet.

The third part is *tawhid al-asma' wa-l-sifat* (oneness of the names and
attributes). The Qur'an names the attributes of God, such as his hands
or his face. These provide the basis for metaphorical explanations and
the use of reasoning. For example, while Ash'aris explain the men-
tioning of God's hands in the Qur'an as the expression of his power,[59]
Salafis strictly reject this approach. Since these things are mentioned
in the Text, they have to be accepted literally without any further
explanation.

Salafis consider the preservation and defense of their understanding
of *tawhid* to be their most important task and fight anything that can
lead to polytheism (*shirk*). Therefore, Salafis fight any innovations
(*bid'a*) that contradict the Qur'an and Sunna, because *bid'a* can lead
to *shirk*. For example, Salafis consider the celebration of the Prophet's
birthday (*mawlid*) *bid'a*, because they do not find any proof in the
scripture.

What makes contemporary Salafis different from other Muslims
who adopted similar creeds, such as the majority of the adherents of
the Hanbali *madhab* (legal school) – or for that matter Muhammad bin
'Abd al-Wahhab, who revived Athari thinking in the eighteenth-
century Arabian Peninsula – is the rejection of *taqlid*, or the exclusive

belief and unbelief. However, the creedal debates within Salafism are usually
complicated and understood only by the most knowledgeable participants of the
movement. Joas Wagemakers, "Revisiting Wiktorowicz: Categorising and Defining
the Branches of Salafism." In *Salafism after the Arab Awakening*, edited by Francesco
Cavatorta and Fabio Merone. New York: Oxford University Press, 2015

[58] Muhammad bin 'uhammad binoi, *Kitab al-Tawhid*. Riyadh: Maktabat al-Haramayn, 2001.
[59] "'Ash'ariyya." In *The Encyclopaedia of Islam*, 2nd edn. edited by Clifford Edmund
Bossworth Leiden: E.J. Brill, 1986.

following of a particular legal authority. In the Sunni context it mostly means refusing the *taqlid* of the four *madhab*s. Instead, Salafis adopt *ijtihad* (independent reasoning) to make legal judgments. Yet the Salafi methodology of *ijtihad* is restricted to looking for proof by the philological reading of the scripture and using *qiyas* (analogy) in cases where there is no direct answer in the scripture.

As a result of this literalist reasoning, Salafis put great emphasis on *'ilm al-hadith* (the science of *hadith*), which is the archaeology of the Text, to find answers to specific questions. Salafi Hadith scholars examine the credibility of a *hadith* by analyzing the chains of transmission (*isnad*). Unlike Ash'aris, however, they believe that it is forbidden to criticize the content (*matn*) of the prophetical tradition. The former might classify a *hadith* as corrupted on the grounds that its substance does not agree with the spirit of the Qur'an.[60]

One of the most important features of Salafism is *al-wala' wa-l-bara,'* which can be translated as "loyalty and disavowal." *Al-wala' wa-l-bara'* divides the world into two separate spheres: one is the realm of Islam and the other is the realm of the *kuffar* (unbelievers), which is necessarily evil. Muslims should feel loyalty and a sense of brotherhood with those who belong to the first realm, while defending the purity of their religion from influences coming from the second. However, Salafis interpret the practice of this concept in different ways.[61] Activist interpretations can even call upon Muslims to physically destroy that which is regarded as un-Islamic, while more quietist interpretations focus only on the avoidance of foreign elements that corrupt the purity of Islam.

Al-amr bi-l-ma'ruf wa al-nahi 'an al-munkar (commanding right and forbidding wrong), or *hisba*, is another important element of Salafi activism. The term refers to the imposition of the moral rules of Islam on Muslims and the prohibition of immoral acts such as deviations from correct religious beliefs and practices, drinking alcohol, committing adultery, and so forth. *Hisba* can be implemented using only a verbal warning, but it can also take the form of violent acts (see Chapter 4).[62]

---

[60] Muhammad al-Ghazali, *al-Sunna al-Nabawiyya Bayn Ahl al-Fiqh wa-Ahl al-Hadith*, 15th edn. Cairo: Dar al-Shuruq, 2007, pp. 39–43.

[61] Wagemakers, "The Transformation of a Radical Concept: *al-wala' wa-l-bara'* in the Ideology of Abu Muhammad al-Maqdisi." In Meijer. *Global Salafism*. pp. 84–87.

[62] On *Hisba* see Roel Meijer, "Commanding Right and Forbidding Wrong as a Principle of Social Action: The Case of the Egyptian al-Jama'a al-Islamiyya," in Meijer. *Global Salafism*.

I.4.2   The Internal Divisions of Salafism

Despite sharing the basics of the creed that sets very strict boundaries on theological thinking, Salafism is far from monolithic. Although Salafis share the concept of *tawhid*, they differ on the methods of purifying Islam. While some exclusively focus on religious practice, others engage in a broader range of activities, from political activism to armed struggle. Perhaps the most influential typology of Salafism, proposed by Quintan Wiktorowicz, classifies the movement into three factions: purists stay away from politics, politicos engage in political debates and challenge existing regimes in peaceful ways, and jihadis who excommunicate contemporary Muslim rulers and intend to impose their vision of pious society by launching armed jihad.[63]

In my view, setting up a general typology to classify Salafis globally is a difficult task since Salafism is constantly evolving. Wiktorowicz's classification thus might only tell something about the Salafis' behavior in a certain sociopolitical context at a certain point in time. It does not inform us, however, about the ideological affiliations of Salafi participants and ignores the transnational linkages and affiliations that have become crucial to the movement. For instance, the *Kuwaiti Jama'iyyat Ihya' al-Turath al-Islami* (Society for the Revival of Islamic Heritage – SRIH), one of the largest and most influential Salafi transnational charities, has a political wing and regularly delegates MPs to Kuwait's legislature.[64] Yet, SRIH's discourse is very close to those scholars who do not participate in parliamentary politics in their respective countries, such as al-Albani and Ibn Baz, or 'Ali al-Halabi (b. 1960), a Jordanian Salafi scholar with a significant transnational following. If we look at the transnational linkages of SRIH, they consist mostly of scholars and groups that are labeled as purists by Wiktorowicz. In other words, members of SRIH might not participate in politics and would not be politicos according to Wiktorowicz's classification if they lived in Jordan instead of Kuwait, for example.

I argue that the stance toward political participation alone does not make purists and politicos different. Instead, I propose to refine Wiktorowicz's typology and look at their discourses and determine the key debates that create differences between different Salafi groups.

---

[63] Quintan Wiktorowicz, "Anatomy of the Salafi Movement," *Studies in Conflict and Terrorism*, 29, no. 2. (2006). This classification has been criticized by many: Thurston argues that separating purists from politicos does not make sense, as purists also frequently comment on certain political issues. Thurston. *Salafism in Nigeria*, location 377.

[64] See Chapter 1 for details.

As Chapter 1 will explain and the book will show throughout, the issue that divides Salafis most sharply relates to the concept of *hukm* (ruling) in Islam. The main debate revolves around the relationship of the ruled to the ruler (*hakim*), and this divides Salafis in both Lebanon and the Gulf into two factions. Following Wiktorowicz, I will call the first faction "purist." The term "purist" is appropriate here, since the main concern of the members of this faction is purifying the minute details of belief and religious practice of Muslims. In order to be able to do so, they need a political order, which grants the necessary stability to carry out the *da'wa*.

This makes purists proponents of unconditional obedience to the ruler as long as he is not an apostate. In addition, they do not allow open criticism of the ruler, only secret advice (*nasiha sirriya*). The purists refer to the Text to support their stance. They commonly quote one of the sayings of the Prophet: "Who sees disobedience of God from his *amir* [ruler] shall hate what this disobedience causes but shall not lift his hands against him."[65] Purists usually cite the example of the first civil war in Islam: "When *fitna* [civil war] occurred in the time of Caliph 'Uthman, some people asked Usama bin Zayd [one of the companions of the Prophet]: 'Don't you rebuke 'Uthman?' He answered: 'Rebuke him in front of the people? I rebuke him only in private but I do not open the doors of Hell in front of the people'."[66] Purists use this to explain that even if it is warranted, open criticism can cause the people to rise up against the ruler and undermine order.

This faction's main concern, however, is doctrinal purity. Yet, some of them participate in parliamentary politics. For example, in Kuwait, purists have regularly been elected to the legislature since the 1980s. To them, political participation is necessary to defend the autonomy of the *da'wa* from its enemies, such as western-oriented liberals and socialists. However, their political aims mainly concern social behavior and the promotion of their understanding of Islam within Kuwait. For instance, partly due to their efforts, in most departments of the University of Kuwait, male and female students have to attend lectures in separate rooms. I call this current "purist-politically oriented." Others, whom I call "purist-rejectionists," reject any political participation, putting forward that in the political arena, Muslims can be affected by those who do not practice religion properly, or even by non-Muslims. Faithful Muslims should only focus on proper daily religious practice. The followers of the Saudi scholar Rabi' al-Madkhali are an example of this group.

[65] See www.binbaz.org.sa/mat/1944 (accessed September 19, 2009).
[66] Al 'Abd al-Karim, *Mu'amalat al-Hukkam*, p. 17.

Those belonging to the second faction, whom I call *harakis* (activists),[67] refuse to obey the ruler unconditionally. They approach religion from an all-encompassing (*shumuli*) viewpoint. They are influenced by Sayyid Qutb's concept of *hakimiyya*, which considers any government that does not govern according to God's law to be illegitimate.[68] *Harakis* also think that a ruler can only be legitimate if the ruled voluntarily perform an oath of allegiance (*bay'a*). Therefore, regimes that come to power via military coups or conquest are by definition illegitimate. They defend their stance by referring to the case of the first four caliphs who followed the Prophet, all of whom were accepted by the majority of Muslims. Although there is no clear reference to this in the Text, this process is in accordance with the consensus (*ijma'*) of the *Sahaba*, the Companions of the Prophet.[69]

Haraki Salafis think that since Islam extends its rulings to every domain of life, politics and the political state of the *umma* should not be neglected. Therefore, the other important point that makes *harakis* different from the purists is that in their discourses, they engage with a wider range of topics.[70] As I show later in this book, Lebanese Salafis in general feel negatively about the Shi'ite Muslims. However, while purists mostly criticize the latter from the viewpoint of doctrines, the *harakis* extensively discuss the Shi'ites' perceived negative role in Lebanese and regional politics, and place them in the center of conspiracy theories.[71] Furthermore, the repertoire of action of *harakis* is also wider than that of the purists. They do not refrain from openly criticizing the rulers, and regard demonstrations as legitimate means.

Jihadis, the third faction, are different from *harakis* in the sense that they believe that removing secular regimes and imposing Islamic legislation could happen only through armed jihad, and that long-range public engagement would not bring results.[72] Yet, *haraki* networks often overlap with that of the jihadis. I encountered many Salafis who firmly believed in the ultimate necessity of armed jihad to abolish secularist

---

[67] I consider the term *haraki* to be appropriate here, since the members of this faction themselves use this term to explain their activist approach toward Islam.

[68] Some of them even add *tawhid al-hakimiyya* (oneness of the governance) as the fourth component of *tawhid*. In the fifth chapter, I will discuss the debate surrounding *tawhid al-hakimiyya* in Kuwait.

[69] See, for example, Hakim al-Mutayri, *Al-Hurriyya aw al-Tawfan*. Beirut: Al-Mu'assasa al-'Arabiyya li-l-Dirasat wa-l-Nashr, 2008, pp. 21–25.

[70] Joas Wagemakers makes a similar point while discussing the internal differences of Jordanian Salafis. See *Salafism in Jordan*, p. 207.

[71] See Chapters 3 and 7.

[72] Joas Wagemakers, "Revisiting Wiktorowicz: Categorising and Defining the Branches of Salafism." In Cavatorta and Merone, *Salafism after the Arab Awakening*.

regimes and establish Islamic governance. However, at the same time, they advocated for participation in parliamentary politics as a temporary means of activism until the circumstances become appropriate to successfully wage jihad.[73] While jihadis often form their own distinct groups and organizations, there are cases when it is difficult to distinguish them from other *harakis* on the ground. During my fieldwork in Lebanon and Kuwait, I met Salafi youths in the networks of *haraki* shaykhs who expressed jihadi views and rejected political participation. Despite this, they networked with others who were inclined toward *haraki* thinking. These young people were constantly challenging each other's views. On some occasions, I even observed jihadis changing their views regarding political participation.

These ideological differences influence the shape of transnational networks in which Lebanese Salafis are linked. As I will show in this book, the difference of views about the relationship of Muslims to the ruler fragmented the Kuwaiti Salafis in the mid-1990s. This, in turn, reshaped the Salafi scene in Lebanon due to the dense interconnections of Salafis in these two countries. While overlaps might exist, the transnational networks that I discuss in this book largely can be characterized as *harakis* or purists.

I.4.3   What Makes Salafism Appealing?

Anthropologists of Islam highlight that many Muslims in the late twentieth and twenty-first century are attracted to religious movements and trends that provide them guidance in rapidly changing and uncertain circumstances.[74] It means offering a way to constantly engage with the scripture and connect one's actions and feelings directly to it.[75]

Salafism fulfills these needs. Anthropologists have noticed a number of similar reasons why individual believers are attracted to Salafism. These include the Salafis' claim to authenticity, that they perform rituals

---

[73] The Kuwaiti Salafi scholar Hamid al-'Ali is a good example. He is a frequent commentator of the website of the jihadi ideologue Abu Muhammad al-Maqdisi. At the same time, he is the former head of the Kuwait political organization al-Haraka al-Salafiyya and encourages political participation. See his fatwa on this issue www.h-alali.org/f_open.php?id=d084c652-dc31-1029-a62a-0010dc91cf69 (accessed June 24, 2015).

[74] Saba Mahmood, *Politics of Piety: The Islamic Revival and the Feminist Subject*. Princeton, NJ: Princeton University Press, 2005; Charles Hirshkind, *The Ethical Soundscape: Cassette Sermons and the Islamic Counterpublic*. New York, NY: Columbia University Press, 2006; Lara Deeb, *An Enchanted Modern: Gender and Public Piety in Shi'i Lebanon*. Princeton, NJ: Princeton University Press, 2006.

[75] Schielke, *Egypt in the Future Tense*, locations 2883–3029; Deeb, *An Enchanted Modern*, pp. 20–23.

exactly as the Prophet did by correctly reading the Qur'an and the Sunna. By extensively referring back to the hadith, Salafis leave no gray areas but provide clear instructions to all aspects of human life: not just how to pray, but, for example, how to dress, eat, or interact with society. By clearly defining the terms of what being a good Muslim means (i.e. perfecting oneself according to what is codified in the scripture), Salafism provides a point of reference, discipline, and clear structure for one's life in highly unpredictable socioeconomic conditions or in time of personal crisis.[76]

As explained in Chapters 4 and 7, these observations are true for Lebanon as well. In a context of constant political instability and uncertain economic conditions, many Sunnis, especially young people, are looking for empowerment and moral support, which they often find in Salafism. Yet only looking at the moral dimensions of the movement would not sufficiently explain why the popular appeal of Salafism in Lebanon has been growing since the end of the first decade of the twenty-first century in particular. Therefore, this book closely examines the evolution of Salafism in light of the transformation of Lebanon's sociopolitical context, and the dynamics of its interconnections with the countries of the Arabian Gulf.

Furthermore, analyzing the sociopolitical context is also necessary to explain the power balance within the Salafi movement in Lebanon. As Wagemakers highlights in his analysis on Jordanian Salafism, in the kingdom, those who he calls quietist, who I would identify as a purist faction, gained predominance.[77] Contrary to Jordan, in Lebanon, *harakis* are dominant. I suggest that the *haraki* message of going beyond doctrinal purity and addressing issues such as the Sunni–Shi'ite sectarian tensions has become more relevant.

I.5   Salafism as a Movement

As the discussion in the previous section shows, Salafis, regardless of factions, share a utopian vision: They are determined to recreate the ideal community of Muslims as, according to their belief, it used to be during the time of the *Salaf*. In many respects, Salafism resembles what Price et al. call "grounded utopian movements" (GUMs).[78] GUMs

---

[76] Schielke, *Egypt in the Future Tense*, 2892–2973.

[77] Wagemakers, *Salafism in Jordan*, especially, pp. 201–225.

[78] Charles Price, Donald Nonini and Erich Fox Tree, "Grounded Utopian Movements: Subjects or Neglect," *Anthropological Quarterly*, 81, no. 1 (2008).

create strong utopias in order to counter different types of oppression and injustice (real and perceived). In other words, the followers of such a movement create a parallel reality to escape from the conditions present in the surrounding world. "Grounded" here means "that the identities, values, and imaginative dimensions of utopia are culturally focused on real places, embodied by living people, informed by past lifeways, and constructed and maintained through quotidian interactions and valued practices that connect the members of a community."[79]

Similarly to the majority of GUMs (including Rastafari or Zapatistas), Salafism is constituted by networks that are largely informal and decentralized. Interpersonal ties make up the core of these networks, which mostly evolve during common activities such as religious lessons held in the mosques or ad-hoc discussions after prayer. Yet, as I explain later, Salafi interpersonal networks in certain cases overlap with formal institutions, in particular charities that finance various humanitarian and religious projects. A collective identity built on shared worldviews and aesthetics, such as performing religious practices in an ostensibly uncorrupted way, a dress code, and specific ways of verbal communication holds these networks together. This book focusses on the characteristic of Salafism as a movement made chiefly of informal networks.[80]

Salafism differs from the majority of the GUMs that are discussed by Price et al. in one important way: While the main goal of these GUMs is to maintain an autonomous, alternative lifestyle for their participants, for Salafis it is equally important to convince others to adopt their worldviews and practices. In other words, their end goal is to export their utopian vision to wider society. Therefore, Salafis actively engage in various preaching activities, such as holding religious lessons in mosques. Salafis are very active on the web and maintain thousands of websites and internet forums in order to spread their ideas. Salafi educational institutions, often financed by the wealthy monarchies of the Arabian Gulf, can be found all over the world.

All this shows that transforming society is of central importance in Salafism. In this process, Salafis often challenge other actors that they perceive as endangering the *da'wa* or who resist the Salafis' attempt to spread their version of Islam. This is particularly obvious in Lebanon,

[79] Ibid., p. 128. The authors give examples of GUMs such as the Rastafari movement or Mexico's Zapatistas.
[80] Chapters 5 and 6 explain the structure of Salafism in detail.

where Salafis contest the legitimacy of Dar al-Fatwa to represent Sunni orthodoxy. In this contestation the Salafis employ their economic abilities, social ties, and mastery of religious knowledge and practices to gain more influence in society. Using Pierre Bourdieu's theory of social reproduction, I will explore and describe how Salafis mobilize finances and build up social networks in order to create and reinforce the public image of exemplary Muslims.

Bourdieu's approach divides society into different but interconnected microcosms called "fields." A field is a configuration of hierarchically arranged positions where agents compete with each other to increase their influence and dominate the field.[81] These positions are defined by the possession of capital, a symbolic resource that enables its possessor to exercise power in a specific field. Within a field, there is a struggle between agents to possess as much capital as possible and thereby achieve a more influential position.[82] There are as many kinds of fields as there are types of capital. For example, it is possible to distinguish economic, political, artistic, or religious fields, each of which are governed by their own logic and rules. Institutions, individuals, and networks make up these fields. For example, the religious field can be composed of churches and mosques, state institutions that regulate religious life, religious centers, religious specialists, and religious movements.

Fields can be overlapping and can influence each other.[83] For example, the religious field can affect the political: The success of Islamic movements might lead to the electoral success of parties with an Islamic orientation, as we could see in several cases in the Middle East, such as the Egyptian elections in 2012.

Beyond field-specific capital, two forms of capital are present and often become a game changer in each field. These are economic and social capital.[84] For example, as this book will show, the acquisition of social capital in the religious field might lead to the increase of economic capital that enables agents of the field to expand their religious infrastructure, and hence reach out for more followers.

---

[81] Pierre Bourdieu and Loic J. D. Wacqant, *An Invitation to Reflexive Sociology*. Chicago: The University of Chicago Press, 1992, p. 97.

[82] David Schwartz, "Bridging the Study of Culture and Religion: Pierre Bourdieu's Political Economy of Symbolic Power," *Sociology of Religion*, 57, no. 1 (1996), pp. 78–81.

[83] Landy, "Bringing the Outside In," pp. 264–266.

[84] Pierre Bourdieu, "The Political Field, the Social Science Field, and the Journalistic Field." In Bourdieu and the Journalistic Field, edited by Rodney Benson and Erik Neveu. Cambridge: Polity Press, 2005, pp. 42–46.

I.5.1   Examining Salafism in the Lebanese Sunni Field

Salafis in Lebanon chiefly (but not exclusively) operate on what I define as the Sunni religious field. This field is composed of persons and institutions that are struggling to dominate or monopolize the creation of religious knowledge and the administration and provision of religious services. The category of agents includes actors such as Dar al-Fatwa and various Sunni Islamic movements. Furthermore, beyond movements and institutions, individuals such as religious scholars, preachers, and Sufi shaykhs are also parts of the field. These agents claim to possess superior knowledge of the wishes of the transcendent, and they compete but often also cooperate with each other to increase their influence within the field.

Religious capital is the field specific capital on the Sunni religious field. Religious capital is manifested in myths, ideologies, religious knowledge, or the mastery of religious practices.[85] In the case of different agents the quality of religious capital can be different. Sufis, for example, claim religious capital on the basis of understanding the esoteric meaning of the revelations and having personal connection to the transcendent that they can pass to others. As I will explain in Chapter 4, Salafi religious capital rests on the ideological foundation that they embody pure and authentic Islam. They cement this foundation by their strict adherence to religious rules (such as dress code and exact performance of religious rituals). Salafism strives to transform the field by imposing its own vision on it. The participants of the movement intend to define the terms of what a good Muslim is. In other words, they want to alter the consensus of the field on what a Muslim should believe and how they should act according to Salafi standards.

Salafism, however, is not just an actor on the Sunni religious field. The latter often overlaps with the political field of Lebanon, revolving around the formal sharing of power between the country's main religious communities. This field emerged in mid-nineteenth-century Mount Lebanon, when the political positions in the country started to be filled according to sectarian affiliation, a system that the modern Lebanese state has inherited.[86] The most visible constituents of the political field are the institutions of the political system, such as the parliament, ministries, and municipal bodies, and the political patrons

---

[85] Pierre Bourdieu, "Genesis and Structure of the Religious Field," *Comparative Social Research*, 13, no. 1, (1991), pp. 22–23.

[86] Engin Akarli, *The Long Peace: Ottoman Lebanon 1861–1920*. Berkeley and Los Angeles: University of California Press, 1993, pp. 82–102.

(*za'im, pl. zu'ama'*), whose position in the field is enhanced both by their following within their religious community and their access to the political institutions.

Agents of the Sunni religious field can influence the political field both directly and indirectly. For example, Salafi shaykhs often support certain candidates during parliamentary elections in exchange for the candidate's political or/and material support in case he/she wins the mandate. Some of the Salafis even became candidates themselves, as happened during the 1996 and 2009 elections.[87] As Chapter 7 will demonstrate, by framing the conflicts of the political field, such as the one between the March 14 and March 8 camps using religious symbols, Salafis gain a significant amount of religious capital.

To facilitate the understanding of how Salafism constitutes an actor on the field and mobilizes capital, I combine Bourdieu's theory with approaches developed by scholars of social movement theory.[88] The concept of collective identity includes values and symbols that hold a group of individuals together and makes them pursue common goals (purifying the belief and practices of Muslims in a certain way in the case of Salafism). Discussing this in Chapter 5 is important to understanding what holds Salafi networks – the avenues of the mobilization of capital – together.

Framing provides a useful tool to explain how these Salafi networks can expand by employing a certain political discourse at a certain time to attract the masses. Framing explores the ways in which individuals can communicate their perceptions of reality. In the case of movements such as Salafism, successful framing activity puts ordinary people's daily acts and experiences in the context of the wider sociopolitical realm; they learn that their actions matter, too.[89] Chapter 7

---

[87] In 1996 Shaykh Da'i al-Islam al-Shahhal was an electoral candidate; in 2009 his cousin Dr. Hasan al-Shahhal ran for office.

[88] SMT intends to understand the emergence and dynamics of social movements that in Mario Diani's definition are "networks of informal interactions, between a plurality of individuals, groups or associations, engaged in a political or cultural conflict, on the basis of a shared collective identity." Mario Diani, "The Concept of a Social Movement." In *Readings in Contemporary Political Sociology*, edited by David A. Snow, Sarah A. Soule, and Hanspeter Kriesi. Oxford: Blackwell Publishers, 2000, p. 13.

[89] Erving Goffman, *Frame Analysis: An Essay on the Organization of Experience*. Boston: Northeastern University Press, 1974; Social movement theorists are particularly fond of employing framing in discussing movement dynamics: David A. Snow and Robert D. Benford, "Ideology, Frame Resonance, and Participant Mobilization," *International Social Movement Research*, 1, no. 1 (1988); Robert D. Benford and David A. Snow, "Framing Processes and Social Movements: An Overview and Assessment," *Annual Review of Sociology*, 26 (2000).

explains how the accumulated religious capital facilitates the success of the Salafis' framing activities.

I.6   Notes on Data Collection

This book is the result of several rounds of fieldwork undertaken between 2009 and 2012. In this period, I conducted more than one hundred semi-structured interviews with Salafis, and participated in their activities, such as Friday sermons, religious lessons, and other informal gatherings. Books, leaflets, magazines, and recordings of sermons that I collected while visiting mosques and Salafi institutions proved to be valuable sources as well.

I first engaged with Salafis while working in Lebanon as the correspondent of the Hungarian daily *Népszabadság* in 2007–2008. Lebanese fellow journalists put me in contact with a few Salafi shaykhs who were willing to be interviewed when I was preparing a report on the aftermath of the battle of Nahr al-Barid. When I returned to Lebanon as a researcher from Utrecht University of the Netherlands to research Salafism, I contacted the same shaykhs whom I had previously interviewed as a journalist. Knowing me as a former journalist, these shaykhs initially showed distrust toward me out of the fear that whatever they say might end up in the media and would shed negative light on them. Yet, I managed to convince many of them to provide information and assistance to my research when I clarified that my aim was not writing news reports anymore, but explaining the dynamics of Salafism to an academic audience. Therefore, I might even help dispel misunderstandings on the movement, such as their often indiscriminate association to terrorism by the western news outlets.

Some of the Salafi shaykhs refused to talk to me. Others agreed to be interviewed, but the only issue they really wanted to discuss was that Salafism had nothing to do with terrorism. Others, who were willing to share a broad range of information with me, thought that our conversation might be beneficial for Salafism. Shaykh Muhammad, a Palestinian shaykh, for example, in our regular meetings strived to convey his narrative on Fath al-Islam, hoping that through my mediation it would reach a broader audience in academia.[90] According to the shaykh, the Syrian intelligence planted the movement, and Salafis in Nahr al-Barid had no role in creating it.

---

[90] Shaykh Muhammad tried to convince me to write a book on Fath al-Islam with him, an offer that I declined.

During the years I spent researching Salafism, a good personal relationship with Shaykh Mohamed emerged. He often invited me to his home in al-Baddawi camp near Tripoli. Such personal bonds that I had with Shaykh Mohamed greatly increased his trust toward me, which led to sharing more information and connecting me to other Salafis.

Those shaykhs who were willing to cooperate with me, such as Shaykh Muhammad, were my gateways to the Salafi community of Lebanon. Some of them, both *harakis* and purists, I interviewed regularly. These religious leaders provided invaluable information to reconstruct the historical trajectory of Salafism, as most of them were not only witnesses to but key actors in the events. My contacts with the shaykhs also greatly helped to earn the trust of young committed Salafis, who were most often students of the shaykhs. I regularly socialized with these young people, and often stayed in their homes during my visits. Similarly to the case of Shaykh Muhammad, my relationship to some of them went beyond my work. 'Uthman, a haraki Salafi in his mid-twenties, whom I introduce in Chapter 5, considered me a friend and introduced me to his family. Forging these social ties with young Salafis contributed to gaining their trust, giving me deeper insights into their lives. They also introduced me to Tripoli's Salafi scene, and helped me gain access to religious lessons and participate in the Salafis' other religious activities.

I also conducted interviews and engaged in random conversations with sympathizers of Salafism who had not fully adopted the movement's rulings, but nevertheless prayed in Salafi mosques and tended to follow the guidance of Salafi religious scholars. Important data were collected from ordinary inhabitants of North Lebanon who could not be called followers of the movement, and from opponents of Salafism, in particular officials of Dar al-Fatwa and members of Hizbullah.

During my field trips to Kuwait and Qatar, my main aim was to interview the Salafi leaders who control the financial capital destined to support Salafi activity abroad. I was granted access to several leading figures and employees of transnational charities in both countries. At the same time, in Kuwait I expanded the scope of my inquiry and also talked to ordinary followers of Salafism and observed their activities. My participation in traditional gatherings (*diwaniyya*) provided space and a sufficiently relaxed atmosphere to establish contact with Kuwaiti Salafis. This allowed me to map the informal social networks that connect the movement in this Gulf monarchy with that in North Lebanon.

During my fieldwork in Europe, I mainly interviewed Lebanese Salafi preachers about their *da'wa* in Muslim minority communities. One of my most productive field trips was to Sweden, where a Lebanese-Palestinian Salafi shaykh whom I had interviewed several times in Lebanon had been appointed as the head of an Islamic center. He let me observe his activities and interview his followers during my short stay, which helped me to understand how transnational networks facilitate the import of Salafi ideas from the Middle East to Europe.

I.7   The Structure of This Book

The first chapter traces the development of Salafism in the Gulf, which is crucial to any understanding of the dynamics of Lebanese Salafism. The first section explains the roots of the fragmentation of the movement in Saudi Arabia, and goes on to describe its transformation in Kuwait. Kuwaiti Salafism is densely interconnected with its equivalent in Lebanon; the Kuwait-based Salafi charity SRIH is one of its main financial supporters. The last section touches upon the development of the other main sponsor of Lebanese Salafism, the Qatari SACF.

Chapter 2 examines how Salafism evolved into a prominent Islamic movement in Tripoli and its surroundings during the 1990s. It shows the historical transformations of the Sunni religious field, and discusses how these changes contributed to the Salafis' accumulation of religious and economic capital.

Chapter 3 further examines the transformation of the Sunni religious field and explains how Salafism in Lebanon split into purist and *haraki* factions. The chapter identifies the selective repression by the authorities and the material support provided by SRIH to the purists as the main factors leading to the disintegration of the once relatively unified Salafi movement in the country. It also shows the dynamics of the purist and *haraki* factions. This chapter also examines how the Arab Uprisings and the subsequent growth of the popularity of Salafism across the Middle East provided Lebanese *haraki* Salafis with an opportunity to rise in prominence.

Chapter 4 focuses on the construction of the religious authority of the North Lebanese Salafi shaykhs, and outlines the importance of the religious specialists in the movement. It traces how the different forms of capital translate to authority. This authority enables Salafis to successfully claim orthodoxy in considerable segments of the Northern Lebanese Sunni population. The decline of the influence of Dar al-Fatwa and the fact that other Islamic movements do not claim orthodoxy contributed to the Salafis' success.

Chapter 5 analyzes the structure and functions of Salafi networks at the local level. It examines the social composition of Salafi networks and the modality of the evolution of interpersonal network ties. This chapter sheds light on the construction of a collective identity among Salafis. Looking at activities such as religious lessons held in mosques and private homes, Friday sermons, and *ad hoc* gatherings it provides insights into how a collective identity among younger believers is created.

Chapter 6 discusses the dynamics of Salafi transnational networking, detailing the ties between North Lebanon and the Gulf. It examines how both the role of informal, interpersonal ties and that played by Salafi charities in the Gulf provide religious, social, and economic capital to the Lebanese Salafis. The last section of the chapter explains how informal links with Europe and the Gulf facilitate the dissemination of the Salafi message. Using two of my case studies from Sweden and the Netherlands, the chapter shows how transnational Salafi networks between Lebanon and Europe function.

The last chapter identifies the significance of "framing" and highlights the process of conversion in the recruitment of passive and active adherents of Salafism. The second half of the chapter examines the appeal of Salafi ideology to young people who feel alienated in North Lebanese society for a variety of socioeconomic and identity-related reasons. These youths become committed followers of Salafism and seek to adopt the movement's rulings after undergoing conversion. Within this context, I will also exemplify how Salafi networking strategies facilitate conversion.

Relatively few scholars have explored the dynamics of Lebanese Salafism in depth. In order to understand that the movement is differentiated and cannot quite be understood using western concepts of organizations, it is necessary to provide a detailed history and analysis.

1   The Transformation of Salafism in the Gulf

This chapter will discuss the development of Salafism in the Arabian Gulf, which forms the essential backdrop to understanding the movement's evolution in Lebanon. A major part of the economic capital of Lebanese Salafis comes from the Gulf. Therefore, the dynamics of Salafism in Saudi Arabia, Kuwait, and Qatar, and the politics of donors such as wealthy transnational charities can play a key role in the configuration of the Salafi scenes in other regions, as has happened in Lebanon.

The existing literature mostly focuses on the fragmentation of Salafism in the Saudi context, but rarely discusses how this affected other Gulf States and shaped the Salafi scene elsewhere.[1] In order to understand the current configuration and diversity of Salafism in Lebanon it is crucial to take a closer look at the dynamics of the Kuwaiti and Qatari Salafi scene. Both countries have become important transnational hubs of Salafism. Their interconnections with Salafi networks in Lebanon are significant: Kuwaiti and Qatari charities have been bankrolling various Lebanese Salafi groups, and their intervention in the intra-Salafi power struggles in Tripoli and its surrounding areas determined the current shape of the Salafi scene there (See Chapter 3).

I hope to provide insight into how the regimes in Saudi Arabia and Kuwait favored purist groups over the *harakis* in order to repel the perceived threat coming from the latter. This contributed to the occurrence of numerous splits within the movement.

---

[1] On the fragmentation of Salafism in the Gulf see Stephane Lacroix, *Awakening Islam: The Politics of Religious Dissent in Contemporary Saudi Arabia* (Cambridge, MA and London: Harvard University Press, 2011). Noorhaidi Hasan provides some insight into how ideological debates in the Gulf affected Indonesian Salafism. See Noorhaidi Hasan, *Laskar Jihad: Islam, Militancy and the Quest for Identity in Post–New Order Indonesia* (Ithaca, NY: Cornell Southeast Asia Program, 2006), pp. 58–62 and 80–92.

1.1   The Fragmentation of Salafism in Saudi Arabia

During and after the liberation of Kuwait in 1991, two ideological streams emerged within Salafism. Transnational social networks have evolved along these ideological lines, which have largely shaped Salafism in different localities.

Over the centuries, the task of the Salafi *'ulama'* class did not go beyond solving religious and mundane problems.[2] They provided answers to questions concerning the minute details of their constituency's daily life, but they almost never engaged in theoretical debates. Very few of them wrote theological treatises with a scope that went beyond the correct performance of the *'ibadat*. Unlike their counterparts in other areas of the Muslim world, they completely lacked a sophisticated perspective and discourse on sociopolitical issues. As a result, they were unable to confirm the legitimacy of the Saudi Kingdom when it was threatened by Arab Nationalists and Leftists during the Arab Cold War.[3]

The Arab Cold War between Egypt and Saudi Arabia lasted from the mid-1950s until 1970. In 1952, a military coup abolished the pro-Western monarchy in Egypt. The new regime, led by President Gamal Abdel Nasser, adopted Arab nationalism as its main ideology and allied itself with the Soviet Union. Cairo also began to support secular Arab nationalist movements worldwide. In the two decades following the revolution in Egypt, Arab nationalist regimes came to power in a number of Arab countries. In 1958, a coup d'état abolished the pro-Western monarchy in Iraq, and in 1962, an Arab nationalist government came to power in post-independence Algeria. In the same year in North Yemen, the monarchy was brought down by 'Abdullah al-Sallal, who became an ally of Nasser. Equally important were the Syrian and Libyan "revolutions" in 1963 and 1969. These countries allied within the framework of the self-declared "progressive" block, led by Egypt, maintained good terms with the Soviet Union, and intended to transform the whole Arab world in accordance with the ideals of Arab Nationalism.

The spread of the new ideology endangered the existence of the traditional, kinship-based Saudi monarchy. In response to the threat, Riyadh created its own alliance structure based on other conservative monarchies, such as Jordan and Morocco, around the rhetoric of *al-ta-damun al-Islami* (Islamic Solidarity).[4] Although the symbolic importance

---

[2] Al-Rasheed, *Contesting the Saudi State*, pp. 62–63.

[3] Stephane Lacroix, *Awakening Islam*, pp. 41–42.

[4] Malcolm Kerr, *The Arab Cold War: Gamal'Abd al-Nasir and His Rivals, 1958–1970*, 3rd edn. (London and New York, NY: Oxford University Press, 1971).

of the kingdom's geographical location – that is, controlling the holy cities of Mecca and Medina – was initially a helpful means of boosting the Kingdom's legitimacy, Saudi Arabia did not possess the resources to compete with Egyptian propaganda.[5] From the end of the 1950s, the Kingdom opened its doors to members of the Muslim Brotherhood who had escaped persecution in Egypt and Syria. The majority of these activists were skilled professionals who could be employed in education and the media. They became the core elements of the anti-Nasser propaganda apparatus whose leading organ was the *Sawt al-Islam* (Voice of Islam) radio station.

At the same time, the Muslim Brotherhood permeated all levels of the education. Due to their dominance in schools and universities and in the media, the foreign Islamists strongly influenced the thinking of a young generation of Saudis. Although the Ikhwan (Muslim Brothers) were forbidden from establishing an official branch in Saudi Arabia, they used their resources to spread their *da'wa* as extensively as possible. Controlling the education system was especially useful for this purpose. In the view of the Brothers, the goal of education was not only learning but also shaping the worldview of young people in line with the Brotherhood's ideals.[6] As Lacroix puts it, the "massive influx of an exogenous tradition (. . .) was the source of a vast social movement that produced its own counterculture and its own organizations and, through the educational system, soon reached almost all fields of the social arena."[7]

This movement is widely called *al-Sahwa al-Islamiyya* (Islamic Awakening, *Sahwa* for short). The *Sahwa* is not exclusively a product of *Ikhwani* ideas, but possesses a hybrid ideology. The *Sahwa* adopted the main elements of the Muslim Brothers' worldview but retained the Salafi creed and jurisprudence.[8] The result is an ideology that only recognizes the right of the one, "true Islam" to exist, and intends to purify religion from *bid'a*. At the same time, it adopts the Muslim Brotherhood's activism, commitment to the Islamization of all spheres of society, and resistance to imperialism and Westernization. In al-Rasheed's words,

while the *Sahwa* may represent itself through increased commitment to ritualistic Islam, it is above all a state of mind that allows a Muslim to have Islam and only Islam as a reference point for all aspects of life, including

---

[5] Nasser became increasingly popular among the rural population and the educated class in Saudi Arabia.

[6] Lacroix, *Awakening Islam*, pp. 42–51.   [7] Ibid., p. 51.   [8] Ibid., p. 54.

public political affairs. At the individual level, Sahwis have a commitment not only to the salvation of the self but also to society.[9]

The *Sahwa* never established a formal organizational structure, or clear-cut hierarchy. Rather, it was characterized by the predominance of loose, informal, interpersonal networks.[10] At the beginning of the movement in the 1970s, the *Sahwa* was on good terms with and was even supported by the Saudi government.[11] In the 1980s, the *Sahwi* presence became so powerful among the educated class that the regime had to side with them in their battle with secular intellectuals, so as not to lose legitimacy in the eyes of a wide segment of the population.[12]

The monarchy came under *Sahwi* attack on the eve of the Gulf War in 1991, when the government allowed American soldiers to land on Saudi soil to defend the country against a potential Iraqi invasion. In public sermons and lectures, *Sahwi* shaykhs openly questioned the ruling system's legitimacy. They decried the official *'ulama'* that had issued a fatwa legitimizing the presence of the US soldiers, calling these scholars *'ulama' al-sultan* (scholars of the rulers), hypocritical and subservient. They were depicted as ready to sacrifice religion for the interests of the regime, to avoid falling out of favor with the Sa'ud clan.[13] The movement also demanded more political freedom and free elections, while at the same time calling for more social conservatism.[14]

However, the *Sahwa* insurgency failed around 1994, and the government once again controlled the public sphere. There are several reasons for this failure. The movement ran out of steam because it had been unable to gain wide grassroots support beyond the educated class. In addition, some countermovements weakened the *Sahwis*, the most important being the Madkhalis or Jamis. Government repression was an important factor as well. Some of the leading figures in the movement were imprisoned for years, and *Sahwis* were fired from their jobs in media and education, posts that were then filled by secular intellectuals and Salafis loyal to the government.

---

[9] Madawi Al-Rasheed, *Contesting the Saudi State: Islamic Voices from a New Generation* (Cambridge: Cambridge University Press, 2007), p. 68.
[10] They dominated many institutions, but unlike the Muslim Brotherhood, they did not have their own organizational networks. Lacroix, *Awakening Islam*, pp. 63–73.
[11] Ibid., p. 152.   [12] Ibid., pp. 129–133.
[13] Sahwis often refer to the former Mufti Muhammad bin Ibrahim (1893–1969) who was always brave enough to oppose the king if he thought that the king's orders contradicted religion. Ibid., p. 149.
[14] Al-Rasheed, *Contesting the Saudi State*, pp. 59–101; Mamoun Fandy, *Saudi Arabia and the Politics of Dissent* (New York; Houndmills: Palgrave, 2001), pp. 21–60.

Despite the weakening of the *Sahwa* within Saudi Arabia, the movement had a great impact on Salafism at the transnational level and played a key role in shaping its contemporary character. The emergence of the movement led to the formation of the *haraki* faction. Foreign students in the Saudi Kingdom who had been inspired by the *Sahwa* and socialized in *Sahwi* circles went on to spread its discourse and worldview in other Muslim countries. Leading *Sahwi* shaykhs, such as Muhammad Surur, Salman al-'Awda, Safar al-Hawali, and Nasir al-'Umar, became transnational authorities. The *Sahwa* also influenced Jihadi thinking; for example, Osama bin Laden socialized in *Sahwa* circles before he left for Afghanistan.[15] As Lacroix shows, other influential jihadi shaykhs such as 'Ali al-Khudayr started their activism in *Sahwi* circles. After the government's crackdown on the movement, they concluded that political activism would not lead to success. They therefore opted to use violence to destroy the Saudi regime and drive its main ally, the United States, from the region.[16]

The example of the Kuwaiti scholar Hamid al-'Ali also indicates the influence of the *Sahwa*. At the beginning of the 1990s, Al-'Ali was counted as one of the *Sahwa*, at least in ideological terms. Later he became one of the leading *haraki* figures in Kuwait. Although he never sided explicitly with the jihadis, many jihadis consider his polemics against the Shi'a or writings on Western imperialism to be authoritative. Al-'Ali usually focuses on diagnostic framing and leaves both the political and the military solutions open. Therefore, he has a large following among both jihadis and politicos.[17]

It is important to note here that the adoption of the revolutionary approach toward *ijtihad* and the *hadith* by one of the greatest Salafi scholars, Nasir al-Din al-Albani (1914–1999), played a crucial role in shaping *Sahwi*, and thereby *haraki*, discourse.[18] This is despite the fact that the shaykh himself was clearly a purist. In theory, traditional Saudi *'ulama'* call for *ijtihad*, but in practice they largely follow Hanbali jurisprudence. In most cases, they abandon a given ruling by the *madhhab* only if they find proof that it contradicts the text. Al-Albani criticized

---

[15] Lacroix, *Awakening Islam*, p. 47.   [16] Ibid., pp. 249–250.
[17] During my fieldwork in Kuwait between February and March 2012, I met several followers of Shaykh Hamid al-'Ali. According to my observations, they are ideologically mixed. Many of them are ideologically close to Jihadis, while others have more moderate views. The moderates then are active in networks affiliated with the main politico organizations in Kuwait, such as al-Haraka al-Salafiyya or Dr. Hakim al-Mutayri's Hizb al-Umma.
[18] Al-Albani was born in Albania, but his family moved to Syria in his early childhood. Salafis regard him one of the greatest *hadith* scholars in history.

this approach, and instead emphasized the need for extensive study of the Hadith. He rejected the *taqlid* of the *madhahib*, instead proposing a wider form of *ijtihad* that requires, in each case, that there be proof by means of an independent reading of the Prophetic tradition, if the Qur'an does not give a clear answer.[19]

This extensive usage of the *hadith* independently of the constraints of the Hanbali School inspired the *Sahwa* and profoundly influenced its discourse. It is also essential to *haraki* Salafis to refer to verified quotations from the Prophet to support their statements and claims in their discourse. When they argue about the necessity of reforming Middle Eastern regimes or ridding the Muslim world of Western imperialism, they support their arguments with proof and references from the corpus. There are plenty of examples of this; one of the most obvious is the book by the Kuwaiti Salafi thinker Hakim al-Mutayri, *al-Hurriyya aw al-Tawfan* (Freedom or Storm).[20] He builds up a system of references to the *hadith* and Qur'anic quotations to prove that, with the revelation, God also created a political system for humans that is based on individual freedom and the free election of leaders.

Another movement played a crucial role in the fractionalization of Salafism; its adherents are commonly called Madkhalis, in reference to one their intellectual founders. Their origins go back to *al-Jama'a al-Salafiyya al-Muhtasiba* (JSM), a group inspired by al-Albani's teachings. They were even more influenced by the shaykh's approach toward the *hadith* than were the *Sahwis*, but, like al-Albani himself, they focused on the ritualistic aspects of Islam. They adopted his theory on Islamic activism, which he called *al-tasfiya wa-l-tarbiya* (purification and education). According to this theory, an Islamic society and state cannot be established until the religion has been purified of every foreign element and of those Muslims who do not apply the teachings of Islam in full. On that basis, the JSM was fiercely critical of Islamic movements that were directly involved in politics, such as the *Sahwa*. The group also distinguished itself by its extreme social conservatism, attacking symbols of "Westernization" under the pretext of practicing *hisba*.[21]

The JSM later split into two factions. The first rejected the rule of the House of Sa'ud on the grounds that they do not have *Qurayshi* origins.[22] This first group occupied the Grand Mosque under the

---

[19] Stephane Lacroix, "Between Revolution and Apoliticism," p. 60.
[20] al-Mutayri, *al-Hurriyya aw al-Tawfan*.
[21] Stephane Lacroix, "Al-Albani's Revolutionary Approach to Hadith," *ISIM Review*, 21, no. 1, 2008, p. 7.
[22] Lacroix, *Awakening Islam*, p. 97.

leadership of Juhayman al-'Utaybi in 1979. The loyalists took the opposite stance, resulting in the movement whose leading figures are Rabi' al-Madkhali (1931–) and the Ethiopian shaykh Muhammad Aman al-Jami (1930–1995). They retained the social conservatism of the JSM and their focus on the *hadith*, but at the same time emphasize that the obligation of unconditional obedience to the Muslim ruler is one of the most important aspects of their discourse. They launch harsh attacks on those who violate this premise. The Madkhalis' most frequent targets are the various Islamic movements, especially the Muslim Brotherhood.

Madkhalis (in Muslim countries) are exceptionally keen to work for state institutions, and they often support those who enter the army or the security services. According to Ikhwani activists from the United Arab Emirates, who I interviewed when they visited Kuwait, there are large numbers of Madkhalis working as agents and officers in their country's internal security agency.[23] During the *Sahwa* insurgency, the state supported the Madkhalis to boost its own legitimacy. Madkhali scholars were appointed as university professors in place of *Sahwis* who had been fired. While the authorities tried to silence *Sahwi* shaykhs by forbidding them from giving sermons, Madkhali shaykhs were encouraged to play public roles.[24]

According to many of my informants, at that time, divisions emerged among Salafis about the nature of a Muslim's relationship to the ruler.[25] As one of my Kuwaiti informants, the *haraki* scholar Shaykh 'Abd al-Aziz al-Jarallah, recalled, this issue had not previously been at the center of Salafi discourse. By contrast, after the Gulf War, "this became the first question a Salafi [individual] was asked about. Anything else became secondary after that."[26] Many *haraki* Salafis claim that the Madkhalis elaborated the thesis of "unconditional obedience to the ruler." When the Madkhalis' numbers increased in educational and religious institutions, they had a significant influence on Salafi discourse. Many Salafis accepted their views on obedience to the ruler even if they dismissed their harsh criticism of those who differ from them or their ultra-puritan lifestyle. This became the main dividing line between Salafis at the transnational level. The Madkhali movement also spread around the globe, despite the numerous internal splits.[27]

Although the Madkhalis are the most vocal in emphasizing the necessity of obeying the ruler, the official Saudi religious establishment

---

[23] Interview, Kuwait, March 4, 2012.   [24] Lacroix, *Awakening Islam*, pp. 214–216.
[25] See Introduction.   [26] Interview, Kuwait, March 9, 2012.
[27] Lacroix, *Awakening Islam*, pp. 218–220.

is the most influential authority within the purist faction. The official *'ulama'* were not always unconditionally loyal to the Saudi rulers; in fact, they often tried to influence the politics of the royal family. The most notable example is when, in 1964, senior Saudi scholars openly demanded that King Saud resign and transfer the power to Prince Faisal, whom the religious establishment favored. Since 1971, the official *'ulama'* 'have been organized under the auspices of the Council of Senior Scholars (*Majlis Hay'at Kibar al-'Ulama'* [CSS]), and since the 1980s they have almost unconditionally endorsed the decisions of the ruling family. The reason for their submission to the authority of the royal family is that the members of CSS realized that without the support of the Sa'ud clan they could not maintain their dominant status in the religious domain.[28]

Today, CSS enjoys a predominant position in the worldwide purist Salafi networks. Purists regard the fatwas of the members of CSS as the most authoritative legal opinions. The publications and sermons of the Council's scholars are globally distributed and widely read by purist Salafis.

1.2   The Fragmentation of Salafism in Kuwait

Kuwait's social and political system differs significantly from that of other states in the Arabian Peninsula. Although Kuwait is a hereditary monarchy, the ruling family has never been able to gain absolute dominance, and the emir has always shared his power with influential elements in society. Today, Kuwait is a constitutional monarchy unique among the Gulf countries, with an elected and functioning parliament, and a mostly free press. Due to this arrangement, control over society has been limited, and unlike in other Gulf monarchies, the flow of ideas and ideologies has been relatively free. The Shi'ite community that makes up around one third of the population was never as severely repressed as in other Arab countries such as Iraq or Saudi Arabia.[29]

This made it possible for Islamist movements to emerge relatively early on, and to be peacefully accommodated in the social and political

---

[28] Nabil Mouline, "Enforcing and Reinforcing the State's Islam." In *Saudi Arabia in Transition: Insights on Social, Political, Economic and Religious Change* (New York, NY: Cambridge University Press, 2015).

[29] Rajab al-Damanhour, "al-Tayyarat al-Shi'iyya al-Kuwaytiyya ... al-Tashakkulat wa-l-Masarat," *Islamonline*, November 3, 2009, http://islamyoon.islamonline.net/servlet/Satellite?c=ArticleA_C&cid=1235628915074&pagename=Zone-Arabic-Daawa%2FDWA Layout (accessed March 5, 2010).

system. The first Islamist movements were the Muslim Brothers, Hizb al-Tahrir, and the Tabligh. Of these, the Muslim Brothers were able to gain significant influence and representation in the political system. Tabligh was the first active puritan movement in Kuwait, and in the 1950s and 1960s had many followers among the locals. Even some of the older Salafi shaykhs became Islamist activists, with the Tabligh.[30] Hizb al-Tahrir, however, while able to attract some Palestinian intellectuals, never enjoyed a significant membership among the Kuwaitis.[31]

Although, according to some accounts, the Salafi message arrived in Kuwait in the nineteenth century from Central Arabia via tribal contacts, the movement was not able to establish itself until the 1960s.[32] At this time, a handful of *Salafi da'is* (preachers) settled in the country to transmit what was, according to them, the "pure form of Islam." The three most famous among them were the Egyptian 'Abd al-Rahman 'Abd al-Khaliq, the Saudi 'Umar al-Ashqar, and 'Abdullah al-Sabt, who belonged to the stateless community (*bidun*) in Kuwait.[33] According to an account by one of the first students of 'Abd al-Rahman 'Abd al-Khaliq, the Salafi *da'wa* began in an informal way at the beginning of the 1960s:

In the beginning we, a few dozen Salafis, only made excursions every night to the beach where we sat around the shaykh and took courses on the Qur'an and Sunna. At this stage we never touched on political or even social issues that went beyond personal, religious behavior. When our numbers became larger, we were able to have our study groups in mosques, until three mosques were entirely Salafi. The continuous arrival of migrant workers definitely increased our numbers.[34]

The movement's first center was the Dar al-Salafi (Salafi House), where the members were able to handle issues in a more official way. These, however, were restricted to collecting *zakat* and voluntary donations (*sadaqat*). As Shaykh 'Abd al-Rahman 'Abd al-Khaliq remembers, in the first years of the *da'wa*, the number of Salafis was still limited:

---

[30] One of them is the prominent Kuwaiti scholar, Nazim al-Misbah. Interview, al-Bayan district, February 20, 2012.

[31] Interview with one of the first Kuwaiti Salafis, Kuwait, January 11, 2010.

[32] Daghash al-'Ajmi bin Shabib, *Umara' wa-'Ulama min al-Kuwait 'ala 'Aqidat al-Salaf* (Kuwait, 2008), pp. 53–61; Ali Fahed al-Zumai, *The Intellectual and Historical Development of the Islamic Movement in Kuwait* (Exeter: Unpublished Ph.D. Thesis, 1988), p. 66.

[33] The *bidun* in Kuwait include those who are long-term residents of Kuwait or are born in the country without proper national identification. Their origins are usually from Saudi Arabia, Iraq, or Syria. Claire Beaugrand, "Framing Nationality in the Migratory Context: The Elusive Category of Biduns in Kuwait," *Middle East Law and Governance*, 6, no. 3 (2014), p. 174.

[34] Interview, Kuwait, January 21, 2010.

People were preoccupied with material goods and did not have many concerns about religion. When I first arrived in Kuwait, I was surprised to see that only old people visited the mosques.[35]

In fact, three important factors played a crucial role in the expansion of the Salafi movement in Kuwait. The first was the 1967 war, and the catastrophic military defeat of Egypt, Syria, and Jordan by Israel. Since this event, throughout the Arab world, "the attraction of Arab nationalism and socialism, dominant in 1967, has declined dramatically, while revivalist Islamism has risen."[36] After this war, for the first time, Arabs blamed themselves, not colonialism, for their defeat. Islamists exploited this situation by arguing "that the war was punishment for misplaced trust in the promise of alien ideologies that had been fostered as a means of mobilizing for modernization and development. The defeat was devastating because the margin of deviance from the faith was great."[37]

The situation in Kuwait was similar. Until the end of the 1960s, the various Arab nationalist movements, mainly the Nasserists, enjoyed overwhelming popularity.[38] However, after the 1967 war, their reputation rapidly declined and the vacuum was filled by an increase in religiosity and, naturally, by the Islamists, at the time dominated by the Muslim Brothers. As my interviewees recalled, in the years following the war, mosques that used to be empty, even at the time of Friday prayers, filled up with young people who had previously attended Nasserist gatherings or Communist organizations. Many people suddenly changed their lifestyles and those who had previously followed a Western lifestyle, now stopped shaving their beards.

The main beneficiaries of this upheaval were the Muslim Brothers, who had been present in the country for almost two decades and had built up their organizational infrastructure. The state also helped them by every possible means, since it saw Arab nationalism as a serious threat, especially because of the enmity between Nasser and the traditional pro-Western monarchies. The Egyptian president's hostility grew in particular after Algerian independence in 1962, when colonialism ceased to be the direct enemy. "Nasir had to find new targets, new 'others'. So Arab nationalist fury was turned against Arab countries that Nasir deemed to be 'reactionary'."[39]

---

[35] Interview with 'Abd al-Rahman 'Abd al-Khaliq, Kuwait, February 13, 2010.
[36] Yvonne Haddad, "Islamists and the 'Problem of Israel': The 1967 awakening," *Middle East Journal*, 46, no. 2 (1992), p. 266.
[37] Ibid., p. 267.
[38] Salih Baraka al-Sa'idi, *Al-Sulta wa-l-Tayyarat al-Siyasiyya fi al-Kuwait: Jadaliyyat al-Ta'awun wa-l-Sira'* (Kuwait: Dar al-Qabas, 2010), pp. 25–33.
[39] Adeed Dawisha, *Arab Nationalism in the Twentieth Century* (Princeton, NJ; Oxford: Princeton University Press, 2003), p. 285.

Salafis were also able to take advantage of the religious upheaval, due to the fact that they already controlled several mosques and had direct access to young people who had recently turned to religion. The other efficient means of transmitting the message was attending *diwaniyya*s, the traditional Kuwaiti (mostly men's) gatherings. These events are usually held weekly in the houses of prominent families and are open to everyone. *Diwaniyya*s are an essential part of the Kuwaiti public sphere, as they provide the main forums for both political and religious debates (see Chapter 6).[40] When members of significant Kuwaiti families became sympathetic to Salafism, the *da'i*s were able to access these *diwaniyya*s and share their teaching with other attendants. They are usually invited weekly or bi-weekly to give lectures and hold study groups for Qur'an or Hadith.[41]

The real breakthrough for Salafis was the restructuring of economic and political power in Kuwait. In the early 1970s, Salafis recruited followers among the influential merchant class. Khalid Sultan, the former leader of the Salafi parliamentary faction, was among them. This also opened the way for them to become part of Kuwait's political map in the long term. In the pre-oil era, the rulers of Kuwait traditionally shared power with the merchant class. The emirs were financially largely dependent on the merchants, as the latter dominated large segments of the population whose livelihoods were based on trade and pearl-diving, and were able to extract revenues from them. However, after the discovery of oil, the power balance changed in favor of the rulers. They became independent from the merchants' revenues and were therefore largely able to exclude the latter from decision-making.

Unlike the other Gulf States, however, in Kuwait, the ruler did not enjoy absolute power, and though the merchants lost most of their official political power, they still constituted an influential segment of the population.[42] They continuously sought new opportunities to regain their former sociopolitical influence, and therefore supported political and religious movements. At the end of the 1970s, scions of influential merchant families became followers of Salafism. This enabled the movement to gain a presence in the financial and trading sector, and receive more funding than before. Since the merchants

---

[40] There are *diwaniyya*s for women as well. The number of the mixed *diwaniyya*s is also growing among the liberal-minded population.

[41] Nowadays, every Kuwaiti Salafi sheikh tends to appear at *diwaniyya*s on a regular basis, and the dates can be found on their websites. See, for instance, the website of Sheikh Salim al-Tawil, a prominent Kuwaiti Salafi scholar: www.saltaweel.com/schedule (accessed 4 November 2016).

[42] Jill Crystal, *Oil and Politics in the Gulf: Rulers and Merchants in Kuwait and Qatar* (Cambridge: Cambridge University Press, 1995), pp. 84–88.

were interested in social and political issues, the voices that grew stronger in the Salafi movement were those keen on seeing religious rulings implemented in public life.

As one of my informants explained to me, at this time, Salafis began involving themselves in more worldly debates concerning politics and society.[43] A few Salafis joined the Muslim Brotherhood or worked with them. The majority, however, remained independent and harshly critical of the Muslim Brothers. According to some accounts, in the 1970s, a "war of ideas" (*harb afkar*) took place between the Muslim Brothers and Salafis in the *diwaniyya*s, mosques, public gatherings, and in the media, which became accessible to Salafis after they had gained sympathizers within the merchant class.[44]

The third factor is the geopolitical change in the region, which favored the Salafis. The Iranian Revolution of 1979 posed an existential threat to the Kuwaiti state. Beside the military threat that came from Tehran, Khomeini's Islamist regime intended to spread the revolution among the Shi'ite communities of the Gulf. Shi'ite militant cells in Kuwait committed several terrorist attacks during the 1980s. In addition, the fact that Islamists were able to come to power and establish a regime based on *shari'a* in Iran (despite the fact that they were Shi'ites) gave the Muslim Brotherhood in countries with Sunni majority new confidence that their project could succeed. The Kuwaiti ruling family was frightened by the prospect of being overthrown by the Islamists. Therefore, to divide the Sunnis, the state began supporting the Salafi movement against the Muslim Brothers, as it had supported the latter at the end of the 1960s against the Nasserists. A further reason for helping the Salafis against the Muslim Brothers was the 1980–1988 Iran–Iraq War. While financing Saddam Hussein's expensive military adventure against an Islamic state, the government needed a form of Islamic legitimacy.

By the early 1980s, the Salafi movement in Kuwait had achieved an unprecedented level of organizational development. While most aspects of the movement's organizational strategy retained an informal character, Salafis gained a strong presence in professional syndicates and student unions, where they competed with the Muslim Brothers. As the next stage in their organizational development, the Salafis of Kuwait established *Jama'iyyat Ihya' al-Turath al-Islami* (Society for the Revival of Islamic Heritage, or SRIH). The society was founded in 1981 with the support of the Kuwaiti state and wealthy merchants

---

[43] Interview with Salim al-Nashi, the former director of the political desk of al-Tajammu' al-Islami al-Salafi (Salafi Islamic Gathering), January 13, 2010.

[44] Falah al-Mudayris, *Al-Jama'a al-Salafiya fi-l-Kuwait: al-Nasha't wa-l-Fikr wa-l-Tatawwur 1965–1999* (Kuwait: Dar Qurtas li-l-Nashr, 1999), pp. 7–8.

who had adopted Salafi ideology. Although, according to its founding documents, SRIH was created for charitable purposes, from the beginning, it covered a wider range of tasks.

In the 1980s, the SRIH served as an umbrella organization for Kuwait's Salafis and provided the institutional framework for engaging in the political process. In 1981, for the first time anywhere in the world, Salafis were nominated for parliamentary elections. At the time, Salafis elsewhere did not support any kind of political participation in secular and parliamentary regimes, since they were heavily influenced by the Saudi religious line, which abstained from any serious political involvement aside from legitimizing the autocratic rule of the royal family. Most Kuwaiti Salafis, however, took a different stance, due to the revolutionary ideology propagated by their main religious authority, 'Abd al-Rahman 'Abd al-Khaliq.

1.2.1   The Thought of Shaykh 'Abd al-Rahman 'Abd al-Khaliq

It is necessary to briefly discuss the philosophy of 'Abd al-Rahman 'Abd al-Khaliq, since his ideas played a crucial role in the development of SRIH. Unlike those of purist Salafis, the majority of the writings of Shaykh 'Abd al-Rahman are related to politics. In the late 1970s, he began publishing weekly in *al-Watan*, one of the biggest Kuwaiti dailies, mainly commenting on contemporary political affairs. In one of his articles, he argues that politics and human development are more important than mere religious practice. Islam, he says, is a total system; politics forms a part of this system and cannot be neglected.

Shaykh 'Abd al-Rahman criticizes the argument that the Prophet did not practice politics in the first Meccan period. According to Shaykh 'Abd al-Rahman, this claim is false, because politics is not only about governing a state. In his words,

the Prophet from the first day of his *da'wa* intended to apply a different dogma from the dominant worldview and wanted to gather people around this dogma ... The Prophet also created a secret society [when the Muslims were oppressed in Mecca], a society that worked publicly to change the social system. He used every available media, like personal conversations, sermons ... the media war against the belief of the *Jahiliyya*, and all of this is politics.[45]

'Abd al-Rahman 'Abd al-Khaliq argues that the purist stance on politics only serves the enemies of Islam who destroyed the Caliphate and then

---

[45] 'Abd al-Rahman 'Abd al-Khaliq, *al-Muslimun wa-l-'Amal al-Siyasi*, undated book, accessible online at: www.salafi.net. (accessed February 5, 2010).

established weak rulers in Muslim countries in order to safeguard the interests of the West. Unlike the purists, he also justifies the establishment of political parties on the grounds that they can raise the flag of Islam, and there is nothing in the Qur'an that prohibits such organizations. He writes that parties and associations are effective tools of *da'wa* in a democratic system, and that it is in the interest of Muslims to preserve this system, since the alternative is military dictatorship. Many purists regard other types of associations, such as charitable organizations, as *bid'a* (invention) and therefore prohibited. In Shaykh 'Abd al-Rahman's view, such associations existed at the time of the Prophet. He mentions the case of Muslims who fled to Ethiopia to escape the repression of the Meccans. Since the Muslims lived in a minority in a predominantly Christian country, they forged close ties with each other and established an association (*jama'iyya*) led by one of the Companions, Ja'far bin Abi Talib.

1.2.2   SRIH after the Liberation of Kuwait

While the Salafi movement had been quite united until 1990 under the umbrella of SRIH, after the liberation of Kuwait from the Iraqi occupation, this was no longer the case. The schism occurred due to debates within the Salafi movement in Saudi Arabia described in an earlier section in this chapter. During the Gulf War, most Kuwaiti Salafis escaped to Saudi Arabia, where they actively participated in these debates. They were able to integrate quickly into the different Salafi networks and groups in Saudi Arabia because they were often connected to the Saudi Salafis through kinship.[46] Many of them became active followers of the *Sahwa* movement. Upon their return to their home country after the war, these individuals became pioneers of the *haraki* wing of Kuwaiti Salafism, as was the case for Dr. Hakim al-Mutayri, Shaykh Hamid al-'Ali, and Dr. 'Abd al-Razzaq al-Shayiji.

During the occupation of Kuwait, others sided with the purist camp, which was represented by the official Saudi *'ulama*. Most probably, this was because the purists did not oppose Kuwait's liberation, even though it was undertaken by Western forces. Many Kuwaitis became influenced by Rabi' al-Madkhali and propagated his ideas upon their return. After the liberation, when most Kuwaiti Salafis returned home, the debates

---

[46] Most Kuwaitis have numerous relatives in Saudi Arabia, especially those who have tribal origins. All of the tribes that are present in Kuwait have extensions in Saudi Arabia.

were exported to Kuwait, and in the 1990s, the local Salafi community split along *haraki* and purist lines. This schism, in turn, had an impact on SRIH. Until that time, the organization had been under the unquestionable leadership of Shaykh 'Abd al-Rahman 'Abd al-Khaliq.

In the first half of the 1990s, 'Abd al-Rahman 'Abd al-Khaliq was suddenly ousted from SRIH and the organization's ideological direction changed. Around 1996, a purist stream gained control over SRIH, led by Shaykh 'Abdullah al-Sabt and Shaykh Hayy al-Hayy, both influenced by Shaykh Rabi' al-Madkhali. According to some of my informants, the purists were given intensive state support, since the ruling family no longer trusted 'Abd al-Rahman 'Abd al-Khaliq and his followers. There were two reasons for this distrust. First, Shaykh 'Abd al-Rahman had personally sympathized with Saddam Hussein prior to the invasion, due to the Iraqi president's anti-Shi'a stance. Although Shi'ites were not the only victims of Saddam's persecution, many Salafis sympathized with him because he harshly repressed Shi'ite Islamic movements such as the Islamic Da'wa Party (*Hizb al-Da'wa al-Islamiyya*).[47] Second, the Kuwaiti state felt threatened by *haraki* Salafis due to their ambiguous stance toward Arab rulers.

The direct result of the expulsion of Shaykh 'Abd al-Rahman 'Abd al-Khaliq and most of his followers from SRIH was an open feud between 'Abd al-Rahman 'Abd al-Khaliq and Shaykh 'Abdullah al-Sabt, his former pupil. Shaykh 'Abdullah al-Sabt attacked one of the books written by 'Abd al-Rahman 'Abd al-Khaliq, *al-Sirat*, in which the latter describes *tawhid al-hukm* (oneness of governance) as an integral part of the pillars of *tawhid*.[48] As 'Abd al-Rahman 'Abd al-Khaliq puts it, "Unifying the *hakimiyya* of God Almighty means that we believe that he is the only one who has the right to govern and he is the source of the law for those who love him and accept [his *shari'a*]. As God said [in the Qur'an] there is no governance except for God [*la hukm illa li-llah*]."[49] Purist Salafis interpreted this as the application of Sayyid Qutb's concept of *hakimiyya* in a Salafi context.[50] According to Qutb, the government should be based on the sovereignty of God, which means that the legal

---

[47] The Islamic Da'wa Party is currently the leading force in the Iraqi government. In the 1970s and 1980s it was led by Muhammad Baqir al-Sadr (1935–1980), one of the most important Shi'ite Islamist thinkers, whose thought has had a great impact on contemporary Shi'ite Islamism.

[48] Salafis usually regard *tawhid al-'uluhiyya*, *tawhid al-rububiyya* and *tawhid al-asma' wa-l-sifat* as the three pillars of Tawhid.

[49] 'Abd al-Rahman 'Abd al-Khaliq, *al-Sirat*, 2000, available online at: www.salafi.net (accessed February 7, 2010).

[50] Interview with Nasser al-Khalidi, January 26, 2010.

system must be entirely based on *shari'a*. The ruler must rule justly, and must be chosen by the ruled, who must then obey the ruler. However, this obedience is based on the ruler's obedience to God.[51]

'Abdullah al-Sabt accused 'Abd al-Rahman 'Abd al-Khaliq of making a covert call for a revolt (*khuruj*) against the ruler and called him a Khariji, after a sectarian movement in early Islam.[52] As 'Abdullah al-Sabt wrote in an article that referred to 'Abd al-Rahman 'Abd al-Khaliq:

> The first Khawarij were repeating the truth but their aim was unjust with it: *la hukm illa li-llah*. They wanted to revolt against the legitimate Caliph of the Muslims ... That happened throughout history [i.e. according to the purist Salafi concept, the Khawarij always existed in Islamic history] and today's Khawarij [*Khawarij al-'Asr*] use the same word: the *hakimiyya* to excommunicate their rulers and legitimize the revolt against them.[53]

In a lecture, 'Abdullah al-Sabt explained that:

> This sentence of *la hukm illa li-llah* is old in the vocabulary of the *khawarij*. They used it to excommunicate the companions [of the Prophet] and to revolt against [the Caliph] 'Ali. [These thoughts] were transmitted among them [to the new generations] and then Sayyid Qutb used them ... then the contemporary *khawarij* developed these and divided *tawhid* into four parts [*aqsam*]: *uluhiyya*, *rububiyya*, *al-asma wa-l-sifat* and *al-hakimiyya*.[54]

Al-Sabt took a strong purist stance, which reflects the desire for order under the leadership of a Muslim ruler, even if he is unjust. He argued that, "there is no intelligent Muslim who thinks that governance is not for God." However, he questioned why it is necessary to emphasize this, since it can be misleading and cause political difficulties. In his article, 'Abdullah al-Sabt explained that the Salafis believe in God's rule, meaning following all of the practices and rulings of Islam, and having a government that assures this (*iqamat al-hudud*). He rejects "the narrow-minded *hakimiyya* " propagated by Islamist movements.

---

[51] William E. Shephard, *Sayyid Qutb and Islamic Activism: A Translation and Critical Analysis of Social Justice in Islam* (Leiden: Brill, 1996), p. 117.

[52] The Khawarij (plural of Khariji) had revolted against the fourth Caliph, 'Ali bin Abi Talib, when he agreed to settle his dispute with the governor of Damascus, Mu'awiya bin Abi Sufyan, by arbitration. Mu'awiya accused 'Ali of hiding the murderers of the third Caliph, 'Uthman bin 'Affan – who was Mu'awiya's relative – and claimed the Caliphate for himself. Some of 'Ali's soldiers did not accept the method of arbitration, since according to them, "God alone has the right to judge [*la hukm illa li-llah*]," which can also be translated as "no governance except for God." 'Khāridjites,' in Bosworth, *The Encyclopedia of Islam*.

[53] Undated audio recording of the debate between Shaykh 'Abd al-Rahman 'Abd al-Khaliq and 'Abdullah al-Sabt.

[54] Ibid.

'Abd al-Rahman 'Abd al-Khaliq responded to 'Abdullah al-Sabt in a religious letter (*risalah diniyyah*). In this, he stated that,

the Khawarij, when they said this word [*la hukm illa li-llah*] to 'Ali bin Abi Talib, were not demanding the application of the *shari'a*, but were disagreeing with him because he accepted the arbitration between him and Mu'awiyah ... Therefore not everybody is a Khariji who uses the words *la hukm illa li-llah*.[55]

He thinks that revolution against the ruler is obligatory only if the ruler is openly an apostate and thinks that manmade law is as good as *shar'ia*, or better. Shaykh 'Abd al-Rahman views the inclusion of *tawhid al-hukm* among the pillars of *tawhid* as a matter of choice, not a matter of sacred principle. There is no reason why a Salafi should strictly hold on to the idea of three aspects of *tawhid*. One may also speak of just one pillar of *tawhid*, or of ten, if one so wishes.

It should be noted that when I asked 'Abd al-Rahman 'Abd al-Khaliq whether it was permissible for the ruled to overthrow the ruler under certain conditions, he refused to give me a clear answer, while the purists who today control SRIH respond with an unequivocal "no." Throughout the 1970s and 1980s, however, when the Muslim Brothers openly criticized the legitimacy of contemporary Arab regimes, including Kuwait, he had always argued that it was not in the interest (*maslaha*) of the *umma* to touch on political issues such as these.

After the emergence of the activist current of Salafism, the Gulf regimes began to worry about potential criticism of hereditary monarchical systems and their alliances with the West. Therefore, the government began to support the purist Salafi faction led by 'Abdullah al-Sabt against 'Abd al-Rahman 'Abd al-Khaliq. By supporting a loyal faction and gaining control over SRIH, the state expected to ensure the loyalty of the majority of Salafis, or at least to depoliticize them. As a result of the internal strife in the organization, the majority of the followers of 'Abd al-Rahman 'Abd al-Khaliq left the organization in 1997 and created their own group under the name of "The Salafi Movement" (al-Haraka al-Salafiyya). After this, the nature of SRIH rapidly changed. Shaykh 'Abd al-Rahman 'Abd al-Khaliq's books disappeared from the organization's publishing houses, and it instead began printing the works of the Saudi religious establishment and works by Kuwaiti scholars with purist views. These publications focus on two main issues: the relationship between the ruler and the ruled, and the question of jihad.

On the relationship between the ruler and the ruled, SRIH has distributed one of the essays of the renowned Saudi purist scholar

---

[55] Ibid.

'Abd al-Salam bin Barjas. Bin Barjas argues that the companions of the Prophet did not revolt against Hajjaj bin Yusuf, the governor of Iraq between 695 and 714, known in the Islamic tradition for his unjust behavior toward his subjects and for his cruelty. According to the author, Hajjaj was no better than contemporary rulers, but the Sahaba abstained from overthrowing him in order to avoid chaos, which potentially would lead to corruption both in religious and worldly matters (*fasad al-din wa-l-dunya*).[56]

Bin Barjas also argues that the ruler must not be publicly criticized, since this can lead to disorder and revolt. The author supports his opinion with a *hadith* about the third Caliph 'Uthman: "When the civil war broke out in the time of 'Uthman, some of the people asked Usama bin Zayd [one of the companions of the Prophet]: You do not criticize Othman? He answered: What? Shall I criticize him in front of the people? No, I only can do it in private and thus not open the door to Evil."[57] This citation also reflects the purist view that open criticism of the ruler is forbidden, and that it should only be done in private by skilled religious scholars. Publicly, the *'ulama'* can condemn those things that violate religious rules, but without directly relating them to the ruler.

The second main topic of the new purist discourse of SRIH is jihad, in response to the increase in terrorist attacks in the last decade on the Arabian Peninsula and elsewhere in the world. SRIH – like other Islamic charities – has been accused of sponsoring jihadi organizations worldwide. The U.S. Treasury Department has accused the organization of giving financial support to two South Asian terrorist groups. The first is the Pakistani group Lashkar e-Tayyiba, which was responsible, *inter alia*, for the December 2001 attacks on the Indian parliament. The second is the Bangladeshi organization Jama'at al-Mujahidin. Both groups are linked to al-Qaeda.[58] On the basis of these accusations, the American government demanded that the Kuwaiti state close SRIH (as the Saudis had done with Mu'assasat al-Haramayn). However, the Kuwaiti government did not fulfill this request, claiming that there was no reliable evidence against SRIH. Most Islamists – even those who were otherwise ideologically opposed to the organization,

---

[56] 'Abd ul-Salam bin Barjas bin Naser al 'Abd ul-Karim, *Mu'amalat al-Hukkam fi Dhu' al-Kitab wa-l-Sunna* (Kuwait: Jama'iyyat Ihya' al-Turath al-Islami, 2009), pp. 11–12.

[57] Ibid., p. 48.

[58] Roy Bhaskar, "Terrorism in Bangladesh: Monster Child of BNP Jamaat," *South Asia Analysis Group*, November 17, 2009, available from www.southasiaanalysis.org/% 5Cpapers36%5Cpaper3509.html (accessed March 17, 2010); "Kuwait charity denies Qaeda links," *Kuwait Times*, June 15, 2008.

including *haraki* Salafis – resisted the ban. Although SRIH avoided the fate of Mu'assasat al-Haramayn, it came under almost total state control, and the purists' dominance became even more overwhelming. To avoid further accusations, SRIH put considerable effort into producing anti-jihadi propaganda. The organization published several books on the topic of jihad, and most of these are freely available in Salafi mosques worldwide. All of these publications reflect a strict purist agenda.

Shaykh Abi Hassan al-Sulaymani wrote *al-Tafjirat wa-l-Ightiyalat* (*The Bombings and the Murders*), one of the most read of these publications. He claims to explain the reasons for jihadi activity and offers solutions to the problem. To him, the main reason for the radicalization of Muslim youth is that some Salafi scholars have begun to openly criticize Muslim rulers, and accuses them of only being Muslims on the surface. This is in reference to *haraki* Salafis, who, according to the author, care little about *da'wa* and only focus on the issue of *hakimiyya*. This way of thinking inspired young people who were ignorant of religious matters to take up weapons against their legitimate ruler. Suleymani thinks that, although contemporary ruling regimes are not truly Islamic, Muslims should not revolt against them. He refers to a *hadith* to support his stance: "Always when an element of Islam is destroyed the people will cling even more to that which remains."[59] The author insists that by this, Muhammad meant that even when a government was not truly Islamic, other aspects of Islam would remain strong.[60]

1.2.3   Salafism in Kuwait after the Split in SRIH

The secession of Shaykh 'Abd al-Rahman 'Abd al-Khaliq's faction from SRIH led to the reorganization of the Salafi movement in Kuwait, which in turn had a serious impact on the transnational movement. Kuwait has become one of the main hubs of transnational Islamic activism. Due to its relatively free environment, it serves as an important meeting point for activists. At the same time, it is one of the most important centers of Islamic financing and charity activity in the world. For these reasons, transnational Islamic networks intersect in the country. Salafis from around the globe frequently travel to Kuwait to mobilize material resources or meet fellow activists. Thus, local transformations in the Kuwaiti Salafi movement tend to have a transnational impact.

[59] Abi Hasan al-Sulaymani, *al-Tafjirat wa-l-Ightiyalat* (Kuwait: Jama'iyyat SRIH al-Islami, 2008), p. 31.
[60] Ibid., p. 32.

The split of Kuwaiti Salafism into two main streams, a purist one and a *haraki* one, defined the character of Salafism in other locations, including Lebanon. Local factions became influential parts, and often the main material sponsors, of larger transnational networks. Therefore it is necessary to briefly describe the main Salafi groupings that emerged after the 1997 split in SRIH before I analyze how they contributed to the transformation of Salafism in Kuwait.

1.2.4   The Purists of Kuwait

Most of the purists identify themselves as close to SRIH, which now serves as their umbrella organization. Although the charitable institution's discourse has changed radically, it is still active in politics and has retained a relatively developed organizational structure in comparison to those of other Salafi groupings.

The members of the largest Salafi parliamentary block, *al-Tajammu' al-Salafi al-Islami* (Salafi Gathering), are closely connected to SRIH. Despite being politically active, they pursue predominantly purist aims in their parliamentary work. They always emphasize the need to obey the emir of Kuwait, and they are mostly concerned with the Islamization of social practices, such as the segregation of the sexes in public institutions and universities, and obliging Muslim women to wear the *hijab* when they appear in public. As one of the Salafi MPs explained to me, the *da'wa* is still developing and is endangered by both Westernized liberals and "extremists." Parliament offers an opportunity to defend the *da'wa*, support legislation that ensures the Islamic character of society, and practice *hisba*. Regarding this latter aspect, he mentioned how Salafis had contributed to the creation of a law that forbade the selling of alcohol on Kuwait Airways flights.[61] The members of *al-Tajammu'* – as Kuwaitis commonly refer to it – are often severely critical of those who are perceived to have insulted the person of the emir, whom they consider to be *wali al-amr*.[62]

At the same time, SRIH preserved the organizational structure that had been established when Shaykh 'Abd al-Rahman 'Abd al-Khaliq had dominated the institute. Although the Salafis who belong to the circle of SRIH tend to rely on informal networks, they maintain a more elaborate formal institutional structure than Salafis elsewhere. At the core of this structure is the charitable organization itself and its

[61] Interview with 'Ali al-'Umayr, January 15, 2010.
[62] "Al-Tajammu' al-Salafi: Narfudu Ayya Massas Bi-l-amir (Salafi Gathering: We Refuse Touching [the Person] of the Emir)," *al-Qabas*, October 12, 2012.

branches in Kuwait's different districts. Besides mobilizing funds to implement projects abroad, these branches also organize local Salafis. They establish local committees (*lajna*), which set up programs for the followers of SRIH.

The other influential purist stream contains those who belong to the Madkhalis, which I categorize as purist-rejectionists (see Introduction). Although fewer in number than the followers of SRIH, they have extended transnational networks in the Middle East, Europe, and Southeast Asia. The Madkhali stream in Kuwait developed around individuals who seceded from the Salafi mainstream when Salafis entered the political process in 1981. During the Gulf War they became close to the circle of Rabi' al-Madkhali. At the beginning of the 1990s, many young Salafis who rejected SRIH's main ideological line became attracted to them. Central to this wing of the Salafi movement in Kuwait are the shaykhs Hamad 'Uthman, Salim al-Tawil, Falah Mundakar, and, from the younger generation, Ahmad al-Siba'i and Muhammad al-'Anjari.

The cornerstone of the purist-rejectionists' discourse is showing unquestioning loyalty to the ruler and being harshly critical of those who – in their opinion – disobey him. Purist-rejectionists interpret the meaning of *khuruj 'ala al-hakim* (see Introduction) in a much narrower way than do other purists. Mainstream purists think that Muslims can disobey the ruler and side with the opposition if the ruler uses extreme and unjustified violence against his subjects. For example, most purist Salafis in SRIH opposed the Syrian and Libyan revolutions, but when the governments of Mu'ammar al-Qadhafi and Bashar al-Assad started to murder large numbers of demonstrators, they felt justified in supporting the revolutionaries.[63] By contrast, Madkhalis attacked SRIH for taking this stance. Shaykh Salim al-Tawil called Bashar al-Assad *wali al-amr*, forbade fighting against his army in a fatwa,[64] and described those Salafis who sent material support to the revolutionaries as *khawarij*.[65]

When I interviewed him, al-Tawil argued that Salafi *da'wa* can abide by a strong ruler who can provide security and essential infrastructure, such as roads, health services, and food. This enables the *da'is* to reach people and enables Muslims to focus on studying the Qur'an and

---

[63] Interview with Khalid Safran, a youth leader of SRIH, Kuwait, March 5, 2012.
[64] www.youtube.com/watch?v=jKblfbmb1E4. Shaykh Salim's fatwa incited a huge campaign against him, led by the Muslim Brothers and the *harakis*. In early March 2012 he was severely criticized in public sermons, on internet sites, and in social media (Facebook and Twitter).
[65] Interview, Kuwait, February 3, 2013.

Sunna, instead of focusing on their very survival.[66] When Muslims start to establish organizations to achieve certain aims, they indirectly contribute to undermining this order. Therefore, even Salafis who claim to believe in unconditional obedience to the *hakim* are in fact partisans (*hizbiyyun*), and he includes SRIH among these. As he explained, by organizing their members, they turn their attention away from the *shari'a* and become loyal to the organization instead. By their political activism and by occasionally forming different opinions to those of the ruler, they challenge the order.[67]

Purist-rejectionists commonly categorize those who do not agree with their views as belonging to *ahl al-bid'a*[68] and openly express hostility toward them. One of the young Kuwaiti Madkhalis told me that he could be friends with someone who drinks alcohol or even a murderer, because he might repent. It is not possible to be friends with someone who is a *mubtadi'* (commits *bid'a*), however, because this might make this person believe that he is right, and such behavior might imply that diversity in *'aqida* is permissible in Islam. Moreover, a murderer usually only kills one person, whereas the *mubdtadi'* kill thousands by legitimizing demonstrations and overthrowing *wulat al-amr* (pl. of *wali al-amr*).[69]

A defining characteristic of purist-rejectionists is their extreme social conservatism. They socialize only with those who hold similar views. Most of them are reluctant to enter those parts of Kuwait that are seen as "secular" and "westernized," such as certain areas of Salmiya. They rarely go to restaurants, as women are also present there. In contrast, purists from SRIH usually do not mind appearing in such places if they have reason to be there (such as an appointment or business meeting), although Salafis generally agree that spending leisure time in shopping malls or "Western-style" cafés should be avoided.

At the same time, the networks of SRIH and the Madkhalis overlap in several ways. Despite the enmity the latter feel to the organization, many SRIH followers attend the religious lessons of the purist-rejectionist shaykhs because they are well-versed in *hadith*. Purist-rejectionists also visit shaykhs associated with SRIH. Scholars such as Hayy al-Hayy or 'Uthman al-Khamis are considered to be close to Madkhali thinking and spend most of their time giving lessons, even though both of them

---

[66] Ibid.

[67] Discussion in one of Shaykh Salim's religious lessons, Kuwait, February 6, 2012.

[68] Only those persons who are knowledgeable in matters of religion are regarded as *ahl al-bid'a*. Those with only an average religious knowledge do not face the same harsh criticism from the Madkhalis.

[69] Interview, Kuwait, March 1, 2012.

belong to the charity (Hayy al-Hayy is a recognized *hadith* expert, while 'Uthman al-Khamis specializes in the refutation of Shi'ite beliefs).

1.2.5   Haraki Salafis

The core of the *haraki* faction in Kuwait is made up of followers of Shaykh 'Abd al-Rahman 'Abd al-Khaliq, who seceded from SRIH in 1997. Although, before the Gulf War, the majority of Salafis in Kuwait could probably be considered *harakis*, *haraki* thinking within the movement developed further after the Iraqi invasion. The young generation of Salafis, in particular, was exposed to the ideas of the Saudi *Sahwa*, and many of them adopted several elements of Saudi thinking. The most important figure of the young generation of Kuwaiti *harakis* is probably Hakim al-Mutayri. He became the de facto leader of the activist-minded youth wing within SRIH that remained loyal to 'Abd al-Rahman 'Abd al-Khaliq.

According to Dr. Sajid al-'Abdali, a veteran *haraki*, before the Gulf war, Hakim al-Mutayri's thinking was rather purist, and he was mostly interested in the issue of *'ibadat*. When the debates between the activist Salafis and the purists started to heat up, he became involved in a network centered on Muhammad Surur Zayn al-'Abidin,[70] a leading figure in the *Sahwa* movement, which radically changed his thinking. Dr. Sajid described Mutayri as an unusually charismatic person who was able to make friends quickly. Within a short time, many young Kuwaitis who had escaped to Saudi Arabia joined him in the al-Qasim region, where he was then residing.

This group, which was led by Hakim al-Mutayri, 'Abd al-Razzaq al-Shayiji, and Shaykh Hamid al-'Ali, established a strong platform within SRIH. When the debate erupted between 'Abd al-Rahman 'Abd al-Khaliq and 'Abdullah al-Sabt, they founded a political organization, *al-Haraka al-Salafiyya* (Salafi Movement), under the leadership of al-Mutayri.

According to Dr. Sajid, the aim was initially not to secede from SRIH, but to establish a new political wing for Kuwaiti Salafis. Al-Mutayri's idea was to create a political platform that would include both the purist-minded Salafi politicians and the *harakis*. He intended to create

---

[70] Muhammad Surur is one of the leading ideologists of *haraki* Salafism. Between the 1970s and the 1990s, one of the two dominant *haraki* networks in Saudi Arabia closely associated itself with his teachings. See Lacroix, *Awakening Islam*, pp. 63–70; al-Rasheed, *Contesting the Saudi State*, pp. 73–77.

it in accordance with the example of the pre-Islamic tribal alliance of *Hilf al-Fudul*, in which everyone could have their own autonomy.

The Hilf al-Fudul alliance was made between five tribes a few years before the Prophet Muhammad's mission. They intended to protect each other's interests against other tribes that were not part of the alliance. At the same time, the participants retained their autonomy; none of them intended to dominate the others.[71] Al-Mutayri wanted to create a Salafi alliance that would respect the differences between the various Salafi groups and would instead unify their lines and promote their mutual interests. The idea did not prove to be viable, mostly because of the purists' firm refusal to cooperate with those whom they considered *khawarij*. Al-Haraka al-Salafiyya soon became a separate *haraki* umbrella organization, connecting – mostly by informal relationships – most activist-minded Kuwaitis.[72]

However, this network of *haraki* Salafis did not remain united for long. Soon, internal differences surfaced. The main cause of the rift was the distinct visions of Hakim al-Mutayri and Hamid al-'Ali. When the former went to obtain his Ph.D. at Muhammad Surur's Centre for Islamic Studies in Birmingham at the beginning of the 2000s,[73] Hamid al-'Ali took over as leader of the "Haraka." While Mutayri had originally wanted it to be an exclusively political organization, Al-'Ali started *da'wa* and charity activities, and transformed al-Haraka al-Salafiyya into a competitor of SRIH. Due to the disagreements, Hakim al-Mutayri established his own political party, *Hizb al-Umma* (the Umma Party), in 2005.

Until the 2011 Arab Uprisings, most of the committed Salafis in Kuwait sympathized with SRIH.[74] Activists usually have only one member in parliament, Walid al-Tabtab'ai, while al-Tajammu' al-Salafi has between eight and ten. Despite this, Kuwaiti *harakis* are important members of transnational Salafi networks. The country is a significant transnational meeting point for activist-minded Salafis. *Harakis* from all around the world frequently pay informal visits to Kuwait in order

---

[71] "Hilf al-Fudul," in Bosworth, *The Encyclopaedia of Islam*.

[72] Interview with Dr. Sajid al-'Abdali, former spokesman of al-Haraka al-Salafiyya, March 4, 2012.

[73] The center was established by Muhammad Surur in the mid-1980s, after he had arrived as an exile in Britain. It functioned as a *haraki* think tank and a key educational destination for the second generation of *haraki* Salafis in the 1990s and 2000s. See Lacroix, *Awakening Islam*, p. 154.

[74] The situation changed when *harakis* took the lead to financially support the armed Syrian opposition. See Zoltan Pall, "Kuwaiti Salafism and Its Growing Influence in the Levant," *Carnegie Middle East Papers*, May 2014, http://carnegieendowment.org/files/kuwaiti_salafists.pdf (accessed May 28, 2015).

to meet individuals such as 'Abd al-Rahman 'Abd al-Khaliq or Hakim al-Mutayri. Prior to the Arab Spring, Kuwait was considered to be the only country in the Middle East in which Salafis did not face pressure from the government and security forces and were able to freely exchange their views. When I interviewed him in Kuwait, 'Abd al-Rahman 'Abd al-Khaliq claimed that the idea that Egyptian Salafis should participate in politics had emerged during the meetings that these Salafis had attended in his house and mosque.[75]

The charitable activities of *harakis* are also significant. Their charitable organization, Mabarrat al-'Amal al-Khayriyya, has projects all over the Middle East and Africa. They cooperate with the Qatari Mu'assasat al-Shaykh 'Aid al-Khayriyya and also raise funds in informal ways. During my fieldwork in Kuwait, I often observed that activists would collect money during *diwaniyya*s and other informal meetings for various purposes, such as helping the revolutionaries in Syria. Large amounts of money went to Northern Lebanon, destined for Syria. However, according to some of my informants in Wadi Khalid, part of this funding is never handed over to the revolutionaries, but is kept by some of the Salafi shaykhs. According to them, this partly explains the increasing material means of some Salafis in the North.[76]

The fragmentation of Salafism in Kuwait is a good illustration of the dynamics of the movement since the Gulf War, and the intramovement transformations that have reshaped the face of Salafism worldwide. Being one of the most important hubs of Salafi transnational networks, the split in SRIH not only influenced the movement locally but also had a significant transnational impact. The reconfiguration of the structure of Salafism in Tripoli and its surroundings is not unique; there were similar developments in Indonesia, for example.[77] Therefore, my analysis uncovers important aspects of the roots of significant developments at the transnational level of the movement, and at the same time provides an important comparative perspective.

---

[75] Interview, al-Bayan district, March 12, 2012.
[76] In the summer of 2011 I conducted many conversations with smugglers in Wadi Khalid, who are currently helping to transfer goods and money to the Syrian revolutionaries.
[77] According to my informants in Jakarta, after the split in RIHS, the charity stopped sponsoring many *harakis* and instead built up an entirely purist network. The agents of RIHS in Jakarta whom I interviewed emphasized the need to obey *wali al-amr* under any conditions, if he is a Muslim. Interview with Ustaz Zarkashi and Ustaz Setiawan, Jakarta, December 11, 2012.

1.3   Qatar as a Main Hub of Haraki Salafism

To understand the development of Lebanese Salafism, it is also necessary to briefly discuss Qatar's position as one of the main transnational hubs of *haraki* Salafism and as a source of sponsorship for the movement. The trajectory of Salafism in Qatar is distinct from Salafism in Kuwait, because of the development of the country's sociopolitical structure.

Between its establishment in the second half of the nineteenth century and the second half of the twentieth century, Qatar, unlike Kuwait, gained little significance in transnational trade and remained one of the poorer areas of the peninsula. As in Kuwait, the small sheikhdom's main income was based on pearl fishing, and the ruler also had to rely on the merchants who controlled the pearling industry. However, the merchants in Qatar were less wealthy and politically much weaker than their counterparts in Kuwait. They were unable to counterbalance the Al Thani ruling clan, which dominated the political leadership.[78]

Because of the unchallenged dominance of the ruling family, no deliberative body emerged in Qatar comparable to the parliament in Kuwait. Despite the country's rapid modernization after oil production began in 1940, the structure of the regime remained intact. Apart from members of the ruling family, no one could participate in political decision-making, and there was also no place for political movements, unlike in Kuwait. In Qatar, Salafis confined themselves to strictly religious matters and never really aspired to assume any political role.

Because of the lack of indigenous religious scholars, *'ulama'* from the Najd settled in the small monarchy and provided religious services. Until the late 1990s, they remained the sole religious authorities. Even in the twentieth century, a local class of religious scholars failed to develop in Qatar, meaning that Saudi shaykhs regularly crossed the border or settled in the country to fulfill the religious needs of the population. These *'ulama'* could be classified as purist, and were close to the official religious establishment of Saudi Arabia.

The Qatari religious field was completely reshaped when, in June 1995, Shaykh Hamad bin Khalifa Al Thani deposed his father, Shaykh Khalifa. Apart from a broad modernization program, the primary objective of the first period of his reign was to rid his country of Saudi patronage. Since gaining independence from Britain in 1971, Qatar's

---

[78] *Crystal, Oil and Politics in the Gulf*, pp. 112–118.

internal and foreign policy had been dominated by its powerful neighbor.[79] The new emir broke with Riyadh and intended to rule independently from the House of Sa'ud. Transforming the religious field was one means of minimizing Saudi influence in the country. Most of the *'ulama'* in Qatar were loyal to Riyadh, rather than to the new ruler. Emir Hamad also feared that these scholars might side with one of the pro-Saudi wings of the royal family to oust him. Therefore, the post-1995 government dismissed the Saudi preachers and replaced them with Egyptians, Syrians, Yemenis, and Saudi *Sahwis*. The cooptation of the latter is important for understanding the establishment of *Mu'assasat al-Shaykh 'Aid al-Khayriyya* (Shaykh 'Aid Charity Foundation – SACF), one of the most powerful Islamic charity organizations and a main patron of Lebanese Salafism.

When the state suppressed the Saudi *Sahwa* insurgency in 1995, many of the activists had to leave the kingdom. Doha offered some of the *Sahwi* shaykhs the chance to settle in the country and work as *khatibs* and imams of mosques. The Qatari government expected these *'ulama '* to be loyal to the ruling family in Qatar due to their persecution in their native country, and because the emir at that time was about to implement similar political reforms to those that they had been demanding in Saudi Arabia.[80] The ruler had two main reasons for hosting and employing the *harakis*. First, they were a means of strengthening his legitimacy against the Saudis, who were likely to seize every opportunity to reinstall their tutelage over Qatar or even annex it.[81] Second, the *Sahwis* were able to cater to the religious needs of the Salafi-minded inhabitants of the country, thereby largely detaching them from the Saudi religious establishment.

The ruler also tried to assure the loyalty of the Sahwis by using patronage to bind them to him. The ruling family generously funded the *haraki* Salafis' activism abroad by giving them part of the personal property and wealth of one of the deceased members of the Al Thani clan, Shaykh 'Aid bin Muhammad (1922–1994). Before he died, Shaykh 'Aid specified in his will that one third of his material possessions should be used to establish a charity. Although the new foundation was not exclusively Salafi, because participants of other Islamic

---

[79] Guido Steinberg, "Qatar and the Arab Spring: Support for Islamists and the New Anti-Syrian Policy," Report: German Institute for International and Security Affairs, February 7, 2012, p. 2, www.swp-berlin.org/en/publications/swp-comments-en/swp-aktuelle-details/article/qatar_and_the_arab_spring.html (accessed June 6, 2013).

[80] I acquired this information while talking to a group of *haraki* Salafis in the office of Dr. 'Abd al-Rahman al-Nu'aymi in Doha in June 2010.

[81] Ibid.

movements were also among its employees, most *haraki* Salafis in the country were connected to it. Since SACF was put in charge of money that came from the royal family, the charity became the clients of the Al Thanis. This is one of the ways in which the Qatari royal family has traditionally ensured the loyalty of different elements of society.[82]

In recent years, SACF has established a worldwide presence by supporting various Islamic NGOs and movements. It has become a key sponsor of Salafism in several regions, including the Middle East and Southeast Asia (especially Indonesia), and its influence in Europe is growing. It supports hundreds of local charities, Islamic centers, and mosques and gives financial aid to relief projects, from well-digging to the building of schools. Unlike Ihya' al-Turath, SACF does not have official branches abroad, but instead sponsors independent local charities or even individuals. However, those who receive financial support often have to be well embedded in transnational *haraki* networks and have to be in personal contact with someone who is influential in the organization (see Chapter 6).

Patronizing an organization such as SACF is also part of Qatar's foreign policy strategy. While before the takeover of Emir Hamad, Qatar's foreign policy largely was in line with Saudi Arabia, since the takeover it not only chose an independent path from its neighbor, but aspires to be a major player in international politics. Unlike Kuwait, the regime in Qatar does not face internal opposition. The country has a largely apolitical indigenous population without sectarian cleavages. Around 10–20 percent of Qataris are Shi'a, but are well integrated. To repel any possible external threats, Doha relies on the US security umbrella.[83] The lack of direct internal or external threats enables the Qatari leadership to focus its energy on increasing the country's international standing.

Qatar's foreign policy strategy revolves around pursuing what Mehran Kamrava calls subtle power. Achieving international prestige and proactive presence on the global stage are among the key components of subtle power.[84] Qatar achieved international prestige by pursuing a hyperactive diplomatic strategy and by establishing nationally identified brands: Qatar Airways, rated as one of the top airlines in the world, and the widely followed Al Jazeera satellite television channel are among the most renowned brands of the country. In recent years,

---

[82] Mehran Kamrava, "Royal Factionalism and Political Liberalization in Qatar," *Middle East Journal*, 63, no. 3 (2009), pp. 407–408.
[83] Mehran Kamrava, *Qatar: Small State Big Politics* (Ithaca, NY and London: Cornell University Press, 2013), pp. 73; 88–90.
[84] Ibid.

Doha has also become one of the world's most active mediators in international conflicts in the Middle East and Africa. For example, it played an essential role in resolving the political crisis in Lebanon in 2008 and ending the civil war in Sudan in 2010.

The activities of Qatari Islamic charities contribute to creating a positive image for the country among Muslim communities worldwide. Relief organizations such as SACF, Qatar Charity, or Rahmat al-Insan Fadila (Mercy is Great – RAF) foundation provide financial support for thousands of local Islamic NGOs across the Muslim world. This projects Qatar as a benevolent country in the eyes of Muslims worldwide, one that contributes something more meaningful for the Umma than empty political rhetoric.

Furthermore, the Islamic charities contribute to Doha's influence on the wider international stage. The recipients of the donations of these charities often belong to Islamic movements, which play an important role on the sociopolitical scenes of their localities. The main beneficiaries of Qatari money are the Muslim Brothers, such as the al-Nahda party in Tunisia or the Brotherhood's Egyptian branch.[85] Nevertheless, Salafis also receive vast amounts of money. Islamic movements are rarely paid directly by the state, but by one of the charities that are patronized by the ruling family. Doha expects its beneficiaries to remain loyal when they gain more influence in society, or even come to power, as happened in Egypt, Tunisia, and Morocco. After the 2013 Egyptian coup that removed Muhammad Mursi from power, and the rise of Emir Tamim to power in the same year, this support has decreased somewhat but by no means disappeared. Among the reasons for the decrease was Saudi Arabia's pressure on Doha to change its policy toward the Muslim Brotherhood, which the regime in Riyadh perceives as a threat.[86]

SACF has become a dominant player in Lebanese Salafism by sponsoring the *harakis*. The organization funds the charitable activities of local shaykhs in Tripoli and the North, pays the salaries of hundreds of preachers, and finances the building and maintenance of mosques and religious colleges. This means that SACF is contributing to the Lebanese *harakis'* ability to continue to compete with the increasingly influential purists, and to retain their influence within the movement at the local level.

---

[85] Steinberg, "Qatar and the Arab Spring," pp. 3–4.

[86] Christian Coates Ulrichsen, "Qatar and the Arab Spring: Policy Drivers and Regional Implications," *Carnegie Middle East Papers*, September 24, 2014, http://carnegieendow ment.org/2014/09/24/qatar-and-arab-spring-policy-drivers-and-regional-implications (accessed May 26, 2015).

1.4   Conclusion

This chapter showed that the purist–*haraki* dichotomy emerged after the 1991 Gulf War as a result of the intra-Salafi debates on the rights of the Muslim ruler. This fragmentation of the Saudi Salafi scene in turn affected the Kuwaiti Salafi scene. During the Iraqi invasion, the majority of the Kuwaiti Salafis escaped to Saudi Arabia and participated in the ongoing debates on the Salafi scene of the Kingdom, and this led to the evolution of the purist–*haraki* division. In 1996, purists took over SRIH and forced harakis to leave and establish their own groups. Subsequently, SRIH became one of the main bankrollers of purist Salafism worldwide. While both the Saudi and Kuwaiti governments favored the purist faction, perceiving *haraki*s as a threat, Qatar provided space for the latter to use the country as a base to extend their influence on the international level. Most *haraki* Salafis in the country became tied in some way to SACF, an Islamic charity that, among others, supported several Salafi groups worldwide.

Highlighting these developments serves as the basis to understand the evolution of Lebanese Salafism. In the following two chapters I will show that Salafism in Lebanon emerged as predominantly *haraki* in orientation with strong links to ideologically similar Salafi charities, such as SRIH before the purists' takeover. This, along with local Lebanese political developments contributed to the fragmentation of the country's Salafi movement. In the mid-2000s, SRIH contributed to setting up a purist network in North Lebanon, while the Qatari SACF played a crucial role in the *haraki* ascendance starting from the second half of the decade and culminating in the post–Arab Uprisings period.

2   Salafi Expansion in the 1990s

Salafis in Lebanon today constitute a religious elite with a large base of passive followers. Salafis control a considerable number of mosques, which enables them to disseminate their ideas while providing everyday religious services. Data from Dar al-Fatwa (the official religious establishment of the Sunnis) shows that the institution administers only 40 of the 110 mosques in Tripoli. Another 40 are under the control of Salafi shaykhs, and 30 mosques belong to different movements such as *al-Ahbash* (a Sufi-inspired movement), *al-Jama'a al-Islamiyya*, and *al-Tabligh*.[1] In *Bab al-Tabbana*, an economically disadvantaged quarter, all seven mosques are under Salafi control. In Wadi Khalid, another region in the North, which has 23 villages and 40,000 inhabitants, 15 of the 30 mosques belong to the Salafis, while the rest are administered by Dar al-Fatwa or privately by Sufi shaykhs. It can therefore be assumed that a significant part of the Sunni population of the North attends Salafi mosques and seeks advice regarding daily religious practices from Salafi shaykhs.

Before the Lebanese Civil War (1975–1990), Salafis constituted a marginal group with no significant political or social influence in North Lebanon. Yet, in the 1990s, Salafis established themselves in Northern Lebanese society and became an influential movement. To understand the reasons for their success, we need to look at the transformations of the Sunni religious field in light of wider sociopolitical processes, and examine how these transformations facilitated Salafism to mobilize capital. As this chapter will show, Salafis did not necessarily exploit the specific transformations of the field strategically and consciously. Rather, they became more relevant due to the way they carried out their *da'wa*. Before discussing the changing dynamics of the Sunni religious field in the 1990s, I provide a brief background on the roots of Lebanese Salafism.

---

[1] The original Urdu name of this latter movement is Tablighi Jamaat, since the movement originated from India in the first half of the twentieth century.

2.1   The Roots of Salafism in Lebanon

According to the contemporary Lebanese Salafi narrative, their movement is one of the oldest Islamic movements in Lebanon, founded in
the late 1940s by Shaykh Salim al-Shahhal (1922–2008), a self-educated
intellectual from the Dinniyeh region. His son, Abu Bakr al-Shahhal,
told me that his father was originally influenced by the discourse of
Muhammad Rashid Rida (1865–1935), who was born in the village of
Qalamun near Tripoli, but spent most of his life in Egypt. At the end
of the 1940s, Al-Shahhal became an enthusiastic reader of the journal
al-Manar, which had been founded by Rida in 1898.[2] While Rida was
a reformist in sociopolitical matters, he adopted a Salafi *'aqida* and a
more scripturalist approach than his mentor, Muhammad 'Abduh.[3] Al-
Shahhal was inspired by Rida's (and his disciples') articles in *al-Manar*
that called for erasing "heretical" Sufi practices and imposing a uniform
way of worship based on a literalist interpretation of the scripture.[4]
As Abu Bakr al-Shahhal recalled, the popularity of Sufi practices and
the impious, "western" lifestyles in Tripoli (including drinking alcohol
and abandoning prayer) greatly upset Shaykh Salim. Therefore, he was
determined to call Tripolitans to a more systematic religious observance
and abandon "heresy."[5]

In the 1960s, Salim al-Shahhal established good relations with
the famous Salafi scholar, Nasir ad-Din al-Albani.[6] Through him, he
was able to connect with Salafi scholars in Saudi Arabia and gain
financial support for his *da'wa* activity. It should be added, however,
that according to his contemporaries, Shaykh Salim did not adopt
the contemporary meaning of the Salafi *manhaj* and did not consider
himself part of the Salafi *da'wa*. He even refused to use the word
"Salafi," and rejected the black and white worldview of today's Salafis.
Rather, he considered himself one of Tripoli's religious intellectuals,
respected by the political leaders of the city.[7]

Al-Shahhal was often invited to advise the leaders of the Karami clan,
Tripoli's most powerful political patrons until the civil war. Shaykh
'Abd al-Ghani, one of the Palestinian shaykhs in Nahr al-Barid camp on

---

[2] Interview with Abu Bakr al-Shahhal, Tripoli, October 29, 2009.
[3] Soage, Ana Belén, "Rashid Rida's Legacy," p. 6.
[4] Lauziere, *The Making of Salafism*, pp. 60–94.
[5] Interview with Abu Bakr al-Shahhal, Tripoli, October 29, 2009.
[6] According to al-Shahhal's son, Abu Bakr, Salim al-Shahhal visited al-Albani several
times in Saudi Arabia, and they exchanged numerous letters. Ibid.
[7] Interview with Hasan al-Shahhal, Tripoli, July 14, 2008; Interview with Abu Bakr
al-Shahhal, Tripoli, October 29, 2009.

the outskirts of Tripoli, remembered that in the 1960s, al-Shahhal used to be the candidate for Hizb al-Tahrir, an Islamist movement that intends to reestablish the Caliphate, in the parliamentary elections. According to the Shaykh, al-Shahhal preferred wearing traditional "Shami" (referring to Greater Syria) garb to Salafi attire: "Salim al-Shahhal with another Shaykh, 'Utman al-Safi, used to stalk the streets of Tripoli wearing turbans, trousers and light shirts. If they observed that somebody's behavior was un-Islamic, they immediately talked to him trying to convince him to change his attitude. They regarded this as part of *hisba* [see Introduction]." Those with whom I spoke, however, stated that they had never heard him express the concept of *al-wala' wa-l-bara'*.[8]

In the early 1950s, Shaykh Salim gathered pious youths from the city and named the group *Muslimun* (Muslims). This group became the nucleus of Lebanon's Sunni Islamic movements. Among the disciples of al-Shahhal were, for example, Fathi Yakan, the founder and first leader of the Lebanese branch of the Muslim Brothers, and Sa'id Sha'ban, the leader of *Harakat al-Tawhid al-Islami* (the Islamic Unification Movement) that dominated Tripoli for two years at the beginning of the 1980s. Many of the central figures in the current Salafi *da'wa* also socialized in the group that was run by Salim al-Shahhal.

However, despite the existence of some Salafis in Tripoli, prior to the Lebanese Civil War, the conditions were not favorable for the movement to gain many grassroots followers. There were three main reasons for this. First, in the 1960s and 1970s, the Sunni masses, especially young people between 18 and 40, were at that time attracted to Nasserism and, to a lesser extent, Marxism. Among this group, levels of religiosity were decreasing. The gradually narrowing religious field was under the firm control of *Dar al-Fatwa*. Shaykhs from the traditional religious establishment were fervent supporters of Arab Nationalism, which therefore gained the sympathy of those who still visited the mosques.[9] In such a climate, Salafis could not find a wide constituency. Those individuals who were keen to follow pietistic trends tended to join one of the well-established and influential Sufi orders.

Second, and more importantly, prior to the civil war, al-Shahhal's group lacked skilled preachers who would be able to appeal to the masses. Even in their social habits, the members of Muslimun did not differ from the more traditional inhabitants of the North. At that time, Salafis focused on a number of narrow issues that were limited to

---

[8] See Introduction.

[9] Interview with Shaykh Khaldun 'Uraymit, a high-ranking Dar al-Fatwa official from 'Akkar. Beirut, August 3, 2008.

personal religious practices.[10] They usually warned people not to follow Sufi practices and to perform religious rituals correctly, but they did not possess the all-encompassing ideology of contemporary Salafis. In other words, they did not challenge Arab Nationalism – some accounts even suggest that al-Shahhal sympathized with it.[11] Third, Salafis lacked transnational support. Even though the Saudi Kingdom was already propagating a general message of Islamic solidarity in the early 1990s, it was not yet exporting Salafism abroad. Although Salim al-Shahhal had good connections in the Saudi religious establishment, he did not gain significant financial support to spread the da'wa.

This situation, however, was about to change. At the end of the 1980s and beginning of 1990s, dozens of graduates of the Islamic University of Medina, who left in the early 1980s when Saudi Arabia started to grant generous scholarships to foreign students, returned to Lebanon. Most of these young shaykhs had adopted the contemporary version of Salafism that had crystalized in Saudi Arabia starting from the 1970s.[12] They were able to mobilize a considerable amount of religious and economic capital to establish their da'wa as an important Islamic movement in the 1990s. This acquisition of capital was facilitated by the ongoing sociopolitical transformations that affected the Sunni religious field. One of the most important changes was the decline of the traditional religious establishment.

2.2 The Weakening of Dar al-Fatwa

Prior to the civil war, the official Sunni religious administration organized under the auspices of Dar al-Ifta' (commonly known as Dar al-Fatwa) dominated Sunni religious life in Lebanon.[13] As most religious scholars belonged to Dar al-Fatwa, there was a clear hierarchy of the 'ulama' class and its members. At the top of this religious hierarchy were those scholars who had been educated in prestigious religious institutions such as al-Azhar in Cairo. The lower level consisted of informally educated shaykhs.

This religious elite had a relationship of mutual dependency with Lebanese Sunni patrons, including political patrons (za'im, pl. zu'ama'),

---

[10] Interview with a former member of Muslimun, Tripoli, November 7, 2009.
[11] Interview with Hasan al-Shahhal, Tripoli, July 14, 2008.
[12] Lauziere, The Making of Salafism, pp. 199–230.
[13] Fuad I. Khuri, "The Ulama: A Comparative Study of Sunni and Shi'a Religious Officials," Middle Eastern Studies, 23, no. 3 (1987).

such as the Karami clan, and local notables (*wujaha'*). The lower-level religious officials did not receive any salary from Dar al-Fatwa, but were directly dependent on financial support from local communities such as villages or city quarters, and needed the backing of their leaders. The high-ranking *'ulama'* filled political positions and depended on government appointments, and therefore needed good relations with the *zu'ama'*. The jurists who administered religious endowments (*awqaf*) had a similar clientelistic relationship. These endowments were mostly financed by patrons, who also had a decisive voice in the committees that elected their administration.[14] At the same time, the *'ulama'* served as an effective tool for the *zu'ama'* to control the population and recruit voters.

In contemporary Northern Lebanon this setting changed and the authority of the official *'ulama'* became contested. This was due to the weakening of the role of Dar al-Fatwa and the disruption of traditional social structures and alliances. During the civil war, when Leftist and Arab Nationalist militias gained prominence at the expense of the traditional *zu'ama'*, the old alliance between the latter and the religious elite also largely disappeared. For a while, the *'ulama'* seemed to have become not only the religious but also the political representative of the Sunni community. This newly gained influence went into reverse after the 1989 assassination of the charismatic state *mufti* Hassan Khalid.[15] His successor, Muhammad Rashid Qabbani, who lacks personal charisma and adequate leadership skills, does not possess his predecessor's level of authority, and is thus unable to influence the political leaders of the Sunni community.[16]

Dar al-Fatwa has also suffered from a serious lack of funding since the end of the 1980s. This is because the traditional Sunni *zu'ama'* lost much of their wealth and influence during the civil war, and therefore

---

[14] Ibid., p. 299.

[15] Jakob Skovgaard-kovgaard, "The Sunni Religious Scene in Beirut," *Mediterranean Politics*, 3, no. 1 (1998), p. Hasan Khalid was killed by a car bomb on May 16, 1989 while returning from a meeting with Prime Minister Michel 'Awn. It is widely believed that the assassination was carried out by Syrian intelligence, because the mufti was a staunch opponent of the Syrian presence in Lebanon and was seeking its elimination. To this end, he was keen to cooperate with 'Awn, who at that time was aspiring to oust the Syrian army from the country. The murder of Hassan Khalid was probably a warning to those who had sided with 'Awn against Damascus. David Grafton, *The Christians of Lebanon: Political Rights in Islamic Law*. London; New York: I. B. Tauris, 2003, p. 130. For a detailed analysis of Michel 'Awn's premiership and his "Liberation War" against the Syrians in 1989–1990, see: Harris, *The New Face of Lebanon*, pp. 243–278.

[16] Qabbani, Hassan Khalid's deputy, was not even granted the title of grand mufti until 1996, when Rafiq al-Hariri helped him to be elected. This is one of the reasons why many regard him as the former Prime Minister's puppet.

no longer support the institution financially. State funding is also very scarce.[17] Therefore, Dar al-Fatwa is unable to employ a sufficient number of religious scholars, and those who are employed receive very low salaries. An imam of a mosque, for example, often earns only between 100 and 200 USD per month, while a *khatib* (a preacher who delivers the Friday sermon) earns less than 100 USD. These wages are far from enough to survive in Lebanon, where living costs are nearly as high as in Western Europe. The financial instability has made it unattractive to the young generation of Sunni religious specialists to join the institution, which in turn has led to a diminishing of Dar al-Fatwa's influence over the population and religious institutions.

At the same time, many of the Sunni religious institutions that had been destroyed in the civil war, such as mosques, schools, and charity endowments, were restored by Islamic movements, which later retained their control over them.[18] Since then, the official Sunni establishment has been unable to gain absolute dominance over the network of mosques and other religious institutions in the country. The institutional weakness of Dar al-Fatwa has left space for the establishment of hundreds of independent Islamic charities that offer their services to members of the Sunni community. Since they do not depend on the official Sunni religious body, they often pursue a very different agenda. Some of them are under the patronage of the *zu'ama'*, while others belong to different Islamic movements, such as the Muslim Brotherhood or Sufi orders.

According to one of my sources from al-Jama'a al-Islamiyya (Islamic Community, the Lebanese Muslim Brotherhood), there are almost 6,000 registered Islamic charity institutions in Lebanon. While many of them exist only on paper, others are active organizations serving the aims of political leaders, Muslim Brothers, Salafis, Sufi brotherhoods, or independent Islamists.[19] Most mosques belong to Islamic movements, and as such are outside of the official religious establishment's control. At the same time, the shaykhs of Dar al-Fatwa have lost their ability to provide for the religious needs of their communities (see Chapter 4). To translate this development into Bourdieu's terms, the amount of religious and economic capital that Dar al-Fatwa possessed has diminished and its position in the Sunni religious field has weakened.

---

[17] Hannes Baumann, "The New Contractor Bourgeoisie in Lebanese Politics: Hariri, Mikati and Fares." In *Lebanon after the Cedar Revolution* edited by Are Knudsen and Malcolm Kerr. London: Hurst, 2013, pp. 128–129.

[18] Skovgaard-Petersen, "The Sunni Religious Scene in Beirut," p. 71.

[19] A vague category, this mainly refers to those who have left al-Jama'a al-Islamiyya or Harakat al-Tawhid al-Islami and administer charity endowments, serving their own aims by using transnational contacts and relations with Lebanese politicians.

This has opened up space for various Islamic movements to accumulate capital and strengthen their own positions.

Salafis benefited from the weakening of the traditional religious elite because they had been known in the communities of the Sunni neighborhoods of Tripoli as individuals who sacrifice most of their time and energy for the sake of the *da'wa* and to fulfill the daily religious needs of ordinary believers. Salafis were active in issuing fatwas, holding religious lessons, and providing personal consultations. A prominent member of Tripoli's Salafi community even admitted to me that if Dar al-Fatwa had fulfilled its task and taken care of the believers, he does not believe that the Salafis would have been able to gain a permanent foothold in Lebanon.[20] Other factors in the rise of Salafism's popularity were the failure of the Muslim Brotherhood type of Islamism and the appearance of wealthy sponsors from the Gulf countries.

2.3   The Failure of the Muslim Brotherhood

At the beginning of the civil war, the alliance between the official religious institutions and their political patrons collapsed. Although Dar al-Fatwa had initially been able to maintain its status as both the religious and the political representative of the Sunnis, the authority of the traditional establishment was now largely diminished in Tripoli.

The city used to be a stronghold of the Left. Going with the dominant flow in the Middle East, local Sunnis were attracted to Arab Nationalism in large numbers after Nasser's ascendance at the beginning of the 1950s. Due to the uneven distribution of wealth in the country, many of Tripoli's Sunni youth joined the Lebanese Communist Party or other radical Marxist groups, such as the Maoist People's Resistance Movement led by Khalil 'Akkawi. The Syrian Social Nationalist Party (SSNP), with its semi-socialist agenda, also had numerous followers. According to contemporary witnesses, these movements pulled the younger generation away from religion: "during the 1970s the Communists and the Qawmiyyun [reference to the SSNP] were able to draw the youth away from Islam. Only the old used to pray and in some regions the mosques were absolutely empty." (Shaykh 'Ali Taha, the imam of Abu Bakr al-Siddiq mosque)[21]

---

[20] Interview with 'Ali Shahadi, Tripoli, August 3, 2011. 'Ali Shahadi is probably the most successful distributor of Islamic books in Tripoli. Due to his multiple contacts in Islamist circles, he is able to constantly observe the dynamics of the city's Sunni religious scene.

[21] Interview, Tripoli, December 5, 2009.

However, at the beginning of the 1980s, the dominance of the left ended, a development partly due to the Middle East-wide decline of the Arab Nationalist and Marxist movements and the rise of Islamism in the region, and partly due to its lack of success in providing a viable alternative for the inhabitants of Tripoli.[22] The Israeli invasion in 1982 and the withdrawal of the PLO from Lebanon was the final blow for the Leftist movement, which then fell into an inexorable decline. One effect of this decline was the expansion of the Sunni religious field. Adhering to religious practices became an important marker of Sunni identity again. As many Tripolitans recalled, in the beginning of the 1980s people who had never prayed before now went to the mosques and learned how to carry out religious practices.[23]

At the same time, the success of the Iranian revolution gave credibility to Islamists who had upheld the possibility of establishing an Islamic state in the region. Local Islamist movements in the city quarters of Tripoli successfully recruited the young people who had previously been drawn to Marxism or Arab Nationalism. Many Leftist and Maoist activists seceded from the left due to its failures in fighting Israel and the Maronite establishment, and joined Islamism.[24] One of them was Khalil 'Akkawi, who converted his Communist group into an Islamist movement.

These Islamist factions then merged into one movement, the Islamic Unification Movement (*Harakat al-Tawhid al-Islami* – IUM), under the leadership of the charismatic Shaykh Sa'id Sha'ban. In 1982, the movement was able to control the city with material support from Yasir 'Arafat's Fatah and the Iranian Islamic Republic. Sa'id Sha'ban announced the founding of an Islamic emirate in the North. The Islamist mini-state was short-lived, however, because the Syrian army that had been occupying Lebanon since 1976 managed to take back Tripoli in 1985. After it was defeated militarily, the movement lost popular support. The main reasons for this were the terror practiced by the IUM during its three-year reign, the internal schisms, and the lack of a unified ideological direction.[25]

---

[22] See: Fida' 'Itani, *al-Jihadiyyun fi-Lubnan: min Quwwat al-Fajr ila Fath al-Islam*. Bayrut: al-Saqi, 2008, p. 74.

[23] Series of interviews with Tripolitans who were adults at the turn of the 1970s and 1980s.

[24] See: 'Itani, *al-Jihadiyyun fi-Lubnan*, p. 74. The left's loss of popularity was partly the result of the split in the PLO into a pro-Syrian and an anti-Syrian faction (led by Yasir 'Arafat) after Damascus' intervention in the Lebanese Civil War in 1976. Fawwaz Traboulsi, *A History of Modern Lebanon*. London: Pluto Press, 2007, pp. 205–219.

[25] The militants of IUM intended to eradicate their political opponents that included leftist movements. In 1983 fighters of the Islamist militia killed dozens of members of

After the collapse of the IUM's Islamic mini-state, there was intensive competition between the different players in the Sunni religious field. Because Dar al-Fatwa was unable to regain its previous role due to financial difficulties and a lack of legitimacy, different Islamic movements were now struggling for the soul of the Sunni community. After the fall of the IUM, the Lebanese Muslim Brothers or *al-Jama'a al-Islamiyya* (the Islamic Group – IG) were able to recruit quite a large follower base. However, after the Ta'if Agreement (1989), which ended the 15-year-long civil war in Lebanon, the movement's influence on the Sunni population gradually declined in the next two decades.[26] There are several reasons for this: First, the IG was unable to establish a clear and long-term agenda in the Lebanese environment. Although it propagated a "moderate Islamic ideology" and accepted Lebanon's multi-confessional political system, the movement's intellectual discourse only attracted a limited segment of the educated Sunni middle class. Due to the hostile Syrian military presence and the continuous harassment by the Lebanese and Syrian security services, and despite the efforts of its activists, the IG was unable to establish and maintain a large charitable network, which would have secured broad-based grassroots support.[27] Second, after the end of the civil war, a number of secessions occurred within the ranks of the Lebanese Muslim Brothers, driven by the growing differences between the pro- and anti-Syrian wings of the IG.[28]

At the same time many activists who had initially benefited from the IG, both financially and in building their social networks, preferred to establish their own patronage and Islamic institutions independently from the Muslim Brothers. Many of my informants who were formerly IG activists recalled how the movement's cadres put personal material interests before ideology. Shaykh Sa'd al-Din Kibbi, one of the prominent Salafi figures, left the Lebanese Muslim Brothers for the same reason. As he told me during my visit to his *ma'had shara'i* (*shari'a* school),

---

the Lebanese Communist Party. Raphael Lefevre, The Islamic Emirate of North Lebanon (Cambridge: Unpublished Ph.D. thesis submitted to the Department of Politics and International Studies at the University of Cambridge, 2016).

[26] In the post–Arab Uprisings period JI's popularity has been increasing. Muhammad Hayik, "Al-Jama'a al-Islamiyya fi Lubnan … An al-Awan," *al-Iylaf*, April 1, 2014, http://elaph.com/Web/opinion/2014/3/891044.html (accessed September 10, 2015); Fida' 'Itani, 'Al-Jama'a l-islamiyya: Lam Nusbih Badilan min al-Mustaqbal…Ba'd', *al-Akhbar*, February 14, 2012.

[27] Interview with ex-IG activist Nasser Naji, April 28, 2012.

[28] The final schism in the IG occurred when the former leader Fathi Yakan left the movement in 2006 and established a new umbrella organization, which draws together Islamists who have allied themselves with Hizbullah, such as Harakat al-Tawhid al-Islami, and other, smaller local groups.

"Islamist ideology legitimated the desire to capture political positions and fill the pockets of IG activists. They did not use material sources to make Islam victorious but used Islam to achieve material benefits." Many former IG voters whom I interviewed had similar views on the movement. When I chatted with ordinary people about their political preferences, they often referred to the Lebanese Muslim Brothers as "*Jama'a baddon al-Kursi bass* [a group interested only in achieving political positions]." Third, the IG's Palestinian members left the group to join Hamas when it opened its offices in Lebanon in 1998. This dealt a severe blow to the movement, because it lost hundreds of activists. Together, these factors led to the decline of the movement's influence in state institutions and in the Sunni religious field.

Salafis gradually were able to fill the space left by the IG. Many former IG supporters who did not want to abandon Islamic activism joined the ranks of Salafis. Some of them told me that the years they had spent in the IG had made it clear to them that building an Islamic state and society should begin with perfecting the beliefs and practices of the grassroots. Otherwise, people would hijack the idea of Islamism to acquire political positions and other personal benefits.[29] IG members were no longer active in giving religious lessons (*dars*, pl. *durus*), which are important tools of mobilization for Islamic movements; the Salafis took over this task from them as well. As early as 2008 and 2009 (my first field trips to the region), I observed that even in one of the main centers of the Muslim Brothers, the Rahma mosque in the Qubba region, Salafi shaykhs were the ones who most often organized religious lessons. In short, the decline of the IG's presence on the Sunni religious field created opportunities for Salafis to accumulate religious capital by appearing as the righteous few who sincerely care about Islam by providing religious services for Muslims.

2.4   Deepening Sectarian Cleavages

Worsening tensions between Sunnis and Shi'ites influenced the structure of the Sunni religious field. Salafis exploited the deepening sectarian cleavages to improve their positions in the field. According to Vali Nasr, "to Arabs and Iranians, Afghans and Pakistanis living in the region, it is an age old scourge that has flared up from time to time to mold Islamic

---

[29] Interview with former IG member Nasser Naji, April 28, 2012.

history, theology, law and politics."[30] Such a flare-up occurred in the years following the 1979 Iranian Revolution. The new Islamic government in Tehran became an existential threat to the Gulf States and other Sunni governments, due to the Iranian regime's intention to export the revolution. Several times, Khomeini expressed his views about the dictatorial and illegitimate nature of the Saudi Kingdom's leadership. He believed that the time had come to abolish autocratic regimes throughout the Islamic world and establish similar ones to that in Iran.

However, the Iranian leader overestimated the capabilities of the revolution and the loss of legitimacy of the Saudi regime. In fact, Sunni Islamists, although inspired by the Islamist takeover in Tehran, were reluctant to acknowledge the Iranian leadership due to its Shi'ite identity.[31] At the same time, in their eyes and the eyes of the wider Sunni public, Saudi Arabia enjoyed a high degree of legitimacy because of the Saudi role in the 1973 Yom Kippur War and the image of the late King Faysal.[32] Saudi-sponsored counterpropaganda was thus able to emphasize the Shi'ite identity of Khomeini and his revolution, and to discredit Iranian claims to pan-Islamic leadership.[33] Moreover, the increasing Shi'ite activism in the Gulf, Lebanon, Pakistan, and India was framed as a threat to the Sunni majority in most of these regions.[34] After that, the already existing socioeconomic cleavages began to take a sectarian shape. This development culminated after the occupation of Iraq by the United States in 2003, when the Shi'ite majority became the dominant force in a previously Sunni-ruled country.[35] Salafis have generally been able to exploit sectarian sentiments, since hostility toward the Shi'ites lies at the core of their ideology. Throughout the Islamic world, they have published books about the *"Rawafid"*

[30] Vali Nasr, *The Shia Revival: How Conflicts within Islam Will Shape the Future*. New York: W. W. Norton, 2006, p. 23.

[31] Walid M. Abdelnasser, "Islamic Organizations in Egypt and the Iranian Revolutions of 1979: The Experience of the First Few Years," *Arab Studies Quarterly* 19, no. 2 (1997); Yvette Telhami, "The Syrian Muslim Brothers and the Syrian-Iranian Relationship," *Middle East Journal*, 63, no. 4, (2009).

[32] King Faysal (1964–1975) is often portrayed as the champion of the Islamic cause due to his support for the establishment of transnational Islamic organizations, such as the Organization of the Islamic Conference (OIC), and for imposing the oil embargo in 1973. His personal image as a pious monarch living a modest lifestyle was in contrast to the hedonistic behavior of his family members. Alexei Vassiliev, *King Faisal: Personality, Faith and Times*. London: SAQI, 2012, p. 287.

[33] Madawi Al-Rasheed, *Contesting the Saudi State: Islamic Voices from a New Generation*. Cambridge: Cambridge University Press, 2007, pp. 104–112.

[34] May Yamani, "The Two Faces of Saudi Arabia," *Survival* 50, no. 1 (2008), pp. 151–154.

[35] For an excellent overview see: Fanar Haddad, *Sectarianism in Iraq: Antagonistic Visions of Unity*. New York: Oxford University Press, 2011, pp. 143–178.

conspiracy against Islam, and spread sectarian hostility from the *minbar*.[36] The Sunni-dominated governments often supported their activism, and their audience grew in this sectarian climate.

Sunni–Shi'ite tensions throughout the Islamic world also provided Salafis with an opportunity to reach a larger Sunni audience. Before the civil war, Lebanon's Shi'ites constituted the most underdeveloped and impoverished community in the country.[37] The majority of Shi'ites lived under the patronage of their traditional *zu'ama'*, and most of the population worked in the agricultural sector or as unskilled workers in cities such as Beirut or Sidon.[38] Compared to Christians or the Sunnis, their middle class was small. This situation changed, however, after the outbreak of the civil war. After the collapse of the state institutions, the Shi'ite *zu'ama'* lost almost all of their power. Shi'ites initially joined leftist movements like the Lebanese Communist Party or the various Palestinian factions. From the beginning of the 1980s, their own sectarian militia, the Battalions of the Lebanese Resistance (*Afwaj al-Muqawama al-Islamiyya* – AMAL) became prominent.

After the 1982 Israeli invasion, partly due to AMAL's inefficiency in dealing with the occupiers and defending its own community from Israeli raids and arrests, the ideology of the 1979 Iranian Revolution became increasingly popular. Groups of enthusiastic Shi'ite youth who had adopted Khomeinism, began launching attacks on the Israeli army. Then the Iranian Revolutionary Guard, which had gained a foothold in the Beqa' Valley in Eastern Lebanon, organized these cells in a single institutional framework. In 1985, the Iranian Revolutionary Guard formed a new organization, Hizbullah (the Party of God). In 1985, due to the organization's paramilitary activity (in particular, employing suicide bombers), Israel withdrew its army from most of the territories it had occupied three years before. By the end of the civil war, Hizbullah had successfully established itself in the Shi'ite community by building charity institutions and fulfilling the tasks of the state (keeping order and security, and providing basic services such as electricity and water), which in some parts of the country were nonexistent at that time.

After the civil war, Hizbullah successfully established itself as a political party. From the 1992 elections onward it became a dominant

---

[36] The *minbar* (pulpit) is used by the preacher in the mosque at the Friday prayer.

[37] Augustus Richard Norton, *AMAL and the Shi'a: Struggle for the Soul of Lebanon*. Austin: University of Texas Press, 1987, pp. 16–18.

[38] About the marginalization of the Shi'ites before the civil war see: Fouad Ajami, *The Vanished Imam: Musa al Sadr and the Shia of Lebanon*. Ithaca and London: Cornell University Press, 1986, pp. 58–72.

force in the Shi'ite community, along with AMAL. Furthermore, the two Shi'ite parties became among the main allies of Syria, which became the power broker in the post–civil war Lebanese political order. Due to the patronage of Damascus, Hizbullah and AMAL disproportionally increased their weight in the political field and no major governmental decisions could be made without their approval.[39] While the majority of Sunnis initially supported Hizbullah, now fears arose that Hizbullah's aim was not only to defend the country against Israel, but also to establish Shi'ite dominance in Lebanon. The Sunni population wondered why Hizbullah and AMAL had the right to control entire neighborhoods in Beirut without the interference of the state.[40] They also felt that members of their community had been deprived of the rights that Shi'ites now possessed. In the North in particular, many believed that the slow progress of the post–civil war reconstruction in their region, compared to the much faster development in the Shi'ite South, was a sign of Shi'a control over state resources.

A segment of these Sunni Muslims, especially young unemployed people in the impoverished neighborhoods of Tripoli without higher education, was receptive to the Salafis' anti-Shi'a rhetoric. Salafi preachers invested their already accumulated religious capital and presented themselves as defenders of *Ahl al-Sunna wa-l-Jama'a* against the "Shi'ite plot" and the "import of Khomeinism." Salafi preachers framed the grievances of these young Sunnis into a historical struggle between the Sunnis, who are the flag bearers of true Islam, and the Shi'ites, who have been corrupting the religion since the first century of Islamic history. Sunni youth in the North felt that these shaykhs were telling the truth when they described the weak position of the Sunnis and their vulnerability to external enemies as a direct result of the spread of heresy.[41] In this case, dynamics of the political field influenced the Sunni religious field where fear from the increasing power of Shi'ite political parties facilitated the accumulation of religious capital by the Salafis. The arguments of the Salafi preachers at the time only appealed to a few young people, but the seeds were sown. This foregrounded the developments fifteen years later when Salafi shaykhs employed the same tropes in their sermons.[42]

---

[39] Harris, *The New Face of Lebanon*, pp. 281–291.

[40] Since the final years of the Lebanese Civil War Hizbullah have controlled large parts of the Shi'ite-inhabited areas of Beirut's southern suburbs (al-Dahiyya al-Janubiyya). See: Mona Harb, "Deconstructing Hizballah and Its Suburb," *MERIP* no. 242, 2007.

[41] Most Salafis whom I interviewed, who had joined the movement in the 1990s, said that the perceived political dominance of the Shi'a drew them originally to Salafism.

[42] See Chapter 7.

2.5 The Emergence of Transnational Sponsors

The oil boom and the increased financial capabilities of the Gulf countries, which enabled Saudi Arabia in particular to sponsor the Salafi *da'wa* worldwide, provided Lebanese Salafis with economic capital that improved their positions on the Sunni Islamic field. The kingdom intended to use its sudden wealth to boost its own status in the international political arena and become the dominant power in the Islamic world.[43] One way to fulfill this ambition would be to reach out to the grassroots in Muslim countries. To this end, Saudi Arabia started to export its own religious ideology, which is identical to Salafism, and financed massive transnational Salafi proselytization in order to dominate the religious discourses in Muslim communities worldwide and suppress hostile ideological currents.

As al-Rasheed put it, this political strategy "aimed to control the minds and hearts of Muslims from Detroit to Jakarta."[44] Saudi Arabia financed the building of mosques, charities, and educational institutions on a global scale, propagating Salafi ideas. Riyadh invested vast sums in spreading religious literature among Muslims around the world to transform their identities in accordance with the Salafi ideal.[45] An important part of this *da'wa* was establishing the kingdom's universities as centers of transnational Islamic education. Since the end of the 1970s, these institutions have educated tens of thousands of foreign students, who have since returned to their countries to spread Salafism.

When the prestigious al-Azhar University of Egypt restricted its scholarships for students from Syria, Jordan, and Lebanon because these countries opposed Sadat's change of policy and Egypt's peace agreement with Israel in 1979,[46] the Islamic University of Medina opened its doors for them. As one of the Palestinian shaykhs from Nahr al-Barid camp recalled, about 50 Lebanese students went to study in Medina at the beginning of the 1980s. Many of them (the shaykh himself among them) had graduated from a religious high school in Tripoli and were supposed

---

[43] Gilles Kepel, *Jihad: The Trail of Political Islam*. London: I. B. Tauris, 2006, pp. 61–80.

[44] Al-Rasheed, *Contesting the Saudi State*, p. 126.   [45] Ibid., pp. 127–131.

[46] Ali E Hillal Dessouki, 'Egyptian Foreign Policy since Camp David.' In *The Middle East: Ten Years after Camp David* edited by William B. Quandt. Washington: The Brookings Institution, 1988, pp. 103–104. One of my informants, Shaykh Muhammad 'Abd al-Ghani, recalled that when he finished high school in Tripoli in 1980 his scholarship to al-Azhar was withdrawn. The Saudi Embassy in Lebanon almost immediately offered him and his fellow students to study in Medina at Riyadh's expense. According to the shaykh, this is how he became Salafi. Interview, Tripoli, April 11, 2012.

to leave for Cairo. When al-Azhar denied them their scholarships, the Saudi Embassy offered to finance their studies in Medina.

The shaykh remembered that unlike al-Azhar or other universities that left much space for pluralism in *'aqida* and *fiqh*, in Medina, Salafism was the only path for a student to follow. After the second year, students whose commitment to Salafism was doubted were asked to leave the university. Upon their return, the Lebanese graduates of the Islamic University of Medina were to transform Salafism in their country from being a marginal group into one of the most important Sunni movements. Among them were Shaykh Salim al-Shahhal's three sons, who, after returning to Tripoli, began building institutions and spreading the Salafi understanding of Islam. Those who studied religious studies in Saudi Arabia often accumulated social capital during their stay in the Kingdom that they could convert into economic capital by establishing connections to charities and wealthy individuals who were keen to support their *da'wa* upon returning home. Shaykh Hilal Turkomani, a popular Salafi preacher in Miryata, remembers how he joined Salafism at the beginning of the *da'wa* in Lebanon

After the fall of the IUM, Salafi shaykhs began gathering young people around themselves. One of them was Usama Qasas. We were 40 young people and Shaykh Usama was our master until his murder by the Ahbash. Then around 1990 Da'i al-Islam al-Shahhal [the son of Salim] returned to Tripoli from Saudi Arabia with a lot of money. He succeeded in surrounding himself with hundreds of young men who became Salafis.[47]

The Syrians, who had occupied Tripoli since the defeat of IUM and created a massive intelligence network in the city, initially gave Salafis carte blanche. One reason was that Da'i al-Islam al-Shahhal told his followers not to vote in the elections.[48] This weakened the political support of Sunni politicians who might challenge the Syrian presence in Lebanon. Second, the Syrian leadership hoped that the growth of the Salafis would fragment the Sunni religious field and prevent the dominance of a single movement such as IG.[49]

In a climate of identity crisis, yet relative political stability, Salafism grew rapidly. Da'i al-Islam al-Shahhal, relying on the funds he received from the Gulf, successfully developed the group established by his

---

[47] Interview with Shaykh Hilal Turkomani, Miryata, October 18, 2009.

[48] Ibid., Al-Shahhal in the early 1990s considered the Lebanese political system illegitimate and urged Muslims not to participate in it, a view that he reconsidered a few years later when he ran as a candidate in the 1996 elections.

[49] Tine Gade, "Sunni Islamists in Tripoli and the Asad regime 1966–2014," *Syria Studies* 7, no. 2 (2015), p. 50.

father into a network of charities and educational institutions that operated not only in the North but also in almost every Sunni region. The organization's name became *Jama'iyyat al-Hidaya wa-l-Ihsan* or Guidance and Charity Society (GCS).

GCS's main supporter was *Mu'assasat al-Haramayn* (al-Haramayn Institution), one of the biggest Saudi charities that frequently sponsor activist Salafis. Thus al-Shahhal's group became part of a wider transnational network that expanded to approximately 50 countries. Al-Haramayn was established in 1988 by 'Aqil 'Abd al-Aziz al-'Aqil, a former Saudi government official and co-worker of the Saudi Red Crescent. The charity set out to help Afghan refugees in North-West Pakistan, but soon extended its activities to several other Muslim-inhabited areas in Asia and Africa. Al-Haramayn also had branches in the United States and Europe. Unlike other Saudi Islamic charities, such as The Muslim World League and the World Assembly of Muslim Youth, al-Haramayn focused on spreading Salafism at the expense of other interpretations of Islam.[50]

Not all successful Salafi preachers received funds from the Arabian Gulf. Among the notable figures who began the Salafi *da'wa* in Tripoli was Shaykh 'Abdullah Husayn, a former physicist who had previously lived in France. Shaykh 'Abdullah, a thin and tall man with a gray beard, often can be seen walking in the old market of Tripoli. He is not a talkative person, but well known for his extraordinary expertise of the *hadith*, and his exact answers when believers ask him for religious advice. He owns a bookstore near the Great Mansuri Mosque, where he sells classical collections of the books of the literalist school.

Although I dropped by his bookstore several times, and the shaykh was rather welcoming, he refused to share his biographical data with me, telling me that he is not an important enough person to be mentioned in an academic study. According to the narrative of some of his students, the shaykh gave up his career in Europe and after a near fatal car accident turned to religion.[51] He changed his life so radically that he does not even allow his children to study in government schools, but educates them at home, as he believes that science courses in secular

---

[50] Yusra Bokhari, Nasim Chowdhury and Robert Lacey, "A Good Day to Bury a Bad Charity: The Rise and Fall of the al-Haramain Islamic Foundation." In *Gulf Charities and Islamic Philanthropy: The "Age of Terror and Beyond"* Edited by Robert Lacey and Jonathan Benthall. Berlin: Gerlach Press, 2014.

[51] Informal conversations with a number of Shaykh 'Abdullah Husayn's students in Tripoli, November 2009. Salafis commonly explain their conversion with some kind of rupture or trauma in their lives. Yet, I could not verify whether the accident was the immediate reason behind Shaykh 'Abdullah's religious turn.

schools are mostly lies. For example, he believes the Earth is flat, and the concept that the planet has the shape of a globe is a lie invented by Europeans to fool Muslims.

Unlike most of the other Salafis in the city, Shaykh 'Abdullah has never had any relations with the Gulf, but adopted Salafi *'aqida* and *manhaj* through his reading. At the end of the 1980s, many young Tripolitan men became Salafis after participating in his study circles. Those who wanted to play an active role in the Salafi *da'wa*, however, later joined other groups that received Gulf funds and offered more opportunities to these young men to pursue their preaching activities.

2.6   The Tensions with al-Ahbash and the Emergence of Salafism on the Sunni Religious Field

By the first half of the 1990s, Salafis had accumulated enough religious and economic capital to establish themselves as a significant Sunni Islamic movement. They were, however, far from dominating the Sunni religious field, which had been highly contested since the second half of the 1980s. In the final stage of the civil war, a fierce competition erupted between different Islamic movements: Four movements – al-Jama'a al-Islamiyya, the Salafis, al-Ahbash (a Sufi-oriented group), and some Sufi brotherhoods – tried to extend their influence. All of the Islamic groups (with the exception of the Sufi brotherhoods) intended to gain as much influence as possible in Sunni religious institutions, especially mosques. From the 1980s until the mid-1990s, there was almost daily violence between al-Ahbash on one side and al-Jama'a al-Islamiyya and the Salafis on the other, as they tried to occupy each other's mosques. This period of tension with al-Ahbash played an important role in the development of the Salafi movement.

Al-Ahbash appeared in Lebanon in the 1960s, when the Ethiopian-born Shaykh 'Abdullah al-Harari[52] succeeded in gathering a considerable number of disciples around him. Al-Harari had left his home country in 1948, when Emperor Haile Selassie's government accused him of collaborating with separatist circles of Harar province and expelled him from the country.[53] He traveled through the Middle East

---

[52] 'Abdullah al-Harari was born in the Ethiopian province of Harar and settled in Beirut in the 1940s. The name al-Ahbash refers to the Shaykh's Ethiopean origins (Habashi, pl. al-Ahbash).

[53] Mustafa Kabha and Haggai Erlich, "Al-Ahbash and Wahhabiyya: Interpretations of Islam," *International Journal of Middle Eastern Studies* 38, no. 4 (2006), p. 522.

and then stayed for a while in Damascus, where he belonged to the Qadiriyya Sufi order. In 1950, al-Harari settled in Beirut, where Dar al-Fatwa gave him an official appointment as a religious scholar. He started his activism more than a decade after his arrival in Lebanon. However, for two decades the movement limited its activities to organizing study groups for the instruction of Harari's disciples. Al-Ahbash gained prominence from 1983 on, when the disciples of al-Harari took over an old charity, *Jama'iyyat al-Mashari' al-Khairiyya al-Islamiyya* (the Association of Islamic Philanthropic Projects), which became their organizational body. The members of the movement then gradually took over more and more neighborhoods in Beirut, filling the vacuum created by the rapidly waning influence of the leftist militias due to the Israeli invasion. They were able to gain a foothold in all of the areas inhabited by Sunnis.

Al-Ahbash can be considered a countermovement to Islamism in general, and to Salafism in particular. Its ideology mostly builds on Ash'arism and the *Shafi'i madhab*. Al-Ahbash's main critique of Islamism is that it transforms religion into a political ideology that intends to capture the state. Al-Ahbash regards Salafis as innovators; al-Harari considers Ibn Taymiyya and Muhammad bin 'Abd al-Wahhab to be *ahl al-bid'a* (knowledgeable persons who distort Islam), because of their literal understanding of the Text. The Salafis' literal understanding of God's attributes has led al-Ahbash to accuse them of anthropomorphism. In general, according to *Ash'ari* thought, a metaphorical interpretation of the Text is necessary in order to avoid anthropomorphism that leads to disbelief. Al-Harari even calls the two scholars "unbelievers."[54] Kabha and Erlich point out that al-Ahbash's message to Muslims is much harsher than that toward non-Muslims.[55] While the followers of the movement take a reconciliatory approach toward the latter, they practice *takfir* (excommunication) toward those Muslims whom they consider extremists.

Al-Ahbash's struggle against Salafism has a transnational dimension and is rooted in the secessionist aspirations of the Harar Province. Salafis gained influence in Harar in the 1940s, and attempted to regain independence from the Ethiopian state and revive the 900-year-old Islamic emirate. The secessionist Salafi organization was defeated in 1948 and its leader, Shaykh Yusuf 'Abd al-Rahman, later emigrated to Saudi Arabia. After he had settled in Medina in 1976, he immediately launched a series of attacks on his old enemy, Shaykh 'Abdullah.

[54] Ibid., p. 528.   [55] Ibid., p. 526.

He was able to convince the highest echelons of the Saudi Salafi establishment to support him in his struggle. The chief *mufti* of the kingdom, 'Abdulaziz bin Baz, even issued a fatwa stating that al-Ahbash was not part of *Ahl as-Sunna wa-l-Jama'a* (the community of Sunnis). According to one of my Lebanese Salafi informants, some Salafi groups in Tripoli received extraordinary levels of funding from Saudi Arabia to finance the struggle against al-Ahbash. I, however, want to stress that this claim is not verified by other sources.

This tension at the ideological level manifested itself in clashes in the streets of Beirut, Tripoli, and other Sunni-inhabited places. Al-Ahbash started to occupy the mosques, even those under the supervision of Dar al-Fatwa, under the pretext that the institutions were too weak to protect places of worship from infiltration by extremists (i.e. the Muslim Brothers and the Salafis). As one Salafi in Tripoli remembers

al-Ahbash usually came to the mosques at the Friday prayer. They waited for the appropriate moment, then started a discussion about a certain topic, like whether the angels are male or female or whether is it permitted for Muslims to use disinfectants containing alcohol. If the *khatib* [preacher] or the imam of the mosque did not agree with them, then they came back later with 20–30 men, beat up respectable scholars, and took over the mosque. After several of these incidents, we [the Salafis] became also violent in this way and began using the same methods.[56]

The tension between al-Ahbash and Salafis culminated when a group of Salafi youth who belonged to *'Usbat al-Ansar*, a militant group in the 'Ain al-Hilwa Palestinian refugee camp in Sidon, murdered the head of the al-Ahbash organization, Shaykh Nizar al-Halabi, in 1995. This event proved to be a constraint for Salafism: The subsequent persecution of Salafis by the Lebanese and Syrian security forces resulted in the movement's current disintegrated, polysepalous nature.

At the same time, the tensions with al-Ahbash also benefited the Salafis' acquisition of religious capital. Due to its violent methods and serious deviations from mainstream (Ash'ari) Sunni Islam, the Sufi-oriented group alienated large parts of the wider Sunni population. Salafi preachers were able to play the role of the defenders of Sunnism in the face of a "deviant" group. They also posed as the representatives of authenticity in the face of dangerous innovations. This was the first time that Salafi preachers were able to attract larger crowds to their Friday sermons.[57] Many followers of Salafism in the North started to

---

[56] Interview, Tripoli, November 7, 2009.
[57] Interviews with Salafi individuals and witnesses to the events. See also Bernard Rougier, *Everyday Jihad*. Cambridge and London: Harvard University Press, 2007, pp. 113–140.

engage in Islamic activism along the lines of al-Ahbash. The movement's combination of personal piety with social work was attractive
to them. These individuals, as they recalled, found the same in Salafism,
but without the "distortions" and "innovations" of al-Ahbash.

2.7   Conclusion

This chapter discussed how the transformations of the Sunni religious
field facilitated the nascent Salafi movement to accumulate religious
and economic capital and grew from a small group to an important
movement in the 1990s. The decrease of the traditional religious elite's
influence provided space for Salafis to accumulate religious capital
by providing religious services that previously had been the task of
Dar al-Fatwa, thereby spreading their own interpretation of Islam.
The diminishing influence of the *Ikhwan* on the religious field made
Salafis appear as among the few who sincerely care about their fellow
Muslims, thereby further increasing their religious capital.

The deepening sectarian tensions between Sunnis and Shi'ites
enabled Salafis to pose as defenders of *Ahl al-Sunna wa-l-Jama'a* against
the threat from the Shi'a community and its militia, Hizbullah. They
accumulated religious capital by framing the tensions of the political
field into the framework of a cosmic Manichean struggle between
Islam and those who intend to corrupt the religion. Wealthy sponsors
from the Arabian Gulf provided Salafis with economic capital that
enabled the latter to build mosques, charities, and religious colleges
to spread their call, thereby increasing their influence on the field.

The tensions between Salafis and al-Ahbash often went beyond
ideological debates, and led to street fights. Although this conflict
ultimately led to a security crackdown on Salafis, they also benefited
from it. Salafi preachers were able to pose as the defenders of Sunnis
in the face of the "deviant" teachings of al-Ahbash. In the 2000s,
however, serious differences emerged within the Salafi groups. In
Chapter 3, I will show how Lebanese Salafism fragmented.

3   The Fragmentation of Salafism in Northern Lebanon

Over the last decade, Salafism in Lebanon has undergone a significant transformation. While the movement was relatively united under the leadership of Shaykh Da'i al-Islam al-Shahhal in the 2000s, this situation later changed. The fragmentation of Lebanese Salafis happened along similar ideological lines as in the Gulf. Yet the disruption of al-Shahhal's network by the Lebanese security services played a decisive role in triggering this development.

With the demise of the *haraki* al-Shahhal's authority, those inclined more toward purist thinking expanded their influence. Lebanese Salafis benefitted from the appearance of the two Gulf charities SRIH and SACF on the Lebanese scene, and this contributed to the cementing of the purist–*haraki* dichotomy. Lately, the power balance between the two factions has been altered in favor of the *harakis*, mostly due to the change of the sociopolitical context hallmarked by the Arab Uprisings. The *harakis* were able to utilize the transformations of Lebanon's political field to accumulate more religious and economic capital than the purists and improve their standing on the Sunni Islamic field.

3.1   The Fragmentation of al-Shahhal's Network

The Salafi community in Tripoli was relatively unified until the second half of the 1990s. Although the Salafis in this city never developed formal organizational structures, they gathered around GCS and its leader, Da'i al-Islam al-Shahhal. As many of my informants recalled, this was due to Shaykh Da'i's prestige, authority and financial power, since he was in contact with many charitable organizations and wealthy individuals in the Gulf, who generously financed the Lebanese Salafi movement. According to Shaykh 'Ali Taha, one of the prominent Salafi *'ulama'* in Tripoli's Tabbana district, "incredible amounts of money arrived from Saudi Arabia – mostly from the *Mu'assasat al-Haramayn* [the Haramayn Institution] – for building mosques, distributing Salafi literature and charitable purposes."[1] Riyadh's generosity was in line with its policy of counterbalancing Iran's effort to win the hearts of the Sunni population in the Middle East.[2] In Lebanon, the Salafis seemed capable of counterbalancing Hizbullah, in its attempt to gain allies among the Islamic movements of the North.

In less than a decade, Da'i al-Islam al-Shahhal was able to establish a charitable and educational network, not only in Tripoli and its extended urban area, but also in all of the country's Sunni regions. This emerging Salafi charitable empire was subsequently dismantled, when the Lebanese judiciary ordered the closure of GCS in 1996, accusing the organization of inciting sectarian hatred. The context of this event was the general crackdown on Islamists after the murder of Nizar Halabi, who had been favored by the Syrian-Lebanese security regime.[3] Al-Halabi was a renowned Ash'ari *'alim* and the leader of al-Ahbash after 'Abdullah al-Harari had retired. On August 31, 1995, he was assassinated by a group of Jihadi Salafis from the 'Ain al-Hilwa camp near Saida. The security regime used the events to justify a crackdown on the entire Salafi movement. The Syrian regime and its representatives in Lebanon argued that al-Shahhal's network was spreading extremist ideas, which had eventually turned many of the young Salafis to violence.[4]

According to Shaykh Da'i's younger brother, Abu Bakr al-Shahhal, some members of al-Ahbash reported to the internal security service that in Ma'had al-Hidaya (Hidaya Institute), one of the Salafi organization's educational centers in Tripoli's Abu Samra district, students were being taught from a book that contained violent anti-Shi'a statements, and talked about the Alavite sect with derogatory remarks as well.[5] As Abu Bakr al-Shahhal explained, a textbook published by GCS contained some pages from this particular book. However, he argued that the teachers avoided discussing these statements with the students, and used a different part of the book for education.

Shaykh Da'i's charity network, however, was able to continue its activities until 2000, when the final crackdown occurred. Da'i al-Islam al-Shahhal's name was mentioned in connection with a jihadi group, which had fought against the army for several days in late 1999 in the

---

[1] Interview with Shaykh 'Ali Taha, Tripoli, December 5, 2009.

[2] al-Rasheed, *Contesting the Saudi State*, p. 105 and pp. 126–133.

[3] According to some sources, the Syrians wanted Halabi to be elected as Mufti of the Republic to control the Sunni religious establishment. Interview with a shaykh in Dar al-Fatwa, Tripoli, November 26, 2009.

[4] Rougier, *Everyday Jihad*, Cambridge, pp. 119–123.

[5] Gade, "Sunni Islamists in Tripoli and the Asad regime," pp. 47–49.

Dinniya region.[6] According to accusations made by the Lebanese judiciary, some of the militants had connections to GCS. After the battle, many members of the organization were arrested, and Shaykh Da'i fled to Saudi Arabia to escape prosecution.[7] GCS was reestablished only after the withdrawal of Syrian forces from Lebanon in 2005.

After the battle of Dinniyya, the policy of the Syrian-Lebanese security regime toward Salafis changed. Earlier in the 1990s, it had considered the Maronite opposition and the remnants of the PLO to be its main enemies.[8] The former were identical to the members and supporters of the Lebanese Forces militia, which fought the Syrian army during the civil war. Later, after the restoration of peace, the Lebanese Forces became one of the strongest Christian political parties. Its leaders opposed the Syrian domination of Lebanese politics and demanded the departure of the occupying Syrian army. Since the Assad regime was unable to reach an agreement with the party, the regime sought the party's elimination. In 1993 and 1994, many members of the Lebanese Forces were arrested. Its leader, Samir Ja'ja', was sentenced to life imprisonment, and the party was banned by the Lebanese judiciary.[9]

The PLO under the leadership of Yasir 'Arafat was also among Damascus' arch-enemies. After Damascus' intervention in Lebanon in 1976 against the LNM, the Syrian army also confronted the PLO, which was the ally of the LNM. The enmity between 'Arafat's organization and Syria continued until the PLO leadership had to relocate to Tunis as a consequence of the 1982 Israeli invasion. After the Ta'if Agreement in 1989, the Syrian intelligence services kept a close check on the remnants of the PLO in Lebanon, preventing it from regaining any of its former influence.[10]

In the face of the threat coming from PLO activists and the still-strong Maronite opposition, the security regime saw the Salafis as a secondary challenge. Before the battle of Dinniyya, the authorities believed that the movement could be contained without having to take security measures. Syrian and Lebanese intelligence believed that any threat coming from the Salafi community could be countered by the presence of many informants among the movement's followers.[11] After the battle, this view changed. Fears arose that the proselytization activity of al-Shahhal's network would lead to a radicalization of northern youth.

[6] Rougier, *Everyday Jihad*, pp. 229–241.
[7] Shaykh Da'i's decision proved to be the right one, as in the same year, the Lebanese military court sentenced him to death in his absence.
[8] Salloukh, "A Brotherhood Transformed."
[9] Harris, *The New Face of Lebanon*, p. 282.   [10] Rougier, *Everyday Jihad*, p. 260.
[11] Rougier, *Everyday Jihad*, p. 261.

The drying up of Saudi financial sources following the 9/11 terror attacks and the subsequent "War on Terror" also contributed to the fissure in the Salafi movement. The United States accused various Islamic charity organizations of directly or indirectly financing terrorists and put pressure on the governments of the Gulf States to control their citizens' charity activities more closely and shut down organizations that might have links to al-Qaeda and other militant groups. The most notable case was the closure of the biggest transnational charity, Mu'assasat al-Haramayn (see Chapter 3). Bowing to American pressure after the 9/11 attacks, the Saudi government forbade local charities to send funds abroad. The authorities also froze the assets of al-Haramayn. The charity, meanwhile, did not comply with the government's instructions. By 2003, al-Haramayn managed to raise considerable funds again. It found ways to get around the ban of transferring money abroad, and started to support its branches in several countries. This resulted in the final shutdown of the institution in 2004 by the Saudi authorities.[12] Having lost their main source of funding, Salafis in Lebanon had to look for alternative channels.

After Shaykh Da'i's escape to Saudi Arabia, Lebanese Salafism underwent transformative changes. Until then, al-Shahhal had been the unquestioned leader of Lebanese Salafism. It appears that there were minor ideological differences between the participants in the movement: Salafism in Lebanon generally followed a *haraki* line. Although they projected the image of a purely *da'wa* movement that was primarily concerned with religious beliefs and practices, under the surface, Lebanese Salafis tried to change public opinion regarding Syria and Hizbullah. At that time in the 1990s, the majority of the Sunni community regarded the Syrian presence as a necessary evil to keep the peace in the country and the Shi'ite party was considered more a resistance movement against Israel than a sectarian militia. Shaykh Da'i's group attempted to undermine these views by preaching anti-Shi'a *khutbas* in some mosques in Tripoli and 'Akkar.[13]

Although some Salafis were more inclined toward purist ideas, they did not oppose al-Shahhal's main *haraki* line. For instance, when Shaykh Da'i ran as a candidate in the 1996 parliamentary elections, he was not publicly criticized by purist Salafis, who in principle rejected any involvement in institutional politics. The Salafis were circumspect because, at that time, Salafism in Lebanon was still in its infancy and was associated with al-Shahhal's name. Most of the Salafi activists in

[12] Bokhari et al., "A Good Day to Bury a Bad Charity," pp. 209–220.
[13] Rougier, *Everyday Jihad*, pp. 254–259.

the country were under his patronage and often received their main income from him. However, when he had to leave the country, the relative unity that Lebanese Salafis had formed around him disintegrated. As one of the veteran Salafis recalled, only al-Shahhal was in direct contact with the Gulf charities, which were the main sponsors of Salafi activities in the North. He distributed the money between the other shaykhs and activists. When he had to leave the country, many of those who used to work with him found themselves without an income.[14]

Although Shaykh Da'i established many institutions, he never managed to establish a sophisticated organizational structure. When he left, his associates and followers did not show much willingness to cooperate with each other. Instead, as my informant remembered, "everyone withdrew to his own mosque or *waqf* "[15] and started to look for alternative sources of patronage, either individually or with a few acquaintances. One of their strategies was to contact al-Shahhal's old supporters. During the 1990s, Shaykh Da'i was considered a successful Salafi leader, and delegations from Saudi, Kuwaiti, and Qatari charities and individual sponsors would therefore visit him, offering their support. Some of those who were around al-Shahhal socialized with these individuals in the Gulf and often made contacts that later proved to be useful.

When al-Shahhal was no longer the main distributor of financial resources, Salafis called these numbers and paid visits to potential donors in the Arabian Gulf. The other strategy was to contact their former classmates and friends from the Islamic University of Medina, who were now well connected to charities, the religious establishment, and businessmen. Many Lebanese Salafis started visiting Saudi Arabia and Kuwait more frequently, and participated in the religious lessons of some well-known '*ulama*' there. According to one of the Palestinian shaykhs from Nahr al-Barid, these were excellent occasions to meet potential donors and build social networks. In Kuwait, for example, the Lebanese visitors who were present at some of these religious lessons were often subsequently introduced in a *diwaniyya* – frequent traditional gatherings in a patron's home – which are the best social opportunities in the Gulf countries to increase one's social capital.[16]

Through increased participation in the transnational movement, Lebanese Salafis socialized in networks that had evolved around

---

[14] Interview, Tripoli, November 9, 2009.   [15] Interview, Tripoli, April 11, 2012.
[16] Interview, Tripoli, October 3, 2009.

different ideological streams. This led to the presence of the *haraki* and purist factions in Lebanon as representatives of larger transnational networks. Purists became particularly influential, since their main focus on the '*aqida* and the '*ibadat* meant that they did not attract the attention of the authorities. It is likely that the security regime also thought that the purist *da'is* would be an antidote to the radicalization of Salafis, due to their refusal to discuss political issues.

The tight security control over Salafis was lifted only after the fall of the Syrian-Lebanese security regime in 2005. On February 14, 2005, a massive car bomb in Beirut killed the former Prime Minister Rafiq al-Hariri. Many believed that Damascus had planned the murder, which was followed by massive demonstrations. The protesters demanded the resignation of the government and the withdrawal of the Syrian army. Whereas anti-Syria rallies in the past had consisted mainly of Christians, now Sunnis and Druze joined as well. At the same time, international pressure on Damascus also grew to implement UN Resolution 1559, which called for the withdrawal of all foreign forces from Lebanon. The Syrian army left the country on April 10, 2005.

With the end of the Syrian occupation, al-Ahbash's influence declined even further. The movement had close relations both to Syria and Hizbullah, and some of its members were even detained in 2005 in relation to the Hariri murder.[17] Many followers of the movement changed heart after Sunni public sentiments turned against Syria. They could not accept the association of the movement with the Assad regime anymore. As a result, the presence of the main rival of Salafism severely decreased on the Sunni religious field expanding the possibilities of Salafis for proselytization.

IG did not emerge as a considerable force after the Syrian uprisings. Divisions emerged in the ranks of the movement over their relationship to March 8 and March 14 camps. A faction, led by the founder of IG, Fathi Yakan (1933–2009), broke away in 2006 and established a separate group under the name Jabhat al-'Amal al-Islami (Islamic Action Front – IAF). Yakan aligned himself with Hizbullah, while the rest of IG stood with the March 14 camp that was supported by the majority of the Sunnis.[18] Even though Hizbullah supported IAF financially, it could never gain much popularity in the political climate

---

[17] Rita Daou, "Al-Ahbash: Shadowy Group at Center of Hariri probe," *Lebanon Wire*, October 27, 2005, www.lebanonwire.com/1005/05102708AFP.asp (accessed October 3, 2016).

[18] Omayma Abdel-Latif, "Lebanon's Sunni Islamists: A Growing Force," *Carnegie Middle East Center*, February 4, 2008, http://carnegie-mec.org/2008/02/04/lebanon-s-sunni-islamists-growing-force-pub-19882 (accessed, February 10, 2008), pp. 2–5.

after the Syrian withdrawal. The loss of one of its chief ideologues and a number of skilled cadres who followed Yakan also weakened IG. As one of Beirut's Muslim Brotherhood members told me, they lost one of the two established and charismatic figures within the movement (the other one was Faisal al-Mawlawi (1941–2011), the then head of IG).[19]

The lack of alternatives after the Syrian withdrawal improved the positions of Salafism on the Sunni religious field and the movement began to flourish in the North. The proselytizing activity of both purists and *harakis* reached unprecedented levels. Both factions received economic capital from donors in the Arabian Gulf. Purists received financial support from the Kuwaiti SRIH, while the *harakis* were sponsored by the Qatari SACF. The increase of their financial capital enabled Salafis to extend their religious infrastructure and reach out to a larger number of Sunnis.

3.2   The Emergence and Development of the Purist Networks in North Lebanon

The emergence of the politico-purist faction in Lebanon correlates with the transformation of the Salafi movement in Kuwait.[20] After purist Salafis had taken over the leadership of SRIH and Shaykh 'Abd al-Rahman 'Abd al-Khaliq had to leave the organization, the charity cut its ties with *harakis* in Lebanon. Since the late1990s, it has been exclusively sponsoring Lebanese purists.

SRIH has been present in Lebanon since 1990, but at that time it was still under *haraki* influence. The charity supported *Jama'iyyat al-Hidaya wa-l-Ihsan* and Da'i al-Islam al-Shahhal. Shaykh Da'i befriended many members of Ihya' al-Turath during his studies in Medina, and one of them was 'Abdullah al-Sabt. These individuals saw potential in Shaykh Da'i to be their agent in Lebanon. Al-Shahhal followed them to Kuwait, where he stayed for a few months. During his stay, he established contacts in Kuwait's *haraki* circles and later became a frequent guest at *diwaniyyas*, conferences, and other Salafi meetings in the country. When he went back to Lebanon in 1990 to start his *da'wa*, SRIH supported him financially,[21] to establish *shari'a* colleges in Tripoli and the southern port city of Saida.[22]

---

[19] Interview, October 27, 2009.   [20] See Chapter 2.
[21] Interview with a Palestinian Salafi shaykh, Tripoli, October 11, 2009, and interview with Shaykh Hilal Turkomani, Miryata, October 18, 2009.
[22] Interview with Da'i al-Islam al-Shahhal, Tripoli, August 9, 2011.

However, when the leadership of the charity changed in 1997, al-Shahhal fell from grace. The new SRIH administration initially tried to convince him to follow a purist *manhaj* and distribute purist literature among his followers. When he refused to do so, the organization cut the financial aid to GCS and started to look for other beneficiaries. As Shaykh Da'i sarcastically noted, the only thing that SRIH considers important is that those who receive their financial aid "must not have *fiqh*."[23] By this, the shaykh expressed the frequent *haraki* criticism against purists: that the latter do not have a sophisticated discourse on public affairs.

After SRIH broke with al-Shahhal, the organization sent only small amounts of money for a few purist individuals to publish booklets or make *iftar* (fast-breaking) for the poor. Large-scale charity work in Tripoli was resumed in the mid-2000s. A member of SRIH's leadership visited Lebanon as a tourist when he met a Salafi in his early thirties, Safwan al-Za'bi. The former invited Al-Za'bi to Kuwait, where he spent some time studying in *halaqa*s (informal religious lessons usually held in the mosque or private homes) and was introduced to leading figures from SRIH. Around 2004, a-Za'bi started to build an Islamic center and a clinic in Tripoli's Abu Samra district using funds he received from Ihya' al-Turath. In 2005, he established the local branch of the Kuwaiti charity under the name *Waqf al-Turath al-Islamiyy* (the Islamic Heritage Endowment – IHE).

IHE became the backbone of the purist networks in North Lebanon. Safwan al-Za'bi was the main agent of SRIH in the country and distributed the funds that arrived from the Kuwait charity. This gave him considerable influence over the North Lebanese Salafi scene until he left the organization in 2011. He launched several projects that drew the majority of the purists into his circle of patronage. The IHE has opened several medical clinics in Tripoli and in the villages of 'Akkar and Dinniya. At the same time, the charity sponsors mosques and local *awqaf* (plural of *waqf*) where the needy receive aid. Al-Za'bi also built an orphanage, financing the education of hundreds of orphans.[24]

Besides alleviating poverty, the IHE emphasizes Islamic education. It sponsors two *ma'ahid shara'iyya* (*shari'a* colleges); one of them is Ma'had al-Bukhari in 'Akkar, the other is Ma'had Tarablus in Tripoli. According to al-Za'bi, some Salafi colleges in Tripoli are spreading

---

[23] Ibid.

[24] Here the category of "orphan," according to the Islamic definition, includes those who have lost their father but whose mother is alive. See: "Yatim," in Bossworth, *Encyclopedia of Islam*.

"extremism and *khariji* ideology" among the youth. By supporting "moderate" teaching institutions, he intends to counterbalance those who endorse a "deviated [*munharif*] *manhaj*."[25] The IHE also organizes *halaqat* in mosques and makes regular payments to purist shaykhs to teach in them. Those who participate in these lessons can receive an *ijaza* (authorization, license) issued by the IHE, which enables them to teach certain religious subjects.

Bankrolling many of Lebanon's purist Salafis enabled Safwan al-Za'bi to start implementing the agenda that been proposed by the Kuwaiti charity. SRIH's main intention was to create a strong purist stream in the country to counterbalance the *harakis*. At the beginning of 2009, many of the *'ulama'* who were counted as representatives of the purist stream and received support from the SRIH signed a document (*al-Manhaj al-Wadih wa-l-Mithaq al-Shadid* – The Clear Methodology and the Strong Agreement) in which they agreed on a number of basic tenets of the method of the *da'wa* that they would follow. This event occurred after serious controversy had arisen between purist Salafis regarding an agreement between Safwan al-Za'bi, the representative of SRIH in Tripoli, and Hizbullah. This document was most likely suggested by SRIH, as a means of creating a loose network among its beneficiaries in Lebanon (and probably elsewhere).

The agreement stresses the need to remain loyal to the Saudi Great *'ulama'* and forbids "mocking them."[26] The second main point is the call to create an Islamic society by peaceful *da'wa* and to exercise stoic forbearance regarding the injustices of the rulers. The document also prohibits revolt against the rulers, even if they are not Muslim, and condemns the understanding of jihad propagated by militant groups. Instead, they call for peaceful coexistence with non-Muslims and respect for "the treaties and contracts made with Muslims and non-Muslims."[27] These points, of course, closely resemble the preferences of SRIH.

The IHE also formed a *fatwa* council composed of some of the most renowned Salafi scholars. Its task was to issue legal opinions in local Lebanese cases where the *fatwas* of the Saudi Great *'ulama'* did not fully apply or were not specific enough. The council, for example, legitimized al-Za'bi's attempt to participate in institutional politics and mobilize

---

[25] Interview with Shaykh Safwan al-Za'bi, Tripoli, September 29, 2009.

[26] This is a reference to those *harakis* who call some of the Great *'ulama'* the "'*ulama*' of menstruation," because of their lack of attention to political issues when lost in the details of daily religious practice, such as how women should worship while menstruating.

[27] See *Al-Sharq Al-Awsat* newspaper, August 20, 2008.

voters for his preferred candidates in a *fatwa*. The writers of the legal opinion state that, "we live in a multiconfessional society where different religious groups and intellectual streams live together. It is not possible for one of them to dominate the others; this is one of the characteristics of Lebanese society." Therefore, "it does not harm the [Muslim] candidate if he uses the parliament as a tool for *al-'amr bil-ma'ruf wa al-nahi 'an al-munkar* [*hisba*] (Commanding good and forbidding evil) and also as a tool for the *da'wa* by offering his thoughts, [especially] if he does that through the media."[28]

The writers of the *fatwa* argue that participating in the election of representatives to parliament is legitimate, since Lebanese law does not oblige them to make decisions that are un-Islamic. It is also possible to elect non-Muslim candidates if they serve Muslim interests. In their reasoning, the authors of the *fatwa* first refer to the Qur'anic exegesis of 'Abd al-Rahman bin Sa'di (1889–1956), a widely-quoted Saudi scholar who followed the example of the prophet Shu'ayb (mentioned in the Qur'an) when he urged Muslims to participate in political life if they lived in a society that had no Muslim majority:

God may defend the believers in many ways, some of which they may know and some they may not know at all. He may defend them by means of their tribe or their *kafir* compatriots, as God defended Shu'ayb from the stoning of his people by means of his clan. There is nothing wrong with striving to maintain these connections by means of which Islam and the Muslims may be defended, and in some cases that may be essential, because *da'wa* is required according to ability.

Based on this, if Muslims help those who are under the rule of the *kuffar*, and strive to make the state a republic in which the religious and worldly rights of individuals and peoples are protected, then this is better than their submitting to a state that denies their religious and worldly rights, and is keen to destroy them and make them its servants. Yes, if it is possible to make the state an Islamic one that is ruled by Muslims, then this should be done, but when this is not possible, the next priority is supporting a type of state where religious and worldly interests are protected. And God knows best.[29]

The *fatwa* also refers to the example of the prophet Yusuf, when he accepted the Pharaoh's offer to be the supervisor of Egypt's warehouses. Although Yusuf had to act according to the law of the Pharaoh and not that of God, by this action, he was able to save his youngest brother. As the Qur'an relates, Yusuf's brothers wanted to return to their homeland, and Yusuf was concerned lest they might harm the

---

[28] *Al-Sharq Al-Awsat* newspaper, August 20, 2008.   [29] Ibid.

youngest brother. He therefore had a precious goblet belonging to the Pharaoh hidden in the latter's baggage, and had his officials carry out an inspection in which they discovered this item. This allowed him to arrest his youngest brother and thereby save his life. According to the authors of the *fatwa*, this means that he "who trusts himself that he is able to be of benefit [to the Muslim community], turn away from corruption and serve the common interest can be a representative in the parliament and [he] who trusts him must vote for him."[30]

The *fatwa* even states that political participation in a non-Muslim country can be a religious duty for Muslims, if, by doing so, they serve the interests of their community. Al-Za'bi claims that due to this *fatwa*, many purist Salafis who had never previously voted went to the ballot boxes during the 2009 elections. He believes that political participation in the secular state defends the *da'wa*. As he explained, since his network mobilizes voters to elect different political bosses in Tripoli, it is in their interest to support Salafis by granting them protection and financial aid, instead of oppressing them.[31]

Safwan al-Za'bi tried to further increase his patronage over the purist Salafis by signing the so-called Memorandum of Understanding (*Wathiqat al-Tafahhum*) between a coalition of purist *'ulama'* led by himself and Hizbullah on August 15, 2008.[32] The document itself contains a number of platitudes, such as accepting the other with all their differences or solving problems through discussion instead of confrontation. The only interesting point is the plan to set up a body of *'ulama'* between the Salafis and the Shi'ites in order to research the differences between Sunni and Shi'a thought. This is a unique initiative on the part of the Salafis, since they usually refuse any such proposition until the Shi'ites denounce their sect and "return" to Sunni Islam. The real significance of the memorandum lies in the Salafi faction's motives and reasons for approaching and signing an agreement with Hizbullah, despite the Salafis' inherent hostility toward the Shi'ites.

The event happened three months after Hizbullah and its allies had launched a military operation and occupied most of Beirut on May 8, 2008. This confrontation had erupted as a result of a three-year-long political conflict between the governing March 14 and the opposition March 8 alliances. The Sunni-dominated government decided to shut down Hizbullah's telecommunications network and sack the

---

[30] *Al-Sharq Al-Awsat* newspaper, August 20, 2008.
[31] Interview, Tripoli, October 13, 2009.
[32] "Wathiqat al-Tafahum Bayn Hizb Allah Wa Ba'd al-Jama'iyyat al-Salafiya Bayn al-Tarhib wa-l-Tahaffuz," *al-Sharq al-Awsat*, August 20, 2008.

pro-Hizbullah airport commander, Walid Shukayr.[33] Hizbullah interpreted these measures as the first step to disarm the movement. In response, the armed brigades of Hizbullah and its allies, among them the secular Shi'ite AMAL and the Syrian Social-Nationalist Party,[34] took over the Sunni districts of Beirut, the power base of the al-Mustaqbal-led government. Fighting erupted between militants of the March 8 alliance and pro-government guerrillas in both the capital and in other regions of the country.[35] During the confrontation, Hizbullah outgunned its opponents, which led to the weakening of the March 14 alliance. Therefore, the Hariri camp had to make concessions to Hizbullah. On May 21, 2008, in an agreement between March 14 and March 8, the former granted veto power to the latter in a newly formed government.[36]

As one of the participants in the Salafi delegation that signed the memorandum explained, after May 8, 2008, there were fears that Hizbullah would try to uproot Salafism in Lebanon.[37] By approaching the party, al-Za'bi's network hoped to protect itself and turn the militia's and its allies' attention, in terms of military security, toward the *harakis*. By doing so, they would secure their autonomy to practice their *da'wa*, which, being purist in nature, is not concerned with the power struggle between the elites of the March 8 and March 14 blocks. Safwan al-Za'bi and his circle also believed that they could sign the memorandum without losing their constituency, because they could not gain legitimacy by focusing on the "Shi'ite conspiracy" against the Sunnis, unlike the *harakis*. Their criticism of the Shi'a focuses on the *'aqida* and other elements of the belief system,[38] and they tend not to connect the alleged "deviations" of the Shi'a to political events and processes.[39] Za'bi also

---

[33] "Lebanon: Hizbollah's Weapons Turn Inward," *International Crisis Group Policy Briefing* (May 15, 2008). www.crisisgroup.org/en/regions/middle-east-north-africa/egypt-syria-lebanon/lebanon/b023-lebanon-hizbollahs-weapons-turn-inward.aspx (accessed November 15, 2012).

[34] "Lebanon: Hizbollah's Weapons Turn Inward," 2008.

[35] "Bab al-Tabbanah Wa Jabal Muhsin: Jarah al-Shamal al-Lubnani al-Maftuh," *al-Sharq al-Awsat*, June 23, 2008.

[36] "The New Lebanese Equation: The Christians' Central Role," *International Crisis Group Policy Briefing* (July 15, 2008). www.crisisgroup.org/en/regions/middle-east-north-africa/egypt-syria-lebanon/lebanon/078-the-new-lebanese-equation-the-christians-central-role.aspx (accessed November 15, 2012).

[37] Interview, December 3, 2009.

[38] This was my experience when I frequently participated in *durus* and lectures by purist Salafis and talked to them during my fieldwork in Lebanon in 2009, 2011, and 2012, and in Kuwait in 2010 and 2012.

[39] This might be changing in the wake of the Arab Spring, due to growing anti-Shi'a sentiment on the Sunni street in the Middle East and the increasing keenness of active participants to understand the context of the events that are now occurring, such as the revolutions and the Syrian civil war. When I spent a long period of time with a purist group with close contacts to SRIH in Kuwait in February 2012, during the *durus*, the

believed that the crackdown on the *haraki* Salafis would come sooner
or later, leading to the imprisonment or exile of most Salafi leaders
in the country. If he were able to secure his position with Hizbullah, he
would have a chance of becoming the most powerful Salafi patron
in Lebanon.

Interestingly, the Memorandum was signed by Dr. Hasan al-Shahhal,
the cousin of Da'i al-Islam and director of *Ma'had al-Da'wa wal-l-Irshad*
(Call and Guidance College), one of the prominent Salafi educational
institutions in Tripoli. Dr. Hasan holds purist views and is well connected to the Saudi official religious establishment that includes purist
'ulama'. When I interviewed Hasan al-Shahhal, he accused Da'i al-Islam
of trying to hijack Salafism for personal political gains. As he told me,
by involving "Salafis in a political conflict [between March 8 and 14]
[Da'i] hopes that al-Mustaqbal would reward him financially or perhaps with a parliamentary seat."[40] Dr. Hasan regarded himself as the
real successor of Shaykh Salim al-Shahhal's *da'wa*, as, according to him,
the latter never wanted to be part of Lebanese politics.[41]

Signing the Memorandum could have been an attractive choice
for Hasan al-Shahhal for a number of reasons. First, the operation of
his *ma'had* was almost entirely financed by SRIH funds distributed by
Safwan al-Za'bi.[42] Considering the similar ideological views Shaykh
Safwan held and the financial resources he possessed it is not surprising
that Dr. Hasan wanted to forge a close relationship with him. Second,
having a considerable purist network with solid financial backing and
secured by a security crackdown standing in alliance with him, he
could hope to match Shaykh Da'is authority.

Shortly after the Memorandum was signed, the Future movement,
one of the most influential Sunni players on Lebanon's political field,
rejected it. Although Safwan al-Za'bi claimed that members of the
latter, such as one of the most influential Sunni MPs, Samir al-Jisr,
supported the Memorandum, the majority were vocal about their rejection.[43] The Future Movement is supported by the Saudi political leadership, while purist Salafis who signed the memorandum possess a
myriad of personal ties to the kingdom's religious establishment. It is
unlikely that these shaykhs would sign the document if the Saudi
'ulama' expressed their rejection. This rather shows that Saudi Arabia
is not necessarily a unitary actor in Lebanon. While the Saudi

Shi'a were not discussed beyond their "doctrinal deviations." However, among
themselves, the participants frequently touched the topic of the Shi'i conspiracy.
[40] Interview with Dr. Hasan al-Shahhal, Tripoli, October 3, 2009.   [41] Ibid.
[42] Interview with Safwan al-Za'bi, Tripoli, October 13, 2009. An employee of the ma'had
verified this claim during an informal conversation in December 2009.
[43] Ibid.

government backs the Future Movement, the religious establishment might consider it important to protect the *da'wa* of purist Salafis, even if it is not completely politically in line with some of Riyadh's protégés.

The attempt to secure an agreement with Hizbullah, however, proved unsuccessful. Al-Za'bi and the other participants had to withdraw, due to the criticism from the *harakis*. Their own purist constituency also reacted in an unexpected way, with many of them expressing open hostility toward al-Za'bi and the *'ulama'* who had supported his initiative. In the long term, the Memorandum of Understanding also led to a breach with Ihya' al-Turath. The Kuwaiti charity initially supported the idea of trying to reach an agreement with Hizbullah and protect the purist *da'wa*. According to one of the leading figures of the Kuwaiti politico-purist stream, the organization convinced al-Za'bi to make the first step and approach Hizbullah.[44]

The Lebanese Salafi broke with SRIH three years later, due to their internal divisions. At the time when the Lebanese group signed the memorandum, SRIH was dominated by a faction that endorsed reducing the Sunni–Shi'i gap, even inside Kuwait. However, this stream lost its influence on the eve of the Arab Spring in 2011, when a radically anti-Shi'a faction took over.[45] Safwan al-Za'bi complained to me that the new leaders of SRIH started to curb his autonomy and wanted to forbid him to participate in politics or defend the interests of Salafis "at the level of civil society." Therefore, he decided to leave the Lebanese branch of the Kuwaiti organization. A new administration took over the Al-Sunna mosque and Islamic center, along with the other charity projects launched by al-Za'bi. The latter started to develop his own local charitable network, *Jama'iyyat al-Ukhuwwa* (the Brotherhood Association), and at the time of my fieldwork he was establishing contacts with individual sponsors and getting financial aid from, as he expressed it, Saudi "state actors."[46]

3.2.1   Purist-Rejectionist Networks

Purist-rejectionist Salafis are also present in Northern Lebanon's Salafi scene. They are more scattered than the politico-purists discussed earlier, and there is no trace of even a rudimentary form of coordination similar to that set up by Safwan al-Za'bi. Purist-rejectionists

---

[44] Interview with Salim al-Nashi'.
[45] Interview Sami al-'Adwani, al-Zahra' district, March 7, 2012, and interview with Safwan al-Za'bi, Tripoli, April 26, 2012.
[46] Interview, Tripoli, April 26, 2012.

usually gather around a shaykh who either studied in Saudi Arabia or is a self-educated individual who gives *halaqat* to young people in his local neighborhood. The faction tends to attract committed Salafis, and the shaykhs who belong to this stream rarely have passive followers. The reason for this tendency lies in their stance toward society and their social habits, which are similar to the Kuwaiti Madkhali movement. Many of them prefer to isolate themselves from the rest of the population. Their only concerns are to follow what is prescribed in the Qur'an and the *hadith* in minute detail, and to create the perfect Muslim individual by perfecting everyday religious practice. Politics and social issues are beyond their concern, since, as one of them explained, "all hardships that we are facing now will be solved when the majority follow what is prescribed in the Scripture."[47]

Besides rejecting participation in institutional politics, they often criticize charities. As a purist-rejectionist shaykh, Shaykh Wisam told me that aside from leading to partisanship (*hizbiyya*), the activities of SRIH and other organized charitable work are contributing to keeping the population of Northern Lebanon in a condition of poverty:

People are accustomed to getting a pittance from the charities or the *zu'ama* to fill their stomachs and they do not have to do anything for it. Therefore they have no aspirations to improve their situation; to learn a profession or open a business. Islam, however, tells people to be hard-working. *Zakat* funds should also help people who want to start an enterprise, as was the case in the time of the Salaf.[48]

Most of these purist-rejectionist individuals spend their free time studying the Qur'an and the *hadith*, reading the books by those *'ulama'* whom they acknowledge, and participating in religious lessons. Their interactions with wider society outside of their workplace is limited to those activities that are considered useful for the *da'wa*.

In Northern Lebanon there are dozens of small purist-rejectionist networks. One of these networks is centered on a highly knowledgeable, Medina-educated individual, Shaykh Ihab. The group has ten to twenty members, mostly university-educated, middle-class young men. Shaykh Ihab's life story mirrors the typical trajectory of a Lebanese Salafi *'alim*. He was born into a secular middle-class family in the 1970s. He described how his mother never put on a *hijab* and his father often cursed God. Despite this, he has had an affinity with religion since his childhood.

---

[47] Interview with Ghassan, Tripoli, April 24, 2012.
[48] Interview with Shaykh Wisam, October 8, 2009.

He recalled that two events pushed him toward Salafism. First, one of his teachers, who was following the *Athari 'aqida* instead of the mainstream *Ash'ari* one, had a great impact on him. Second, he went to al-Azhar University in Egypt to take a summer course. After finishing his daily lessons at al-Azhar, he usually went to visit the *halaqat* of a Salafi shaykh in Cairo. The arguments he heard in Egyptian Salafi circles made more sense to him than what he had learned in al-Azhar. After returning to Lebanon, he joined the local Salafis, participated in religious lessons every day and visited both *haraki* and purist groups. Despite the objection of his parents, he accepted a scholarship to Medina University. In Saudi Arabia, he became a student of Shaykh Rabi' al-Madkhali.

During the *halaqat* of Shaykh Rabi', Shaykh Ihab met a couple of students from Kuwait who invited him to their country, where he worked for two months. There, he met Shaykh Salim al-Tawil and became close to the local Madkhali networks. Incongruously, while he was sharing activities with the Kuwaiti purist-rejectionists in the *halaqat*, he also met some individuals who were close to Ihya' al-Turath. When he went back to Lebanon, he found work as a clerk at the Sunna Islamic Center that had originally been built by Safwan al-Za'bi. The income he earned there enabled him to settle in Tripoli and start his *da'wa* activity in Abu Samra, his neighborhood.[49] Middle-class young men from the same district and also from al-Qubba joined him and participated in his weekly *halaqat* in the Sunna mosque. Shaykh Ihab's network rarely interacts with that of other Salafis in Lebanon. At the same time, they form part of the transnational circulation of Salafism. Shaykh Ihab's students often benefit from their teacher's contacts in Kuwait. Some of them have traveled to the Gulf emirate to participate in purist-rejectionist study circles, find a job, or pursue their studies. Kuwaiti shaykhs such as Salim al-Tawil, Ahmad al-Siba'i, and Hamad 'Uthman are frequently followed by group members on social media platforms such as Twitter.

3.3 The *Haraki* Network in Northern Lebanon

After the Syrian army left Lebanon, the security services' pressure on *haraki* eased significantly. After five years of passivity following the crackdown that had occurred in the wake of the battle of Dinniyya

---

[49] Interview, Tripoli, April 28, 2012.

in 2000, they were able to relaunch their activities. Shaykh Da'i al-Islam al-Shahhal returned to Lebanon after being exonerated of all the charges against him. He reopened GSC and attracted many young Salafis to the group. Some of his former associates also rejoined his circle.[50] Due to his transnational contacts and access to financial aid from the Gulf, he was able to reestablish himself as a patron.

The conditions after the Syrian withdrawal were generally favorable for *haraki* Salafis. For the upcoming elections in May 2005, two big coalitions were formed from the opponents and the supporters of Syria. The former camp, called "March 14," a mix of Sunni, Christian, and Druze parties, was led by the son of Rafiq al-Hariri, Sa'd. For March 14, it was crucial to gain the majority of the votes in Northern Lebanon to win the elections. Therefore, they made an alliance with *haraki* Salafis led by Da'i al-Islam al-Shahhal, who helped them to mobilize voters. In exchange, the Salafis received material support from the Hariri clan to relaunch their charity networks, which had been disrupted by the security regime.[51]

The escalating Sunni–Shi'ite tensions after the Hariri murder also proved to be favorable for *harakis* to gain more followers. As mentioned in Chapter 2, sectarianism between the two Muslim communities was already present after the end of the civil war, although it was rather limited in extent. However, the situation changed radically in 2005. Between 1992 and 2005, Hizbullah was satisfied with holding one of the largest parliamentary blocs in the country, but did not participate in the cabinet. Hizbullah chose not to engage with governance because it enjoyed enough political protection from the Syrians, who effectively controlled the extremely fragmented political mosaic of Lebanon. Therefore, Hizbullah was able to maintain its image as a pan-Islamic and national resistance movement that transcended sectarian divisions. However, this protection was lifted and pro-Western, anti-Syrian forces gained a majority in the cabinet after the 2005 elections. These latter demanded the full implementation of UN resolution 1559, which included the disarming of Hizbullah in addition to the withdrawal of Syrian forces. The Shi'ite movement therefore sent its own representatives to the government to create

---

[50] Interview with Da'i al-Islam al-Shahhal, Tripoli, August 9, 2011.

[51] Interview with Fida' 'Itani, a leading journalist on the *al-Akhbar* newspaper and a frequent publisher on Salafism in Lebanon, Beirut, October 6, 2009. See also: Fida' 'Itani, "Al-Sa'udiyya Fi Lubnan Tarablus Wa al-Ma'raka al-Akhira li-Tawhid al-Sunna 3/3," *al-Akhbar*, September 4, 2008.

political cover for its armed wing. By doing so, however, it became part of the sectarian struggle.[52]

Gradually, the image of the Party changed from a national resistance movement to a sectarian militia that wanted to dominate other confessional communities. Sectarian divisions increased more sharply after the disastrous economic and social consequences of the 2006 war between Israel and Hizbullah. The result of this chain of events was that anti-Shi'a sentiments spilled over from the circles of Islamists and intellectuals and took deep root among the wider Sunni population. Hizbullah has been framed by the media and even by the 'ulama' of Dar al-Fatwa as part of a sectarian struggle across the Middle East between the Sunnis and Shi'ites, and as the Lebanese agent of Iran, a state that wants to rule the whole region and ultimately eradicate Sunni thought.

The *harakis* utilized this environment to increase their positions on the Sunni Islamic field. Their anti-Shi'a framing – which portrayed the Shi'ites as part of a global conspiracy against Islam that has been going on for centuries – proved credible in the eyes of many Sunnis in the North, thereby increasing their religious capital. *Haraki* Salafis were not only regarded as masters of the scripture, who know how the Prophet prayed or lived his daily life, but also as those who can offer guidance based on a profound knowledge of the Qur'an and the Sunna, a time that most Sunni Muslims perceived as challenging.[53] Furthermore, having increased their religious capital, *haraki* shaykhs also accumulated economic capital by forging a close relationship to the Sunni political elite. The Hariri clan, in order to secure a majority among Sunnis in Lebanon, provided financial assistance to Haraki-Salafis in exchange for their political support, in election times.[54]

The appearance of the Shaykh 'Aid Charity Foundation (SACF) greatly increased the capabilities of the *harakis*. The leadership of the Qatari charity saw an opportunity to establish a strong presence in Lebanon after the Syrian withdrawal. They first established connections with Lebanese Salafis through one of the charity's high-ranking officials, a veteran Lebanese *haraki* called Shaykh Khalid Za'rur. In the 1990s, Shaykh Khalid was a close associate of Da'i al-Islam al-Shahhal and spent a few months in prison after the battle of Dinniyya. Upon his release, he settled in the Gulf and became an activist in the local

---

[52] "Hizbollah and the Lebanese Crisis," *International Crisis Group*, October 10, 2007. www.crisisgroup.org/~/media/Files/Middle%20East%20North%20Africa/Iraq%20 Syria%20Lebanon/Lebanon/69_hizbollah_and_the_lebanese_crisis.pdf (accessed October 3, 2010), pp. 1–3.

[53] See the discussion on anti-Shi'a framing in Chapter 8.

[54] Several lower ranking *haraki* preachers told me this in Tripoli between 2009 and 2012.

haraki networks. In the early 2000s, he found employment at SACF and was made responsible for the charity's foreign relations.[55]

In 2005 Shaykh Khalid reconnected with the Lebanese *harakis* and offered them sponsorship. SACF, for example, helped Da'i al-Islam al-Shahhal to reopen his radio station, Iza'at al-Qur'an (The Qur'an Broadcast), which had been banned by the authorities in 2000. Dozens of other Salafi shaykhs received financial support for charitable and *da'wa* purposes. Almost all of the renowned *haraki 'ulama'* at the center of significant local sub-networks received support from SACF. Among them were Shaykh Zakariya al-Masri, an influential preacher from Tripoli's Qubba district, and Shaykh Salim al-Rafi'i, probably the most popular religious scholar in Northern Lebanon. Several lesser-known shuyukh also received significant material support to build mosques and boost their *da'wa* in and around Tripoli.

Besides contributing to the preaching activity of local Lebanese shaykhs, SACF directly employs a large number of *da'is* in the Sunni-inhabited areas of Lebanon. As Khalid Za'rur explained to me, the organization pays them a fixed monthly salary, which in 2009 was USD 400–600, two to three times higher than they would receive from Dar al-Fatwa. Furthermore, SACF covers the maintenance of their mosques, reimburses the cost of petrol, and sponsors the printing and distribution of *da'wa* material such as leaflets and booklets. In turn, the *da'is* spread Salafism among their local communities. Usually a *da'i* is in charge of a small mosque, where he delivers the Friday sermon and organizes daily religious lessons. At the same time he provides advice to the inhabitants of his village or neighborhood on daily religious issues.[56]

Within a few years, SACF was able to establish a huge network of religious schools, mosques, and Salafi missionaries in Northern Lebanon. Shaykh Khalid Za'rur elaborated that the organization tried to establish coordination and cohesion between the members of this network. It never aspired, however, to create a sophisticated institutional structure similar to that of the Muslim Brotherhood. SACF appointed a mediator in Lebanon, an ex-Maronite convert, Rabi' Haddad. His task was to organize a regular forum, *al-Liqa' al-Salafi* (Salafi Meeting), where *harakis* would have the opportunity to discuss and establish cooperation in matters of charity or politics.

By 2010, due to favorable local conditions and financial support from SACF, a large, decentralized network of *haraki* Salafis had emerged.

---

[55] Interview with Shaykh Khalid Za'rur, Doha, July 29, 2010.
[56] Interview with Shaykh Khalid Za'rur, al-Waqra, August 1, 2010.

Although Da'i al-Islam al-Shahhal likes to pose as the leader of the Lebanese Salafis in his media appearances, in reality, he does not even have authority over the majority of the *harakis*. A number of other shaykhs, all of whom can claim popular support and access to sponsorship from charities in the Gulf, and to Lebanese political patrons, lies at the center of the extended sub-networks.

3.3.1   The Network of Shaykh Salim al-Rafi'i

During my fieldwork, I discovered a *haraki* sub-network that competes with that of al-Shahhal in terms of influence and the number of followers. It is centered on Shaykh Salim al-Rafi'i, who is regarded by many as the most renowned and respected Salafi *'alim* in Lebanon. He became an Islamic activist in the IUM in the mid-1980s, when it had controlled Tripoli for nearly two years. When the Syrians conquered the city, he was forced to seek refuge in Germany. After studying in several universities in the Middle East and South Asia, and graduating from the Islamic University of Medina, he established himself as the main religious leader of the Syrian-Lebanese-Palestinian community in the Kreuzberg district of Berlin. As the imam of the al-Nur Islamic center and Mosque, he fought against, as he put it, the "erosion of the traditional values of Muslims and their westernization."[57]

When he had to leave Germany and return to Lebanon in 2005, he had already built up a vast transnational network of Salafis based in Europe and financial donors based in the Gulf. His rhetorical skills, modest lifestyle, and access to material resources enabled him to establish himself as one of the main Salafi authorities in Tripoli. Upon his arrival, he became the imam of the huge al-Taqwa mosque in the al-Tabbana district, where he quickly built up a vast follower base. Following the outbreak of the Arab Spring and the Syrian revolution in particular, he declared the events the beginning of a new Sunni ascendance, whereby the *umma* would break the chains of "Western colonialism" and would curb the Shi'ites' attempt to "dominate the region" and "destroy true Islam."

His rhetoric, which was thick with conspiracy theories, proved attractive to the masses of Sunnis in Tripoli. The Sunnis felt economically and politically marginalized, for which they blamed the West, Hizbullah, the Shi'ite community, and the Assad regime in Syria, a government which they regarded as one of the closest allies of the Shi'ites. At the time of my last visit to Lebanon in the spring of 2012,

---

[57] Interview, Tripoli, August 2, 2011.

between 3,000 and 4,000 people listened to his Friday sermon at the al-Taqwa mosque. Reflecting his ability to seize the opportunities created by the climate of the Arab revolutions, the Shaykh 'Aid Charity Association, and (according to some rumors) the Qatari state provided him with financial support every month.

Shaykh Salim gathered many of the younger Salafi shuyukh in the al-Tabbana region and al-Mina, where he controls the more modest but nevertheless important 'Uthman bin 'Affan mosque. He uses his access to Gulf funds to help these young preachers to build up their *da'wa*. In exchange, he relies on them for political support. For example, the shaykhs urge their own constituents to vote for Shaykh Salim's candidates during elections. Along with heads of local families, they also participate in the *shura* (advisory), which was established by Shaykh Salim in 2012. The council is destined to "make the Muslims take their affairs into their own hands."

Shaykh Salim and other shuyukh who belong to his network attract large numbers of local youth in al-Tabbana to join their movement. Working-class and lower-middle-class young people in the district were traditionally recruited by militias that fought under the successive banners of Marxism, Arab Nationalism, and Islamism in the Lebanese Civil War against the Christians, and then against the invading Syrian army in 1985 and their Alawite allies who inhabit the neighboring Jabal Muhsin. These armed factions regrouped when the conflict between the Sunnis of al-Tabbana and the Alawites re-erupted as part of the events surrounding May 8, 2008. Since then, there have been clashes between the two communities in the area every year. Recently, Salafis have been able to win over many militiamen, if not the majority of them. Since the beginning, the conflict between the Alawites and the Sunnis has been sectarian, and Salafis frame it as a Muslim struggle against those who are trying to destroy Islam from within (the Alawite sect is widely regarded as an offshoot of Shi'a Islam). Besides providing religious legitimacy for their fight against the Alawites, Salafis also provide these young men with material help and monthly salaries.[58]

3.4   The *Haraki* Ascendance after the Arab Uprisings

In the post–Arab Uprisings environment, the *haraki* stream has started to flourish in Northern Lebanon, taking over much ground from the

---

[58] An average salary is between 400USD to 600USD. Some of the leaders earn between 1000USD and 2000USD. Interview with a group of young Salafis from al-Tabbana, April 25, 2012.

purists. This reflects developments at the transnational level, when the revolutions in 2011 led to the rapid expansion of *haraki* Salafism and to a decrease in the popularity of the purists. The main reason for this change of fortunes is that the purist shaykhs supported the autocratic Arab regimes until the last moment, and issued *fatwas* against the demonstrations all over the Middle East. They were quick to label the protests against dictatorship as *"khuruj 'ala al-hakim "* and *fitna* (civil strife), labels that imply the right of the ruler to suppress the protestors.[59]

Shaykh Abu al-Hasan al-Sulaymani, a renowned purist scholar,[60] argued that "the Muslim ruler has the right to be obeyed [by the ruled] in what is accepted by the religion[61] and there cannot be any reason which allows the revolt against him ... because the Prophet has forbidden the dethronement of the ruler as long as he is Muslim." He justifies his argument by referring to a *hadith*: "'Ibada bin Samit[62] told us: God's Prophet called us [to accept him as leader] and we pledged allegiance to him. Among other things he obliged us to listen to him and obey him ... and not to contest the rulers only if we see that they commit such acts which make them unbelievers." According to this scholar, even if the ruler takes the property of the people unjustly, the ruler's orders have to be implemented.[63] Another purist *'alim* argued on the eve of the Arab Spring that people should not demonstrate to achieve freedom, since "the human being and the *jinn* have been created for worshipping God and not for freedom."[64] This stance largely alienated their follower base in the Middle East. After some hesitation, the *harakis*[65] supported the revolutions, and subsequently their popular support multiplied.

---

[59] Purist scholars across the Middle East issued hundreds of fatwas denouncing the revolutions and urging the people to stay at home instead of demonstrating.

[60] Al-Sulaymani (b. 1958) is originally Egyptian but currently lives in Ma'rib in Yemen. http://sulaymani.net/index.php?option=com_content&view=article&id=99:2009-07-03-15-20-57&catid=29&Itemid=59 (accessed August 22, 2015).

[61] Here the meaning is that the ruler has no right to order people to neglect religious duties such as prayer.

[62] One of the companions of the Prophet.

[63] Fatwa of Shaykh Abu al-Hasan al-Sulaymani. See the discussion on www.kulalsalafiyeen .com: www.kulalsalafiyeen.com/vb/showthread.php?t=48698 (accessed February 10, 2013).

[64] Shaykh 'Abd al-Malik al-Ramadani, a prominent Algerian Salafi scholar, posted this opinion on his Facebook page on April 10, 2011. www.facebook.com/Abdulmalek .Ramdhani.

[65] Some *haraki* shaykhs, such as Zakariyya al-Masri in Tripoli, at the very beginning of the Arab Spring expressed fears that the demonstrations might be connected to a Western conspiracy. Khutba of Shaykh Zakariyya al-Masri, Hamza mosque, Tripoli, January 21, 2011.

After the demise of authoritarian governments in Egypt, Tunisia, and Libya, *haraki* Salafi activism throughout the Middle East reached unprecedented intensity as the lifting of state control created opportunities to spread their message more openly than before. As many reports suggest, after the pressure from the authorities disappeared, the Salafi presence increased in the Middle Eastern public sphere, especially in Egypt and Tunisia.[66] During the decades of authoritarian rule in these countries, Salafis, while mostly avoiding direct political involvement, were able to develop deep roots in society. Their informal networks provided material help and patronage for the youth who were struggling to find employment and make a decent living,[67] and fulfilled the spiritual needs of many through a discourse that provided easy access to religious rulings.[68] Before the fall of the Arab dictatorships, Salafis achieved considerable success in attracting people despite having to keep a relatively low profile and occasionally (in Egypt) or continuously (in Tunisia) facing persecution from the authorities.[69]

After the fall of the regimes, the movement increased its *da'wa* activity and became a key player in politics – particularly so in Egypt, where the Salafi al-Nur party won 25 percent of the votes in the last elections. When the pressure from the authorities disappeared, the Salafi *da'is* intensified their proselytizing activities on the streets, neighborhoods, and university campuses. By combining their demand for the introduction of Islamic rulings to regulate public morality with an emphasis on social justice as one of the core tenets of Islam, they appeal to significant segments of post-revolutionary societies.[70] Salafis promise equality and

---

[66] Ghassan Ben Khalifa, "The Secret of the Salafists' Appeal in Tunisia," *Al-Monitor*, May 1, 2013, www.al-monitor.com/pulse/culture/2013/05/disadvantaged-tunisian-youth-embrace-salafism.html?utm_source=&utm_medium=email&utm_campaign=7110#ixzz2SBxLTKd9 (accessed May 7, 2013); Khalil al-Anani, and Maszlee Malik, "Pious Way to Politics: The Rise of Political Salafism in Post-Mubarak Egypt," *DOMES*, 22, no. 1, (2013).

[67] Al-Anani and Malik, "Pious Way to politics," pp. 60–62; Amel Boubekeur, "Salafism and Radical Politics in Postconflict Algeria," *Carnegie Papers*, no. 11, September 2008. http://carnegieendowment.org/files/salafism_radical_politics_algeria.pdf (accessed September 10, 2008), pp. 14–16.

[68] Samuli Schielke, 'Being Good in Ramadan: Ambivalence, Fragmentation, and the Moral Self in the Lives of Young Egyptians', *Journal of the Royal Anthropological Institute*, 15, no. s1 (2009), pp. s29–34.

[69] A few months before the revolution, the Egyptian government forced the Salafi Satellite channels to close, and arrested and tortured many of the *'ulama'*. Dina Muqallid, "al-Fida'iyyat al-Diniyya: al-Ighlaq Laysa Hallan," *al-Sharq al-Awsat*, 21 October 2010; al-Anani and Malik, 'Pious Way to Politics', p. 59. In Tunisia Salafis were not visible before the revolution, due to harsh oppression by the Ben Ali administration. However, their powerful appearance in the public sphere after the fall of the regime indicates that there was indeed successful *da'wa* activity before the 2010 uprisings.

[70] When discussing the issue of social justice, Salafis often refer to the hadith that describes God saying: "My worshipers, I have forbidden injustice for Myself, and did so for you."

social justice after decades of corruption, and many people in the region appear to find them a credible alternative to democratic activists.

The recent growth of *haraki* Salafism in Tripoli is connected to the aforementioned ascendance of the movement at the transnational level. In Northern Lebanon in the last few years, many lower-middle-class and working-class Sunnis descended into apathy, due to the lack of opportunities to improve their lives and the widespread corruption. After the outbreak of the Arab revolutions, many felt that while there was change in the Arab world, in Lebanon everything was stagnating or even becoming worse. When Salafism grew stronger in the aftermath of the revolutions throughout the Middle East, large numbers of Lebanese Sunnis thought that the movement could offer an alternative for them as well. This does not mean that they would endorse direct political participation by Lebanese Salafis, but that they are attracted to the movement's call for social justice and the argument that Muslims' lives will improve if they perfect their religious practices.

The Syrian revolution played an especially important role in this process. The events in the neighboring country have had a profound sociopolitical impact on Lebanon. As Syria has always played a significant role in Lebanese politics, it is no wonder that the conflict that erupted in 2011 fueled further antagonism between Lebanon's pro- and anti-Assad camps. The political cleavages quickly took on sectarian overtones and added to the Sunni–Shi'i tensions, since the vast majority of Shi'ites support Hizbullah and its allies as well as the Syrian regime's suppression of the revolutionaries. If Assad were to fall, the Shi'a community would lose a regional patron, and this loss would lead to a decline in the Shi'a's political and economic power.

By contrast, most of the Sunnis sympathize with the revolutionaries. Sunni Muslims have been alienated from the Syrian regime several times in the past. Most recently, the Assad regime was accused of orchestrating the assassination of Rafiq al-Hariri, and the Sunni community has sided against Assad and his allies ever since. At the same time, many Sunnis have relatives in Syria who are fighting against Assad, or who have been victims of the regime. In this climate, the *haraki* Salafi framing of the events as being part of a Manichean struggle between Islam and those who have corrupted it – i.e. the Shi'a – resonates with Lebanese Sunni. Salafis are also perceived as playing the most active role in helping

So you shall not be unjust to one another." Salafi shaykhs who became prominent supporters of the Arab Uprisings such as the Egyptian scholar and media person Muhammad Hassan argue that it means that the state should ensure the just redistribution of wealth and look after the poor. See his Friday sermon on April 13, 2012, www.youtube.com/watch?v=DS94626zVR8 (accessed October 8, 2016).

Syrian refugees and aiding the revolutionaries at home. Many of the inhabitants of Northern Lebanon think that the Salafis deal honestly with the money that they receive to care for the refugees or to send to Syria. This perceived integrity contrasts with the behavior of many members of other Islamic movements or Dar al-Fatwa shaykhs, who often misuse the financial resources destined for the Syrians.

The opportunity that emerged for the *harakis* with the outbreak of the Arab revolutions has been widened by the leadership crises within the Lebanese Sunni community. In June 2011, the Sunni-led Lebanese governing coalition, with Sa'd al-Hariri as prime minister, was brought down by disputes over the special tribunal investigating the murder of Rafiq al-Hariri.[71] The new government, led by Najib Miqati, enjoyed the backing of Hizbullah and did not represent the vast majority of the Sunnis.[72] Losing control of state institutions led to a significant decrease in the power of the Hariri clan.[73] Many Sunnis started to question the ability of Sa'd al-Hariri to lead the community, as he lost power despite the fact that his coalition had won the 2009 elections.

Doubt has also arisen as to whether the *zu'ama* deserve to be the representatives of the community. Miqati lost popularity after his pact with the Shi'a that allowed him to serve as prime minister. Many Sunnis started to look beyond their traditional community leaders for guidance. This led to the increase of the importance of certain actors at the Sunni religious field. A large number of Sunni Muslims felt that, just as in Egypt and Tunisia, it would be worth giving Islamic movements a chance to prove their leadership skills. Among them was a popular movement that emerged around Shaykh Ahmad al-Asir, the Muslim Brotherhood, and *haraki* Salafism, which proved to be the major beneficiary of this process.

The Muslim Brotherhood considerably increased its popularity among the Lebanese Sunnis after the Arab Uprisings. Its Lebanese manifestation, IG, reorganized its lines and put a younger and more capable generation of cadres into key positions. According to a leading figure of the Kuwaiti Muslim Brotherhood, the latter provided large sums of money to IG to carry out charitable activities.[74] The Brotherhood's win in the elections both in Egypt and Tunisia increased IG's credibility.

Perhaps the best-known figure in the international media who gained fame by utilizing the sociopolitical climate after the Syrian uprising is

---

[71] Waard Vloeberghs, "The Hariri Political Dynasty after the Arab Spring," *Mediterranean Politics*, 17, no. 2, (2012).

[72] "Sha'biyyat Miqati Fi Tarablus Tadannat," news program on LBC, November 19, 2011.

[73] Vloeberghs, "The Hariri Political Dynasty," (page numbers are not available).

[74] Interview with a leading official of the Kuwaiti Muslim Brotherhood's charity wing, *Jama'iyyat al-Islah al-Ijtima'i* (Social Reform Society), Kuwait, March 3, 2016.

Shaykh Ahmad al-Asir, the imam of Bilal bin-Rabah mosque in Sidon. Before the Arab Uprisings, al-Asir was a relatively unknown figure. He rapidly gained popularity among both working- and middle-class Sunnis of the city when he organized rallies in Sidon, where he fiercely attacked Hizbullah and stood with the Syrian armed opposition. While the media and even some academic experts focus on al-Asir Salafi, he never has been embedded in Lebanon's Salafi networks. Haraki Salafis considered him as an ally, and often appeared together with him in demonstrations and rallies.

A Salafi scholar close to Shaykh Salim al-Rafa'i told me that al-Asir agrees with the Salafis on their political views but he does not follow a Salafi *manhaj*.[75] Al-Asir started Islamic activism with the Muslim Brotherhood, and later he joined the Tabligh. Even in his rallies in 2011 and 2012, he frequently appeared in a dress associated with members of the latter. While he reportedly left Jama'at al-Tabligh in the early 1990s, he continued to proselytize in the same way, such as organizing *khuruj* (proselytizing tour) three times a month.[76] These activities, however, would be condemned by Salafis as *bid'a*.[77] Al-Asir's protest movement ended in 2013 after a clash between his supporters and the Lebanese security forces. When the judiciary issued an arrest warrant against him, he went into hiding in the 'Ain al-Hilwa refugee camp near Sidon until his arrest in 2015.[78]

Among the Sunni movements, Tripoli's Salafis were perhaps the most successful in turning Lebanon's changing sociopolitical conditions to their advantage.[79] The legitimacy of the *zu'ama* has been somewhat weakened, but it appears that the Salafis are filling this vacuum. There is another reason why they are able to do so: According to some reports, the financial abilities of the Hariri clan were severely weakened after Sa'ad lost the premiership.[80] Charities belonging to the family stopped operating in some northern areas due to lack of funding.

---

[75] Interview with Shaykh Tawfiq, Tripoli, April 18, 2012.

[76] Al-Asir's opinion on music and dance, for example, is much more forgiving.

[77] In the Salafis' view there is no indication in the scripture that someone must organize *khuruj* in a certain regularity. Establishing a rule to practice it three times a month might mislead others by making them believe that *khuruj* is part of the religion.

[78] Radwan Murtada, "Nass Muhaddar li-'Itirafat Ahmad al-Asir," *Al-Akhbar*, August 27, 2015, www.al-akhbar.com/node/240889 (accessed November 3, 2016).

[79] After the Arab Spring, ordinary Sunnis in Tripoli often told me that Salafis should be given a chance to show whether they are capable of being the leaders of the Sunni community. Leadership of a community in patriarchal societies such as Lebanon and the rest of the Arab world is not confined to institutional politics. In exchange for their subordination and support, the leader is expected to look after his followers in socioeconomic matters and provide individuals with advice in their spiritual and material lives.

[80] Vloeberghs, "The Hariri Political Dynasty."

At the same time, due to their direct contact with the Syrian rebels, Lebanese Salafis receive increasing amounts of financial support from the Gulf. Therefore, they gained additional followers by taking over the role of Hariri's social support networks.

The favorable conditions created by the Arab revolutions led to the *haraki* shaykhs being regarded by a large segment of the people as potential leaders. For many, they appear to be the ideal representatives of Sunnis, who claim authority by acting in accordance with the foundational texts of Islam. They underscore this by successfully taking care of the spiritual and mundane needs of the community. As one of my informants explained:

The *zu'ama* care about filling their pockets and if their interests demand it, they even make a deal with Satan. Salafis are different. They act in accordance with what God and the Prophet said. Today they are the ones who are really standing up against the Shi'a and Hizbullah ... They also do not distribute money before the elections only, but always help the needy.[81]

3.4.1   Hay'at 'Ulama al-Muslimin and the Apex of the Harakis' Influence

The continuing of the two-decade-long weakness of Dar al-Fatwa contributed to the *harakis'* success in making their voice heard. Dar al-Fatwa was technically paralyzed due to a row between the Mufti of the Republic, Muhammad Rashid Qabbani, and the Future movement. The strife happened over al-Mustaqbal's attempt to curb the power of the mufti and take from him the supervision of the country's Sunni *waqfs*.[82] Qabbani instead allied with Sunni politicians close to the March 8 camp. This resulted in a split within the ranks of Dar al-Fatwa's officials. One faction supported Qabbani in his attempt to preserve the prerogatives of the mufti, while others sided with al-Mustaqbal. The latter also accused Qabbani of stealing from the movement.[83]

In 2013, Qabbani called for early elections for Dar al-Fatwa's governing body *al-Majlis al-Shara'i* (Shari'a Board) in order to secure a majority for members loyal to him.[84] The shaykhs allied to al-Mustaqbal rejected the

---

[81] Interview, May 3, 2012.
[82] 'Abd al-Kafi Samad, "Dar al-Fatwa wa-Ri'asat al-Hukuma: Sira' al-Marja'iyyatayn," al-Akhbar, July 31, 2013, http://al-akhbar.com/node/188051 (Accessed November 3, 2016).
[83] Raphael Lefevre, "The Roots of Crisis in Northern Lebanon," *Report*, Carnegie Middle East Center, April 2014, http://carnegieendowment.org/files/crisis_northern_lebanon .pdf (accessed January 28, 2017).
[84] Ibid.

results and acknowledged the legitimacy of the previous *Majlis* only. This resulted in the existence of two Shari'a Boards, formalizing the split within the ranks of the official religious establishment. Dar al-Fatwa's legitimacy was further weakened and it became even more difficult to provide religious services to the country's Sunni population.

This situation emboldened *haraki* Salafis to openly challenge Dar al-Fatwa and pose themselves publicly as those who truly represent the Sunni community. In 2012 they opened an institution that many see as a competitor to the official religious establishment. The new body, called *Hay'at 'Ulama al-Muslimin* (Committee of Muslim Scholars - CMS) was originally the idea of Shaykh Salim al-Rafi'i. Yet, CMS included not only Salafis but also scholars from IG, shaykhs who were employed by Dar al-Fatwa but were dissatisfied with its inefficiency. Some of them were even Sufis.[85] The first head of the organization was the representative of the Muslim Brotherhood, Shaykh Ahmad al-'Umari, who was then followed by Salim al-Rafi'i after the end of his six months' term. The membership reached four hundred shaykhs soon after founding and covered all Sunni-inhabited areas of the country.

The founders of CMS claimed that they wanted to provide an institutional framework for scholars and preachers who are active among the Sunnis of Lebanon in light of Dar al-Fatwa's apparent inability to be so. Prominent members of the committee argued that the current official Sunni religious establishment, because of its divisions, is unable to effectively deal with the most important grievances of the Sunni community.[86] Indeed, the tasks that CMS' founders proposed to fulfill are similar to those of Dar al-Fatwa. The organization issues fatwas, supervises religious institutions such as colleges and mosques, and provides charity.

Perhaps the most unifying cause of CMS' members was the support of the Syrian opposition against the Assad regime and their frustration over Hizbullah's involvement in the conflict. CMS organized numerous demonstrations in support of the revolution and provided material aid for the Syrian refugees in Lebanon and those who were affected by the conflict in Syria. It also played the role of mediator in August 2014 between the Lebanese army and factions from al-Nusra Front

---

[85] Conversation with Raphael Lefevre, the specialist of Carnegie Middle East Center on North Lebanon, Singapore, September 2, 2016. Email correspondence, January 23, 2017.

[86] Report of the Lebanese al-Jadida TV Channel. October 10, 2012 and Interview woth Shaykh 'Adnan al-Umama on the Lebanese MTV TV channel 4 January 2014; CMS's website: www.olama-lb.com/ar/index.php/2016-01-04-14-27-15 (accessed November 14, 2016).

and ISIS during the battle of 'Arsal. In the fighting, the militants captured dozens of soldiers and policemen. CMS intended to secure their release by its intervention.[87]

CMS is often blamed for getting directly involved in the civil war in Syria. During the battle of Qusayr between April and June 2013, when Lebanese Hizbullah fighters directly faced Sunni youth who fought on the side of the Syrian opposition, Shaykh Salim al-Rafa'i called for sending Lebanese Sunni fighters. He argued during a meeting of the *shura* on April 22, 2013 that since Hizbullah justified its military intervention in Syria as protecting Lebanese Shi'ites who live in Syrian villages, Lebanese Sunnis should protect their fellow Sunnis in Syria.[88] According to one of the aides of al-Rafa'i, CMS organized and sent 700 Sunni fighters to Syria. The center for enlisting them was the shaykh's Taqwa mosque.[89]

Furthermore, CMS often addresses the perceived oppressed status of the Sunni community in Lebanon at their events. Preachers frequently point to the "Iranian plan" to subordinate Lebanon with the help of "Tehran's agent" Hizbullah. For example, during the clashes between Sunni militias in al-Tabbana and Alavite militants in Jabal Muhsin that flared up in 2011 after relative stability since 2008, scholars of CMS called the Lebanese army an accomplice of Hizbullah. Allegedly, the army detained dozens of Sunni youth from al-Tabbana, but did not do touch the fighters of the main Alavite militia of Jabal Muhisn, the Arabic Democratic Party, led by Rif'at 'Aid. As Shaykh Salim al-Rafa'i put it in 2013 in a press interview, such behavior proves that the army implements the Shi'ite party's agenda to subordinate Sunnis in order to dominate Lebanon.[90]

CMS' popularity started to grow rapidly as it was capable of regularly gathering thousands of participants for its events. Many of the members of CMS were able to mobilize considerable economic capital and followers individually, such as the case with the *haraki* Salafis such as Shaykh Salim al-Rafi'i, Zakariyya al-Masri. Joining forces made them considerable actors on the ground. Most of CMS' leading faces, such as

---

[87] Martin Jay, "Fighting rages in Arsal with Muslim scholars caught in the crossfire, three soldiers released." *An-Nahar English*, August 5, 2015, http://en.annahar.com/article/158221-fighting-rages-in-arsal-with-muslim-schom-scholars-caught-in-the-crossfire-three (accessed November 14, 2014).

[88] www.youtube.com/watch?v=odu5_oOZxQw (accessed January 31, 2017).

[89] "Imam Masjid al-Taqwa Hukima bi-Sanatayn: Qumtu bi-Khata' Shara'I," *al-Diyar*, June 2, 2016, www.addiyar.com/article/1195835 (accessed October 5, 2016).

[90] "Cleric accuses Lebanese army of plotting with Hezbollah to fight Sunni youth," *The Daily Star*, July 3, 2013.

Salim al-Rafi'i, 'Adnan Umama, Ra'id Hulayhil, Zakariyya al-Masri, and Hasan Qatarji came from Lebanon's *haraki* Salafi networks. Ahmad al-'Umari and Malik Judayda were perhaps the only significant figures who were not participants of the Salafi movement. This made the Committee an important vehicle for the *harakis* to increase their influence. Leaders of CMS' *haraki* Salafi shaykhs appeared in the national and international media not as representatives of one Islamic movement among others, but as among the most important religious leaders of Lebanon's Sunni community.[91]

At the time of writing in October 2016, it remains to be seen whether CMS will preserve its position as an important actor on the Sunni Islamic field. The conflict within Dar al-Fatwa was resolved in August 2014 by electing Shaykh 'Abd al-Latif Daryan as Mufti of the Republic. During the elections, CMS tried to exert its influence on Dar al-Fatwa, but Daryan easily defeated its candidate, Ahmad Darwish al-Kurdi (Daryan got seventy-four votes against al-Kurdi's nine).[92] Yet, the election of the new mufti did not solve the institution's financial problems and inability to take bold political stances that would reflect the opinion of the majority of the Sunnis. The row was resolved by means of a regional compromise between Saudi Arabia and Syria, mediated by Egypt. These countries historically influence the internal politics of Dar al-Fatwa. Furthermore, the institution depends on the political patrons of the Sunni community, as the latter have a key role in electing the former's high ranking officials, including the mufti.[93]

Yet, internal fractionalization is already taking place within CMS. A group of *haraki* Salafis led by Shaykh Salim al-Rafa'i intends to transform the organization into a political party. Most members of the Muslim Brotherhood who participate in CMS, however, oppose this plan, as it would become a direct competitor of IG.[94] Furthermore, as a former member of CMS who is affiliated to the Muslim Brotherhood

---

[91] CMS' mediatory role in the Arsal battle was among the most important of these appearances. In August 2014 a battle broke out between the Lebanese army, and al-Nusra front and the Islamic state in the border town of 'Arsal when the militants infiltrated from Syria. Al-Nusra and IS captured 24 service men from the army and the police, and held them hostage. 'Ulama' from CMS ventured to mediate between the army and the militants in order to release the captives. Shaykh Salim al-Rafi'i claimed the Committee had a role in freeing thirteen captives.

[92] "Derian Elected Lebanon Mufti in Show of Sunni Unity," *The Daily Star*, August 10, 2014.

[93] Rougier provides a good description on the election mechanism within Dar al-Fatwa: *Everyday Jihad*, pp. 127–133.

[94] Skype interview with a member of CMS who asked me not to disclose his name, September 27, 2016.

told me, differences in religious views between the Salafi *'ulama'* and the *Ikhwan* often appear. For example, in 2014 Salafi shaykhs verbally attacked *Ikhwani* scholars because the latter participated in the celebration of the Prophet's birthday (mawlid), which the Salafis regard as *bida'*.[95]

As in other Middle Eastern countries, purists in Lebanon distanced themselves from supporting the Arab Spring, and many of them openly sided against the protests. Safwan al-Za'bi frequently told the media that revolution is not the way to change sociopolitical reality. According to him, the current events in the Arab world are leading to the return of Western colonization.[96] He is critical of the *harakis*, especially Shaykh Salim al-Rafi'i, for employing populist rhetoric to serve their own interests instead of considering what would benefit the *Umma*. In his opinion, the *harakis'* activities will result in chaos and civil war. He thinks that Lebanese Salafis should not focus on appealing to the masses, but instead should pursue the *da'wa* among those who are willing to change their lives fully in accordance with the "true principles of Islam," even if they are few.[97] Some purists have even distributed leaflets containing the *fatawa* of Saudi shaykhs against the revolutions.

Many of the purist Salafis refuse to criticize or support the recent revolutions in the Arab countries. Instead, they withdraw to teach the minute details of religious practice, largely neglecting their surroundings. One of my purist informants, the imam of a small mosque in the district adjacent to the Citadel in Tripoli, thinks that the actions of al-Za'bi and other opponents of the revolutions are foolish. In this imam's opinion, "clearly, the majority of Ahl al-Sunna [in Northern Lebanon] are enthusiastic about the Arab Spring. Therefore, openly siding against [the protests] is unwise on the part of [purist] Salafis. Through their harsh rhetoric, they lose the respect of the people while not gaining anything." He thinks that purists should refrain from talking about the demonstrations, and should instead focus on the *da'wa*: "If the number of true Muslims becomes more than the *muqassirun* [sing. *muqassir* – those who do not accomplish fully their religious duties], they will recognize that *al-khuruj 'ala al-hakim* will not lead to any good."[98]

[95] Personal conversation with Fadi Shamiyya, a political analyst for IG, Kuwait, September 23, 2014.
[96] http://arabi-press.com/index.php?page=article&id=4591.
[97] Interview, Tripoli, April 26, 2012.   [98] Interview, Tripoli, May 3, 2012.

3.5   Conclusion

In the 2000s, the Lebanese Salafi movement split into purist and *haraki* factions. Due to selective repression by the security services, Da'i al-Islam al-Shahhal's network disintegrated at the end of the 1990s. Since al-Shahhal, who had been the main distributor of money from Gulf charities, was forced into exile, Lebanese Salafis needed to look for alternative sources of sponsorship. Those who were inclined toward purist thinking received massive support from SRIH, which contributed to the emergence of a strong purist stream in North Lebanon.

The *haraki* faction reemerged after the Syrian army's withdrawal from Lebanon in 2005 to become the dominant faction of the country's Salafi scene. Due to the Sunni–Shi'i tensions, the *harakis'* stridently anti-Shi'a rhetoric became attractive to many Sunnis. The appearance of the SACF on the Lebanese scene greatly increased the influence of the *harakis*. The charity established a large network of religious colleges, mosques, and *da'is* across the country. The Hariri clan's financial assistance also increased the *harakis'* economic capital.

The post–Arab Uprisings context was favorable to *harakis* across the Arab world. In addition, in Northern Lebanon many people saw *haraki* Salafis as alternative candidates for leadership of the Sunni community, in view of the declining legitimacy of political patrons such as Sa'd al-Hariri or Najib Miqati. *Haraki* Salafis reached the apex of their influence when their representatives managed to become the most influential figures in CMS, an organization that gathered Sunni religious scholars with various affiliations.

Historical transformations, such as the Hariri murder, the Syrian withdrawal from Lebanon in 2005, and the Arab Uprisings, were crucial for Salafis to increase their positions on the Sunni religious field. Yet, to exploit the historical moments, Salafis had to have the ability to acquire and invest various forms of capital. The next chapter will discuss the movement's acquisition of religious, social, and economic capital.

4   The Authority of Salafi Shaykhs

I met Fu'ad, a middle-aged Sunni, in the 'Uthman bin 'Affan mosque after the religious class delivered by Shaykh Tawfiq, one of the prominent Salafi scholars of Tripoli's Mina district. Fu'ad approached the shaykh after the *dars* held between the *maghrib* and *'isha'* prayers asking him for advice in solving a minor misunderstanding with his adolescent son. I asked him why he did not go to Dar al-Fatwa, since the institution provides similar services. He replied that he only goes to Dar al-Fatwa when he needs official documents such as a marriage certificate.[1] For other religious services or advice, he mostly asks Shaykh Tawfiq or another Salafi shaykh. He trusts Salafis because "they demonstrate extraordinary religious commitment and are close to the people, while the officials of Dar al-Fatwa mostly sit behind their desks and show up on Friday only when they deliver a sermon."

Fu'ad's attitude toward Dar al-Fatwa is fairly common. During my fieldwork I observed that many Salafis provide the same services that would be the task of the official *'ulama'*. Among these are issuing verbal and written fatwas, providing religious counseling, and giving religious lessons in the mosques. Salafi shaykhs are especially active in resolving social disagreements and conflict. It turned out that this is one of the most effective tools to increase their social standing.

This chapter discusses how Salafi shaykhs claim and establish their authority by accumulating religious, social, and economic capital. I show how, by investing the various forms of capital, Salafism contests the legitimacy of Dar al-Fatwa to marking the boundaries of orthodoxy in Lebanon. Salafis strive to transform the Sunni religious field by making their version of Islam the orthodox one and defining what a good Muslim is.

By building on religious, social, and economic capital, *harakis* and purists construct their authority in a similar way. The major difference

---

[1] In Lebanon all marriages are performed by the respective confessions' official religious representative institutions. In the case of Sunnis it is Dar al-Fatwa.

in this respect between the two factions is their engagement in dispute resolution. Purists rarely engage in such activities for ideological reasons, while *harakis* utilize it to increase their influence.

4.1 Religious Authority in Salafism

Religious specialists or men of religion (*rijal al-din*) in the local Lebanese context constitute a wide category that includes all those who perform religious services. In this sense, it includes religious scholars, Sufi shaykhs, and some of the Islamists.

The authority of men of religion relies on their claim to possess *'ilm*, or knowledge.[2] The nature of *'ilm* can vary, and can be both scholarly and esoteric.[3] The Salafis claim scholarly knowledge since they entirely reject Gnosis. The privileged position of the possessor of the former "rests upon achievements in learning and specifically his supposed mastery of the revealed canon together with related juridical and perhaps other texts."[4] In other words, the possession of *'ilm* confers the ability to bring the divine order from the abstract to real life. The religious authority of men of religion is based on the social perception that they have the ability to translate what God has revealed to be intelligible for those who are not trained to fully understand scripture. In this sense, the instructions coming from them generally represent God's will.

Salafis construct their authority on the claim that their teaching represents Islam exactly as God revealed it. They argue that they preserve and spread the "undiluted" version of the religion in a world where foreign elements entered Islam and corrupted it. In short, Salafis claim that their teachings, in contrast to other Islamic trends and schools of thought, constitute right belief, or orthodoxy.

Orthodoxy is manifested by a huge body of intellectual tradition accumulated over the centuries.[5] Since there is no institutional body to define right belief and distinguish it from heresy, orthodoxy "lies inside the discursive tradition of jurists who write creeds."[6] It is caught up in an ongoing discursive process to continuously interpret and reinterpret it.

---

[2] Patrick Gaffney, *The Prophet's Pulpit* (Berkeley, Los Angeles, London: University of California Press, 1994), p. 34.

[3] For a more detailed discussion see: Ernest Gellner, *Muslim Society* (Cambridge: Cambridge University Press, 1983), pp. 1–85.

[4] Gaffney, *The Prophet's Pulpit*, p. 39.

[5] Norman Calder, "The Limits of Islamic Orthodoxy." In *Interpretation and Jurisprudence in Medieval Islam*, edited by Norman Calder (Aldershot: Ashgate, 2006), p. 67.

[6] Ibid., p. 69.

Prior to the twentieth century, jurists rarely attempted to interpret the Qur'an and the Sunna independently, disregarding the views of earlier scholars. At the same time, most of them intended to understand the context in which a certain ruling was revealed and then reinterpret it in accordance with contemporary circumstances. The jurists also made an effort to understand Divine Law, but never could be sure that their opinions were correct. Therefore, in a given locality conflicting opinions and interpretations were often accepted as within the boundaries of orthodoxy.[7] In other words, orthodoxy was constructed by discourses that were accepted in a given locality as orthodox. Its limits were blurred and never clearly defined.[8]

To Salafis, however, the meaning and scope of Islam is clear: The rulings of the scripture are self-explanatory and are not subject to reinterpretation. They believe that in the majority of cases, Muslims can be sure of God's will. God's word is valid at all times and in all circumstances and has the same meaning regardless of context. In this sense, Islamic law functions in a similar way to modern positive law. According to Salafis, Muslims must focus on the exact implementation of the *shari'a* and disregard any contextual considerations. They usually argue that humans should not search for any kind of logic in the Divine Law or link it to moral imperatives, which can alter the original meaning. This is because while a specific ruling might sound illogical or even immoral, later its rightfulness will be proven. Salafis believe that only a very minor part of Islamic law is open for debate and can be a subject of difference in opinions.[9]

Salafis generally argue that the decline of the *Umma* in modern times is due to the fact that Muslims have made space for pluralism in theology and jurisprudence (*fiqh*) and different methods of interpreting the Text, instead of relying on a literal interpretation. They have also validated *taqlid* and the hegemony of the *madhahib* (as explained in the Introduction). In order to reverse this decline, Salafis believe that Muslims must adopt their version of right belief and abandon all other practices, methodologies, and interpretations. Salafi authors have been prolific in explaining their understanding of orthodoxy and why

---

[7] Muhammad Khalid Masud, "Ikhtilaf al-Fuqaha: Diversity in Fiqh as a Social Construction." In *Zainah Anwar, Equality and Justice in the Muslim Family* (Petaling Jaya, Malaysia: Musawah, 2009), pp. 65–86.

[8] Richard C. Martin and Abbas Barzegar, "Formations of Orthodoxy: Authority, Power and Networks in Muslim Societies." In *Rethinking Islamic Studies: From Orientalism to Cosmopolitanism*, edited by Carl W. Ernst and Richard C. Martin, (Columbia: The University of South Carolina Press, 2010), pp. 183–191.

[9] Gauvain, Richard, *Salafi Ritual Purity: In the Presence of God* (London and New York: Routledge, 2013), p. 101.

anything else should be rejected. One of the most systematic and influential writers on this topic is Shaykh 'Abd al-Rahman 'Abd al-Khaliq, who has significant readership among Lebanese Salafis.

Shaykh 'Abd al-Rahman, as the pioneer of the Kuwaiti Salafi *da'i*, illustrates how Salafis intend to establish orthodoxy by setting the terms of the discourse. In his book *Khuṭuṭ Ra'isiyya* (Main Guidelines) he argues the necessity to impose Salafism on the whole Umma, and recommends the unification of the methods and sources of jurisprudence (*fiqh*) and the erasure of all other Islamic schools of thought.[10] He recommends the creation of a Qur'anic encyclopedia (*mawsu'a qur'āniyya*). This would contain the "exact, correct meaning" of all words and terms to be found in the Qur'an. After this, it would be forbidden to interpret the Qur'an in any way other than that based on the "correct meaning." Similarly, an encyclopedia of hadith would be created, containing all correct (*sahih*) *ahadith*. Books that contain corrupted narrations or chains of transmission (*isnad*) would be burned. The *ijma'* of the Sahaba and the consensus of the Salafi scholars on matters where the Text does not give exact instructions (*ijma'*) would be codified as well.

After the destruction of the non-acceptable books all *fatwas* would have to be issued according to these rules, and the methodology of *fiqh* would thus be unified. This would mean the exclusion of the *ra'y* and any kind of logical or metaphorical interpretation. According to Shaykh 'Abd al-Rahman, the biggest obstacle to achieving this aim is the existence and availability of the "old books" of jurisprudence, which "charm" and influence the reader to stray from the straight path. Therefore, of these huge Islamic collections, only those should be kept that agree on the aforementioned sources of *fiqh*. He argued that purifying Islam from all deviations would lead to the creation of an ideal Muslim society, and Islam would reemerge as the leading civilization of the world.

Other Islamic movements often allow diversity in their lines in terms of *'aqida* and *fiqh*. For example, many members of the Muslim Brotherhood follow Ash'ari *'aqida*, while others believe in the Salafi creed. In addition, many of them practice the *taqlid* of a *madhab*,[11] and some are involved in Sufism as well. The reason is that the aim of the movement is to implement sociopolitical agendas based on Islam, not to set the boundaries of right belief. Unlike Ikhwanis, the whole program

---

[10] This stance is surprising from 'Abd al-Rahman 'Abd al-Khaliq since he is one of the most willing among Salafis to cooperate with other Islamic movements.

[11] In my experience, Ikhwani activists only follow those rulings of the *madhahib* that concern personal matters. In politics and public issues, they accept the legal reasoning of their respective local Muslim Brotherhood organization. Interview with a Lebanese Ikhwani activist, Beirut, October 6, 2009, and interview with the head of a local office of the Kuwaiti Muslim Brotherhood, Kuwait, February 4, 2012.

of Salafism revolves around the exact definition of orthodoxy. Salafis see Islam as a sociopolitical project based on *tawhid*. As Haj puts it, "*tawhid* presumes the existence of a (moral and historical) community, one in which Muslims are bound to each other through a set of authoritative texts and practices."[12] In Salafism, these authoritative texts and practices are clearly defined. Tawhid can be maintained by a moral community whose worldview, thinking, and actions are directed by their abstract concept of orthodoxy. Therefore, the aim of Salafism is to reorder the orthodoxy that is accepted by the Umma and lead Muslims back to the true form of Islam by purifying their belief and practices.

A vanguard of religiously educated individuals, shaykhs, who control mosques, charity endowments, and religious colleges makes up the core of Salafism. A small number of committed activists and a wide passive follower base of ordinary believers surround these shaykhs and seek religious services from them. Salafis in Tripoli and the surrounding area fulfill the many tasks that are normally associated with men of religion. These include preaching and teaching in and outside of the mosque, giving non-binding legal opinions (*fatwa, pl. fatawa*), and advising people in matters of religion and life. The shaykhs also visit families, comfort the sick and the dying, and mediate in social conflicts. They also provide material aid and access to patronage. Due to the weakening of the official religious establishment, Salafis are gradually taking over its role.

Sunni orthodoxy in Lebanon has been traditionally represented by Dar al-Fatwa. Although most of its religious rulings are issued in the framework of the Shafi'i and Māliki *madhahib*, the institution leaves room for interpretation. It never has attempted to draw clear boundaries of orthodoxy. Salafis, however, exploit their advantageous situation to impose their own static concept of orthodoxy. Until the Lebanese Civil War, the Sunni religious community was relatively well organized under the auspices of Dar al-Fatwa. The mostly Ash'ari *'ulama'* shared the religious domain with various Sufi *tariqas* and, from the beginning of the 1960s, the Muslim Brotherhood, which was then still in its infancy. Dar al-Fatwa lost much of its influence during the civil war and the popularity of the Sufis was also diminished. Salafis filled the vacuum left by the former, and were able to exploit the fact that the reputation of the *'ulama'* associated with Dar al-Fatwa suffered a significant decline in the twenty-first century.

These scholars are traditionally educated in one of the major Islamic learning centers in Egypt, Syria, or the Lebanese branch of al-Azhar.

---

[12] Samira Haj, "Reordering Islamic Orthodoxy: Muhammad Ibn 'Abdul Wahhab," *The Muslim World*, 92, no. 3, (2002), p. 339.

Today, due to their financial weakness, the official religious institutions are unable to provide Sunni religious scholars with a decent living. The salaries of the shaykhs are below the Lebanese average, and most of them are employed on a contractual basis.[13] This means that being a religious scholar at Dar al-Fatwa is one of the least prestigious jobs among those that require higher education. Parents usually discourage their children from studying religion, and instead persuade them to become medical doctors or engineers.

Those who complete their studies at one of the Lebanese Sunni Islamic educational institutions, such as the Lebanese branch of the Egyptian al-Azhar University, the Da'wa Faculty (*Kulliyyat al-Da'wa*), or al-Awza'i University, are therefore often pursuing religious studies because they do not have another choice. Many of them come from families that cannot afford to support them financially during their university years. For them, one of the religious institutions is an attractive option, since they offer students free accommodation, food, and often a modest scholarship.[14] Others are unable to gain admission to most Lebanese universities due to their low high-school grades. They regard Islamic institutions as an easy way to acquire a degree.[15]

Many of my interviewees expressed their disappointment with the religious elite. They felt that some shaykhs are exploiting Sunni Muslims' traditional respect for the *'ulama'*.[16] According to them, shaykhs who engage in charitable activities often steal part of the donations and use this to improve their own economic situation. People often contrast the hedonistic lifestyle of the Dar al-Fatwa shaykhs with the puritanism and helpful attitude of the Salafi shaykhs. Most of the Salafis indeed have a strong missionary mindset. They sacrifice much of their time to serve their communities; changing and purifying their religious practices and helping them solve socioeconomic problems.

It thus not surprising that these graduates are unable to compete with Salafis, who are usually filled with a high degree of missionary zeal. Salafi shaykhs persuade their constituency to affirm their authority on the basis that they represent right belief. They often argue that the

---

[13] See Chapter 3.   [14] Rougier, *Everyday Jihad*, 2007, pp. 213–215.

[15] One of the professors at al-Awza'i University in Beirut expressed his dissatisfaction with the commitment and performance of the students in his institution. Interview, Tripoli, April 11, 2012. See also interview with Shaykh Muhammad al-Masri, Tripoli, May 5, 2012.

[16] In certain cases some shaykhs even use their status to cover up their criminal activities. These stories are circulating among ordinary people, further corroding respect for the *'ulama*. See: Radwan Murtada, "Marmulak al-Lubnani: Mawlana al-Nassab, Man Yuhasibahu?," *al-Akhbar*, September 27, 2011.

current miserable, poverty stricken state of the Sunnis in Lebanon, and in the North in particular, is the result of their abandonment of true Islam. The only way to change this situation is to adopt the uncorrupted version of Islam, which is identical to Salafism.[17] Salafis often argue that "deviant" schools of thought, such as Sufi orders, which have spread throughout history in Tripoli, have led Sunnis astray. Therefore, it is now the task of Salafi men of religion to enlighten ordinary believers about true Islam and guide them in order to abandon *bid'a* and *shirk*. This topic sometimes features in Friday sermons, but Salafi shaykhs discuss it more often during religious lessons.

4.2   Authority and the Possession of Capital

The fact that a growing number of Sunni believers accept the Salafis' claim for orthodoxy is the result of their possession of sufficient religious, social, and economic capital.[18] The possession of religious capital is essential in defining the ability of the men of religion to persuade others to accept their reasoning. However, acquiring social and economic capital increases the social standing of the shaykhs, which adds to the credibility of their religious claim. The more people Salafis are able to convince of the Salafis' concept of religion as equal to orthodox Sunni Islam, the more they manage to reshape the Sunni religious field.

4.2.1   Religious Capital

Religious capital is manifested in myths, ideologies, religious knowledge, or the mastery of religious practices.[19] In the case of Salafism, demonstrating knowledge of the Qur'an and hadith is only one aspect of religious capital. Perhaps more important than this is that many Salafis successfully create their own image as the ideal Muslims in the eyes of many regular believers. This means practicing "mild asceticism," which includes adopting social norms, dress code, and cultural practices specific to Salafism.

Weber distinguishes two types of asceticism: an extreme or "world-rejecting" one and an inner-worldly one. Proponents of the first type withdraw from society and the enjoyment of worldly pleasures.[20]

---

[17] See Chapter 8.   [18] See Chapter 1.

[19] Pierre Bourdieu, "Genesis and Structure of the Religious Field," *Comparative Social Research*, 13, no. 1, (1991), pp. 22–23.

[20] Max Weber, *Economy and Society: An Outline of Interpretive Sociology* (Berkeley, Los Angeles, London: University of California Press, 1978), p. 542.

Those who follow moderate or mild asceticism intend to live a virtuous life while actively interacting with wider society.[21] These individuals regard themselves as instruments of God, meaning that their practice of asceticism often turns to activism in order to purify the surrounding society.[22]

Unlike the followers of other schools of thought, Salafis claim that it is possible to exactly know from the *hadith* collections how the Prophet and his companions acted.[23] Hence, in Salafism moderate asceticism means strictly obeying Islamic law and imitating the behavior and morality of *al-salaf al-salih*, and resisting temptations that do not fit this picture. For example, Salafi shaykhs in Tripoli actively try to avoid places where music can be heard since they consider it forbidden in Islam.[24] They also avoid relaxing in the popular cafes and restaurants of the city. As Shaykh Mahir, a young Salafi scholar from Tripoli's al-Qubba region told me, these places are "convenient for Satan" to lead the believer astray because of the presence of women and loud music. He explained that the "seductive chaos" there makes Muslims forget about God.[25]

Another manifestation of *zuhd* is performing prayer always right after the call for prayer (*adhan*). While most people do not get up for the dawn prayer, Salafis do it without exception.[26] The shaykhs whom I interviewed also regularly do optional fasting (*sawm al-nafil*) such as fasting three days every month.[27] Unlike the majority of men in Lebanon, Salafis never smoke, since in their view it is forbidden by the *shari'a*.[28] Wearing simple clothes is another form of mild asceticism. Wearing fashionable, expensive clothes is strictly rejected by Salafis.

---

[21] Ibid.

[22] Throughout history, a wide range of movements has adopted such attitudes, including Cistercians, Calvinists, and even Communists. Walter E. A. van Beek (ed.), *The Quest for Purity: Dynamics of Puritan Movements* (The Hague: Mouton de Gruyter, 1988).

[23] Gauvain, *Salafi Ritual Purity*, p. 101.

[24] Most Salafi scholars consider music and singing *haram*. Some, like Muhammad bin 'Uthaymin, permit the melodic recitation of poetry. Jonas Otterbeck, "Wahhabi Ideology of Social Control versus a New Publicness in Saudi Arabia," *Contemporary Islam*, 6, no. 3, (2012), p. 347.

[25] Interview, Tripoli, April 3, 2012.

[26] People usually pray dawn prayer after they get up in the morning.

[27] Abdul Kader at-Tayebi, "Voluntary Fasting in Islam," www.sahihmuslim.com/sps/sp.cfm?subsecID=IBD09&articleID=IBD090001&articlePages=1, (accessed March 16, 2015).

[28] Muslim scholars disagree on smoking: Some consider it *makruh* (discouraged); others forbid it. Salafis generally agree with the latter view referring to a *hadīth* that considers everything *haram* that harms human health. See the *fatwa* of one of the most renowned modern Salafi scholars, Ibn Baz: www.binbaz.org.sa/mat/12026, accessed March 16, 2015.

As Shaykh Mahir explained, *zuhd* is an instrument to create the pure Muslim self. He referred to the highly respected Saudi scholar, Muhammad bin 'Uthaymin (1925–2001), who distinguished between two types of purity (*tahara*): sensory purity (*tahara hassiyya*) and abstract purity (*tahara ma'nawiyya*).[29] While the former means ritual purity, the latter refers to the purity of the soul and is related to the Salafi understanding of monotheism (*tawhid*). As Shaykh Mahir clarified, *tawhid* is the exclusive submission to God. Whatever distracts this submission, such as contacting (*tawassul*) deceased holy persons or materialism, falls into the category of polytheism (*shirk*).[30] *Zuhd* is the method for getting rid of *shirk* and reaching this ideal state.

When discussing *tahara* and *zuhd*, Shaykh Mahir also referred to the works of the classical scholar Ibn Qayyim al-Jawziyya.[31] According to Ibn Qayyim, *tahara* means the perfection of one's deeds ('*amal*) and manners (*akhlaq*), and purification (*tazkiya*) of the heart from the sin and ignorance that would otherwise lead to *shirk*.[32] In Ibn Qayyim's opinion, adopting a moderate lifestyle helps to achieve this. He uses clothing as an example: Some of the *ahadith* (in his view) forbid dressing in the skin of the tiger and other predators, for the reason that the behavior of those who do so might become similar to that of the predators. Men are prohibited from wearing gold and silk for the same reason: this leads to a hedonistic lifestyle and increases greediness.[33] According to Shaykh Mahir, if these attributes are attached to someone, this leads to *shirk*, since the individual will prefer material goods and pleasures to the fear and love of God.

This argument was repeated in a public lecture I attended in Kuwait given by the previously mentioned Shaykh 'Abd al-Rahman 'Abd al-Khaliq. As he put it, "everything in Islam [has been created] for purity." Perfect purity is represented by *tawhid*. All the rulings of the *shari'a* are created to establish *tawhid*, and by that their aim is purification (*tazkiya*). As the shaykh explained, *shirk* is equal to pollution (*danas*),

---

[29] Muhammad bin Salih al-Uthaymin, *Kitab al-Tahara*, www.ibnothaimeen.com/all/books/article_18041.shtml (accessed August 7, 2012).

[30] Tawassul is common Sufi practice and still widely present in Northern Lebanon.

[31] Ibn Qayyim (1292–1350) was the disciple of Ibn Taymiyya. Due to his extensive scholarship on *fiqh* and *hadith*, modern Salafi scholars relied on his works when they elaborated their *manhaj*. See also Caterina Bori and Livnat Holtzman, 'Introduction' in *Essays in the Legal and Theological Thought of Ibn Qayyim al-Ğawziyyah* edited by Caterina Bori and Livnat Holtzman, (Rome: Istituto per l'Oriente C.A. Nallino, 2010).

[32] Ibn Qayyim al-Jawziyya, *Ighathat al-Lahfan Min Masayid al-Shaytan*, http://saaid.net/book/search.php?do=all&u=%C7%C8%E4+%DE%ED%E3 (accessed August 7, 2012), pp. 52–53.

[33] Ibid., p. 54.

"the *mushrikin* (those, who commit *shirk*) are impure. Their body and their clothes can appear clear but as long as they stick to *shirk* and apostasy, their soul and feelings are embedded in pollution." Any addition to the divine system of the *shari'a* is pollution as well. Ritual practices (*'ibadat*) serve to reach *tawhid* and by this, purity as well. When somebody neglects a part of them, their soul becomes polluted. Implementing the rules of Islam leads to a pure soul and later to Paradise. If a Muslim dies and his soul is still impure, he goes to Hell for a certain period of time, until he has been purified from breaking the system of the *shari'a*.[34]

Purity also manifests always wearing "*libas shara'i* [religiously proper clothing]," which in turn contributes in creating a truly Islamic appearance and avoiding imitation of unbelievers (*tashabbuh bi-l-kuffar*). Salafis also distinguish themselves by applying a distinctively Islamic vocabulary when they communicate with others. They avoid using English and French loan words, which are common in Lebanese colloquial Arabic, and frequently use religious references in their daily conversations. For example, they avoid greeting Muslims with "*marhaba*" (the common form in Lebanon); instead they use "*al-salamu 'alaykum.*" To thank someone, they frequently say "*jazakum Allah khayran* [May God reward you]." When they argue, they often quote a *hadith* to prove their opinion.

The image of the shaykhs is further strengthened by the manner in which they communicate with other people. Some of the *'ulama'* of Dar al-Fatwa are surrounded by a climate of royalty, and they spend more time in the company of political leaders than of ordinary people. Salafis, by contrast, are more approachable. Their constituents often recall their avoidance of arrogant behavior and tendency to deal with everyone as equals, not as superiors. Most Salafi shaykhs are easily approachable in their homes, often without previously asking for an appointment. They spend a lot of time providing consultancy (*mushawara*) to believers in both religious and mundane matters.

Zuhd does not mean, however, that one has to get rid of material pleasures altogether. Enjoying them in accordance with the rulings of the *shari'a* even pleases God. Some of the Salafi shaykhs in Tripoli are quite affluent. Shaykh Ghassan, a Lebanese Palestinian scholar, who owns clothing stores in the proximity of Nahr al-Barid refugee camp north of Tripoli explained that there is nothing wrong with being rich.

---

[34] Public lecture given by Shaykh 'Abd al-Rahman 'Abd al-Khaliq, Kuwait, al-Salam, Badriyya al-Hajiri Mosque, March 10, 2012.

What is important here is that "you should not be happy when you acquire them and should not be sad if you lose them. Your trust, love and fear of God have to overshadow these."

Instead, according to the shaykh, the individual should use material goods to please God. He considers his wealth as a tool provided by God to help fellow Muslims and spread the *da'wa*. He argued that owning businesses made him materially independent and he does not need to "serve a political patron or cut a slide from charity donations" in order to get by. He partly finances his Islamic Center inside the camp and contributes to microfinance projects to enable poor people to open their own small businesses. By performing mild asceticism, Salafi shaykhs intend to be seen by their constituency as perfect Muslims, those who do not only preach the truth but also embody it by their behavior and practices.

Practicing mild asceticism and following Islamic Law, however, does not automatically translate into authority. The question here is how is this mild asceticism transformed into authority? Islam, according to Salafism, is a total system; its rulings extend to all aspects of human life and mirror the perfect divine order on earth. Therefore, the *shari'a* is a system that represents purity; anything that lies outside its framework is tainted. Imitating the behavior of the Prophet and reaching purity through *zuhd* means getting closer to the divine order, which is manifested by *tawhid*. Purification therefore means restoring order by eliminating that which leads to its disintegration. In the eyes of ordinary believers, Salafis represent this divine order by their intention to live a "perfect Islamic life."

Although a significant segment of the Sunni Muslim community in the North considers the shaykhs to constitute ideal Muslims, most ordinary believers do not become committed Salafis. Their ideals of Islamic morality, which are often represented by Salafism, coexist with other, often contradictory, ideals in other fields of life. This aspect of Salafism has been observed by researchers elsewhere as well. In Schielke's analysis of the morality of young Egyptian Muslims, for example, he observes that "people can argue for very conservative and strict standards of gender relations at one time, but express rather liberal ideals of romantic love at other times."[35] Both Schielke and Peterson refer to this phenomenon as Salafi mood (*mazaj Salafi* – a term they adopted from the late Egyptian expert on Islamic movements, Husam Tammam [1972–2011]), in which individuals embrace

[35] Ibid., p. 30.

Salafism as the uncorrupted form of Islam, but do not follow its path of perfection, which includes *zuhd*.[36]

I made similar observations when interviewing the Salafi constituency in Tripoli. Young people often praise and respect the shaykhs because they do not share their lifestyles. As one of them, Ziad, told me about one of the Salafi scholars, "[h]e is perfecting himself in religion while we are wasting our time in the cafés with meaningless things." Though Ziad admired the shaykh for living a pure life, he explained that he would not be able to adopt a similar lifestyle. He argued that life in Lebanon is full of temptations; he cannot resist occasionally going out with girls, not to say spending nights with friends smoking and often discussing religiously unacceptable topics. He also mentioned that most of the time he even fails to get up for the dawn prayer. This makes him respect Salafis more, who would never miss it for the sake of sleeping.

Not all Salafis are held in high respect in the community, though. People often talk negatively about those who suddenly dress in Islamic clothes, grow beards, memorize a few *ahadith*, and claim to be shaykhs. These individuals are ridiculed when they enthusiastically try to advise others on how to live a proper life. This indicates that becoming an authentic Salafi shaykh should be the result of a long process of learning and perfecting one's religious practices. The image of the Salafi is the image of the ideal Muslim due to the continuous efforts he has made to reach a state of purity. As one of the shaykhs explained to me, purity is the result of long practice, learning, and *zuhd*. The *zahid* (who performs *zuhd*) should try to abstain from telling even small lies, should resist temptation for years, and must devote large parts of his free time to religious activities.[37] It is common in the case of puritan movements that their vanguard transforms its mild asceticism into activism to rid society of its corruptions and purify it in the same way as they purified themselves. *Hisba* became a central element of Salafism as the vehicle of internally purifying the religion from what are identified as "foreign elements."[38] The implementation of *hisba* needs the acceptance of the larger community. Therefore, those Salafi shaykhs who already possess a high degree of religious capital can successfully engage in this kind of activism.

---

[36] Schielke, *Egypt in the Future Tense*, location 2873; Jennifer Peterson, "Going to the Mulid: Street-Smart Spirituality in Egypt" In *An Anthropology of Everyday Religion: Ordinary Lives and Grand Schemes*, edited by Samuli Schielke and Liza Debevec (New York and London: Berghahn Books, 2012), p. 122.

[37] Interview with Shaykh Haytham al-Sa'id, June 23, 2012.

[38] Roel Meijer, "Commanding Right and Forbidding Wrong as a Principle of Social Action: The Case of the Egyptian al-Jama'a al-Islamiyya." In Roel, *Global Salafism*.

Hisba traditionally has three dimensions; in Lebanon it is mostly performed by "heart" and "tongue," since neither the state nor the wider community would tolerate serious actions by "hand" (i.e. vigilante activism), such as forcing music stores to close, or forbidding shops to sell alcohol. Rather, the Lebanese shaykhs constantly remind people about the need to believe in the correct way and abandon deviations like Sufi practices. They argue that the Sunnis in Lebanon can only be saved if believers stick to the right *'aqida*. In their view, the sect is threatened from two sides. First, by the Shi'a who want to dominate the country and turn Sunnis into second-class citizens. Second, by the West, which wants them to turn their back on Islam and follow secularism. In the current climate of sectarian tensions and socioeconomic frustration, this kind of *hisba* meets a positive response. Many ordinary Sunnis think that the Salafis are the only ones who truly care about the fate of the community and who dare to stand up to Hizbullah.

The Salafis' religious capital serves as the basis of their authority. Since many regular believers respect Salafis because of their perceived mastery of religious knowledge and exemplary lifestyle, this religious capital can be turned to social capital if the shaykhs manage to build strong social relationships among their community.

4.2.2   Social Capital

The notion of "social capital" is derived from the assumption that social relationships can lead to the acquisition of certain profits or benefits. Bourdieu defines social capital as "the aggregate of the actual or potential resources which are linked to possession of a durable network of more or less institutionalized relationships of mutual acquaintance or recognition."[39] That is, group membership, networks of friends, followers or access to patronage networks increase someone's social capital. The importance of social capital is that it can be converted into other forms of capital, such as economic or religious capital.[40] These two forms of capital also can be converted to social capital.

In our case, Salafis invest their religious capital to gain social capital. Salafi shaykhs utilize their image as perfect Muslims to engage in activities that are perceived as serving the community, and which in

---

[39] Alejandro Portes, "Social Capital: Its Origins and Applications in Modern Sociology," *Annual Review of Sociology*, 24, (1998), p. 3.
[40] Ibid., p. 4.

turn – if successfully carried out – further increase the shaykhs' social standing. I observed that looking after young people and correct behavior is an important source of social capital for Salafis. Salafi shaykhs and their students often engage in conversations with young people who are on what is perceived as the "wrong path." They try to persuade them to abandon womanizing, drinking, or hanging out with friends on the street and in cafés. Salafis try to convince these young people to pursue their studies or work instead, and they often help them find a job. I observed that the shaykhs sometimes sacrifice a lot of their time to give extra religious lessons to young people, and these activities often mean that Salafis are held in greater esteem by other family members. Salafis regard this activity as part of *hisba*.

Another more important source of social capital for Salafi shaykhs is mediating in cases of social disputes and conflicts. Most often, haraki shaykhs perform mediatory tasks; purists engage in such activities very rarely, and if they do, they resolve only relatively minor issues, such as marital disagreements. To purist shaykhs, the root of social conflicts that need mediation is society's ignorance of scripture, especially the *ahadith*. Therefore, Salafis should focus on leading people back to the morality of the Qur'an and Sunna. This would minimize the occurrence of major disagreement between Muslims.[41]

Harakis argue that disagreements between the *sahaba* happened even in the time of the Prophet. In their view, religious specialists should consider mediating as one of their main tasks. If Salafis withdrew from such tasks, they would delegate conflict resolution to the secular court system that is based on manmade law instead of God's law, or individuals, such as tribal and other community leaders who are often not familiar with the *shari'a*. This also demonstrates the *harakis '* attitude toward public engagement that is derived from their conceptualization of Islam as all encompassing; therefore, no aspects of life should be neglected.[42]

Just as in other Middle Eastern countries, often the state does not interfere directly in disputes over property or even in cases of accidental killing. Instead, the community has the opportunity to solve these issues according to local traditions. Mediation is usually performed by highly respected individuals, such as the *zu'ama* or religious leaders. The latter have even more potential to be effective in settling disputes, since they are supposed to be independent of clan

---

[41] I discussed this issue with several purist Salafis in Lebanon in July 2012.
[42] See Introduction.

affiliations and local power struggles.[43] Today people perceive that Salafis fulfill most of these requirements. The shaykhs that are invited to perform such tasks are usually those who possess the trust of the community due to their high level of religious capital. In addition, when a conflict is solved, the shaykh's prestige increases and he gains even more followers.

Mediation is an integral aspect of the part of the Islamic justice system that is concerned with dispute resolution. Its preferred outcome is *sulh* (amicable settlement), as distinguished from *tahkim* and *qada'*, which are reached after the parties subject themselves to a decision by a third party.[44] The secular judiciary, which was first installed in Lebanon with the beginning of the French mandate in 1920,[45] has not been able to fully replace traditional dispute solution mechanisms for three main reasons.

It is frequently the case that one or both of the quarrelling parties do not accept the secular judge's decision if no informal reconciliation has been made. After the Lebanese court's verdict has been enforced, they often seek justice themselves, which can have tragic consequences. A Salafi shaykh in one of the Northern Lebanese Palestinian refugee camps gave me an example. At the beginning of the 1990s, a secondary school student killed one of his classmates during a fight (accidentally, according to the shaykh). The religious leaders of the camp immediately started a process of mediation between the killer's and the victim's families. However, at the end of the mediation, the victim's father refused the reconciliation and instead demanded the death of his son's killer, who was fifteen years old at the time. Since the shaykhs were unable to reach a solution, the case was delivered to the Lebanese court and the killer was handed over to the state authorities. The victim's father found the seven-year sentence handed to his son's killer insufficient and maintained his demand that he be killed.

Today there are increasing fears in the camp that the tensions between the two families will erupt. For the past twenty years, the vendetta had been prevented because the killer's family had a good

---

[43] Martin van Bruinessen, *Agha, Shaikh and State: On the Social and Political Organization of Kurdistan* (Utrecht: Ph.D. thesis submitted at Utrecht University, 1978), pp. 64, 290.

[44] In the case of *tahkim*, the disputants can withdraw from the arbitration process before the decision. By contrast, during *qida'*, it is impossible to withdraw, and the disputants have to follow the process until the end and subject themselves to the judge's decision. See: Aida Othman, "'And Amicable Settlement Is Best': Sulh and Dispute Resolution in Islamic Law," *Arab Law Quarterly*, 21, (2007), p. 68.

[45] Elisabeth Thompson, *Colonial Citizens: Republican Rights, Paternal Privilege, and Gender in French Syria and Lebanon* (New York, NY and Chichester: Columbia University Press, 2000), p. 58.

relationship with powerful individuals in the neighboring Syrian regime and controlled certain smuggling routes between Syria and Lebanon. Since the Syrian revolution, the family's former influence has been shaken and there are fears that the victim's family will attempt to take revenge.[46] If mediation leads to *sulh*, it restores stability, and tensions never flare up around the same issue again.

The second reason why the Lebanese judiciary system is unable to replace the traditional mechanisms of conflict resolution is its inefficiency. Most verdicts are only reached after a long time. In disputes over money, in particular, one should not expect a quick decision from the Lebanese court. Judges are considered corrupt and winning a case often depends on having political contacts. In contrast, Salafi shaykhs are usually regarded as unbiased and trustful, which is why most people prefer to ask the shaykhs to solve these cases. As one of my informants, a Salafi shaykh with decades of experience in mediation, told me, it sometimes takes the Lebanese court ten years to come to a decision on disputes involving larger amounts of money (starting from 20,000 USD). Salafi shaykhs can solve such issues in a few months by proposing a solution that is acceptable for all parties involved.

The third reason is the suspicion of the Northern Lebanese Sunni population toward the state. In general, people feel that the government is neglecting the region because it is home to the Sunni community. These feelings of unease toward the state increased after 2011, when Prime Minister Saad al-Hariri resigned and Najb Miqati's new government included the Shi'ite Hizbullah. These particular events led many Sunnis to feel alienated from the Lebanese state and its institutions. Although Dar al-Fatwa also offers religious mediation, it is associated with the state and the institution is seen as weak and incompetent; therefore, people often avoid turning to it. Due to the mistrust of their political leadership and feeling disenfranchised, Lebanese Sunnis are increasingly turning to what they perceive to be their true religious identity and their traditional social institutions. Therefore, those shaykhs who are well integrated in their local communities are gaining prominence. At present, most of these shaykhs are Salafis.[47]

Mediation leads to an increase in the shaykhs' social capital, which they can exchange, in turn, for other forms of capital. Successfully achieving *sulh* reinforces the social position of the shaykhs. People

---

[46] Interview with a religious leader of the camp, Tripoli, April 14, 2012.
[47] One prominent Dar al-Fatwa official admitted to me that most of the mediators in social conflict in Tripoli are Salafis. Interview with a Dar al-Fatwa official, Tripoli, April 29, 2012.

respect and trust them more, and their embeddedness in social networks increases. Successful mediation often helps the shaykhs to access
material resources. Furthermore, the acquired social capital might also
facilitate the dissemination of their message.

The shaykhs reported that they were usually invited to all events
of the families that they had helped to achieve *sulh*. Salafi shaykhs
are therefore frequent guests at weddings, which provide an excellent
opportunity for *da'wa*. At the weddings of conservative Sunni families,
men and women celebrate in segregated places. At a certain point
during the event, the Salafi scholar who is present is invited to give a
small lecture. The wedding also serves as an open forum for ordinary
individuals to approach the shaykh and ask their questions about
religion.

In Northern Lebanon, social conflicts can have serious consequences.
Retreat means losing face in society, while ongoing, unresolved disputes can lead even to armed clashes and huge human and material
losses. Obviously, ordinary people hold those who can help the parties
to reach a settlement that is acceptable for all in high esteem. Therefore,
the Salafi shaykhs' mediation activities, among other factors, make
a substantial contribution to increasing their religious authority and
influence in the Sunni community. As a result, they gain social and
material resources to extend their *da'wa*.

4.2.3   *Economic Capital and Patronage*

Possessing economic capital is important in creating the authority
of Salafis. Besides their access to donors in the Arabian Gulf, the
economic capital of the Salafi shaykhs is often gained due to their links
to the Lebanese Sunni community's political patrons. The latter provide material resources for Salafis to pursue their proselytization activities. The shaykhs, in exchange, mobilize their followers to serve the
purposes of the patrons.

While patronage is present in different degrees almost everywhere, it
is particularly salient in the Middle East. Of all the Arab states, patronage is probably the most visible and prominent in Lebanon. There are
two main reasons for this: First, in certain regions the presence of the
state is negligible and the provision of basic services for the population
depends on political patrons (*za'im*, pl. *zu'ama'*). This is especially true
in parts of the North, such as the Dinniyya region or 'Akkar.

The second factor lies in the unique characteristics of the Lebanese
patronage system itself. Prior to the Arab Spring, in all of the other

Middle Eastern countries, one group or family, who built alliances with certain groups to maintain power, dominated the political system.[48] This arrangement still exists in most of the Arab states. In such cases, the dominant group constitutes the top of the patronage system. Other patrons depend on them and are simultaneously the clients of the rulers.[49]

The structure of patronage in Lebanon is different. There is no dominant group that has been able to take over the state. The *zu'ama'* compete with each other for influential positions in the state administration. They regularly need to fill government offices in order to get access to state resources and distribute them among their clients, thereby retaining their status as *zu'ama'*. In order to achieve this, patrons need to mobilize their clientele at the time of elections and collect enough votes to return to parliament.

The contemporary Lebanese patronage system is rooted in the Ottoman era. Between the late eighteenth and early nineteenth centuries, the society of Mount Lebanon was dominated by *muqta'ji* families. The *muqta'jis* were formally appointed by the Ottoman administration in order to collect the taxes. In exchange they got a share of the revenues, and Istanbul did not interfere in the internal affairs of the territory controlled by the *muqta'jis*. The legitimacy of the *muqta'ji's* rule was not based on coercion, but on the personal allegiance of the peasants on his land. Sectarianism was not involved in this form of patronage; in most cases, the landlord was Druze while the peasants were Maronites.[50]

After the civil war in 1860, the religious community became the main component of the identity of the population, and not belonging to a certain patron. Therefore, patronage itself was defined by the religious community. After this time, patrons and clients mainly belonged to the same sectarian group. Following the emergence of the modern Lebanese state, first during the French mandate from 1920 and then from independence in 1943, patronage became tied to the state institutions. In this system, patrons mobilize their constituencies during elections. Between elections, the patrons expect their clients to support them in

[48] Stephen King, *The New Authoritarianism in the Middle East and North Africa* (Bloomington: Indiana University Press, 2009).

[49] Nazih N. Ayubi, *Over-stating the Arab State: Politics and Society in the Middle East* (London and New York, NY: I. B. Tauris, 2006); Mohamed Fahmy Menza, *Patronage Politics in Egypt: The National Democratic Party and Muslim Brotherhood in Cairo* (London and New York, NY: Routledge, 2013).

[50] A. Nizar Hamzeh, "Clientalism, Lebanon: Roots and Trends," *Middle Eastern Studies*, 37, no. 3, (2001), pp. 168–169.

times of political turmoil. For example, the client might take the patron's side in demonstrations, and even in times of armed conflict.

Today, patronage in Lebanon can be regarded as modern because most of the clientele, unlike in the eighteenth and nineteenth centuries, do not have moral bonds to their patrons. They serve them only for material reasons. Furthermore, contemporary Lebanese patronage is not exclusive. Unlike earlier, a client now can serve more than one patron at a time. Due to the special features of the Lebanese election system, patrons usually compete with each other in the same sectarian group[51] while making alliances with patrons of other confessions. The major cleavages between different political coalitions in Lebanon define the political map of Tripoli and the North. In the predominantly Sunni region, patrons ally themselves with the pro-Western and pro-Saudi March 14 movement and with the pro-Syrian March 8 grouping. Until recently, Salafis were usually well integrated into one of these patronage networks.[52] The highest number of them supports the political camp led by Sa'd al-Hariri. Hariri, though originally from Sidon and residing in Beirut, has a vast patronage network in the North. He is also supported by local patrons, who are allied with his block and receive political backing from him. For example, most of the *harakis* have access to Hariri's patronage network. The most famous "Hariri clients" include Da'i al-Islam al-Shahhal, Salim al-Rafi'i, Zakariya al-Masri, and Rai'd Hulayhil (see Chapter 3).

The former prime minister, Najib Miqati, is the most powerful local patron in Tripoli. After a political crisis in 2011, the billionaire allied himself with the pro-Syrian side. In spite of the fact that this camp contains the Shi'ite Hizbullah, Miqati has several clients from the Salafi movement. However, these belong either to the network of Muhammad Khodor or Safwan al-Za'bi. The former rejects the anti-Shi'a stance of the majority of the Salafis and argues that of all those in the region, only Hizbullah has a truly Islamic, purist project. The latter argues that only peaceful coexistence with Shi'ite political forces will create the stability necessary for the *da'wa*.

Patronage networks are structured by a hierarchy of "dominance relations." Typically, there are several figures that mediate between

---

[51] In each electoral district there is a certain number of seats in each of the communities, so electoral competition cannot result in a decrease in the number of parliamentary seats held by one of the sects, Bassel F. Salloukh, "The Limits of Electoral Engineering in Divided Societies: Elections in Postwar Lebanon," *Canadian Journal of Political Science*, 39, no. 3, (2006), p. 640.

[52] After the Sunni Zu'ama lost much of their influence in the wake of the Arab Uprisings in 2011, many of the *haraki* Salafis became more independent from them.

"the little man" and the "big man."[53] Salafis typically play the role of the mediator or middle-man between ordinary people and the zu'ama. The shaykhs are in a good position to benefit from Lebanese patronage networks. They possess the ability to mobilize followers for the patrons. For the patron himself, relying on Salafis and paying them to mobilize followers for elections costs less than attempting to directly mobilize large numbers of people. Naturally, Lebanese patrons have their masses of supporters, but they are unable to reach out in this way to all the people whose vote or presence in demonstrations is needed. If they are using the Salafis as middle-men, they need to finance the shaykhs. The latter persuade their constituencies to vote for the candidates supported by the patron. At the same time, most of the shaykhs receive funding from other sources as well, which is used for the patron's needs when Salafis have to take sides with one of the political camps.

Their relations with patrons enable Salafis to provide a wider range of services to their followers. Since they often receive large amounts of money from the zu'ama, they are able to give more material incentives to their constituencies. This might take the form of direct financial aid in the case of a death in the family, paying for medical treatment, or paying the tuition fees of students from poor families. During my fieldwork in North Lebanon, I had a chance to examine the mechanism of patronage and how Salafis utilize it. One of the best examples of a Salafi who actively serves one or more patrons is Shaykh Safwan al-Za'bi. I interviewed him about this issue in the summer of 2011. He always talked openly about his cooperation with the zu'ama and justified it by stating that this is how Lebanese society works.

Shaykh Safwan mentioned a case in which he had interceded on behalf of his client with one of the zu'ama. In the first case, Ahmad, the head of a lower middle-class family from the Dinniya district, added a new floor to his house without a permit from the municipality. When officials from the municipal council found out, they ordered the man to be fined an extortionate amount. According to Shaykh Safwan, the sum reached almost 50,000 USD. Ahmad turned to Shaykh Safwan for help, since the shaykh has strong ties with some of the patrons in Tripoli, most notably Najib Miqati, the current prime minister, and Mouhammad Safadi. After a few phone calls to Miqati's close aides, the issue was settled within a short time. Ahmad no longer needed to

---

[53] Gero Erdmann and Ulf Engel, "Neopatrimonialism Reconsidered: Critical Review and Elaboration of an Elusive Concept," *Commonwealth & Comparative Politics*, 45, no. 1, (2007), p. 107.

pay a fine and he received the permit from the municipality retro-
actively. Shaykh Safwan declared that Ahmad deserved to be helped
because he is a devout Muslim and urges his family members to
practice their religion properly. During the elections, Shaykh Safwan
is also able to mobilize a number of voters like Ahmad.

Safwan explained that the logic of patronage is such that these people
are afterward expected to show their devotion and appear regularly in
one of his mosques. Maximizing his number of followers increases his
social status among the Salafis in Lebanon. According to him, under-
taking da'wa in this manner has two aims. First, it shows the way of true
Islam to many people, even if some of them initially started to follow
it out of financial interest. Second, having a significant follower base
attracts more funds from the Gulf States. Furthermore, it helps him
to build stronger relationships with the zu'ama. In times of political
turmoil, Salafi shaykhs such as Safwan are expected to visit the patron
with a delegation. Such visits form part of Lebanese politics and demonstrate that there are plenty of people who stand on the za'im's side.
Safwan also mobilized his clientele during the elections. He made a list
of four candidates: two belonging to the Hariri camp, and the other two
to the March 8 grouping. According to Safwan, such moves further
increase his financial options, since he receives payments from all the
candidates he has supported.

The acquisition of economic capital and patron–client relationships in
the Salafi movement are often not linked to the zu'ama. Salafis frequently provide services to individuals without indirectly recruiting
them for the za'im. As I previously have shown, Salafis have access to
the funds of Gulf charities. At other times they possess the necessary
religious and social capital to convince their local supporters to donate
for certain purposes. I observed such a case when I spent a few days in
the Wadi Khalid region in the summer of 2011. One of my informants,
shaykh 'Imad, who is a prominent Salafi shaykh in the region, played
an active role in helping Syrian refugees who had fled from the repression of the ongoing demonstrations. An older Syrian woman's leg had
been broken because security forces back in her hometown had beaten
her up. When she arrived in Wadi Khalid, she was already in a critical
condition. Shaykh 'Imad gave her shelter in his home and spared no
expense in organizing her care in a good hospital and collecting the
30,000 USD needed for her operation. He was able to get one third of
the money from families in Wadi Khalid who sympathized with the
Salafis or the Syrian revolution. The network of Shaykh Da'i al-Islam al-
Sahhal, to which Shaykh 'Imad is also connected, donated 10,000 USD.
Surprisingly, the rest of the money came from the Red Cross. Shaykh

'Imad got in touch with the Lebanese representative of the organization, despite the fact that Salafis often blame the Red Cross for being a tool of the Western "colonizing powers."

4.3   Capital and the Construction of Religious Authority

One might ask why Salafism and not another proselytizing movement, such as Jama'at al-Tabligh,[54] succeeded in establishing a high level of religious authority among Lebanese Sunni Muslims. Al-Tabligh has been present in Lebanon since the 1970s, and is one of the most active proselytizing movements among the Sunni community. Similarly to Salafism, it calls on Muslims to live a more pious lifestyle and never neglect their worship activities. Yet, despite their long and persistent *da'wa*, al-Tabligh arguably has much less influence on the Sunni religious field than Salafism.

When I was living in Tripoli, and frequently socialized with local Sunni Muslims, they sometimes talked about al-Tabligh. They usually described the followers of the movement as good but simple individuals, who love the Prophet Muhammad and are very pious. Yet, according to Salafis, their knowledge is limited, and they do not do much beyond calling people to pray and fast regularly. Even the literature (mostly booklets) that members of the movement distribute focuses on ritual and largely avoids discussing issues related to social or political matters.[55] At the same time, according to al-Tabligh's teachings, abandonment of worldly goods and focusing on proselytization are advisable for Muslims.[56] This is contrary to the thinking of Salafis, who argue that there is no reference for such a demarcation in the scripture, as religion encompasses everything, including the material world and everyday practices.

In other words, al-Tabligh builds on a religious capital derived from a very narrow focus on rituals and call for an almost world-rejecting asceticism in the Weberian sense. For example, Sunni believers rarely, if ever, go to members of al-Tabligh for counselling in social issues, and do not ask them to resolve disputes. It is also unheard of in Lebanon

---

[54] See Introduction.

[55] In Lebanon the most frequently distributed books by al-Tabligh are the translated works of the Indian Muhammad Zakariyya Kandahlawi (1898–1982). Among these are *Fada'il al-Qur'an*, *Fada'il al-Hajj*, *Fada'il Ramadan*, and *Fada'il al-Dhikr*.

[56] The movement clearly separates the realm of religion (*din*) and material world (*dunya*), a much criticized aspect by Salafis, who regard this distinction *bida'*. See Farish A. Noor, p. 72; Yoginer Sikand, p. 184.

that a member of al-Tabligh establishes contacts with political patrons in order to acquire economic capital to be able to provide financial benefits to his followers.

In the sociopolitical context of Lebanon after the Arab Uprisings, the Salafis' combination of the three forms of capital transforms to authority more effectively than that of al-Tabligh's approach. By being able to provide answers to almost all aspects of life by employing their knowledge on the scripture, and taking care of the material needs of the community, Salafis appear to many as the ideal Sunni leaders. The cases of Shaykh Tawfiq and Shaykh Hisham illustrate how the Salafis' accumulation and investment of capital works to consolidate their authority.

4.3.1   Shaykh Tawfiq of the Mina District

Shaykh Tawfiq, a middle-aged Tripolitan, is one of the leading Salafi preachers in the Mina district. The district itself differs significantly from the other parts of Tripoli. In general, inhabitants of the Mina lead more secular lifestyles than elsewhere in the city. The proportion of middle-class citizens among the population is also significantly higher than in most other districts. Tripoli's only street with bars is also in the Mina district. However, there has always been a devout Muslim part of the population, and the growing number of Salafis also points to the locals' increasing religiosity. When I started researching Salafism in Lebanon in 2009, there were only a dozen or so committed Salafis in the Mina district. In 2012, I found hundreds in the same part of the town.

During my fieldwork, I lived in the Mina. Being a resident of the district, it was impossible not to come across Shaykh Tawfiq. The medium-built, agile, and fast-talking scholar, with his slightly stooped back and dark-gray beard, often could be spotted on the streets that lead to the seaside, usually in the company of local men. When I was researching the resolution of social disputes, many residents of the district told me that Shaykh Tawfiq should be the first person to be interviewed.

First, I joined the shaykh's religious lessons in the 'Uthman bin 'Affan mosque, which is maintained by the network of Shaykh Salim al-Rafi'i. These lessons are free and open to the public. After frequently appearing in these lessons, and establishing a rapport with the shaykh, I was able to have longer conversations with him not only about his dispute resolution activities but also about his life-trajectory as a Salafi 'alim. Being settled in the Mina and having local friends whom the shaykh knew was perhaps the main reason why the shaykh was not reserved to talk to me. He developed a strong interest in religion during his teen years in the late 1970s. He studied under the direction of a local shaykh of the Mina, who was not Salafi, but an Ash'ari who graduated at al-Azhar in Cairo. In the beginning of the1980s, when IUM took full control over the district, he joined the movement and, as he described it, became active in the da'wa under the movement's protection.

As Shaykh Tawfiq told me IUM spread religious fervor in the city that had been on the road to "atheism" due to the presence of the various secular Arab Nationalist and Marxist currents. Therefore, most of those who wanted to lead Tripoli back to Islam supported the movement. As the shaykh recalled, at that time it was not known that "IUM is the agent of Khomeini's regime."[57] During this period, as a young da'i, Shaykh Tawfiq became well known for spending most of his time organizing religious lessons for the youth of the Mina, and collecting alms for the needy in the war-torn city. In the mid-1980s he received a scholarship to the Islamic University of Medina. As the shaykh recalled, during his five years' stay in Saudi Arabia, his professors highlighted the mistakes of his previous Ash'ari teacher; therefore, he adopted Salafism both as "'aqida and manhaj."

Shaykh Tawfiq also identifies with the haraki faction, due to the influence of his professors, who came from Syria, Egypt, and Sudan; before adopting Salafism, they were members of either the Muslim Brotherhood or Hizb al-Tahrir.[58] This background provided them with affinity to consider global political and social issues, and not to "be lost only in minor details of worship." At the university in Medina he also met and acquainted other Lebanese students who later became the pioneers of the da'wa in their country. Among these was Shaykh Da'i al-Islam al-Shahhal, who upon return to Lebanon offered Shaykh Tawfiq a teaching job at his newly established al-Hidaya college.

Shaykh Tawfiq's studies in Medina and his previous reputation as an enthusiastic young man who lived for serving the Muslim community established his religious capital. This capital increased due to his

---

[57] Shaykh Sa'id Sha'ban, the leader of IUM, received financial support from Iran that was crucial to holding IUM together. Currently, IUM is an ally of Hizbullah, and many Sunnis regard it as the agent of the Shi'ite militia in the Northern Sunni heartland. See Chapter 2.

[58] Most of the teaching staff of the Islamic University of Medina were foreigners, often with previous experience in Islamic activism as members of different Islamic movements. Many adopted Salafism due to the influence of the Saudi religious environment. Farquhar, Circuits of Faith, pp. 93–95.

proselytization activities in the two decades after his return. Inhabitants of the Mina appreciate his readiness to consult them in religious and mundane matters, and the fact that he holds religious lessons frequently, usually four times a week. Shayk Tawfiq's contact with Shaykh Da'i enabled him to acquire economic capital in the form of donations from Saudi Arabia and Kuwait. He was able to use the money he received through al-Shahhal's network to provide financial assistance to those who were in immediate need, such as people who needed medical care, which is usually very expensive in Lebanon.

As Shaykh Tawfiq told me, after Shaykh Da'i had to flee to Saudi Arabia in 2000, and his network dispersed, he still maintained contact with some donors in Kuwait. He also found employment as a teacher in *Ma'had al-Amin* (al-Amin College) in the al-Zahiryya district, which remained under the control of *haraki* Salafis even after the crackdown of al-Shahhal's network. When Shaykh Salim al-Rafa'i returned from Germany to Lebanon in 2006, he became a close friend of Shaykh Tawfiq. Today, Tawfiq is the leading figure of al-Rafa'i's network in the Mina.

Shaykh Tawfiq's religious and economic capital provided him with authority that made it possible for him to become a successful mediator and resolve social disputes in his city district. The Shaykh told me that he regards mediation as part of *hisba*. According to him, disputes erupt between individuals when they violate the *shari'a*. By intervening in their conflict, the religious scholar leads the believers back to the way of Islam and preserves the social order defined by God. In the opinion of the Shaykh, those who perform this part of *hisba* must be well embedded in society.

Shaykh Tawfiq mostly solves conflicts within families, such as disagreements between family members and disputes over money and property. He mentioned a typical case that had recently arisen in the Mina district. A disagreement occurred between a father and his adult sons over *nafaqat 'ala al-walidayn* (financial support for the parents). In Islamic law, sons have to give part of their monthly income to their father if he does not have enough money to support himself and his wife(s).[59] The sons refused the payment, saying that their father had a decent income and they were therefore not obliged to support him. The father, however, argued the opposite and prepared to file a complaint

---

[59] Plenty of *fatwas* have been issued on this topic by muftis with various intellectual backgrounds. See, for example: http://olamaa-yemen.net/main/articles.aspx?article_no=9458 (accessed August 5, 2012); http://fatwa.islamweb.net/fatwa/index.php?page=showfatwa&Option=FatwaId&Id=56749 (accessed August 5, 2012).

in the secular court. To avoid the shame that a lawsuit between father and sons would bring on the entire family, other family members asked the shaykh to intervene.

As Shaykh Tawfiq explained, in this case his persuasive skills and contact with other kin members and family friends proved to be as important as his knowledge of the *shari'a*. The shaykh's recommendation was twofold. First, by quoting from the Qur'an and the Sunna, he reminded the sons of the need to obey their parents. It might be legitimate but it is not ethical for a son to inquire whether his father is really in need of financial support or not. Providing as high a living standard as possible for one's parents is dear to God and will be rewarded. Second, he argued that if Muslims were unable to agree among themselves and had to go to the non-Muslim court,[60] it would signify the weakness and disintegration of the Sunni community. As he was able to gather family friends and kin to support his stance, the sons agreed to pay the *nafaqa* for the father. In private he interpreted this event as having intervened as one of the *'ulama'* of the Sunnis who guards the values and integrity of the community, especially in times of danger. When Sunni Muslims need a third, secular or non-Muslim party to solve their differences, it is a sign of fragmentation within the *Umma* and gives the green light to Hizbullah in particular, to strengthen its domination over the country.

After such a successful reconciliation, the members of the family will become supporters of Salafism, most likely as passive participants. Solving a serious problem increases the shaykh's reputation in the eyes of those who were involved. After this, they are likely to accept the opinion of the shaykh in other matters as well. There is a high chance that many male family members will attend Shaykh Tawfiq's Friday sermon instead of sermons by those who belong to Dar al-Fatwa or other movements. As a result, they will encounter the Salafi framing of contemporary events, which might influence their worldview.

4.3.2   Shaykh Hisham: The Intercommunity Peacebroker

Unlike Shaykh Tawfiq, who operates in an urban milieu, Shaykh Hisham, a Palestinian scholar in his mid-thirties, established his authority as a scholar and mediator in an environment dominated by Palestinian refugees and rural Lebanese Sunni communities. Shaykh Hisham

---

[60] The judge in the Lebanese court can be also a Christian, Shi'ite, or Druze.

is among the dozens of Salafi shaykhs in the Nahr al-Barid refugee camp (about 30–40,000 inhabitants), that lies 15 km to the north of Tripoli, and was almost completely destroyed in a battle between a group of jihadis and the Lebanese army in 2007.[61]

Salafism gained ground in Nahr al-Barid in the early 1990s, roughly at the same time as the establishment of Da'i al-Islam al-Shahhal's network. Previously, in the 1980s dozens of Palestinian students received scholarships to study at the Islamic University of Medina. Upon returning to the camp, they became the backbone of the movement in the camp.[62] In the early 1990s Shaykh Da'i incorporated most of these shaykhs into his network by offering them financial support that he received from the Gulf. Due to this material benefit, the Palestinian shaykhs built nine Islamic centers in the camp, each of them attached to a mosque, where they performed various preaching activities, such as religious lessons. These centers also became the base for providing charity to the needy Palestinians.

As Rougier explains, the decreasing legitimacy of the nationalist movements (both the secular PLO and the Islamist Hamas) in the camps facilitated the Salafis' attempt to carve out a niche for themselves in Palestinian society. Salafism gave Palestinians an alternative identity that dissociated them from the series of defeat and humiliation they historically faced, and reconnected them to the *Umma*, where national and ethnic belongings are invalid.[63]

Shaykh Hisham is an imam of a mosque, and runs one of the nine Islamic centers together with three other shaykhs, among them Shaykh Ghassan.[64], the founder of the center. Due to my acquaintance with Ghassan, Shaykh Hisham was relatively open to talk about his life and activities when I interviewed him several times in 2012 in Minya region, adjacent to Nahr al-Barid, where he stayed in the home of his Lebanese wife. His parents came to Lebanon as children with the first waves of Palestinian refugees in 1948. His father, who was a militant in Fatah for a short time, worked most of his life as a brick maker. Yet, he managed to educate his three sons at universities. Shaykh Hisham studied engineering in Beirut, but left his studies after two years. He told me that with an engineering degree he would never get a job in Lebanon, as the employment of Palestinians is legally restricted.[65] Instead, "God opened the way to invest [his energy] to serve Muslims," and became a religious scholar.

---

[61] See Introduction.   [62] Rougier. *The Sunni Tragedy in the Middle East*, pp. 124–125.
[63] Ibid., p. 125.   [64] See also Chapter 6.
[65] Palestinians are excluded from a number of syndicated professions, such as law, medicine, and engineering. In addition, they cannot own a taxi or bus used for

Shaykh Hisham does not have an official degree in religious studies, but he studied under the Salafi shaykhs of the camp in informal ways, and spent a few months in Saudi Arabia on several occasions after performing Hajj or *'umra*, and joined the religious lessons of renowned Saudi Salafi *'ulama.'* Despite the lack of formal Islamic education, Shaykh Hisham is acknowledged by the community and by other Salafi shaykhs as someone who has deep knowledge and devotion to pursue the *da'wa*.

During his trips to Saudi Arabia, he established a social network that helped him to acquire donations from charities in the Kingdom and Qatar, and from wealthy individuals as well. This money added up to what others (particularly Shaykh Ghassan) received through their personal contacts in his Islamic center. Using funds from the charities, he provided financial aid for people in the camp and also outside in the surrounding impoverished Lebanese Sunni areas. This earned him the reputation of someone who truly cares about his fellow Muslims. Shaykh Hisham is a good example of how the investment of religious capital can provide someone with religious capital.

Shaykh Hisham often goes to give the Friday Sermon in the nearby Lebanese Sunni villages, where he maintains a good relationship with the leading personalities and the most significant families. His dense social networks in both communities enable him to mediate in disputes between Lebanese and Palestinians. Most of the time, he is invited to mediate in cases of manslaughter and accidental killing. According to him, during such mediation one of the biggest challenges is maneuvering in the framework of three legal systems: Lebanese law, the *shari'a*, and customary (*'urfi*) law. At the same time, his embeddedness in the Salafi networks of the North facilitates dispute resolution. This is a typical case that was mediated by Shaykh Hisham:

In 'Akkar, a Palestinian bus driver ran over two Lebanese schoolboys and one of them died from his injuries. The case was particularly sensitive because the driver was working illegally, using a bus with a private number. If the victim's family refused to solve the case via mediation, the driver would face a much harsher sentence than usual. Lebanese law, however, leaves room for mediation and *sulh*. In a case of accidental killing, the suspect is held in one of the police stations (and not in jail) until the case is solved. When the judge is convinced that a

public transport. Nada al-Nashif and Samir El-Khoury, "Palestinian Employment in Lebanon: Facts and Challenges," *International Labour Organization Report*, 27 February 2014, pp. 100–101.

real *sulh*[66] has occurred, he drops the charges between the two families. In the bus driver's case, the negotiations began three days after the deceased boy had been buried.[67]

Their work was facilitated by the fact that the victim's family had a close relationship with Salafi shaykhs in 'Akkar. Along with other lower-ranking shaykhs from his Islamic center, Shaykh Hisham started to negotiate a solution with these Salafi shaykhs, who represented the family. The scholars together proposed a solution and presented it to the two families. Traditionally, a certain amount of blood money (*diyya*) has to be paid, even in cases of accidental killing, and the Prophetical Tradition has historically stated how much should be paid as *diyya*.[68] However, in the modern application of Islamic criminal law different amounts of blood money can be set.[69] In Lebanon, customary law sets the amount at 10,000 USD. In view of the poor economic situation of the suspect's family, the Salafi shaykhs asked the victim's family to forgo the *diyya* and make other demands that would be even dearer to God. After long talks, the father of the victim agreed to waive the *diyya*, and instead asked the bus driver to go on pilgrimage to Mecca in the same year for the sake of his son's salvation.

The case illustrates the effectiveness of Salafi informal networks in the north of Lebanon. It is unlikely that the victim's family would have forgone the blood money for a shaykh from Dar al-Fatwa who lacked a scholarly network. In this case, though, they considered it more import-ant to please the Salafis whom they follow, and to strengthen the relationship with them (which was possibly also a patron–client rela-tionship), rather than asking for a 10,000-USD *diyya*. At the same time, the deal was worth something to both parties: The Lebanese Salafis who represented the victim's family earned a favor from the Palestinian one, and the Palestinian bus driver became obliged to Shaykh Hisham.

---

[66] The judge has to be assured that the two families have been truly reconciled and no *tha'r* (vendetta) will be committed afterwards. Interview with Shaykh Hisham, al-Minya, May 2, 2012.

[67] ing to customary law, negotiations can begin three days after the death, when the deceased has been buried. Second and third-level relatives of the killer also have to be present at the ceremony.

[68] "In early Islam, the standard bloodprice was given a monetary value of 1,000 dinars or 12,000 (according to the Hanafites 10,000) dirhams. This equals 29.7 or 35.64 kg of silver or 4.25 kg of gold." Rudolph Peters, *Crime and Punishment in Islamic Law* (Cambridge; New York: Cambridge University Press, 2005), p. 51.

[69] "Diya," in Bossworth, *The Encyclopaedia of Islam*. The amount of *diyya* usually differs according to country or region. See: Tahir Wasti, *The Application of Islamic Criminal Law in Pakistan* (Leiden and Boston: Brill, 2009), p. 179, 228; Gunnar Jochen Weimann, *Islamic Criminal Law in Northern Nigeria: Politics, Religion, Judicial Practice* (Amsterdam: Amsterdam University Press, 2010), pp. 23, 27, 109.

4.4   Conclusion

In this chapter, I traced how the different forms of Bourdieuan capital translate to authority, and contribute to the success of Salafism by transforming the Sunni religious field. This authority enables Salafis to successfully claim orthodoxy in considerable segments of the Northern Lebanese Sunni population. The steady decline of the influence of Dar al-Fatwa and the fact that other Islamic movements do not claim orthodoxy contributed to the success of Salafis.

In the case of the Salafis, religious capital signifies their religious knowledge, mastery of rituals, and commitment to what they define as a pure Islamic lifestyle. Those who gain the respect of everyday believers can turn their religious capital to social capital, especially if they provide various services to the community. *Harakis* often perform mediation in social disputes. For that reason, those Salafi shaykhs who are successful mediators build up dense social networks, which constitute social capital.

The social capital of the Salafi can be converted to economic capital. Those shaykhs who have a considerable following can become middlemen in patronage networks. They can mobilize their followers during elections or other occasions to serve the purposes of a political patron. The patron in turn provides material resources for shaykhs, which they can use to strengthen their *da'wa* activities.

Harakis and purists establish their authority in a similar way, but often utilize it differently. The high level of religious legitimacy of the *harakis* gives credibility to their framing activities, which explain current Lebanese and regional political events through the lens of the Salafis' antagonism toward Shi'ite Muslims and their belief that Sunnis are oppressed by other communities.

This chapter has shown how important the shaykhs are in the Lebanese Salafi movement. The following chapter will help us to gain more insight into how this significant role of religious specialists has influenced the structure of Salafism in Lebanon.

5   The Structure of Lebanese Salafi Networks at the Local Level

In the previous chapters I showed how Lebanese Salafis managed to accumulate various forms of capital to increase their influence on the Sunni religious field and set out what it means to be a good Muslim. This chapter turns to examine the internal makeup of Salafism and identifies the "glue" that binds its networks together. For my analysis, I will apply a social network approach and benefit from the literature on collective identity.

The structure of contemporary Salafism differs substantially from other mainstream Islamic movements, such as the Muslim Brothers or *Hizb al-Tahrir* insofar as it lacks elaborate institutional structures. Although there are formal organizations and institutions such as charities and religious colleges, informal networks dominate the movement. In Salafism, unlike in other movements, there is no clear hierarchical structure of authority, and membership is even less clearly defined.

If we think about Salafism as composed of networks and approach the topic from a traditional network theory perspective, individuals, groups, and associations are the nodes of networks that are connected to each other by direct or indirect ties ("spokes"). These ties are direct if the nodes are linked to each other in "explicit interaction and interdependence."[1] They might be personal relationships (either virtual or real), for instance, and intergroup or organizational contacts. Indirect ties exist when nodes are not linked directly but some kind of relationship can be assumed between them, such as participating in the same activity or belonging to the same movement. In the case of Salafism, due to the predominance of informal, interpersonal relationships, I will consider individuals as nodes in the networks.

A very important question is how to define whether a specific node is part of a movement's networks or not, since movement actors may

---

[1] Mario Diani, "Introduction: Social Movements, Contentious Actions, and Social Networks: From Metaphor to Substance?" In *Social Movements and Networks*, edited by Mario Diani and Doug McAdam (Oxford: Oxford University Press, 2003), p. 7.

belong to multiple social networks at the same time. In discussing this we might benefit from the relevant parts of the social movement literature. Social movement scholars show that certain ties facilitate, while others impede, participation in a movement.[2] If the facilitating ties are predominant, the individual joins the movement's activities. Melucci, for example, emphasizes the importance of having a collective identity that draws people into and keeps them in interpersonal networks.[3] Usually, collective identity is signified by a set of shared values and discourses. In our case, we must ask how do networks link different nodes in the Salafi movement, and how does Salafism's network structure facilitate the participation of individuals? Precisely how is the structure of Salafism different from other Islamic movements?

5.1   Specific Features of the Structure of Salafism

Salafis do not mobilize against the state or the capitalist economic system. Normally, Salafis are not (or only indirectly) interested in such goals. The aim of the movement is changing the individual. The networks of Salafism transmit symbols and values, and economic capital to promote a certain lifestyle, to make the Salafi vision of life become the accepted social norm. We can observe that collective action in Salafism resembles that of what Haenfler et al. call "lifestyle movements."[4] Salafis, participate in collective action primarily on the individual level with the subjective understanding that others are performing similar actions. In doing so, they collectively add up to social change.[5] Networks serve to facilitate this "individualized collective" action. They provide space for individuals to express their identity and moral support to adopt or maintain the Salafi way of life, and in that way to export their value system to the wider society.

---

[2] For example, patronage ties might facilitate social movement mobilization if the patron supports the movement, but impede it if he/she is against it. Jeffrey Broadbent, "Movement in Context: Thick Networks and Japanese Environmental Protest." In *Social Movements and Networks: Relational Approaches to Collective Action*, edited by Mario Diani and Doug McAdam (Oxford: Oxford University Press, 2003).

[3] Alberto Melucci, "The Process of Collective Identity," in Johnson and Klandermans, *Social Movements and Culture*; Carol M. Mueller, "Conflict Networks and the Origins of Women's Liberation." In *Social Movements: From Ideology to Identity*, edited by Enrique Larana, Hank Johnston and Robert R. Gusfield (Philadelphia, PA: Temple University Press, 1994);

[4] Ross Haenfler, Brett Johnson and Ellis Johns, "Lifestyle Movements: Exploring the Intersection of Lifestyle and Social Movements," *Social Movement Studies*, 11, no. 1 (2012).

[5] Ibid., p. 5.

When Salafis engage in "conventional" collective action, by, for example, mobilizing to put pressure on the government, they are often unsuccessful. In the spring of 2012, several Salafi shaykhs repeatedly called for demonstrations to demand the release or trial of a number of Salafis and Islamists who had been arrested by the government.[6] Despite the huge effort they put into mobilizing people to protest, the results were rather modest. The majority of committed Salafis ignored the call, on the grounds that demonstrations would not serve the interest of the detainees, but would only downgrade "God's call" to a "political organization such as the Muslim Brotherhood."[7] Most of the participants in the demonstrations appeared to be young (aged 16–25), unemployed men who had little relationship with Salafism. When I interviewed some of the participants, they declared that they joined the protest in the hope of "having some fun."

The mobilizing structures of the Salafi movement consist almost exclusively of informal networks. Informal contacts are essential in all movements and they cannot be equated with formal organizational structures. But in the case of some movements, informal ties are dominant and formal structures play a limited role. Salafism is among these movements, and this is true for both *harakis* and purists. Even Salafi political parties use largely informal ways of mobilization. For example, *al-Tajammu' al-Salafi* in Kuwait (see Chapter 1) failed to establish an effective, top-down institutional system.

There have been several discussions of the significance of informal social networks in Islamic movements.[8] However, most of these informal networks are organically connected to the movements' formal organizational bodies and are influenced by their decision-making mechanisms. It is difficult to imagine the Muslim Brotherhood or *Hizb al-Tahrir* without their sophisticated institutional structures. Informal social networks are connected to these structures and facilitate the effective functioning of the formal organizations.[9] In other words, the formal organizational and the informal parts complement each other and are of equal importance in the dynamics of the movement.

---

[6] After the battle in Nahr al-Barid camp in 2007, several young Salafis were arrested and accused of having been in contact with Fath al-Islam and other jihadi organizations. Many of them were still in jail five years later, and a trial date has not been set.

[7] Interview, Tripoli, May 9, 2012.

[8] Diane Singerman, "The Networked World of Islamist Social Movements." in Wiktorowicz, *Islamic Activism*; Janine A. Clark, "Islamist Women in Yemen: Informal Nodes of Activism." In Wiktorowicz, *Islamic Activism*.

[9] Formal institutions in the Muslim Brotherhood are strong at the local level. At the transnational level, informal, interpersonal networks are predominant. See Alison Pargeter, *The Muslim Brotherhood: The Burden of Tradition*, Kindle e-book edition (London: SAQI, 2010), location: 2091–2965.

The Muslim Brotherhood's organizational structure consists of two main parts that coordinate with each other: the political body and a large network of densely interconnected charitable institutions. Salafism does not possess this kind of formal institutional structure. While mainstream Islamist movements are more or less centralized, at least at the local level, the opposite is true for Salafism. Salafis often deny, and usually do not even recognize, that they are part of a movement. As many of my informants in Lebanon and Kuwait explained, they are simply following "pure Islam," free from any kind of innovation and heretical practices. For them, doing this cannot be identified with a kind of "*haraka* " (the Arabic term for "movement").[10]

There are at least two reasons for this exclusive reliance on informal ties. First, informal networks avoid repression more effectively. The most important reason why Salafis avoid formal organization, however, is the fact that Salafi teachings themselves reject it. Formal institutions create divisions among Muslims, while Islam intends to unify Muslims in one body. Therefore, formal institutions are often regarded as *bid'a* and establishing them leads Muslims away from the true path. They commonly refer to this as *hizbiyya* (partisanship), which is inherently dangerous as the individual may become loyal to the organization instead of to God. The prominent Lebanese purist scholar, Shaykh Sa'd al-Din al-Kibbi, explained to me that, "the Ikhwan replaced God with the organization. What you, as a Muslim, have to sacrifice for God, they do it for the organization."[11] As Muhammad bin al-'Uthaymin (1925–2001), one of the most prominent Salafi authorities, wrote:

I think that *Ahl al-Sunnah wa'l-Jama'ah* should unite, even though they differ in the ways in which they understand those texts that may be interpreted in different ways. This is a matter in which there is room for difference, may God be praised. What matters is harmony and unity. No doubt the enemies of Islam want the Muslims to be divided, whether they are enemies who express their enmity openly or they are enemies who make an outward display of friendliness towards Muslims and Islam, but that is not real. We must be different [from other communities] by being united, because unity is the characteristic of the saved group.[12]

According to Shaykh Rabi' al-Madkhali, the scripture clearly forbids the establishment of any kind of organization. In one of his books,

---

[10] This also resonates with the stance of the most influential Salafi scholars of the Saudi religious establishment. See the fatwa of Shaykh Salih al-Fawzan, a member of the Council of the Senior Scholars: www.alfawzan.af.org.sa/node/9917 (accessed August 4, 2014).

[11] Interview with Shaykh Sa'ad al-Din al-Kibbi, 'Akkar, October 12, 2009.

[12] Sermon of Shaykh Ibn 'Uthaymin, undated, available online at: www.ibnothaymeen .com/all/khotab/article_460.shtml (accessed October 12, 2010).

which is critical of Islamist movements and activist Salafism, he refers to Qur'an verses to underscore his stance: "Hold fast to God's rope all together; do not split into factions";[13] "As for those who have divided their religion and broken up into factions, have nothing to do with them [Prophet]";[14] "This is My path, leading straight, so follow it, and do not follow other ways: they will lead you away from it."[15] According to the author, when Muslims stopped paying attention to these verses, this led to the decline of the *umma*. In his opinion, Muslims from Morocco to Indonesia would have been able to liberate their lands from the armies of the unbelievers at the time of decolonization had the colonial powers not spread the idea of partisanship, which led to the formation of Islamist movements. These, along with their secularist counterparts, keep the Muslims scattered and allow the unbelievers to indirectly influence and govern Islamic countries.[16]

5.2   The Structure of Salafi Networks in Northern Lebanon

Salafis in the Middle East generally use indigenous patterns of mobilization when utilizing informal networks.[17] Since formal institutions in the Arab countries are usually weak and unreliable and generally distrusted – there has always been a high level of informality in everyday social exchanges – people in the Middle East almost exclusively use informal social contacts to fulfill their daily needs and interests. To give some examples, patron–client relationships are predominant in the distribution of goods, material aid, and jobs.[18] Historically, the organization of religious life and education has also mostly been informal. Until the twentieth century, religious knowledge was predominantly transmitted informally in study circles held in the mosques, and this type of education continues to fulfill a

---

[13] *Al 'Umran* 103, translated by Abdel-Haleem.   [14] *al-An'am* 159, ibid.

[15] *al-Ana'm* 153, ibid.

[16] Rabi' bin Hadi al-Madkhali, *Jama'a Wahida La Jama'at Wa Sirat Wahid La 'Asharat: Hiwar Ma' 'Abd al-Rahman 'Abd al-Khaliq* (without date and publisher).

www.rabee.net/show_des.aspx?pid=1&id=17&gid= (accessed October 11, 2011).

[17] Wiktorowicz, "The Salafi Movement in Jordan," p. 221.

[18] Guilain Denoux, *Urban Unrest in the Middle East: A Comparative Study of Informal Networks in Egypt, Iran and Lebanon* (Albany: State University of New York Press, 1993), pp. 16–20; 29–44. Suad Joseph, "Brother/Sister Relationships: Connectivity, Love and Power in the Reproduction of Patriarchy in Lebanon," *American Ethnologist*, 21, no. 1 (1994). See also Jenny B. White, *Civic Culture and Islam in Urban Turkey* (New York, NY: Routledge, 1996).

significant role alongside the *shari'a* faculties to this day.[19] Movements in the Middle East have traditionally utilized these channels. These indigenous parts of Middle Eastern civil society constitute the main avenues of mobilization for Salafism.

The shape of Salafi networks in North Lebanon is influenced by the movement's structure of authority. The movement's sub-networks that constitute the basic elements of larger networks are more vertically shaped than those in other countries, such as Kuwait.[20] This is due to the exceptionally significant role played by the shaykhs. These subnetworks are grouped around a religious leader and consist of his students and passive followers in the neighborhood where his activities are concentrated. The subnetworks connect to each other to constitute larger network structures at the local and transnational levels.

5.2.1   The Men of Religion

At the top of the subnetworks are those individuals who are either associated with outstanding piety or with performing religious tasks, or both. They are considered part of the religious elite. Most of them perform religious tasks such as giving sermons, holding religious lessons, taking care of mosques or administering religious endowments. Generally, they are given the title "shaykh" by their followers. This is a wide category, however, which includes individuals who possess different levels of religious knowledge. Some of them are recognized scholars or influential preachers with huge follower bases, while others are less educated, are only influential within their neighborhoods and are counted followers of other shaykhs. To draw a clearer picture of the category of the Salafi shaykhs, I classify them in two different subgroups.[21]

The *'ulama'* are the most knowledgeable and educated members of the Salafi community. Modern Western literature usually considers the *'ulama'* class in Sunni Islam to consist of those who possess some kind of formal religious education. According to Meir Hatina, the *'ulama'* are

---

[19] Almost all students at formal Islamic educational institutions, such as al-Azhar, told me that they participated in informal study circles on at least on a weekly basis besides their official curricula.

[20] According to my observations, many Kuwaiti shaykhs have much less authority over committed Salafi activists than their counterparts in Lebanon. Active participants often do not belong to one shaykh's network, but visit many. The reason for this probably lies in the fact that the average Kuwaiti Salafi is not dependent on a shaykh's patronage, unlike the Lebanese.

[21] Here I should stress that the following classification is blurred and can be applied only to the situation in Lebanon.

those "who acquired their formal religious training and credentials in established madrasas and religious colleges, and were identifiable by their attire of cloaks and turbans ('ama'im)."[22] The problem with this definition is that it does not cover fully those whom the wider Sunni community consider to be 'ulama'. Although most of the Salafis in Lebanon who belong to this class studied either at the Islamic University of Medina or in one of the Lebanese Salafi colleges, this is not always the case. To give an example, Shaykh Nur al-Din 'Ammar, a leading scholar from the Dinniyeh region, east of Tripoli, has never studied at any kind of religious college or university. He does not even possess a formal *ijaza* (license) from a recognized scholar. Rather, he acquired his knowledge in a wholly autodidactic fashion. Despite this, Shaykh Nur al-Din is regarded as one of the most knowledgeable Salafis in Lebanon. Thousands ask him to issue *fatwas*, and on Fridays around 600 people usually appear in his mosque to listen to his sermon. He has acquired wide recognition as a *hadith* scholar and arbitrator in the semi-tribal society of al-Dinniyeh.

In my opinion, Muhammad Qasim Zaman's definition of the *'ulama'* is most accurate. He argues that "it is a combination of their intellectual formation, their vocation, and crucially, their orientation viz., a certain sense of continuity with the Islamic tradition that defines the *'ulama'* as *'ulama'*..."[23] As Zaman explains, this is what distinguishes the *'ulama'* from modernists and Islamist intellectuals. The latter often share the belief "that one does not necessarily need that tradition [i.e. the Islamic intellectual and religious tradition] to understand the 'true' meaning of Islam, and that one certainly does not need the *'ulama'* to interpret Islam to the ordinary believers. That authority belongs to everyone and to no one in particular."[24] Although Salafis emphasize the need for everybody to be able to read and understand the Text, and will accept anyone's opinion after being assured by studying the sources, many of them still stress that the *'ulama'* are indispensable. According to them, society is in need of experts on the Qur'an and the Sunna who can draw the boundaries of religious interpretation. Furthermore, they also believe that it is important not to dismiss the intellectual tradition of Islam; that is, to use those parts of this tradition that are acceptable according to the Salafi interpretation. In Salafi writings – at least in the

---

[22] Meir Hatina, *Guardians of Faith in Modern Times: 'Ulama in the Middle East* (Leiden: Brill, 2009), p. 1.

[23] Muhammad Qasim Zaman, *The Ulama in Contemporary Islam* (Princeton, NJ: Princeton University Press, 2002), p. 10.

[24] Ibid., p. 10.

purist ones – when discussing a certain issue, the renowned 'ulama' of past centuries are usually quoted.

With this in mind, the description of 'ulama' should be applied to those who match the following criteria: first, those who rely on the Islamic intellectual tradition in building their religious authority. They act on this authority and provide the services the community expects from the 'ulama', such as providing believers with the interpretations of the scripture they need to live their daily lives as pious Muslims and performing certain religious services such as giving sermons or holding religious lessons. The second condition is to be recognized as an 'alim (religious scholar, sing.) by a substantial part of the fellow 'ulama' and the wider Sunni community. This last criterion is very important in light of the fact that many Salafis who are not considered 'ulama' still fulfill similar religious duties. Universal recognition, however, is prevented by the fact that many critics regard Salafism as a heretical and superficial ideology. Many Ash'ari 'ulama' with a Sufi orientation believe that a Salafi cannot be a scholar because what he represents is not 'ilm. A shaykh from Dar al-Fatwa told me that Salafis lack insight into the real meaning of the Scripture, and that their methods are instead confined to "hadith hustling," a term borrowed from Muhammad al-Ghazali.[25] Neither do Salafis recognize Sufis as 'ulama'. I have encountered activists who use the term 'alim only to refer to Salafi scholars, because those who follow other creeds and manhaj are "inventors" (mubtadi'un) and do not deserve to be regarded as scholars. Purist Salafis very often do not recognize harakis as 'ulama'. For example, both Shaykh Ihab and Safwan al-Za'bi told me that they do not recognize Shaykh Salim al-Rafa'i as an 'alim, although the latter is recognized by many non-Salafi religious specialists as such. They called him an agitator (muharrid) who misuses the scripture to disseminate political propaganda under a religious cloak.[26]

The 'ulama' are the backbone of the Salafi movement in Lebanon. Some of them even have transnational influence: Their publications are read in several Middle Eastern countries and Europe and they are in contact with other Salafi mosques, groups, and charities abroad. However, the majority of the Salafi 'ulama' only have local influence, which does not extend beyond their city quarters or villages. The 'ulama' are usually imams of mosques, or directors and senior teachers of religious colleges (ma'ahid shara'iyya). Usually, they have a number of students who regularly attend their religious lessons, which they give

[25] Interview, April 25, 2012.   [26] Interviews, Tripoli, April 26, 2012 and April 29, 2012.

in the mosques or in their homes. The *'ulama'* teach these religiously committed young individuals according to their specialization. Some shaykhs are experts in the *hadith*, while others are distinguished in *fiqh*. Most of the *'ulama'* are full-time religious scholars and earn their income exclusively from their religious activities. They tend to receive a salary from the *waqf* they administer – the money in many cases comes from sponsors in the Gulf – or from the college or university where they teach. Some of them also have private businesses, like Nur al-Din 'Ammar, who is a successful merchant as well.

To the category of the lesser-ranking shaykhs belong those individuals whose knowledge does not compare with that of the *'ulama'* but who are still counted among men of religion (see Chapter 4). In Northern Lebanon, people simply call these people "shaykhs" or sometimes *da'i*-s (preacher). Most of these individuals have never had any kind of religious education aside from participation in informal study circles. Despite this, they still possess a much higher level of knowledge about religion than ordinary people. Moreover, they are counted among those who have an outstanding level of religious commitment, since they tend to be established members of the Salafi *da'wa*. Therefore, the authority of these shaykhs is not built on *'ilm* (knowledge) to the extent that this is true of the *'ulama'*, but more on their mild asceticism. This piety is translated into deeds that are usually interpreted as sacrifices for the well-being and good of the community. This is because lesser-ranking shaykhs usually perform religious tasks without getting any kind of reward in return. Most of them earn their income from having a job or working in their own or others' private business.

These shaykhs have similar duties to the *'ulama'*. Many of them give *khutba*-s on Friday, hold religious lessons, and issue fatwas, although not on the same level as the *'ulama'*. They usually preach in small, less frequented mosques or *musallas*,[27] often in suburbs or villages. Their sermons are much simpler than those of the *'ulama'*, and their religious lessons are mostly attended by ordinary, less educated people. Those who intend to continue learning on a higher level usually go to the *'ulama'*. It is often the case that those who initially become involved in Salafism start taking lessons from these lesser-ranking shaykhs. If they want to deepen their knowledge, they start visiting the study circles of an *'alim*. The fatwas issued by the latter are only verbal and deal with simple issues in which it is possible to reach a conclusion with a somewhat limited knowledge of the *shari'a*. For more difficult issues,

---

[27] The term *"musalla"* in the Sham region means a building or space designated for prayer, but smaller than a mosque.

believers turn to the *'ulama'*. I want to emphasize that there are no clear boundaries between the two categories. While certain individuals might refer to a shaykh as *'alim*, others might refuse to do so, on the grounds he still does not possess enough knowledge.

5.2.2   Active Followers of Salafism

Shaykhs are usually surrounded by a relatively small but growing number of active followers; in Tripoli alone, I would estimate this to consist of between three and four thousand individuals, mostly young people aged between 18 and 45, from all social classes. They follow a Salafi lifestyle by trying to apply all of the rulings of the Salafi interpretation of Islam. Wearing a beard and (most of the time) Islamic clothing is therefore mandatory for them. They also try to perform all Islamic rituals in what Salafism deems the correct manner.

The majority of them have particularly close bonds with one specific shaykh whom they regard as their spiritual leader. They attend his lessons and listen to his sermons more frequently, and often receive economic support from him in exchange for assisting him in his activities. The shaykh can even pay a regular salary to those disciples who assist him, for example, in taking care of the mosque. Others regularly visit families who belong to the shaykh's constituency but whom he does not have the time to visit personally. Students also can fulfill a quasi-secretarial function by editing the shaykh's publications or arranging for the printing and distribution of books and leaflets for the wider follower base. The relationship between students and shaykhs is not mainly based on economic considerations, as the amount of money that these disciples receive is not particularly high, mostly 200–300 USD a month.

Having a special relationship with one mentor, however, does not prevent these committed Salafis from joining the study groups of other shaykhs and scholars, and some of them visit a different mosque each week to listen to the Friday sermon. Different shaykhs focus on different disciplines, and students prefer taking lessons from the most renowned shaykh in every field of Islamic sciences. Therefore, it is not unusual to see these committed Salafis visiting the study group of a *haraki* shaykh about *fiqh* one day, while on another day they might be present at a *hadith* lecture by a purist scholar. When I asked why they did this, they usually answered that Muslims should listen to the opinions of more than one person; otherwise this can lead to *bid'a*, or in the worst case, *taqdis* (sanctification) of persons, which is regarded as a lesser *shirk*. The most candid of them also gave me another reason: Many young Salafis aspire to become *da'is* and highly respected *'ulama'* in the future. Finishing their studies at universities in Saudi Arabia or Kuwait greatly facilitates their careers. Since Salafi shaykhs have extensive transnational contacts, having more than one influential shaykh among their close contacts naturally increases their chances and can help to further these young people's ambitions.

Ideologically, it is not always possible to classify these aspiring scholars. They are frequently in contact with both *haraki* and purist *'ulama'*, and read the literature of both factions; they may even vacillate between purist and jihadi teachings. In extreme cases, they can be the pupils of an ordinary *haraki* or purist shaykh who does not support violence, but secretly visit militant cells and slowly adopt their way of thinking. That happened with four of the students of a prominent Palestinian *haraki* shaykh in the Nahr al-Barid refugee camp. They regularly attended the lessons of their mentor, who is highly critical of *jihadis*, and aided him in performing his daily religious duties. However, in 2007, when a battle broke out between Fath al-Islam and the Lebanese army, they fought in the front lines on the side of the militants. Two of them were killed, and two were captured and are still being held in the Roumiyeh prison. The *haraki* shaykh suspects that they had been influenced by radical shaykhs years before the incident.[28]

One should note here that horizontal, interpersonal relationships are especially dense among these young, committed Salafis, and sometimes even stronger than the vertical bonds to the shaykhs. Through these networks, they exchange not only ideas but also material resources. Being Salafi gives them a sense of belonging to a community other than their kinship group. During my fieldwork, I observed the presence of such informal associations between these committed Salafis. They often help each other find jobs or just survive the harshness of the economic conditions in North Lebanon. Such voluntary, informal associations are extremely important in the organization of society in the Middle East.

These associations are not forged on the basis of kinship; rather, religion and predicament (i.e. similar economic conditions) are the organizing factors. Since these young men come from various economic backgrounds, the only factor that creates a kind of group identity is Salafism. As one of my informants explained, there are two reasons for

---

[28] Interview, Tripoli, November 24, 2009.

helping each other. First, Salafis have the sense of belonging to the vanguard representing the true community of God[29] in a society that is composed of a mosaic of different sects and ethnic groups – most of whom are heretics and unbelievers in their eyes. Believers should help each other in order to defend *Ahl al-Sunna wa'l-Jama'a* in this environment. Second, Salafis can rely on each other and expect that the other will return the favor, since honesty forms a major part of their religion. In other words, these networks are held together by ideology and reciprocity.

During fieldwork in Lebanon between 2009 and 2012, I was able to follow a case that illustrates the mechanism of the informal associations. One of my informants, Hasan, helped one of the members of the local Salafi network to get out of a hopeless economic situation. Hasan belongs to the network that has developed around one of the famous Salafi educational institutions, Dar al-Hadith. By teaching there and participating in the religious lessons given by different shaykhs, he managed to get access to various patron–client networks. When one of his Salafi acquaintances, Ahmad (22), from Tripoli's Tabbaneh district, lost his father in a car accident, Hasan was able to help him. The family's only income came from Ahmad's father's business. After his death, they had to find a way to survive, since they could not expect any long-term assistance from their relatives, who live in impoverished city quarters or in the villages of 'Akkar province (north of Tripoli). Hasan was able to ask one of the shaykhs teaching at Dar al-Hadith to donate money to the family from the funds provided by the Shaykh 'Aid Charity Association. Following this emergency solution, Ahmad got a job in Qatar thanks to the contacts that the same shaykh had there.

5.2.3   The Passive Followers

After the shaykhs and the active followers at the third level, we find what I will call the shaykhs' passive followers: they are numerous, but their level of commitment is more moderate than that of the active Salafis. These individuals are ordinary people who are attracted by the Salafis' religious knowledge, ascetic behavior, and perceived altruistic social activities (see Chapter 4). This means that the Salafis possess varying degrees of authority over them. Common to the group, though,

---

[29] He purposefully called it *shi'at Allah* (*shi'a* means party or community in Arabic).

is the fact that they do not fully apply the rulings of Salafism: they may shave their beards, they may smoke, and in some cases, their wives and daughters do not wear headscarves; yet they do take part in Friday prayers and listen to sermons, and they may even attend the shaykh's religious lessons.

Many of the passive followers have regular contact with the shaykh, and they may ask services of him, such as arbitration in disputes. These networks are held together not only by religious sentiment; patronage also plays an important role, as it does throughout Lebanese society. Families living in dire economic conditions often receive support from the *waqf* administered by the shaykh. In return, they attend the shaykh's Friday sermons and send their children to him to teach them religion. At the same time, Salafi shaykhs often receive economic support from their followers, who pay their *zakat* to the *waqf* or even give voluntary support. As Shaykh Ra'id Hulayhil, the director of *Ma'had al-Amin* (Amin Religious School), told me, a large part of the income of Salafi educational institutions and endowments comes from the merchant families of Tripoli.

The social composition of the passive followers is quite diverse and members of almost all segments of society are present among them, although in my observations, the majority belongs either to the pious middle class or to the urban poor.[30] The former sympathize with the Salafi shaykhs for two main reasons. First, for the members of the pious middle class, belonging to Sunnism and the larger Islamic *umma* has always been an important aspect of their identity. Historically, and in the twentieth century at least, they have always sided with those political forces that in one way or another gained legitimacy due to their attempts to unify the Islamic Nation against foreign oppressors.[31] In Chapter 2, I showed that Arab Nationalism and the Muslim Brotherhood type of Islamism lost much of their credibility in the eyes of Lebanese Sunnis. This contributes to the Salafis' chance to gain followers among the members of the pious middle class. As mentioned earlier Salafis blame both secular nationalists and Islamists for the current miserable predicament of Muslims. They say that these political movements have adopted a way of thinking and action that is alien to the religion. In their view, the movements have contributed to the loss of the tradition of *Ahl al-Sunna*, which is rooted in Islam, leading in particular to the sociopolitical decline of the Sunnis in Lebanon. Salafis

---

[30] I use here the terms of Gilles Kepel; Kepel, *Jihad*, pp. 1–22.

[31] Khalaf, *Civil and Uncivil Violence in Lebanon*, pp. 113–114; Sune Haugbolle, *War and Memory in Lebanon* (New York, NY: Cambridge University Press, 2010), p. 35.

often pose as those who will revive this tradition and thereby improve the situation of the Sunni community.[32]

Second, members of the pious middle class frequently interact with the shaykhs in socioeconomic matters. Since many Salafis belong to the latter group, this presupposes strong ties with them. Beyond using the religious services provided by Salafis, merchants or professionals often are connected to them via patron–client networks.

Salafis are also able to relieve the suffering of the Sunni urban poor in the Tabbana and Qubba districts. Many of them are unemployed and find it extremely difficult to provide for their families. Salafis are able to utilize their frustration and recruit followers among them. Preachers argue that the dominant political forces have neglected the northern territories of Lebanon because they are populated mostly by Sunnis. In their discourse, they often draw comparisons between the dynamic economic development of the Shi'i South and the poverty-stricken North. They claim that the Shi'i community wants to dominate Lebanon and weaken the Sunnis as much as possible (see Chapter 7). At the same time, Salafis are quite active in supporting poor Sunnis, by occasionally giving them financial aid, and helping them to find jobs, which further increases the number of their followers.

Passive followers do not exclusively listen to Salafi rhetoric. They are also receptive to the messages of other currents in Islam, such as the Muslim Brothers, *Tabligh*, Sufis, or the *Dar al-Fatwa* shaykhs. In the contest for the soul of Sunni Muslims, the Salafis have fierce competitors. At the time of writing, however, it seems that Salafis are gaining more ground among ordinary Sunnis than other Islamic movements.

5.2.4 The Difference between the Haraki and the Purist Networks

Haraki and purist networks are similar insofar as they rely on informal ties, and the shaykh–follower relationship dominates their structure. Yet, during my fieldwork I discovered some differences. Purist networks generally contain fewer passive followers, and the ratio of committed Salafis in them is somewhat higher. It means that, for example, in religious lessons held by purist Salafi shaykhs I could see fewer ordinary believers. More often than in the case of *haraki*s these lessons were dominated by the active participants.

---

[32] Salafis tend to ignore the fact that the traditions of the Lebanese Sunni community are largely rooted in Sufism.

The main reason for this difference is that purists in general spend much less time dwelling on actual political issues than the *harakis*. Politico-purists only participate in politics to secure the autonomy of their *da'wa* and increase their economic capital by having the backing of the Lebanese *zu'ama*.[33] As I pointed out earlier, purists in Lebanon chiefly criticize the Shi'ites' religious beliefs but often refrain from linking the latter's ostensible heresy to contemporary conflicts in the Middle East. Unlike the purists, in the case of the *harakis* (as I discussed in Chapter 3 and will show in Chapter 7 more in detail), the conspiracy theories that they create on the basis of the Shi'ites' ostensible distortion from true Islam play a great role in increasing the *haraki* Salafis popularity.

While *haraki* Salafi shaykhs often attract hundreds, sometimes thousands of attendees to their Friday sermons (such as in the case of Salim al-Rafa'i and Zakariyya al-Masri), purists most often only attract dozens who to their *khutba*. Many of the audience are themselves committed Salafis. The purist sermons rarely touch popular topics such as Sunni–Shi'ite tensions and the Syrian conflict. When purist shaykhs talk about the latter, they usually condemn both the Syrian regime's atrocities and the Salafi members of the armed opposition, such as *al-Nusra* front. Yet, most frequently, purist sermons are about topics such as how marriage looks in Islam, or the necessity to respect and obey someone's parents. Purist shaykhs in their religious lessons discuss issues that touch minute details of worship, or teach a book from one of the classical scholars such as Ibn Taymiyya or Ibn Qayyim that is often not interesting and inaccessible for ordinary believers but attractive to committed Salafis.

5.3   The Evolution of Extended Networks

In order to understand how the subnetworks discussed in Section 5.2 evolve into larger network structures, I first have to explain what makes the networks of Salafism cohesive and distinguishable from other networks. A system of shared values and symbols, commonly referred to as "collective identity," plays an important role in this.

According to the observations of scholars who have focused on social movements in the west or Islamic movements, such as the Muslim Brotherhood, the collective identity of these movements presupposes

---

[33] See also Chapters 3 and 4.

a clear entity with a declared aim of achieving a specific kind of societal change.[34] The collective identity of members is based on the perceived existence of a clearly defined movement. Salafism, however, is a different case. Often, Salafis do not identify themselves with a movement; they do not even recognize that they belong to a movement. Many of them say that Salafism is an idea (*fikr*), which is equal to the pure version of Islam followed by the Prophet and the first Muslims. They refuse to regard Salafism as one of the many Islamic movements, which they often regard as aberrant (*dall*). According to my observations, the average Salafi sees himself as an individual who intends to fulfill what God demands from him, whether it be performing rituals or correcting the belief and practices of other people. He does not regard himself as an activist, only as someone who has a special commitment to his religion.

In light of the above, we need a different way to approach the construction of collective identity in the case of Salafism. Here, the concept of "aesthetic formations" elaborated by Meyer is very useful. She argues that a sense of belonging emerges between individuals when they share the same rituals, the same ideals of dress and behavior, and even the same notion of how to use language in everyday conversations.[35]

Groups that are held together by their "shared sensory experiences"[36] are known as "aesthetic formations."[37] As my field observations showed, the concept of aesthetic formations applies to Salafism in North Lebanon. The shared sensory experiences of Salafism are manifold. Here, I summarize the most obvious and common experiences that play the most important roles in constructing the movement's collective identity.

Dress codes are one of the main distinguishing features of Salafism. If somebody lets his beard grow long and shaves his moustache, it strongly indicates that he sympathizes with Salafi ideas. This can be complemented with a *dishdasha*, an ankle-length robe. As I laid out in Chapter 4, Salafis also use a distinct form of everyday discourse. Salafis prefer to attach religious references to almost every subject of

---

[34] Holland et al., "Social Movements and Collective Identity," p. 97; Khalil al-Anani, *Inside the Muslim Brotherhood: Religion, Identity, and Politics* (New York, NY: Oxford University Press, 2016), pp. 34–49; 118–134.

[35] Birgit Meyer, "From Imagined Communities to Aesthetic Formations: Religious Mediations, Sensational Forms, and Styles of Binding." In *Aesthetic Formations: Media, Religion, and the Senses*, edited by Birgit Meyer (New York, NY: Palgrave Macmillan, 2009) p. 5.

[36] Ibid., p. 9.   [37] Ibid., pp. 6–11.

conversation and frequently quote a *hadith* to prove their statements, even when discussing mundane matters. Salafis tend to frame even minor events in daily life according to their worldview, especially in religious matters; their discourse is almost completely lacking in ambiguities.

Their everyday talk is infused with symbols from the Qur'an. For example, a young Salafi shaykh in one of the old quarters of Tripoli once gave me the following explanation for why children are often impolite in his neighborhood: "In our quarter people do everything mindlessly and God is not in the center of their lives. When a husband and wife make love they neglect to perform two sets of prayers (*raka'tayn*) before the act. Therefore Satan penetrates the wife together with the husband and their child is affected by the Devil."[38] Among the important shared sensory experiences are the performing of rituals such as prayer in what is regarded as the correct way and using symbols such as a black flag with *la ilaha ill-allah* (there is no God but God) written in white script.

Having shared sensory experiences implies having a similar world-view. These sensory experiences, however, take on varying significance in the lives of different individuals. It is possible to observe that they play a more important role in the lives of committed Salafis than those of passive followers, for example. The latter rarely follow the code of dress, but most probably do adopt certain elements of the Salafi universe of discourse, such as framing current sectarian tensions in terms of the Manichean conflict between *iyman* and *taghut*. The more important a role they play in someone's life, the more likely he is to be involved in a Salafi network. In other words, the more the elements and symbolism of Salafism form part of someone's social identity, the more he will participate in the movement's activities and the more likely he will be to identify with those who adopt the same elements and symbolism of Salafism as "we." Approached in this way, collective identity in Salafism is highly fluid and dynamic. It is often temporary in the case of many of the movement's followers.

This is particularly the case during sectarian tensions. Since the start of the Arab Spring and the Syrian revolution of 2011, which has been accompanied by increasing Sunni–Shi'i sectarianism, many Lebanese Sunnis have started to associate themselves with Salafism. During my stay in Tripoli at the time, I observed many ordinary Sunnis adopting the Salafi framing of the Syrian revolution as one of the signs of

---

[38] Interview, Tripoli, May 4, 2012.

Judgment Day (*'alamat al-sa'a*). Some individuals whom I had known previously, and were not particularly religious, now referred to Salafism more frequently in their everyday discourse. The displays of their mobile phones were decorated with symbols that are common among Salafis, such as quotes from the Qur'an and Hadith written in a modest style of Arabic calligraphy, or pictures of some of the renowned Salafi scholars, such as al-Albani. The shaykhs are often referred to as the leaders of the community.

Salafi network hubs usually evolve around activities that are intended to create, strengthen, and reinforce collective identity. These can be organized activities, such as the Friday sermon and religious lessons, or *ad hoc* ones, such as evening meetings between friends or discussions in the mosque. These gatherings are at the heart of the movement's network structure, as they provide space to establish interpersonal contacts. At the local level, informal, interpersonal gatherings are dominant due to the smallness of the geographical area, the feebleness and underdeveloped nature of the Lebanese state, and the cost of the modern communications infrastructure. The patterns of network intersections not only play a role in creating and transmitting symbols and other nonmaterial resources, but also fulfill important functions in the socialization of members. They provide them with space and opportunities to establish interpersonal contacts inside the movement and beyond, such as accessing patronage networks. These activities are not limited to religious lessons, evening gatherings, and discussions after prayers, but these three are the most influential.

During my fieldwork, I regularly attended Salafi *durus* religious lessons, evening gatherings, and after-prayer discussions. My close relationship to a number of young, committed Salafis was essential to gain access to these activities. Among these young people, my acquaintance to two seekers of knowledge (*tullab 'ilm*) was crucial to get deeper insight into the inner dynamics of Lebanese Salafism. The first is 'Uthman, a shopkeeper from al-Tabbana district in his mid-twenties. The second, 'Adnan, is a former soldier. Both of them belong to Tripoli's lower-middle classes and show exceptional eagerness in religious learning.

I met 'Uthman in late 2009 on central Tripoli's al-Tall square, where he managed his older brother's perfume shop. A friend, a middle-class Tripolitan trader who owned a cloth outlet in the area and whom I acquainted outside of my research, introduced me to him. Although 'Uthman had taken over the shop management two months earlier, he was already well known among the other traders of the area for his enthusiasm and knowledge of religion. My friend, who knew of my interest in Salafism, thought speaking to 'Uthman would be beneficial as 'Uthman was a Salafi himself. After chatting with 'Uthman a few times in his shop, he invited me to his house and introduced me to some of his friends. The fact that I had a friend among the traders of the area and was not unfamiliar to others in the area (as I also frequently stopped to drink a cup of coffee at one of the local coffee stalls and chatted with customers there) was immensely helpful to dispel his initial suspicion that I might work for one of the intelligence services.

'Uthman lived in the al-Tabbana district, where after years of saving he managed to establish himself financially; he bought a two-room apartment and got married. He came from a nonreligious family; 'Uthman himself was not a practicing Muslim until the age of nineteen when he first met shaykh Kamal who started to proselytize among the youth of al-Tabbana immediately after graduating from the Islamic University of Madinah. 'Uthman told me that even before becoming *multazim* he was very much interested in reading despite never getting beyond elementary school, and collected a lot of books mostly about history and Arabic literature. Shaykh Kamal convinced him that by reading about Islam, his passion about books would have an aim beyond just being a hobby. He would construct his way to Paradise by learning to distinguish true Islam from what the *mubtadi*'s (innovators) teach. 'Uthman finished a course on *'aqida* in Da'i al-Islam al-Shahhal's Ma'had al-Hidaya and became well connected in Tripoli's *haraki* networks. He participated at least once or twice a week in a religious lesson given by one of the Salafi shaykhs either in al-Tabbana or al-Qubba regions. He became one of my most important gateways to observe these lessons.

'Adnan, the other important person who helped me to participate in Salafi activities, is also a member of Tripoli's lower middle classes. When I first met him in 2011, he was in his early thirties. After studying mathematics for three years at the Lebanese University's Tripoli campus, he left higher education and became a soldier for three years. Later, he worked in a supermarket as a cashier. In 2011 and 2012, during my interviews, he did not work at all, in order to focus all his energy on the study of religion.

Unlike 'Uthman, 'Adnan came from a family that belongs to the pious middle class in the Qubba district. His father, a former militiaman in the Iraqi Ba'th Party,[39] was religious "in the traditional way" as 'Adnan described it, manifested by "fasting and praying without

---

[39] The Socialist Arab Lebanon Vanguard Party (*Hizb Tali'at Lubnan al-'Arabi al-Ishtiraki* - SALVP), or, as it is commonly known, the Iraqi Ba'th Party, was founded in Beirut

understanding why, (. . .) just simply because he inherited from his father" and occasionally participating in the *dhikr*s of the Qadiriyya Sufi order. 'Adnan, who in high school was interested in natural sciences, found his father's way "backward (*mutakhallif*)." Starting from the second year of high school he denied the existence of God. He told me that he even liked making jokes about Islam and even cursed.

One of his friends with Salafi leanings introduced him to the purist-rejectionist Shaykh Ihab (see Chapter 3). After long discussions, the shaykh convinced 'Adnan that science and religion go together as all rulings of God have a purpose that science approves.[40] While 'Adnan found a network of friends among Shaykh Ihab's students, he is not a purist-rejectionist himself, as he often joins religious lessons of scholars who are affiliated to the politico-purist network that emerged around Safwan al-Za'bi's Waqf al-Turath al-Islami. I met 'Adnan through Shaykh Safwan, who described him as an extremely eager and active *talib 'ilm* who could help me gain insight into how Tripoli's Salafis live.

Both 'Adnan and 'Uthman were eager to bring me to join Salafi activities, although for somewhat different reasons. The latter continuously wanted to convince me to convert to Islam. The former, also closer to my age, considered me as a colleague, a fellow *talib 'ilm*. He believed that as a researcher, I am looking for the truth but not in the right place. Perhaps by learning more about the true Islam I would be enlightened.

5.3.1 Religious Lessons

Religious lessons (*durus*, sing. *dars* or study circles – *halaqat*, sing. *halaqa*) are one of the earliest forms of knowledge transmission in Islam,[41] and remained the main method of religious education in the Muslim world until the twentieth century, when a modern, classroom type of learning became predominant. Religious lessons are also an integral part of the public space, since they serve as a forum for the exchange of views and for community affairs and other kinds of information. Historically,

in 1966. After the split of the Pan-Arab Ba'th party into a Syrian and an Iraqi wing in 1966, SALVP became affiliated to the latter.

[40] The Salafi prohibition of music was among the examples 'Adnan gave me, which is derived from one of the *ahadith*. He read an article online about how music disturbs the brainwaves and makes concentration difficult while studying. For him, the Prophet revealed this 1400 years ago.

[41] Jonathan Berkey, *The Formation of Islam: Religion and Society in the Near East, 600–1800* (Cambridge: Cambridge University Press, 2003), p. 225.

Islamic movements have utilized them as one of the chief avenues of mobilization.[42] Salafism in Lebanon has evolved from the *durus* and they remain one of the most important hubs in its network structure at the local level.

The lessons in Tripoli are held both in mosques and in private homes. Most *durus* are held by shaykhs. Other people can also give lessons, as long as they possess a certain level of religious education (the title of shaykh is not usually attached to their name). For example, professionals, doctors, and engineers who are well read in religious sciences and are widely thought to be knowledgeable are frequently invited by mosques to give lessons, mostly once a week or once every two weeks. During my fieldwork in Tripoli, I observed that the Salafi-oriented mosques I visited also promoted other *durus* given by Salafis in other places. The lessons are usually held after the *'asr* (mid-afternoon) or the *'isha'* (evening) prayer, mostly on Tuesdays, Thursdays, and Saturdays.

Although a wide range of religious lessons is available, taught by shaykhs with different affiliations (from Sufism to the Muslim Brotherhood), Salafis are especially active in teaching them. This is because they regard these lessons as being one the most effective means of *da'wa*, due to their informal character: They are based on discussions between the shaykh and the audience. Drawing on my observations, I estimate that about 60 percent of the study circles are held by Salafi individuals in Tripoli. In the surrounding areas of the city, this percentage is even higher. I witnessed three types, or three levels, of religious lessons in the area. Most of the lessons are held for the *'amma* or ordinary people. In such cases, the attendees do not have any substantial religious education but they do have a certain interest in expanding their religious knowledge. The second level is visited by *Talabat al-'Ilm* or "knowledge seekers." These individuals intend to deepen their knowledge of the religious sciences and often aspire to be shaykhs in the future. The third level is for the preachers of the mosques who are themselves part of the vanguard of the Salafi movement.

Religious lessons continue to be at the center of the public sphere in Tripoli. Many people visit them in order to expand their religious knowledge and to seek answers to questions about daily life. Therefore, these lessons provide an excellent opportunity for the Shaykhs to disseminate the message of Salafism. For most people in Tripoli and North Lebanon, *durus* are one of the main ways to access a somewhat deeper level of religious knowledge and to synthetize and reaffirm

---

[42] Clark, "Islamist Women in Yemen," pp. 174–177.

what they have learnt from other sources. When a Salafi shaykh gives the lesson, he obviously gives answers from a Salafi viewpoint and shapes the religious imagination of the participants in a way that is identical to Salafism. Due to the Salafis' extended religious authority in the North, religious lessons are currently strongly influencing the religious behavior of the participants.

At the same time, religious lessons function as spaces where people can establish new interpersonal relationships and connect to networks; often friendships emerge, especially between the younger participants. Those who participate frequently also have the chance to get closer to the shaykhs and establish contacts that can facilitate their lives in mundane matters such as access to patronage or receiving charity. The religious lessons are also occasions on which committed Salafis can regularly meet each other. Therefore, they serve as important spaces for exchanging information about intramovement matters.

'Uthman frequently brought me to attend the lessons of Shaykh Kamal, who had *haraki* leanings. The thirty-two-year-old *'alim* gives most of his lessons to ordinary people three times a week in different mosques in al-Tabbana. Perhaps most frequently, he teaches in the 'Ibad al-Rahman mosque, which is located in the middle of the city quarter, where he has a stable schedule every Thursday between the *maghrib* and *'isha'* prayers. I often participated in his religious lessons in this mosque because its imam personally gave his approval for me to join, which made the other participants more welcoming.

Shaykh Kamal's lessons were usually attended by a handful of men (between ten and twenty, although during Ramadan, the number of the participants can reach fifty), although their number has been growing substantially since I first started conducting fieldwork in Tripoli in 2009. The lessons are attended by both Sunni Muslims who live secular lifestyles, and by committed Salafis. There was always a "core" of participants who regularly participate in the same lessons, but there is also a high degree of fluctuation. Most of the participants, due to al-Tabbana's social makeup, belonged to the pious middle-class and the urban poor. The majority were shop keepers, mechanics, and workers who often had no stable jobs.

Shaykh Kamal usually begins his lessons with a reading from one of the collections of the prophetical tradition. He chooses a *hadith* that can be interpreted to give an answer to a topical social problem or ethical question. Most of the lessons touch on issues like how to solve disputes over property or money, how to treat women, divorce, or the importance of performing religious rituals regularly and in the correct way. Since the Arab revolutions, politics has become a frequent topic of religious lessons. After reading the original text, the shaykh explains the meaning in colloquial language. Then, the attendants are free to ask questions. In the next phase, Shaykh Kamal comments on the content of the *hadith* in order to raise a current issue. After giving his opinion on the given problem or question, the audience is free to ask further questions. During a religious lesson, which usually lasts between forty minutes and one hour, two or three *ahadith* are discussed.

These study circles – unlike the *khutba* or lessons that take the form of a lecture – feature a fair amount of give and take between the shaykh and his audience, and they also differ from religious lessons in other places. For example, Richard Antoun describes religious lessons in a Jordanian village that are characterized by a top-down structure. The shaykh dominates the discussion and the audience does not challenge his arguments in any way.[43] In Tripoli, the situation is different. On many occasions, I noticed members of the audience expressing their own opinions and adding their own arguments or interpretations of the texts. This is especially true if a large number of committed Salafis are present. In some cases, the purpose of their presence is to challenge the shaykh, whose opinions they disagree with. Fierce debates often arise between the participants themselves, which continue even after the formal end of the lesson.

'Adnan frequently brought me to the lessons of Shaykh Ihab. Shaykh Ihab's lessons are quite distinct from Shaykh Kamal's. They are not advertised or open to the public, only to a small number of committed Salafi youth. If somebody wants to join, it is necessary to have the prior agreement of the shaykh and the other participants. Shaykh Ihab is a young man in his early thirties and belongs to the purist faction. He holds a Master's degree from the Islamic University of Medina and also studied at the study circles of Rabi' al-Madkhali and other purist authorities. When he came back from Saudi Arabia around 2007–2008, he started to teach some of the enthusiastic youth.

In his religious lessons, Shaykh Ihab does not focus on the basics, but instead reads and explains a book (at that time, *al-Fatawa al-Kubra* by Ibn Taymiyya[44]) that requires advanced religious knowledge.

---

[43] Richard T. Antoun, "Themes and Symbols in the Religious Lesson: A Jordanian Case Study," *International Journal of Middle East Studies*, 25, no. 4 (1993), pp. 610–611.

[44] This collection of Ibn Taymiyya's fatwas is one of the main classical sources of contemporary Salafism. Most of the active participants learn some of the volumes (it consists of six volumes) with instruction from a more knowledgeable individual during informal religious lessons. The fatwas touch on various topics, such as matters of theology, creed, or *hadith*.

Consequently, the discussion afterwards is more sophisticated as well. When I was observing the *durus*, strong friendships had evolved between the participants in Shaykh Ihab's *halaqat*, who frequently engage in *da'wa* activities together. For example, from time to time they travel to the Dinniya region, where one of the young men has a house in one of the villages. They spend one or two nights there holding discussions on *'aqida* and *fiqh*. On these occasions some of the villagers also join them, and they answer their questions regarding religious matters. During the day, they often travel around the neighboring towns and villages and visit Salafis living there. Religious lessons perhaps provide one the most structured spaces for knowledge transmission in the Salafis' case. Yet, besides religious lessons, there are other important, more spontaneous spaces for religious exchanges.

5.3.2   Evening Gatherings

In evening gatherings (*sahrat*, sing. *sahra*) mostly young people gather at the home of one of them or just on the street in their neighborhood. Such events are common in every Arab society. In some places they are even institutionalized, such as the *diwaniyyas* in Kuwait. In Tripoli *sahrat* are largely informal, but nevertheless play a significant role in the everyday lives of the city's inhabitants. *Sahrat* in Tripoli are mostly spontaneous, and people usually participate in such events once or twice a week. The participants are friends and family members, and generally belong to the younger generation in their twenties and thirties. Unlike the *diwaniyyas* where people discuss certain topics or engage in activities like playing music or reciting poems, in the *sahrat* they talk about various issues in daily life. When Salafis hold these gatherings, the sahrat are dominated by topics related to Islam.

I participated in several *sahrat* in 'Uthman's house. Beyond joining *durus*, at least once a week, he invites his friends for *sahrat*, mostly on Thursday or Friday evenings. Most of the participants are young men of the same age or a little older. When I attended *sahrat* in 'Uthman's home, there were usually about six or seven people there. Most of them lived in the same street as 'Uthman, and others knew him from the mosques that he usually attends. We started with coffee and small talk. After a while, religious topics came up. Usually, we would discuss some *ahadith* that arose in relation to our previous conversation, or questions such as whether the *khimar* (a piece of cloth covering the

Muslim woman's face) is obligatory for women or not.[45] At the time (in 2011 and 2012), our discussions frequently touched on the Syrian revolution. The Salafis expressed their reading of the events in accordance with their dualistic worldview. In their opinion, the revolution was a struggle between Islam and the realm of unbelief. The Syrian opposition belonged to the first category, while those who opposed them to the second.[46] They often give weight to their words by showing and exchanging videos, uploaded to their mobile phones, about martyrdom or how the regime's soldiers are abusing the symbols of Islam. Once they even discussed Yusuf al-Qaradawi's last statements on his website, vehemently opposing his interpretations of parts of the Qur'an.[47]

It is obvious that these *sahrat* are important spaces for reinforcing and strengthening collective identity. Since non-Salafis often participate alongside Salafis, these events play a key role in exporting the movement's ideas and in recruitment as well. Just as in the religious lessons, networks frequently intersect in the evening gatherings. Since there is a high degree of fluctuation in the participants, due to the highly informal character of these events, new contacts are often established. Younger shaykhs also show up from time to time to maintain and strengthen contact with their constituency and perform *da'wa* among the uncommitted participants.

5.3.3   Discussions after Prayer

Many of my Salafi informants told me that after performing prayers, they often sit down with other Salafis in the mosque for 10–20 minutes. I witnessed these discussions a number of times myself when either 'Uthman or 'Adnan made it possible for me to attend them. During these occasions, the conversation often evolves into a discussion about religion. This is the most spontaneous form of collective gathering in the movement, yet it provides an opportunity for the circulation of discourse and the strengthening of network ties.

---

[45] There is a disagreement between Salafis regarding this matter. According to al-Albani there is no evidence in the Text that women have to cover their faces, while many *ahadith* point out that the face can be exposed. Others argue the opposite. See: http://maktabasalafiya.blogspot.com/2011/06/shaykh-alabanis-position-of-niqab-of .html (accessed October 7, 2012).

[46] See also Chapter 7.

[47] Purist Salafis often disagree with al-Qaradawi's views. They have been criticizing him publicly, especially since the 2011 Arab Spring, mostly because al-Qaradawi, based in Qatar, is a vocal supporter of the revolutions.

In Islam, praying in the mosque is preferred to performing prayer at home. Therefore, when they are not preoccupied by more urgent matters, Salafis usually pray in the mosque.

People usually spend a little more time in the mosque after the afternoon prayer (*salat al-'asr*), reading the Qur'an or simply chatting. My Salafi informants tended to use these occasions to discuss current religious topics. As one of them explained, these small after-prayer gatherings are excellent opportunities for expanding one's religious knowledge. Since many Salafis do not always pray in the same mosque, these after-prayer discussions allow them to exchange their views with many different people. At most of these meetings the participants talk about different interpretations of parts of the Text, like Qur'an verses or *ahadith*. These discussions are often connected to actual political or social issues such as the clashes between the Sunni militias of al-Tabbana and the 'Alavites in Jabal Muhsin. Another frequent topic is the Shi'a's perceived attempt to sideline Sunnis in Lebanon.

Like *durus*, these small meetings after prayer are primary spaces in which to establish and maintain network ties and circulate within the movement. One of my informants described their importance very eloquently:

Even though I do not have time to go frequently to participate in *halaqat* and spend much time with people who have the same views on Islam, meeting with other Salafi friends in the mosque after the *'asr* prayer shows me that there is still a community of Muslims who give religion priority in their lives. Ten minutes of chat in the mosque gives me the sense of belonging to a true brotherhood and reinforces my commitment to the Book and what the Prophet taught us. Otherwise I would be too preoccupied with daily problems to pay enough attention to God, like most of the Muslims in Tripoli.[48]

Religious lessons, *shahrat*, and discussions after prayers function as important "free spaces" for Salafism in times of political repression. When it is difficult to express one's views openly or act freely in wider society, free spaces provide opportunities for participants of movements to discuss their beliefs and ideas and exchange information, skills, and expertise without risk.[49]

For Lebanese Salafis, both after the battle of Dinniya at the turn of 1999 and 2000 between Salafi militants and the Lebanese army, which was followed by a huge wave of arrests and the oppression of Islamic

---

[48] Interview with an active participant of Salafism, August 1, 2011.
[49] Francesca Polletta, "Free Spaces in Collective Action," *Theory and Society*, 28, no. 1 (1999).

movements, and after the battle of Nahr al-Barid in 2007, it was not safe to communicate openly and engage in obvious *da'wa* activity. For example, criticizing Shi'is or Hizbullah during the Friday sermon could lead to imprisonment. At this time, the movement's activities largely withdrew to the *halaqat*, *sahrat*, and to other forms of informal, private discussions. Narratives and discourses, as well as solidarity and network ties, were preserved and have been utilized during the current period of upheaval in Lebanese Salafism.

5.4   Formal Institutional Structure

Salafism in Lebanon has a loose institutional structure consisting of religious colleges and charity institutions. However, there are no formal links connecting them, only informal ties based on interpersonal relations. These institutions nevertheless play an important role in the movement, as network intersections both at the local and transnational levels. In Tripoli and its surroundings there are approximately seven or eight religious colleges (*ma'had shara'i*). Most of them provide their graduates with secondary school degrees, and some of them have been granted the right by the Islamic University of Medina to award Bachelor's and Master's degrees (as in the case of Shaykh Da'i al-Islam al-Shahhal's *Ma'had al-Hidaya wa'l-Ihsan*. The *ma'had*s are central hubs in interpersonal networks, since many of the Salafi shaykhs in Tripoli gain their main income by teaching in one or more of these institutions. Therefore, the *ma'had*s function as spaces for networking, and strong friendship networks usually emerge around the employees and the students.

The colleges also play an important role in conveying the Salafi message to society. People who do not know much about Salafism often join them for one or two courses in order to extend their religious knowledge. They function as alternatives for those who are otherwise unable to get any kind of education. The *ma'had*s also run summer courses for primary and secondary school students, where they gain a basic knowledge of religion (according to the Salafi understanding).

Other types of formal institutions are charities in the form of *waqf*s. Sometimes they are connected to mosques and *ma'had*s and take part in financing their maintenance. More often, the *waqf*s provide financial and other types of support and alms to those who are living in poverty or cannot pay their medical costs.

The networks that intersect in the informal activities and the loose network of *ma'had*s and *waqf*s have resulted in a polysepalous movement structure that lacks significant formal organization. Leadership in Salafism is largely based on personal charisma and access to financial resources. Some Salafis have attempted to streamline the movement, at least in Tripoli, without any success. Most of these initiatives have met fierce resistance from the majority of Salafis.

Initiatives to create a loose organizational framework, one that can draw Salafis and their supporters together regularly to adjust their activities and exchange information without creating a formal leadership structure and imposing obligations, have been more successful. In the first half of 2012, *haraki* shaykhs under the leadership of Salim al-Rafi'i and Zakariyya al-Masri created a weekly *shura* (council).[50] It consists of two levels; one for the *'amma* (ordinary people) and one for the *khassa* (elite), in which prominent shaykhs participate. The former is held every Monday in the Taqwa mosque after *salat al-maghrib* (late afternoon prayers). Usually between five and ten shaykhs participate, along with leading figures from local families (mostly from the Tabbana and Qubba districts) and a number of young Salafis and sympathizers.

This event provides a forum to discuss the affairs of the communities in different city districts. It makes decisions on such matters as whether they should fight the Alawites in Jabal Muhsin and organize a militia against them, or whether they should instead rely on the Lebanese Army and the government's other security forces. The idea of organizing demonstrations in support of the Salafi detainees (mentioned earlier) also emerged from the *shura*. During the council, Salafis also raise money for Syrian refugees. Quite obviously, the aim is to utilize the temporarily heightened popularity of the Salafi shaykhs (as a side effect of the Arab and the Syrian revolutions) and promote them as de facto leaders of the Sunni community in the North.

Many Salafis distance themselves from this *shura*, accusing Salim al-Rafi'i in particular of using it to promote his personal ambition of becoming the leading religious authority in Tripoli. One of the prominent purist shaykhs told me that it is incorrect to call such a gathering a *shura*. In his view, *shura* should be called together by *wali al-amr* and not an imam of a mosque, "even if he receives a lot of money from Qatar and Sa'd al-Hariri."[51]

---

[50] The *shura* (consultation in Arabic) is rooted in Arab tribal traditions and refers to a consultation body. In early Islamic history it was the advisory body of the Rashidun Caliphs. Later it was reinterpreted several times. In the Arab Gulf, the advisory bodies of the rulers are also called *shura*, as are the different decision-making councils of Islamic movements such as the Muslim Brotherhood or Hizbullah. See "Shura," in Bosworth, *Encyclopaedia of Islam*; Ahmad Nizar Hamzeh, *In the Path of Hizbullah* (Syracuse and New York, NY: Syracuse University Press, 2004), pp. 45–48.

[51] Interview, April 26, 2012.

The second level of the *shura* is more exclusive and secretive, and includes only an inner circle of Salafi shaykhs. As a researcher, I was not allowed to participate. According to one of its members, this circle decides which issues to discuss at the gathering that is open to the *'amma*. The Committee of Muslim Scholars that I discussed in detail in Chapter 3 also grew out of the *shura* by expanding the latter to include Salafi shaykhs from outside of Tripoli, and non-Salafis as well. It remains to be seen, however, whether CMS accomplishes institutionalization of *haraki* Salafism. *Haraki*s of Tripoli too, even though to a lesser degree than purist Salafis, are deeply suspicious of formal organizations, which might not play in favor of CMS in the long run.

5.5   Conclusion

In Northern Lebanon, local Salafi networks stand and fall with the authority of the shaykhs. Salafis mainly rely on informal structures due to the repression they face by the state authorities, and because Salafi teachings often reject formal institutions because the latter is seen as creating divisions among Muslims.

In these networks, religious leaders, surrounded by both active participants and passive followers, are the most important nodes. As we saw, *haraki* networks are more extended among passive followers, while the ratio of committed Salafis is higher in the purist networks. Moreover, these networks are held together by a collective identity that is based on shared sensory experiences, such as performing rituals in the same way, having the same ideas of dress, and having the same concept of using language in everyday conversations. Salafi networks usually evolve around activities that reinforce this kind of collective identity, such as religious lessons, evening gatherings, and discussions after prayer in the Lebanese case.

Lebanese Salafism also possesses a loose institutional structure, which is composed mainly of religious colleges and charity endowments. However, unifying the ranks of Salafis within one clear-cut political organization has so far proved impossible. Setting up a loose organizational framework, such as the *shura*, which has been created by some of the prominent Salafi shaykhs in Tripoli, seems to be proving a more successful initiative. Yet, it remains to be seen whether the evolution of this *shura* to CMS will be a successful venture in terms of organizing Salafis.

Analyzing the network structure at the local level is crucial for understanding the evolution of transnational networks, as I will show in the cases of Sweden or Kuwait in the next chapter.

6   Transnational Networks of Lebanese Salafis

Local Salafi networks extend beyond Lebanon's borders; they form parts of large, transnational webs. Using ethnographic data from three countries, this chapter will look at how interpersonal networks evolve from Lebanon to other countries, with a special focus on the function of transnational charity organizations. Just like local networks, transnational Salafi networks are also largely informal – institutional structures are not elaborate but are rather embedded in a dense web of informal links.

In the first part of the chapter, I examine the structure of transnational networks, show the role of shaykhs, active participants and charities in them, and discuss the different character of *haraki* and purist networks. In the second half of the chapter, I illustrate the significance of informal networking and the Salafi charities in the Gulf, using the examples of two Salafi shaykhs who became participants in the movement in Lebanon, but later pursued their *da'wa* in Europe.

6.1   Transnational Networks in the Muslim World, Past and Present

Since the emergence of Islam, there have been extensive transnational exchanges in the Muslim world. In the pre-modern period, social networks connected the Middle East with Africa and Central, South, and Southeast Asia.

Religion was the key motive for travel and establishing transnational links with other Muslims. The annual pilgrimage to Mecca (*Hajj*), for example, served as a major source of the establishment of long-distance contacts, and was encouraged by Islamic teachings.[1] People in the medieval Dar al-Islam frequently traveled thousands of miles to visit

---

[1] Eickelman and Piscatori, *Muslim Politics*, p. 5.

the shrines of holy persons (*wali*). These shrines often constituted nodes of extended Sufi networks: In the medieval Muslim world, Sufi *tariqas* connected regions such as Central Asia and Anatolia,[2] India and Southeast Asia,[3] and Yemen and the Malay Archipelago.[4] These orders provided assistance to their followers, even if they had to travel large distances.

Networks often emerged of centers of worship and religious learning. Travel for the sake of studying (*rihla li-talab al-'ilm*) was of fundamental importance in facilitating exchange between Muslim societies.[5] Seeking knowledge in highly respected centers of learning such as the sacred cities of Hijaz, or in intellectual centers such as Cairo, often increased the religious authority of scholars after they had returned home.[6] For example, already before the twentieth century, large numbers of Muslims from the Malay Archipelago stayed in Mecca and Medina for years after performing the Hajj in order to obtain religious knowledge. Some of the most renowned scholars among them played a crucial role in spreading the Sufi intellectual tradition and establishing affiliation to Sufi orders in their home regions.[7]

Religious networks were often intertwined with trade in the premodern Islamic world. Through its religious and trade networks, the Hadrami (from Hadramaut) diaspora established a presence in several parts of the Islamic world. In Southeast Asia, East Africa, and Malabar they married local women, created communities with a creole identity and extended civil society networks. "Throughout this space, a Hadrami could travel and be put up by relatives, who might be Arab uncles married to foreign, local aunts."[8] '*Ulama*' as well as merchants could rely on these contacts during their travels or when setting up their businesses or activities in a foreign place with a Hadrami community.

This mobility was further supported by the political systems of the Islamic world: Pre-colonial Muslim societies were ruled by sultanates

---

[2] Dina Le Gall, *A Culture of Sufism: Naqshbanīs in the Ottoman World, 1450–1700*. Albany: State University of New York Press, 2005.

[3] Ahmad Fauzi Abdul Hamid, "The Impact of Sufism on Muslims in Pre-Colonial Malaysia: An Overview of Interpretations," *Islamic Studies*, 41, no. 3 (2002).

[4] Ibid.

[5] Sam I. Gellens, "The Search for Knowledge in Medieval Muslim Societies: A Comparative Approach." In Dale F. Eickelman (ed.), *Muslim Travellers: Pilgrimage, Migration, and the Religious Imagination Comparative Studies on Muslim Societies* (Berkeley and Los Angeles: University of California Press, 1990).

[6] Ibid.

[7] Martin van Bruinessen, "The Origins and Development of Sufi Orders (tarekat) in Southeast Asia," *Studia Islamika*, 1, no. 1 (1994), pp. 6–10.

[8] Engseng Ho, "Empire through Diasporic Eyes: A View from the Other Boat," *Comparative Studies in Society and History*, 46, no. 2 (2004).

"based on the concept of protection as business."[9] The sultan protected the population in a given territory against local violence and external threats. In return, subjects paid taxes that supported the ruler and his army.[10] This form of governance did not involve the concept of territorial sovereignty. Borders were not static, and more importantly, rarely impeded the freedom of movement. The only boundary that set limits to the pre-modern Muslim transnational networks was the end of Dar al-Islam ("the whole territory in which the law of Islam prevails"[11]).

The imposition of colonial rule and, later, the creation of nation states and national boundaries did not impede Muslim transnationalism significantly. With the development of transportation and communication technologies in the twentieth century, Muslim connectivity increased. In Robertson's words, organizational and technological advancements have led to the compression of the world and the emergence of a global field.[12] In this, "individuals and societies become part of a larger system of societies and identify themselves in relation to global standards."[13] Today, the different parts of the Middle East are connected to each other and to other parts of the world through charity networks, business enterprises, and informal, interpersonal, and computer-mediated networks. This has created a transnational Muslim civil society in which transnational movements, such as Salafism, are embedded.

The high density and quick expansion of Salafi transnational networks can only partly be explained by the development of transportation and communication technologies. At the same time, Salafis have a special keenness for establishing transnational contacts and networking.[14] Salafis, as previous chapters have shown, attach little importance to local culture and traditions. They feel at home wherever Islam can be practiced and where they can lead a pure lifestyle (i.e. *halal* food and relative freedom of worship). Therefore, they easily travel large distances for the sake of the *da'wa* or to acquire knowledge by studying under a certain shaykh or in a respected institution such as the Islamic University of Medina.

---

[9] Cornell, "'Ibn Battuta's Opportunism." In Cook and Lawrence, *Muslim Networks*, p. 33.
[10] Ibid., pp. 33–40.   [11] "Dar al-Islam," in Bossworth, *Encyclopaedia of Islam*.
[12] Roland Robertson, *Globalization: Social Theory and Global Culture* (London: SAGE Publications, 1992).
[13] Chandrashekhar Bhat and K. Laxmi Narayan, "Indian Diaspora, Globalization and Transnational Networks: The South African Context," *Journal of Social Science*, 25, nos. 1–3 (2010) p. 14.
[14] Laurent Bonnefoy, *Salafism in Yemen: Transnationalism and Religious Identity* (London: Hurst & Company, 2011), p. 139.

In addition to the Salafis' affinity for building transnational contacts, Lebanese culture also has a strong tradition of transnational networking. Since the second half of the nineteenth century, hundreds of thousands of Lebanese have migrated and settled in West Africa, the Americas, Australia, and Europe to find new business opportunities and employment.[15] In many cases, the Lebanese diaspora established dense trade links with their mother country,[16] which nowadays serve as a main source of investment and income for the Lebanese economy.[17] Family networks and social networks that transmit political and religious ideas are also significant.[18] For example, migrants are often involved in public debates and engage in sociopolitical activism in Lebanon.[19]

Since the establishment of "Greater Lebanon" in 1920, Lebanese Sunnis have continuously tried to reconnect with the larger Sunni world, often by being proponents of ideological streams that promise the unification of the *Umma*.[20] This mindset also enhances the establishment of transnational connections, especially with locations that are perceived as centers of Sunnism, such as the monarchies of the Arabian Peninsula in our case.

6.2   The Structure of Salafi Transnational Networks

Transnational connections can be direct and interpersonal, maintained by visits and communication by phone or via the internet. At the same time, indirect ties also play an important role.[21] Someone can be connected to a transnational network by having ties to someone else in his local networks who in turn possesses transnational contacts. For example, an active participant of Salafism who does not have direct

---

[15] Lebanese migrated from their country in several waves. Most of them were either skilled migrants looking for opportunities abroad, or people fleeing from economic hardship and violence. See Paul Tabar, "Lebanon: A Country of Emigration and Immigration" (Report, Center for Migration and Refugee Studies at the American University of Cairo, 2007), http://schools.aucegypt.edu/GAPP/cmrs/reports/Documents/Tabar080711 .pdf (accessed December 19, 2015).

[16] Mara A. Leichtman, "The Legacy of Transnational Lives: Beyond the First Generation of Lebanese in Senegal," *Ethnic and Racial Studies*, 28, no. 4 (2005).

[17] Tabar, "Lebanon: A Country of Emigration and Immigration," pp. 15–17.

[18] Ibid., pp. 672–675; 677–680.

[19] Dalia Abdelhady, "Beyond Home/Host Networks: Forms of Solidarity among Lebanese Immigrants in a Global Era," *Identities*, 13, no. 3 (2006), pp. 441–445.

[20] See Chapter 5.

[21] See also: Yanjie Bian, "Bringing Strong Ties Back In: Indirect Ties, Network Bridges, and Job Searches in China," *American Sociological Review*, 62, no. 3 (1997) pp. 368–372.

interpersonal ties outside of Lebanon can still be connected transnationally by being close to an *'alim* who is a frequent traveler and maintains a considerable social network in the Gulf countries. Many beneficiaries of Gulf charities are connected to these organizations indirectly through a Lebanese agent (see also Chapter 3).

Belonging to the purist or the *haraki* Salafi factions significantly shapes the structure of transnational links. The structure of these networks depends on whether its members belong to the purist or *haraki* Salafi factions. Networks usually evolve along purist or *haraki* ideological lines. My observations indicate that transnational links within the respective factions are much denser than between purists and *harakis*. As I explained previously, the participants of the two factions often prefer radically different methodologies for purifying people's belief and religious practices.[22] *Harakis* often engage in sociopolitical activism, while purists mostly focus on perfecting the minute details of religious practices and belief. The different views about the ruler's role are a particular cause of mistrust between them, and they disparagingly label each other "innovators" (*mubtadi'*) or *murji'a* (one whose actions do not reflect his belief). Therefore, transnational contacts that link *harakis* and purists are relatively rare.

Although the structures of the purist and *haraki* networks are similar at the local level, the situation is rather different at the transnational level. Transnational purist networks are generally more hierarchical than the *haraki* ones. At the top of the purist networks we find a few renowned scholars (mostly from the Gulf) whose fatwas are widely followed, from Europe to Southeast Asia. For example, the founders of the Indonesian purist militia, Laskar Jihad, had to ask for fatwas from the highest purist Salafi authorities in Saudi Arabia and Yemen before they could legitimize their involvement in the sectarian conflict in Maluku.[23] The involvement of the Saudi Arabian and Yemeni authorities was necessary despite the fact that Muslim participation in the civil war in Maluku was defensive jihad in the Salafi mindset, which is *fard 'ayn* (a personal duty) for the believers in any given country.[24] The purist *'ulama'* in the Gulf also played a role in the disbandment of Laskar Jihad. In 2002, the leader of the group, Ja'far Umar Thalib, referred to the fatwa of Rabi' al-Madkhali when he announced its dissolution.[25] The fact that

---

[22] See Chapter 1 and Chapter 2   [23] Hasan, *Laskar Jihad*, pp. 117–118.
[24] Muhammad bin Salih al-'Uthaymin, *Kitab al-Jihad*, www.ibnothaimeen.com/all/books/article_18093.shtml (accessed April 4, 2013).
[25] Noorhaidi, *Laskar Jihad*, p. 225.

the fatwas of the local Salafi shaykhs were not enough to justify the actions of the militia illustrates the vertical nature of purist transnational networks.

The great scholars of the Gulf possess significant religious authority over the Lebanese purists as well. As mentioned in Chapter 3, Lebanese purists established a fatwa council consisting of local scholars. However, this council only issues independent legal opinions when the fatwas of the Saudi Great 'Ulama' are not specific enough. Most of the fatwas issued by this council simply interpret the opinion of the scholars in the Gulf and apply it to local circumstances. When an ordinary believer asks for a fatwa from a Lebanese purist 'alim, the scholar tends to refer back to legal opinions given by the Great 'Ulama'.

Haraki transnational networks are much more horizontal. They are rarely structured around a few renowned shaykhs. When networks in distinct localities establish links to each other, their relationship tends to be more equal than in the case of the purists. Ideology plays a major role here; when Salafism in Saudi Arabia fragmented during and after the 1990–1991 Gulf crisis, harakis complained about the overwhelming domination of the Great 'Ulama' in the religious field and their monopoly in interpreting the Scripture. They regard this as a distortion of the teaching of Islam, which advocates the individual freedom of the learned (those who are capable of understanding the Qur'an and Sunna) to interpret the Text.[26]

Lebanese haraki shaykhs, although usually well connected to the Gulf, act rather independently. Although shaykhs such as 'Abd al-Rahman 'Abd al-Khaliq, Hamid al-'Ali, Safar al-Hawali, and Nasir al-'Umar are widely respected, they cannot issue orders to haraki shaykhs in other localities. Lebanese activist scholars usually produce independent fatwas. Shaykh Salim al-Rafi'i argued that idolizing shaykhs in the Gulf technically elevates them to the position of Christian priests.[27] He referred to the following Qur'anic verse: "They take their rabbis and their monks as their lords (instead of God)."[28] In Shaykh Salim's opinion, local Salafi shaykhs also can be highly knowledgeable and almost certainly have deeper insights into what is going on in their own community and their country. They should turn to the word of God directly and should not unconditionally accept the opinion of the Great 'Ulama'.

---

[26] Al-Rasheed, Contesting the Saudi State, pp. 71–72; 213.
[27] Interview, Tripoli, July 7, 2011.   [28] Surat al-Tawba, aya 31 (my own translation).

6.3 Links of Lebanese Salafis to the Gulf

Lebanese Salafis (both purists and *harakis*) tend to extend their networks in the direction of the Arabian Gulf: mostly Saudi Arabia, Kuwait, and Qatar. The Gulf is a main source of funding and a center of learning for them. Networking with Salafi groups in the Gulf often provides valuable religious capital, or social capital that can be converted into other forms of capital, such as religious and economic capital. These forms of capital are acquired as a result of establishing contacts in the monarchies of the Arabian Peninsula.

6.3.1 Acquiring Religious Capital

Lebanese Salafis acquire two forms of religious capital in the Gulf. The first form exists in the "embodied state" in the Bourdieuian sense, which refers to knowledge, such as the mastery of religious text and elaborate knowledge of religious rituals.[29] If they can afford it or if they possess the right contacts, Salafis travel to the Gulf countries to pursue their religious studies. Ideally, they enroll in degree programs at the prestigious universities, such as the Islamic University of Medina, Umm al-Qura University in Mecca and Imam Muhammad Ibn Sa'ud Islamic University in Riyadh. A less prestigious but still favored destination is the Shari'a Faculty of Kuwait University, where many renowned Salafi scholars teach (such as Hakim al-Mutayri or Hamid al-'Ali).

Traveling to the Hijaz to perform *'umra* (lesser pilgrimage)[30] can also be combined with religious learning. The *'umra* visa might grant the bearer a three- or six-month stay in the Holy Places. After performing the rituals, Salafis often visit the *halaqat* of renowned shaykhs residing either in Mecca or Medina. Among the most prestigious religious lessons are those of Shaykh Abu 'Abdullah al-Lahaydan, Rabi' al-Madkhali, and Safar al-Hawali. Some of the Lebanese stay in Mecca or Medina for a few weeks or months to pay regular visits to some of these *halaqat*.

Besides the "embodied state" of religious capital, studying in the Gulf provides students with what one might call the recognized or "institutionalized state" of religious capital.[31] In the case of Salafis, this mostly means religious authority. Saudi Arabia, and the Gulf in general,

---

[29] Bradford Verter, "Theorizing Religion with Bourdieu against Bourdieu," *Sociological Theory*, 21, no. 2 (2003), p. 159.

[30] The direction of the *'umra* is also the *Ka'ba*, but it is not compulsory, involves fewer rituals, and can be performed at any time of the year.

[31] Verter, "Theorizing Religion with Bourdieu against Bourdieu," p. 160.

is regarded as the center of learning for Salafis. Those who belong to the Salafi community in Northern Lebanon, and those ordinary inhabitants who sympathize with Salafism, presuppose that an individual who has studied in the Gulf has acquired a superior level of knowledge.

Possessing a degree from one of the universities in the Gulf elevates one's credentials in the Lebanese Salafi community. A shaykh who has a Bachelor's or Master's degree from Medina or Umm al-Qura can potentially attract more active participants and passive followers than someone who is self-educated or has a degree from a Lebanese Islamic educational institution.[32] Being a graduate of one of the learning centers of the Gulf also paves the way for the shaykhs to get a job at one of the Salafi colleges of Tripoli, or to access funding from the Gulf.

Participating in the *halaqat* of some of the famous Salafi scholars in Saudi Arabia might also increase the individual's religious authority. He can claim that he is the student of some of the most renowned Salafi *'ulama'*, or can simply say that he studied in Mecca or Medina. In the eyes of the passive followers, this still elevates his status above those who never studied in the Gulf. In purist-rejectionist circles, however, it is often more respectable to have spent a period of time visiting the *halaqat* of Shaykh Rabi' al-Madkhali in Medina or Shaykh Salim al-Tawil in Kuwait than to have graduated from one of the Islamic universities. This is because there is a significant *haraki* and non-Salafi presence in the *shari'a* faculties there, which might corrupt an individual's beliefs. While Saudi Islamic universities teach a curriculum created according to a Salafi framework, many of the foreign students, and even professors, are not Salafis.[33] Although, as discussed in Chapter 1, the Saudi government in the early 1990s replaced many haraki and non-Salafi employees of the universities with purists, the former were nevertheless not completely wiped out. Purists think that instead of avoiding interaction with these people completely, they might even convince someone with a "pure" belief to follow their "corrupted" ways.

6.3.2   Acquiring Social Capital

Establishing and maintaining contact with Salafis in the Gulf countries increases the social capital of Lebanese Salafis. During my fieldwork,

---

[32] Although there are exceptions: Shaykh Nur al-Din 'Ammar, whom I mentioned in Chapter 5, never had any formal education, yet he can be considered one of the most renowned Salafi scholars in Lebanon.

[33] Farquhar, *Circuits of Faith*, pp. 129–154.

I observed how Lebanese Salafis start and maintain relationships with the monarchies of the Arabian Peninsula.

I classify transnational exchanges between Salafis as taking place on two main levels: On the first level, links are developed and maintained between the shaykhs. The second level concerns the contacts among active followers and between active followers and shaykhs. Passive followers do not usually form an integral part of these transnational exchanges, unless someone asks for a fatwa from a Gulf-based shaykh by telephone or online. However, in my experience, these practices are not yet widespread among ordinary Lebanese Salafi sympathizers.

1. *The level of the shaykhs.* This level includes both links between the shaykhs themselves and between the shaykhs and the sponsors. Transnational contacts between the *'ulama'* are often established during their student years at one of the universities in the Gulf, mostly in Saudi Arabia. My acquaintance to Shaykh Mahir, a preacher in his early thirties from the al-Qubba region in Tripoli, was particularly useful to understand the Saudi universities' role in transnational networking. Shaykh Mahir owns a smartphone shop in one of the main streets in al-Qubba, but in his free time he teaches in Zakariyya al-Masri's Hamza mosque and deepens his religious knowledge. Previously, he spent four years at the Islamic University of Medina acquiring his degree. He told me how he used to spend most of his free time with three other students, who came from Saudi Arabia, Kuwait, and Mauritania. He described how their worldview was shaped when they participated in extracurricular activities, mostly in the *halaqat* of *haraki* shaykhs such as Safar al-Hawali.

After they graduated, they maintained regular contact, with the exception of the Mauritanian student, who after returning to his home country had limited ability to use the internet and travel abroad. Shaykh Mahir, however, often communicates with the other two. They exchange messages almost daily via Facebook and follow each other on Twitter. Since his graduation, Shaykh Mahir has visited them both in Kuwait and Saudi Arabia a couple of times. These occasions provided him with the opportunity to further expand his network and even to acquire some financial support to pursue his *da'wa* activities.[34]

Network ties also often emerge during various formal and informal visits abroad. Such travel can be for a purely social purpose, to look for financial aid, or to participate in Islamic conferences. The latter are usually exceptional opportunities for transnational networking. Such

[34] Interview, Tripoli, April 11, 2012.

events are often organized by one of the Salafi centers or charity organizations in the Gulf. The Kuwaiti SRIH, for example, frequently sets up such events in Kuwait. On many occasions, the organizers have invited renowned scholars from Saudi Arabia or Egypt to give lectures.

These conferences provide space for shaykhs who already know each other to maintain relationships or to forge new ones. At the same time, these events are excellent opportunities for contacting potential sponsors. At conferences in the Gulf, participants are often invited to spend the night at the house of one of the local Salafis after the seminars. The meetings in the evening function as one of the most effective platforms for making contact with others. In the relaxed environment of the informal home gatherings, Lebanese Salafi shaykhs often make valuable contacts that provide them with access to charities or other kinds of patronage. Salafis from the Gulf frequently introduce like-minded movement members to businessmen, who are willing to sponsor certain *da'wa* activities.[35]

During my fieldwork in Kuwait, I often participated in *diwaniyyas* and could observe informal transnational exchanges between Salafis. According to Kuwaitis, these events have been organized since the founding years of the country, and can be traced back to old tribal traditions. The *diwaniyya* is usually hosted by the head of a prominent Kuwaiti family on a given day each week (usually a Tuesday or a Saturday). After the *maghrib* (evening) or *'isha'* (night) prayers, men (usually members of the extended family, friends, clients of the host, or those who wish to discuss something with him) gather in a specific place in a Kuwaiti house that has been created for *diwaniyas*. The people sit back against the wall, to the right and left of the host. A servant offers them drinks, usually tea or Arabic coffee.

The discussions in the *diwaniyyas* cover a range of issues. Sometimes people gather at a *diwaniyya* only to socialize or to watch an important football match. *Diwaniyyas* for poetry are also popular. More important are those *diwaniyyas* where people discuss economic or political issues. The fate of millions of dollars can be decided at such gatherings (rather than in the offices of Kuwait City's skyscrapers). At election time, *diwaniyas* can be extremely crowded, as key campaigning takes place there.[36]

---

[35] Series of interviews with Lebanese Salafi shaykhs in Tripoli during July–August 2011 and April–May 2012.

[36] On the role of diwaniyyas in politics and as forums for public debates see Mary-Ann Tétreault, "Bottom-Up Democratization in Kuwait." In *Political Change in the Arab Gulf States: Stuck in Transition*, edited by Mary Ann Tétreault, Gwenn Okruhlik, and Andrzej Kapiszewski (Boulder, CO: Lynne Rienner Publishers, 2011).

Usually, the time and place of a *diwaniyya* is advertised online, indicating the accessibility of such events.[37]

Salafis from other Middle Eastern countries or Europe often participate in *diwaniyas* when they visit Kuwait. My Lebanese Salafi informants who frequently visit the Gulf emirate also make use of the social opportunities these gatherings provide. One of the most important functions of the *diwaniyya* is providing a "free space"[38] for transnational actors to exchange information. *Diwaniyyas* are protected by Kuwaiti law. According to Kuwaiti law, the state has no right to put them under surveillance or curb their freedom by any means.[39] Therefore, they can hold free and open discussions. Salafis from abroad are often brought to different *diwaniyyas* by their local contacts. As Salafis from Tripoli who are frequently in Kuwait told me, most of the time during the *diwaniyyas* they only exchange ideas with others and establish new contacts. Kuwaiti Salafis often ask them to talk about the situation in Lebanon and how they perceive the threat from the Shi'ite community and Hizbullah.

Diwaniyyas also provide space to establish contact with charities. For example, to receive support from SRIH, it is usually necessary to have previously established contact with shaykhs who are associated with the charity. Funds also can be collected from individual donors who might not even be Salafis. Since SRIH often covers only part of the expenses, the extra funds collected during trips to the Gulf emirate can be very important. Salafis usually ask for extra support for their *ma'had shara'i*, to be able to provide more alms for the poor or to publish books and leaflets. Kuwaiti donors usually offer their *zakat* or pay *sadaqa*.[40]

2. *The level of the active followers.* The transnational networks of committed Salafis are less dense than those of the shaykhs, mostly because the young men tend not to have the financial means to travel to the Gulf frequently. Despite this, active participants can gain social capital, which they convert into religious capital (knowledge) and economic capital.

Committed Lebanese Salafis often mix with young Salafis from Kuwait or Saudi Arabia who are visiting Lebanon. Activists from Western Europe

---

[37] www.dewan.ws/ (accessed April 18, 2011).
[38] Polletta, "'Free Spaces' in Collective Action."
[39] Mary Ann Tétreault, *Stories of Democracy*, pp. 278–281.
[40] Interview with a prominent Palestinian shaykh from Nahr al-Barid, April 23, 2012, and personal conversations and observations during fieldwork in Kuwait, February–March 2012.

and Australia are also a frequent presence in the Salafi religious colleges. Longlasting links and networks can emerge from these encounters, sustained by the internet. Twitter, Facebook, and online Salafi forums enable the movement's followers to transcend locality and create communities that are established purely on the grounds of shared ideology. My data show that these transnational networks can evolve either around certain websites, such as www.kulalsalafiyeen.com, or unfold on social media.[41] For Lebanese Salafis, however, the internet is not yet an effective tool to communicate with their larger audience due to connectivity issues. Despite this, committed Salafis who are willing to sacrifice more time and effort to acquire knowledge and establish contacts with fellow Salafis in other countries are active online. They connect to the internet mostly in internet cafes or, if they can afford it, use expensive and still unreliable mobile data networks.

Members of transnational Salafi networks rarely know each other personally and are only familiar with each other's virtual profiles. In other cases, networks on Facebook and Twitter often evolve after the network's members have previously established personal contact. These networks have a stronger impact, at least in the case of the Salafi youth in Northern Lebanon, and last longer. I had frequent conversations with Khalid, a twenty-five-year-old Kuwaiti Salafi and student at the Islamic University of Medina during my fieldwork in Kuwait in 2012. His family owns a villa in the Dinniya region, close to Tripoli.[42] Since his childhood, he has spent most of his summers there. When he is in Lebanon, he often socializes with fellow Salafis from the villages in the Dinniya region or Tripoli. He told me how four or five years ago, when he left Lebanon at the end of the summer, he would hardly maintain contact with these young people due to the lack of means of communication. In the past few years, however, internet access has become more widespread and even people from poor economic backgrounds can have connections at home. As Khalid told me, he is now able to add many of his Lebanese acquaintances to Facebook and Twitter, and exchanges between them have become quite frequent.[43] They share articles, e-books, and religious materials or inform each other about what is happening in the Salafi communities in Kuwait, Lebanon, and Medina (Khalid is a student there).

---

[41] Kulalsalafiyeen.com is one the most popular Arabic language purist Salafi internet forums. It is supervised by the prominent Jordanian 'alim, 'Ali al-Halabi.

[42] Kuwaitis often buy properties in Lebanon in which they spend the summer, when the weather in Kuwait is unbearably hot.

[43] Interview, Kuwait, February 30, 2012 and March 5, 7, and 14, 2012.

In other cases, however, especially if personal visits are relatively frequent, Salafis in the Gulf can help their Lebanese acquaintances to find a job and establish themselves in one of the Gulf monarchies. I briefly encountered two Lebanese Palestinians in Kuwait who were assisted by the twenty-two-year-old Faisal, one of the students of Shaykh Salim al-Tawil, whose study circles I frequently visited while staying in Kuwait. Faisal told me that the Palestinian youths were connected to him through another student of Shaykh Salim, whom they had previously met in Lebanon. Faisal was helping the youths to secure new jobs after their previous contracts had ended. He mobilized his local contacts and access to patronage to find employment for his protégées. He explained to me that he was doing all of this because he sees the young Palestinians as "right-thinking," and after their return to Lebanon they would spread the right form of the *da'wa* and challenge the *mubtadi*'s (who commit harmful innovation – *bid'a* – in religion).[44] Even though most of the Salafi networks' connections are still personal, and often aided by technology, certain institutional contacts play key roles in mobilizing resources. These institutional contacts most often link Salafis to transnational charities.

6.4   The Role of Transnational Charity Organizations

Gulf-based charities as main sponsors of Salafi activism are among the most important elements in Salafi transnational networks.[45] Previously, I mentioned that two large Gulf relief organizations play a crucial role in the Salafi field in Northern Lebanon. Since it split in 1997, SRIH has sponsored the purist Salafis, while Mu'assasat al-Shaykh 'Aid al-Khayriyya (Shaykh 'Aid Charity Foundation – SACF) finances the North Lebanese *haraki* network.

Islamic charity organizations emerged in the 1970s due to three main factors: The first was the six decades of ongoing wars, civil conflicts, and humanitarian disasters in the Muslim world. The second factor was the 1973 oil boom, which enabled the Gulf States to finance charity activities. The third factor was the need of the Saudi Arabian monarchy and the other monarchies in the Arabian Gulf for legitimacy, especially after the Iranian Revolution. Supporting transnational charities was an excellent way to gain legitimacy, because it improved the reputations of

[44] Interview and observation, Kuwait, February 11, 2012.
[45] Salafi political parties have emerged in Egypt, Tunisia, and Yemen, but they are not yet significant transnational hubs.

these monarchies in the eyes of Muslims worldwide.[46] Funding charitable activities gave credibility to the conservative Sunni monarchies' counterpropaganda against Iran's revolutionary ideology.[47] The Soviet-Afghan War (1979–1989), which caused millions to flee, triggered Islamic charity activity as both individual donors and the Gulf States poured money into charity organizations.[48] The peripheries of Islam in Africa likewise provided opportunities for charitable activities intertwined with *da'wa*. Here, Gulf charities partly justified their intervention with the perceivably Christian missionary activities of Western charities.[49] In poverty-stricken countries such as Chad, these institutions found fertile ground to spread their ideologies among local Muslims, and to convert others to Islam as well.[50]

In the beginning, the profile of most Islamic charities represented the ideology of the Muslim Brotherhood. This is because most of the employees of the charities used to belong to the Ikhwan, as in the 1970s; they were the ones who possessed the skills and education needed for relief work. Salafis also refrained from participating in the newly established charity organizations, due to their rejection of formal organizations that are not mentioned in the Scripture (as *waqf*, for example), labeling them *bida'*. This attitude began to change from the 1980s onward, when the Saudi government started to spread its Salafi ideology worldwide. The senior *'ulama'* affiliated with the state issued fatwas that legitimized charity organizations. In addition, many of the new generation of Salafi scholars, especially the *haraki* ones who were influenced by other Islamist currents, no longer thought that all organizational forms were unacceptable. Since then, transnational charities have come to constitute one of the most important pillars of Salafism.[51]

Transnational Salafi charities differ from other relief organizations in many respects. Probably the most important distinctive feature is that in the activities of Salafi charities, "Islam and aid are intimately intertwined."[52] As I have often heard from members of these institutions, the aim of relief work should not only be the alleviation of

---

[46] Marie Juul Petersen, "Islamizing Aid: Transnational Muslim NGOs after 9.11," *Voluntas*, 23, no. 1 (2012) p. 133.

[47] See Kepel, *Jihad*.

[48] For a more detailed analysis, see Pall, *Lebanese Salafis between the Gulf and Europe*, pp. 79–82.

[49] Marie Juul Petersen, "Trajectories of Transnational Muslim NGOs," *Development in Practice*, 22, no. 5–6 (2012), p. 767.

[50] Mayke Kaag, "Aid, UMMA, and Politics: Transnational Islamic NGOs in Chad." In *Islam and Muslim Politics in Africa*, edited by Benjamin F. Soares and René Otayek (New York, NY: Palgrave Macmillan, 2007).

[51] Pall, *Lebanese Salafis*, p. 82.   [52] Petersen, "Islamizing Aid," p. 140.

poverty; charity work has to be done for the sake of God. It means the recipients should benefit regarding the prospect of their hereafter. This is especially true in the case of Salafi charities. With their charitable activism, Salafis usually intend to convince others to adopt their practice and lifestyle, while Muslim Brothers allow for a wider range of diversity.[53]

The institutional structure of the two charities, SRIH and SACF, share some similarities. Unlike charities linked to the Muslim Brotherhood and the mainstream secular or Christian relief organizations, these charities lack an elaborate organizational framework.[54] Informal exchanges are still significant in their operations, despite the increasing observance of the state authorities over charities in both countries. After the purist takeover in 1997, SRIH started to cooperate more closely with the Kuwaiti state and the authorities of the host countries in which SRIH has a presence. An official from SRIH told me that before launching any major projects, they consult the royal family of Kuwait and ask for their approval.

In Lebanon, for example, the local agents of SRIH are obliged to report to the Kuwaiti Embassy whenever they receive a large amount of money, 100,000 USD or more, from the mother institution. After the 9/11, 2001 attack, the Kuwaiti state imposed increased control on Islamic charities.[55] The authorities tightened their grip even more in 2013, as part of a campaign to curb the funding of militant groups in Syria.[56]

Similarly, the Qatari charity sector was rather disorganized before the 9/11 attacks. Although Qatari charities had not been accused by the United States of financing terrorist groups yet, in anticipatory obedience, Doha implemented a rather strict regulatory framework. The Qatar Authority for Charitable Activities (QACA) was created in 2004 to supervise and control the activities and financial transactions of charitable organizations, which are based in the country.[57]

---

[53] On the differing views of Salafis and Muslim Brothers on diversity in belief and practice see Commins, *The Wahhabi Mission and Saudi Arabia*, pp. 141–143.

[54] On the charities of the Brotherhood see Quintan Wiktorowicz, *The Management of Islamic Activism: Salafis, the Muslim Brotherhood and State Power in Jordan* (Albany, NY: SUNY Press, 2001), pp. 83–110.

[55] "Kuwait moves to tighten grip on Islamic charities," *Middle East Online*, March 2, 2005, www.middle-east-online.com/english/?id=12865 (accessed July 27, 2015).

[56] "Kuwait steps up controls on Islamic charities," *The National*, August 5, 2014, www.thenational.ae/world/middle-east/kuwait-steps-up-controls-on-islamic-charities (accessed July 27, 2015).

[57] Abdul Fatah S. Mohamed, "The Qatar Authority for Charitable Activities (QACA) from Commencement to Dissolution (2004–2009)." In *Gulf Charities and Philanthropy*, edited by Lacey and Benthall.

Although QACA was dissolved in 2009, its functions were delegated to the Ministry of Social Affairs.[58]

While all activities of SACF are closely monitored by the Qatari state, informal social networks still play very important roles. Unlike SRIH, SACF does not have any official branches in foreign countries. On paper, they only subsidize projects launched by independent local charities. However, in many cases, dense informal, interpersonal networks connect these formally unattached institutions to the mother organizations in Qatar and Kuwait. These allow the leadership in the Gulf charities to control their beneficiaries effectively. During my fieldwork, I observed how aid is distributed in North Lebanon. The main agent of SACF in Tripoli is Shaykh Khalid Za'rur. Although he was the charity's international relations chief for several years, since his resignation, he has not had any official links with the charity. Today, Shaykh Khalid works for a Qatari company as a real estate agent. However, he has kept his network ties to the leadership and advisory board of SACF, and distributes the charity's money in Tripoli and the Dinniya region.

I was a frequent visitor to Shaykh Khalid's office[59] in *Sahat al-Nur* (Star Square) in the center of Tripoli during the summer of 2011 and spring of 2012. While he was mostly busy with his clients and business partners, sometimes local Salafi shaykhs also appeared. They usually came to discuss the possibility of receiving subsidies to build a mosque or pursue their *da'wa* activities. When the amount of money required is only a few thousand or tens of thousands of dollars, Shaykh Khalid has the authority to decide. Once the proposed plan is approved, the beneficiary has to prepare a formal application and send it to SACF's headquarters in Qatar. Upon receiving it, they transfer the money to the recipient. If the amount of requested aid is more than the abovementioned sums, either the recipient has to visit Qatar or some members of SACF's leadership visit Lebanon to inspect the proposed project.

Embeddedness in the informal networks of Salafism is essential for someone to become a local representative of a transnational Gulf charity. None of the agents of SACF or SRIH in Lebanon whom I interviewed went through any formal recruitment process. They achieved their positions through the transnational networks of friends and fellow Salafi *'ulama'* whom they had encountered both in Lebanon and the

---

[58] Ibid., p. 279.
[59] I would use the internet in his office, where he had installed a much faster connection than was available elsewhere in the city. During the time I spent there, saving my fieldwork notes and checking my emails, I had plenty of opportunity for observation.

Gulf countries. This was the case with Safwan al-Za'bi.[60] Khalid Za'rur's network evolved through his business activity in the Gulf, while the Lebanese Palestinian Shaykh Ghassan was able to establish his contacts with SACF after years of tirelessly networking with Salafis from the Gulf and Europe.[61]

6.5   The Links of Lebanese Salafis to Europe

The networks of Lebanese Salafis also extend to various European countries, since Europe is a destination where they can expand their *da'wa*. A relatively high number of Lebanese Salafis hold leading positions in European Muslim communities and have become important nodes of the transnational networks of the movement.

The Muslim communities of Western European countries have become fertile grounds of the Salafi *da'wa* since the 1980s. Most academic works on European Salafism argue that the alienation of second and third generation immigrant youth and their search for an alternative identity greatly facilitated the growth of the movement.[62] These young people feel excluded from the societies they live in, but at the same time they cannot adopt the traditional religious identities of their parents. Many of them are looking for "authentic Islam," which they often find in Salafism.[63]

Salafism is usually spread in Europe by individuals who were born in Europe and became influenced by the movement's ideas while studying in the Gulf, or by Middle Eastern Salafis who settled in Europe. In the following, I will present a detailed account of the life story of a Lebanese Palestinian Shaykh who carries out *da'wa* in Sweden. The case illustrates important aspects of the nature of Salafi networking: how a Lebanese shaykh becomes part of the transnational movement, how he establishes contacts with transnational charities through informal networking, and how his interpersonal links enable him to start a career as a preacher in Western Europe

---

[60] See Chapter 4.
[61] The Palestinian shaykh asked me to make him anonymous. Ghassan is not his real name.
[62] Sadek Hamid, "The Attraction of 'Authentic' Islam: Salafism and British Muslim Youth." In Meijer, *Global Salafism*; Mohamed-Ali Adraoui, "Salafism in France: Ideology, Practices and Contradictions." In ibid.; Martijn de Koning, "Between the Prophet and Paradise: The Salafi Struggle in the Netherlands," *Canadian Journal of Netherlandic Studies*, 33–34, no. 2–1 (2012–2013).
[63] See especially Martijn de Koning, "Changing Worldviews and Friendship: An Exploration of the Life Stories of Two Female Salafis in the Netherlands." In Meijer, *Global Salafism*.

6.5.1   Shaykh Ghassan: Between Nahr al-Barid and Sweden

I first started to interview Shaykh Ghassan in 2009, but I managed to continue meeting him several times during my field trips to Lebanon and then to Sweden over the course of four years. Shaykh Ghassan's case demonstrates that Salafis are exceptionally mobile, even in comparison to the activists of other Islamic movements.

Shaykh Ghassan was born in the first half of the 1970s in Berlin, where his father was a guest worker. The family returned to Lebanon and settled in the Nahr al-Barid camp when Ghassan was about five or six years old. While his parents were not practicing Muslims, Ghassan had two uncles who were deeply religious and with whom he had a very strong relationship. Under their influence, he became interested in Islam from an early age. As an adolescent, he became involved in the vibrant religious life of Tripoli in the 1980s. He visited a different mosque almost every day, where he participated in the *halaqat* of shaykhs from various Islamic movements, such as the Ikhwan, al-Ahbash, Sufis, and Salafis. At the age of fifteen, Ghassan joined the *Qadiriyya* Sufi order, where he, as he emphasized, became an exceptionally active member

As he explained, the "Salafi turn" in his life occurred when he started to take lessons from a "*taqlidi* [traditional]" shaykh who followed an *athari 'aqida*.[64] The scholar advised him to stick to the Qur'an and Sunna, since these two sources are not controversial, unlike Sufi practices. After his studies with this shaykh he gradually distanced himself from the Sufis. At this time, Shaykh Ahmad al-Hajj, one of the prominent Salafi scholars of Nahr al-Barid today, returned from Saudi Arabia after finishing his studies and started his *da'wa* among the youth of the camp. Ghassan joined the group of young people that surrounded him, left Sufism for good, and adopted the Salafi *manhaj*. During his high-school years, he studied in Shaykh Da'i al-Islam al-Shahhal's Ma'had al-Hidaya. According to him, his experiences at the college made him decide to dedicate his life to the *da'wa*. Later he graduated from Jinan University in Tripoli in *shari'a* law and started to teach in Tripoli's Salafi colleges.

After receiving his bachelor's degree in the mid-1990s, he began working in the various *ma'had*s, and got involved in the transnational Salafi movement. According to his account, the years he spent lecturing in Tripoli were crucial in building up his transnational interpersonal network, which led him to become one of the main authorities among Lebanese Palestinian Salafis and an important transnational *da'i*.

---

[64] See Chapter 1.

In other words, this was the period when he collected social capital that he later converted into religious and economic capital.

As he told me, before the battle in Dinniya in 1999, there was a lively Salafi community in Tripoli. There were many Australian Lebanese and European Muslim students of Arab, Albanian, and Bosnian origins who were pursuing their studies in the Salafi religious colleges. Shaykh Ghassan was a well-liked teacher and he forged close relationships with some of his students outside of the classroom as well. Some students from Germany "praised his qualities" in front of the leadership of a Salafi mosque in Berlin. As a result, he received an invitation to undertake a *da'wa* tour in the German capital. During his trip, he delivered a series of lectures and issued many fatwas. He also had the opportunity to get closer to a number of leading European Salafi scholars, who later proved to be beneficial to his career.

For Shaykh Ghassan, the other source of connections with transnational networks was the milieu around Shaykh Da'i al-Islam al-Shahhal. The young *da'i*, described by many as capable and tireless, quickly became close to the shaykh, who was then the main Salafi leader in Lebanon. As I mentioned in Chapter 3, shaykhs and agents of charity organizations from the Gulf frequently visited al-Shahhal. On these occasions, Shaykh Ghassan acquired many contacts in Qatar and Saudi Arabia, which he employed to boost his *da'wa* activities. From the second half of the 1990s he frequently traveled to the Gulf to participate in conferences or learn from prominent scholars in their *halaqat*. Unlike many other Lebanese Salafis, he could afford such trips even without external financial help, since he owned a number of successful businesses in Nahr al-Barid. During one of these visits, he was introduced to the leaders of SACF in Doha and was granted subsidies for spreading Salafism among the inhabitants of the Palestinian refugee camps. As Shaykh Ghassan explained, after this introduction, he became part of a "powerful" network, which opened doors to more effectively fulfill his mission to spread the "correct form of God's religion."

After several years of cooperation with the Qatari charity organization to implement local charity projects, mainly in Nahr al-Barid and the surrounding areas (which are mostly inhabited by Lebanese Sunnis), in 2011 Shaykh Ghassan was appointed as one of the heads of a Swedish Islamic center sponsored by SACF. During our interview in Sweden, he told me that he was recommended by European Salafis whom he had met during his *da'wa* tour in Germany and travels to the Gulf. He thinks that the strongest aspect of his candidature was his educational background in administration and accounting. After graduation in *shari'a*, he had acquired a degree in the latter subject, and is therefore able to contribute to the financial management of the center, besides providing religious services. By working as the imam and *khatib* of a mosque in the city of Orebro and directing the Islamic center that is attached to the mosque, Shaykh Ghassan became the center of a transnational network connecting Scandinavia and Lebanon. Although he spends most of his time in Sweden, he goes back to Lebanon every year for a couple of months to take care of the affairs of his institution, Dar al-Arqam, in Nahr al-Barid.

In the summer of 2012, after Shaykh Ghassan agreed to host me, I spent several days at the Orebro Islamic center interviewing cow-orkers and ordinary believers, and observing the activities there. The institution is one of five similar establishments built by SACF in Sweden. Completed in 2007, about 5,000 people visit the establishment regularly. Most of them have Somali origins, but there are Afghans, Iraqis, Syrians, Egyptians, and Bosnians as well. As members of the mosque's leadership committee told me, the arrival of Shaykh Ghassan "brought fresh blood to the Islamic center," which is attempting to "purify the erroneous religious customs" of the local Muslims.[65] In fact, Shaykh Ghassan started his new appointment with exceptional activity.

One of the first initiatives that Shaykh Ghassan launched upon his arrival in Sweden was to start the *da'wa* among university students and young professionals aged 25–35. He gathers these young men every two weeks. After a religious lesson, they continue with a small socializing event in the community hall of the mosque. He tasked a thirty-two-year-old Afghan Tajik computer programmer, Ansare,[66] with attracting his Muslim friends and acquaintances to these events. When I interviewed him,[67] Ansare told me that he did not know too much about Islam and was unable to recognize the different movements and schools of thought. He was only able to learn the very basics of religion from his parents, who belonged to the working class and were "not really practicing." Ansare thinks that many young Muslim professionals of the same age are in the same position: They have a working-class family background with parents who had little to pass on to their children about Islam. At the same time, society does not fully accept them as Swedish, despite the fact that they have received a Swedish education and are native speakers. For most of them, the only identity they can adopt – as has been underscored by several academic

---

[65] Interview with a shaykh from Syria, June 26, 2012.
[66] "Ansare" is the Swedish spelling; the original Arabic or Tajik transcription would be "Ansari."
[67] Interview, June 25, 2012.

studies on European Islam[68] – is being Muslim. According to Ansare, many who belong to this demographic respond positively to Shaykh Ghassan's call, since at least "they get some answer [to the question of] who they are."

One of the most interesting aspects of Shaykh Ghassan's activism in Orebro is how he works on expanding his *da'wa* to neighboring Scandinavian countries. After his arrival in Sweden, he proposed that other members of SACF's network who are based in Norway and Finland should coordinate their activities. In 2011, they launched a yearly Qur'an-memorizing course at the Orebro center in the summer holidays. The four-week-long course was being held while I was there, giving me an opportunity for observation. Most of the participants were aged between twelve and sixteen and more than half of them came from Finland, Norway, and other, distant parts of Sweden. SACF fully financed both their travel expenses and stay in Orebro. During the period they spent in the Islamic center, the students learned a couple of *suras* from the Qur'an by heart. After the memorizing sessions, Shaykh Ghassan, along with some other scholars who were affiliated with the institution, gave them Arabic lessons and an introduction to *fiqh*.

The shaykhs who belong to SACF's network frequently visit each other's mosques to give guest lectures and *halaqat*. The Qatari charity also gives financial aid to some of the originally non-Salafi mosques in localities where there is a considerable Muslim population. In exchange, these institutions let Salafi *da'is* visit them and deliver lectures. Shaykh Ghassan himself often travels to smaller towns in Sweden and elsewhere in Scandinavia. According to Shaykh Ghassan, these trips are especially beneficial for the *da'wa*. As he told me, there are hardly any trained religious scholars in the smaller towns of Scandinavia, and local mosques even lack basic religious literature. The Salafis usually offer to send some additional copies of the Qur'an, hadith collections, and books such as al-Albani's *Sifat Salat al-Nabi*, 'Aid al-Qarni's *La Tahzin* (Don't be Sad!), or 'Abd al-Rahman 'Abd al-Khaliq's *al-Usul al-'Ilmiyya li-l-Da'wa al-Salafiyya* (The Scientific Roots of the Salafi Da'wa). If they have the

---

[68] Studies on European Muslims that are based on ethnographic data often conclude that second- and third-generation European Muslims can accept neither the identity of their parents and grandparents nor that of the host country, where they feel excluded or rejected. Islamic movements, which claim to represent authentic Islam, usually appeal to them. Martijn De Koning, "Changing Worldviews and Friendship: An Exploration of the Life Stories of Two Female Salafis in the Netherlands." In Meijer, *Global Salafism*; Mohamed-Ali Adraoui, "Salafism in France: Ideology, Practices and Contradictions." In Ibid.; Sadek Hamid, "The Attraction of 'Authentic' Islam: Salafism and British Muslim Youth." In Ibid.

capacity, the Salafi centers send scholars to these places on a fortnightly or monthly basis to give lessons or lectures or deliver the Friday prayer.

Shaykh Ghassan told me that he intends to establish a more intensive relationship between his Lebanese and Scandinavian networks. In his opinion, European Muslims should have a better understanding of the concerns and sufferings of their Middle Eastern brethren. Therefore, he plans to bring some of his more enthusiastic students from Sweden to Tripoli, to stay for a while in the Nahr al-Barid camp. He thinks that directly experiencing the difficulties of the Palestinians and Sunni Lebanese in the North, and the injustices that Muslims are facing (from the side of Hizbullah and the Lebanese government), would strengthen their feeling of belonging to the *Umma* as an identity that is superior to all other identities. Besides, these young European Muslims would have the chance to improve their Arabic and religious knowledge by learning in Dar al-Arqam, or even participating in one of the summer schools[69] organized by the institution. Shaykh Ghassan will start sending his students to Lebanon as soon as the security situation in the country improves.[70]

This ethnographic case study on Shaykh Ghassan's activism exemplifies the nature of Salafi transnational networking. He built his *da'wa* almost entirely on informal, interpersonal networks. Even his cooperation with SACF cannot be described as formal and institutional. Officially, he is not a SACF agent. He receives money from the institution because he belongs to a network of friends and fellow Salafis who maintain close personal links with the leadership of SACF. Salafis like Shaykh Ghassan choose this type of networking not only because they are suspicious of formal institutional structures; informal links, even at the transnational level, provide fewer chances for the various state authorities to interfere, because they are more difficult to monitor. A similar transnational networking strategy can be observed in my other European case study, a Dutch *haraki* network, which is also connected to Lebanon.

6.5.2   A Lebanese Network in the Netherlands

Abu Adham, the leader of a Dutch *haraki* network, has followed a somewhat different trajectory than Shaykh Ghassan, yet he shares some

---

[69] Interview, Orebro, June 23, 2012.

[70] At the time of the interview, the country was significantly destabilized by the Syrian civil war. Violence, abduction, and murders were occurring regularly in Northern Lebanon, making it rather unsafe for foreigners.

similarities as well. Although I received his mobile number from a colleague of mine at Utrecht University, who used to pray for a while in Abu Adham's mosque, the shaykh was willing to talk to me due to my personal connections to many Lebanese Salafis. He allowed me to visit his mosque in The Hague several times, and also agreed to speak about his life. Like Shaykh Ghassan, Abu Adham established himself as a result of having become part of the transnational Salafi movement. His transnational networking also largely lacks institutional aspects, and rather relies on informal and interpersonal exchanges. Like Shaykh Ghassan, Abu Adham serves as a hub of networks that connect European Muslims to their country of origin. He spends most of his time in the Netherlands, although he also travels extensively within Europe and to the Gulf and Lebanon. Finally, Abu Adham has a similar goal to that of Shaykh Ghassan: to urge Muslims to focus on their membership of the *Umma* and not to adopt a European identity, which might drive them away from their religion.

Abu Adham – who is now in his mid-fifties – began his life as an Islamic activist in al-Ahbash circles when he was a teenager, as did many other Lebanese Salafis.[71] After a few months, he left this Sufi-oriented group and became a Salafi, as the student of Shaykh Salim al-Shahhal. Shaykh Salim treated him like close family, and he spent several years in his house. When he finished his secondary education in Tripoli, Shaykh Salim helped him to gain a scholarship to the Islamic University of Medina in Saudi Arabia, where he completed a Master's degree. After graduation, he became the imam of a mosque in the United Arab Emirates. He had to leave the country after several years because, as he explained, he did not belong among the government shaykhs (*mashayikh al-sulta*): in other words, because he was *haraki*. He is convinced that those *'ulama'* who follow the prescriptions of the faith and refuse to bow in front of the rulers are not welcome in Gulf countries. He even accuses the government of the Emirates of supporting Sufis in order to weaken Salafi influence. When staying in the Emirates, however, the shaykh came into contact with a group of Dutch Salafis, who invited him to their country to lead their group.

Until recently, he was regarded as one of the most influential Salafi leaders in the Netherlands, with hundreds of committed followers and thousands of sympathizers. Considered a skilled orator, his Friday sermons attracted a considerable number of believers. Even after he

---

[71] Abu Adham is not the real name of the shaykh. He would prefer his name not to be mentioned in any publication.

was removed from his position due to disputes among Dutch Salafi leaders, he retained considerable influence among Dutch Muslim Youth. In the Netherlands, the shaykh regards preserving the identity of Muslims as his main task; he wants to prevent them from becoming westernized. He urges them not to see themselves as Europeans, but rather stresses their membership in the global Islamic community. At the same time, he urges Muslims in the Netherlands to vote in elections, preferably for Muslim candidates or those who do not contradict the interests of Muslims.

The shaykh is still in contact with Lebanese Salafis from the *haraki* network. He visits Tripoli from time to time, occasionally taking some of his students there to become acquainted with local Salafis. There is, however, no indication of any organized relationship between the Dutch Salafi group and the Lebanese network. The shaykh's visits may well reflect his wish to maintain contacts there as a precaution, just in case he has to leave Europe one day, as has happened to other Lebanese Salafi scholars, such as Omar Bakri, Salim al-Rafi'I, and Ra'id Hulay-hil.[72] When I asked him about his activities during his visits to Lebanon, he told me that he mostly meets fellow Salafis and updates himself about the current situation in the country. He stressed that it is import-ant for a preacher to have a comparative perspective on what is going on in distant territories of the *Umma*, so as to make his audience aware of the needs and problems of Muslims. According to him, he needs to inform the Dutch Salafis of the threat that Ahl al-Sunna face in Lebanon from the Shi'a and Hizbullah. Being aware of the nature of the Shi'ite conspiracy[73] enables Muslims in the Netherlands to understand why they need to be cautious with Iraqi Shi'ites who have taken refuge in the Netherlands and, in the opinion of the shaykh, are continuously attempting to harm the Sunnis.[74]

---

[72] Omar Bakri was the head of Hizb al-Tahrir and later the Salafi group al-Muhajirun in Great Britain. In 2005 he left the UK for Lebanon, where he was informed by the British authorities that he would not be allowed to return. "Cleric Bakri barred from Britain," *BBC News*, August 12, 2005, http://news.bbc.co.uk/2/hi/uk_news/4144792.stm (accessed April 3, 2009). Salim al-Rafi'i was banned from reentering Germany in 2006, where he had been the head of an Islamic center in Berlin (see Chapter 4). Ra'id Hulayhil, who had been a prominent Salafi leader in Denmark, was part of a campaign launched by a group of Muslim scholars in 2005 against the publication caricatures by the Danish Jyllands-Posten magazine depicting the Prophet Muhammad. As he told me, due to the subsequent public criticism against him he left for Lebanon in 2006. Interview, Tripoli, November 6, 2009.

[73] See Chapter 7.

[74] At the time of my interview, a disagreement had occurred between the constituency of a Shi'a mosque and the followers of the shaykh.

My interviews with the shaykh shed light on how his Lebanese origins influence his style of activism. On one occasion, we talked extensively about how he perceives the importance of coming from the Sham (Greater Syria) and not, for example, from the Gulf. He explained that Lebanon gave him a kind of "global outlook" (*tafkir 'alami*).[75] Historically, the region has always been a hub of trade routes and a meeting point between East and West. Migration and long voyages have formed part of the inhabitants' lives for thousands of years. Nowadays, large migrant communities originating from Lebanon or Syria can be found throughout the world. Families even urge their members to seek their fortune in Western countries and in the Gulf States.

Salafis from the Gulf usually refuse opportunities to spend a certain period of time in a Western country. They often express fears that they might not find an appropriate environment there in which to live life fully according to *shari'a*. As the shaykh told me, "'*asabiyya* [here meaning kinship bonds] and racism prevent Salafi *da'is* from the Gulf from coming to Western Europe. They are nothing without their tribes, often they do not have an independent personality. Although God created us to individually worship Him, they are nothing without their tribe."[76] This is why the shaykh thinks that *da'is* from the Gulf issue thousands of fatwas for Western Muslims without ever leaving their home towns. He also regards this as the main reason why most of the Salafi *da'is* in the West come from Syria, Lebanon, and Jordan, or have Palestinian origins. As he explained, due to his Lebanese origins, he is able to bridge cultural differences with his mostly Moroccan constituency. "Moroccans have their own *'asabiyya*, which is different from that of the Middle East. You have to find a way to talk to them – people from the Gulf are unable to understand this."[77]

According to the shaykh, another distinguishing feature of Salafis of Lebanese, Syrian, or Palestinian origin is their mostly different understanding of *al-wala' wa-l-bara'*. He argued that for many Salafis in the Gulf, this doctrine not only means an obligation to hate that which is un-Islamic in religion but also to avoid and hate all non-Muslims and heretics. Even one of the greatest Salafi authorities, 'Abd al-'Aziz bin Baz, warned in many of his lectures against friendship with or positive feelings toward unbelievers.[78] The Dutch-Lebanese shaykh, however,

---

[75] Interview with Abu Adham, The Hague, July 6, 2011.   [76] Ibid.   [77] Ibid.
[78] See, for example, www.ahlalhdeeth.com/vb/showthread.php?t=88912 (accessed April 3, 2015).

thinks that *al-wala' wa-l-bara'* means only the hatred of certain beliefs and actions of those who are not Muslims or who do not practice Islam properly, and this hatred should not be extended to their persons. "Muslim men are allowed to take Christian or Jewish wives. They marry them because they are affected by their beauty or thinking. So how could they hate them at the same time?"[79] The shaykh also thinks that Muslims can befriend non-Muslims, because in this way, they may be a positive influence on them.

The biographies of these two shaykhs illustrate how transnational Salafi networks evolve and operate. Informal networks are crucial to access the resources necessary to become a transnational preacher. The way opens to institutional links, such as transnational charities, via informal contacts.

6.6   Conclusion

The linkages of Lebanese Salafis extend to multiple locations around the globe; in this chapter I took a closer look at the ties to the Gulf and Western Europe. Informal ties are predominant at the transnational level as well, while formal organizational ties are less prominent and embedded into the more extended informal networks.

The structure of the *haraki* and purist networks is rather distinct on the transnational level. This is due to the different degree of authority of the *'ulama'* in these two factions. Purist scholars based in the Gulf have a bigger influence on their constituency abroad than the *harakis*. This results in a rather hierarchical structure of the purist transnational networks, while *haraki* networks are more horizontal.

The countries of the Arabian Gulf are at the center of Salafi transnational networks and constitute important sources of religious and social capital for Lebanese Salafis. Studying in the Gulf provides them with religious capital both in its "embodied" and "institutionalized" state. Building contacts with Salafis in the Gulf also often grants access to wealthy donors and charities, or can be helpful for someone to find a job in one of the Gulf monarchies.

While Gulf countries are sources of sponsorship and religious inspiration for Lebanese Salafis, Europe is a destination for *da'wa*. Shaykhs from Lebanon who studied in the Gulf and possess strong

---

[79] Interview with Abu Adham, The Hague, July 6, 2011.

social capital there often become important religious leaders in European Muslim communities, as the case studies on Shaykh Ghassan, who settled in Sweden, and Abu Adham, who established himself in the Netherlands, showed. Both shaykhs largely rely on informal links and their mission is similar: to convince European Muslims not to adopt a European identity, but rather a universalist Islamic one envisioned by Salafis. This universal identity then is reinforced through framing activities.

7 Recruitment

Salafi success in contemporary Lebanon can be only partially explained by the mindset of Salafis, the movement's historical development, and the structure of their local and transnational networks. Understanding Lebanese Salafism also requires an understanding of methods and strategies they use to attract followers. First, I should clarify what "recruitment" means. For Salafis, recruitment does not mean attracting registered members, since the concept of membership does not exist in Salafism (see Chapter 5). Recruitment is about convincing people to adopt their worldview and lifestyle. Many people who adopt Salafi practices or elements of Salafi discourse do not see themselves as Salafi, but in most cases the researcher should regard them as belonging to the movement due to their worldview and activities.

Framing and the Salafi ideology's appeal to young people are the main factors that enable successful recruitment for the movement. Ordinary believers tend usually to be attracted by the Salafis' successful framing activities. Salafis provide plausible explanations for the day-to-day problems of Lebanese Sunnis, and offer appealing and seemingly simple solutions. The success of Salafi framing is strengthened by the articulators' (i.e. the Salafi shaykhs') high degree of religious authority, which is due to their accumulation of religious, economic, and social capital (explained in Chapter 4). The frustration and insecurity young people experience have become fertile ground for Salafis to convince these individuals to transform their lives in accordance with Salafi norms. Due to the successful networking and *da'wa* strategies, the number of active adherents is also growing rapidly.

7.1   Recruitment through Framing

My interviews with individuals who are involved in Salafism at different levels show that many people first became sympathizers with the movement because they accepted the Salafi interpretation of the world around

200

them.[1] The discourse they hear during the Friday sermon, which is repeated during *halaqat* or informal conversations, resonates with their own experiences and helps them to construct an understanding of their external environment. The concept of framing is especially useful for studying and explaining this process. Goffman calls "frames" the "schemata of interpretation," which "enable users to locate, perceive, identify and label a seemingly infinite number of concrete occurrences defined in its terms."[2] In other words, frames are prisms through which past and present events, and the logic of "the world out there," can be interpreted.

The discussions of social movement theorists on framing are especially useful to understand how Salafis attempt to convince potential adherents and constituents to adopt the movement's discourses and practices. Frames that call for collective action – in the case of Salafism individualized collective action, as Chapter 5 explains, have three core tasks: "diagnostic," "prognostic," and "motivational framing."[3] The first one aims to identify the problem and its sources, and the culpable agents. In prognostic framing, the frame articulators propose a solution to the problem detected in diagnostic framing.[4] Motivational framing "provides a 'call to arms' or rationale for engaging in ameliorative collective action."[5] For successful mobilization these three core tasks usually have to be contained in a movement's framing.[6]

Salafi ideology plays a central role in creating collective action frames. The main reason is that the aim of Salafism is to make others accept its ideology as the only truth, and a system of ideas that can provide explanations for all aspects of human life. One of the main elements of Salafi ideology is conceptualizing the world as a place of struggle between good and evil, or truth and falsehood (*sira' bayn al-haqq wa-l-batil*). The good side is manifested in Islam. Those who follow the right *'aqida* and *manhaj* belong to the good side. Any deviation from Islam forms part of the realm of *batil* (or *kufr* or *taghut*). According to the Salafi concept, correct deeds (*sahhat al-a'mal*) can be derived only from the right *'aqida*. Deviant belief can only result in deviant acts.[7] The Muslims' task in this world is to correct their own and others' belief, so as to erase wrongful acts and create an ideal life-world for the whole of humankind.[8]

---

[1] Interviews and field observations between September 2009 and May 2012.
[2] Goffman, *Frame Analysis*, p. 21.
[3] Snow and Benford, "Ideology, Frame Resonance, and Participant Mobilization."
[4] Ibid., pp. 615–617.   [5] Ibid., p. 617.   [6] Ibid., p. 615.
[7] www.saaid.net/Doat/almuwahid/003.htm (accessed January 10, 2013).
[8] Most of the Salafis I interviewed gave this answer to the question, what is the aim of the *da'wa*? For example, interview with Shaykh 'Abd al-Rahman 'Abd al-Khaliq, Kuwait, March 11, 2012.

The world thus is engaged in a Manichean struggle, with clearly defined sides.[9] On the good side there is *Ahl al-Sunna wa-l-Jama'a* and on the bad side is *Ahl al-Batil* (the community of wrongfulness), which consists of all those who deviate from the right path. Salafi writings, both purist and *haraki*, often repeat that these two sides are engaged in a continuous struggle against each other. Yet, *harakis* utilize this concept of Manichean struggle more effectively to gain followers than purists. This is because purists intend to face the challenges coming from *Ahl al-Batil* only by perfecting the minute details of their religious practice and dissociate themselves as much as possible from the customs and practices of non-Salafis and non-Muslims. They rarely engage in public affairs and discuss actual politics.

The publications of Lebanese purists almost never focus on issues beyond individual religious practice and conduct of behavior. The purist Center for Islamic Scientific Research (*Markaz al-Bahth al-'Ilmi al-Islami*) funded by Shaykh Sa'd al-Din al-Kibbi in 'Akkar, and one of the beneficiaries of SRIH publishes a monthly journal entitled "Islamic Scientific Research" (*al-Bahth al-'Ilmi al-Islami*) that contains research articles written by mostly purist Salafis. The majority of these articles focus on correct worship, the relationship between wife and husband, and some theoretical issues that concern theology and jurisprudence. Actual politics are touched occasionally and in indirect ways. For example, one article in the journal was published in 2015 after ISIS had burned Jordanian pilot Mu'adh al-Kasasiba alive as a retaliation to Jordan's air raids against the organization.[10] The author Muhammad 'Ali al-Hawamila argues, pointing to the scripture, that retaliation in kind is not allowed by using fire. Qisas also can be implemented after *wali al-amr* orders it. Yet, the article does not explicitly mention Kasasiba's case.

Haraki Salafis establish their discourse that is related to public affairs on the basis of the struggle between good and evil. Shaykh Zakariyya al-Masri (b. 1960) is perhaps the most established *haraki* Salafi writer in Lebanon. Since the early 1990s, he has authored dozens of books and articles that have been published mostly by his institute, the Hamza Center (Markaz Hamza'). Al-Masri, a personal friend of the leaders of the Saudi Sahwa movement, argues that the forces of *taghut*

---

[9] Salafis often refer to the 32nd *aya* in *Surat Yunus*: "That is God, your Lord, the Truth. Apart from the Truth, what is there except error?" Abdel Haleem, *The Qur'an*, p. 131.

[10] Muhammad 'Ali al-Hawamila, "Harq al-Insan bi-Da'wa al-Qisas: Dirasa Firqhiyya Muqarina," *al-Bahth al-'Ilmi al-Islami*, July 1, 2015.

in the contemporary historical era are manifested in secular ideologies, such as Capitalism and Communism.[11] The proponents of the these, although they struggle with each other, unite their forces against Muslims. Al-Masri also argues that the Shi'ites, who pretend to be Muslims, but in reality belong to the realm of unbelief, ally with the secularists against Sunnis.[12]

Al-Masri's books are widely read by *haraki* Salafis in Lebanon, but they reach only a very limited audience beyond that. The Friday sermon is the most common way for Lebanese Salafis to transmit their message to the masses. Unquestionably, the most popular preachers in the city of Tripoli and also probably in the whole North are Salafis from the *haraki* faction. Purist preachers do not attract mass audiences, since they have refused to support the revolutions, labeling them illegitimate. Furthermore, purist sermons usually focus on issues that deal with religious practices and belief. For this reason, only dozens of people appear at the Friday sermons of purist shaykhs.

In contrast, Shaykh Salim al-Rafa'i in the Taqwa mosque on the border between the city center and the al-Tabbana district, and Shaykh Zakariyya al-Masri in the Hamza mosque of al-Qubba attract thousands of people every Friday. In addition, hundreds often gather to listen to the *khutba* of other, less renowned Salafi shaykhs all over the city. The most common topics of discussion in the past few years have been the role of Hizbullah, the social and economic deprivation of the Sunnis, and the Arab revolutions. The Salafi worldview and universe of discourse provide the toolkit to formulate from these topics diagnostic frames that identify for the audience what causes the Lebanese Sunnis' ostensibly oppressed situation both in political and economic terms.

7.1.1   Shi'ites as Enemies of Islam

In the diagnostic framing of *haraki* Salafi shaykhs, every adversity that Lebanese Sunnis are facing has been caused by the enemies of Islam, who are trying to weaken and crush the religion, such as Shi'ites who throughout the history of Islam have been conspiring against Sunnis.

---

[11] Zakariyya al-Masri, *Istratijiyyat al-Sahwa al-Islamiyya fi-Kayfiyyat al-Ta'amul ma'al-'Almaniyya al-Shariqiyya wa-l-'Almaniyya al-Gharbiyya: Fikra Islamiyya Jami'a* (Tarablus: Markaz Hamza, 2009).

[12] Zakariyya al-Masri, *Dawr al-Imbaraturiyya al-Shi'iyya al-Shuyu'iyya* (Tarablus: Markaz Hamza, 2007).

Anti-Shi'ism is a cornerstone of Salafi ideology and appears in the vast majority of the *khutbas*. As discussed in Chapter 4, Salafis present themselves as the "ideal Muslim" who follows every aspect of their understanding of Islam as the manifestation of purity. The Shi'a, who in the Salafi view corrupt the perfect belief system, represent "pollution [*najas*] in the body of the *umma*."[13] The hostility toward the Shi'a has been present in the *Athari*[14] school since its early days. Ibn Hanbal was the first to call the members of the sect *rafida* (sing. *rafidi*).[15] The term means "rejectionists" and refers to the Shi'ite denial of the legitimacy of the first three Caliphs.[16] Ibn Taymiyya and his students, such as Ibn Qayyim al-Jawziyya, also expressed enmity toward the sect's doctrines. The foundations of contemporary Salafi anti-Shi'ism, though, were laid out by Muhammad bin Abd al-Wahhab and the Najdi *'ulama'* in the eighteenth and nineteenth centuries.[17] Salafis today criticize the Shi'ite belief system in three main aspects. First, Salafis accuse the Shi'a of believing that the Qur'an was altered (*tahrif al-Qur'an*) when it was put together during the rule of 'Uthman bin 'Affan (644–656 AD). During the process, some *aya*s that proved Ali's right of succession were changed or erased.[18] The second accusation is that the Shi'a cursed and excommunicated many of the *Sahaba*, including the first three Caliphs and those who supported Mu'awiya against 'Ali.[19] Third, Salafis believe that the excommunication of the Sunnis is an essential part of Shi'ite theology. According to them,

---

[13] This view was expressed to me during numerous interviews and conversations with Salafis in Lebanon and elsewhere in the Middle East between 2009 and 2012.

[14] See my discussion of the Athari school of thought in the Introduction.

[15] Guido Steinberg, "Jihadi Salafism and the Shi'is: Remarks about the Intellectual Roots of anti-Shi'ism." In Meier, *Global Salafism*, p. 133.

[16] The Shi'ites claim that the first three Caliphs, namely Abu Bakr, 'Umar, and 'Uthman, unlawfully ascended to the throne, denying the right of 'Ali to immediate succession after the death of the Prophet. Ethan Kohlberg, "The Term 'Rāfida' in Imāmī Shī'ī Usage," *Journal of the American Oriental Society*, 99, no. 4 (1979), p. 677.

[17] Muhammad bin 'Abd al-Wahhab, *Al-Radd 'ala al-Rafida*, n.d. www.tawhed.ws/r?i= 1381 (accessed January 10, 2013).

[18] The notion of *Tahrif al-Qur'an* is indeed expressed by some Shi'ite texts, but Twelver Shi'ites in general reject it. See Muhammad Ismail Marcinkowski, "Some Reflections on Alleged Twelver Shi'ite Attitudes Toward the Integrity of the Qur'an," *The Muslim World*, 91, nos. 1–2 (2001). However, the belief in the forgery of the Qur'an is not entirely extinct. When I was staying in South Lebanon in the summer of 2006, I had conversations with Shi'ite shaykhs who still upheld such views, although they can be considered a negligible minority.

[19] See, for example, the lecture of the renowned Kuwaiti Shaykh 'Uthman al-Khamis: www .youtube.com/results?search_query=عثمان+الخميس+شيعة&oq=عثمان+الخميس+شيعة&gs_l=you tube.3. . .22784.40892.0.41275.19.14.1.4.4.0.595.4080.1j3j6j2j0j2.14.0. . .0.0. . .1ac.1.11.you tube.FmZzX2PMH38 (accessed January 4, 2013); Bin 'Abd al-Wahhab, *Al-Radd 'ala al-Rafida*.

Shi'ites believe that they have the right to kill the Sunnis and can take their property legally. Such acts are even dear in God's eyes.[20]

Almost all Salafis agree with these three points and claim that those Shi'ites who are aware of their doctrines and do not reject them (i.e. the *khassa* or elite) are unbelievers.[21] *Harakis* go even further and claim that these deviations make the Shi'a masterminds of conspiracy against the Sunnis. This view originates from the Syrian Muslim Brothers at the beginning of the 1980s, who saw the alliance between the Assad regime and Khomeini's Iran as part of the Shi'ites' continuous attempts throughout Islamic history to dominate the Middle East and oppress Sunnis.[22] *Haraki* Salafis worldwide adopted this frame to explain the role of the other major Muslim sect in the contemporary Islamic world. It is also a chief element in Shaykh Zakariyya al-Masri's and Salim al-Rafa'is rhetoric. In one of his *khutbas*, the former argues that the Shi'ite sect is the direct result of the *taghut* 's eternal attempt to destroy the *haqq*:

After the Prophet extended his rule over the whole of the Arabian Peninsula by conquering Mecca and starting the wars with the Byzantines with the raid of Tabuk [*Ghazwat Tabuk*],[23] and after Abu Bakr eliminated the *Ridda*,[24] the Muslims began under[the latter's] leadership to conquer Persia and the Byzantine Empire. This continued under the rule of 'Umar bin al-Khattab and 'Uthman bin al-'Affan until the Muslim armies arrived at the borders of China in the East and the [western] coasts of North Africa in the West. These [events] shook the world and woke the resentment of [those who hate Islam]. The leaders of the Persians and the Greeks gathered to find a way to face this great Islamic expansion. They formed a secret organization to hit Islam from inside ... by pretending [by a group of people] to convert and spread the division and internal strife among Muslims. 'Abdullah bin Saba', a Yemeni

---

[20] Interviews and conversations with Salafis in Lebanon and the Gulf between 2009 and 2012. This view is also expressed in Shaykh 'Uthman al-Khamis' lecture and can be detected on various Salafi websites and internet forums. See, for example, Ramadan al-Ghannam, "Falsafat al-Qatl wa-l-Ightiyal Fi al-Fikr al-Shi'i," *Almoslim.net*, March 22, 2012. www.almoslim.net/node/162346 (accessed January 5, 2013).

[21] Most Salafis agree that *'ammat al-shi'a* or ordinary Shi'ites should not be excommunicated until they individually prove that they deserve it.

[22] Steinberg, "Jihadi Salafism and the Shi'is," pp. 116–121.

[23] According to the Islamic tradition, in 630 BC Prophet Muhammad led a campaign against the Byzantines stationed in Tabuk, North Arabia. Although the Muslim army did not make contact with the enemy, some local chiefs submitted to them. See: "Tabuk." In Bossworth, *Encyclopaedia of Islam*.

[24] Here the *Ridda* means a series of battles between the early Muslims and the tribes that terminated their allegiance to the Islamic state in Medina or refused to pay taxes during the Caliphate of Abu Bakr (632–634). In Islamic historiography these tribes left Islam, and this is why they had to be fought. See "al-Ridda." In Bossworth, *Encyclopaedia of Islam*.

Jew, was given this dangerous diplomatic [sic!] task. He pretended to accept Islam with a group of fellow Jews to mobilize Muslims against their Caliph in the capital city of the Islamic Empire.[25]

According to Shaykh Zakariyya, 'Abdullah bin Saba''s activity led to several uprisings in different parts of the Caliphate, and he was also behind the murder of the Caliph 'Uthman. Later, after the death of the Caliph 'Ali (who followed 'Uthman), bin Saba' and his followers started to mix the doctrines of Islam with old Zoroastrian beliefs and invented Shi'ism by associating divine attributes with 'Ali and his descendants, the twelve Imams. The mission of the "Shi'ite religion" – as many of the Salafi preachers refer to it, denying that the sect is part of Islam – is to undermine and destroy Islam. Zakariyya al-Masri and other preachers often present the example of the Fatimid Caliphate[26] and the Safavid Empire[27] as the attempt of the *"Majus "* (reference to Zoroastrians) to destroy Sunnism. Similarly, they accuse the Shi'ites of allying with the Crusaders and cooperating with the Mongols to conquer Baghdad and abolish the Abbasid Caliphate.[28]

The Salafi shaykhs warn that the series of Shi'ite conspiracies has been continuing in the twentieth and twenty-first centuries. In their reading of events, since the Islamic Revolution (1979), Iran has been trying to dominate the Middle East. First, the Iranians tried to achieve this by spreading their ideology by direct military means, but they failed to do so, because "Iraq with the leadership of Saddam Hussein made their aspirations fail and resisted them with the support of the Gulf countries."[29] After that, Iran began to mobilize the Shi'ite minorities throughout the Islamic world to spread the revolution. They incited the Shi'ite communities in Saudi Arabia and Iraq to revolt. Salafis believe that the Iranian leadership has a secret alliance with the United States. Shaykh Zakariyya al-Masri often claims that the regime in Tehran helped the Americans to conquer Afghanistan and Iraq by supporting local Shi'ite minorities against the Taliban, "that held the ideology of unifying Muslims under the banner of the Caliphate," and Saddam Hussein, who "turned from nationalist to Islamist at the last period of his rule."[30] According to Salafi preachers, the other

---

[25] Khutba of Shaykh Zakariyya al-Masri, Hamza Mosque, Qubba district, Tripoli, February 11, 2011.
[26] al-Masri, *Dawr al-Imbaraturiyya al-Shi'iyya al-Shuyu'iyya*, pp. 37–38.
[27] Ibid., pp. 86–87.   [28] Ibid., pp. 84–86.
[29] Salafis usually argue that the 1980–1988 Iraq–Iran war was provoked by the latter, and depict Saddam Hussein as a hero who stopped Iran with the help of the Gulf monarchies, which financed his military. See, for example, Al-Masri, *Dawr al-Imbaraturiyya*, p. 35.
[30] Interview with Sheikh Zakariyya al-Masri, Tripoli, November 10, 2009.

ally of Iran is *al-'Almaniyya al-Sharqiyya* (Eastern Secularism), namely China and Russia, which also intend to weaken Islam in order to subjugate their own minorities and achieve control over the Middle East's resources. Salafis also think that the Shi'ites have been in a secret alliance with the Jews since the dawn of Islamic history, and that they now cooperate with Israel. With all of this, they imply that the Shi'ites are prepared to ally with non-Muslim powers, and even atheists and Communists, simply to destroy Sunnism.

Salafi preachers commonly frame contemporary events in Lebanon as part of this global Shi'a conspiracy against Islam. Most of them have adopted Zakariyya al-Masri's reading of the country's history since the civil war.[31] According to the shaykh, Iran intends to convert the whole country to Shi'ism. In order to realize this, Tehran has allied with the *Nusayriyya*[32] (the Syrian regime dominated by the Alawites).[33] As Shaykh Zakariyya explains, the Iranians began to execute their plan during the civil war, from the beginning of the 1980s onward. They established Hizbullah, which, since that time, has constantly been trying to rid the country of its Sunni population. They initially supported the Shi'ite AMAL militia in its military campaign against the Palestinians in the second half of the1980s (the event known as *Harb al-Mukhayyamat* or "the war of the camps").[34] Their plan was "to weaken *Ahl al-Sunna* by ridding them of their military power,"[35] represented by the Palestinian factions.

In the common Salafi rhetoric, Tripoli is the last stronghold of *Ahl al-Sunna* in Lebanon, and the Shi'ites realized that it should be broken before they would be able to take over the country. Iran therefore assisted Syria in wresting the city in 1985 from the IUM. The IUM

---

[31] Shaykh Zakariyya al-Masri, probably the most notorious anti-Shi'a cleric in Tripoli, is regarded as "the authority [*al-marja'iyya*]" in the "scientific inquiry" about the "truth about the Shi'ites." Many local Salafi shaykhs have studied at his Islamic center and *halaqat* or read his books.

[32] Nusayriyya is a reference to the Alawite sect. The term is mostly used by Sunnis and has a pejorative meaning.

[33] The Alawites are part of Shi'ite Islam and constitute the majority of the population on the Syrian coast. They have dominated Syrian political life since the Assad clan, an Alawite family, came to power in 1970. See: Patrick Seal, *Asad: The Struggle for the Middle East* (Berkeley and Los Angeles: University of California Press, 1995).

[34] The war in the camp lasted between 1985 and 1989. After Israel had withdrawn from most parts of Lebanon in 1985, the PLO started to gain a foothold again in South Lebanon. Hafiz al-Asad, in order to boost his own dominance in the country and avoid a possible second Israeli invasion, helped the secular Shi'ite AMAL militia to sweep the PLO factions out of Beirut, Sidon, and the Southern regions. Harris, *The New Face of Lebanon*, pp. 195–197.

[35] Interview with Sheikh Zakariyya al-Masri, November 10, 2009.

was formed by different local Islamic movements that were controlling different quarters of Tripoli. Their intention was to establish an Islamic emirate in North Lebanon. According to the Salafis, Tehran prevented the IUM from introducing Islamic rule by buying the leader of the movement, Shaykh Sa'id Sha'ban, by promising him the presidency of an Islamic state in Lebanon that was to follow the template of Iran. However, when the Syrian army took over the city, none of the Ayatollahs' promises came true. Instead, Islamists and Salafis had to face long persecution by the agents of the Ba'th regime and Hizbullah. The "sincere" members of Harakat al-Tawhid were either arrested or left the movement. The rest sided with the Syrians and the Shi'ite militia. Since then, the Alawites of *Jabal Muhsin* who, according to the Salafis, helped Assad's army to slaughter the Sunnis upon the takeover of the city, and the IUM have been the main agents of Shi'a influence in Tripoli.[36]

When Salafi preachers discuss contemporary events in Lebanon that involve Hizbullah or are related to the Shi'a in other ways, they frame them using the Shi'a conspiracy theory. Hizbullah is regarded as the Trojan horse and main agent of the "Persian conquest." In one of his sermons, Zakariyya al-Masri states that Israeli military exercises between May 31 and June 4, 2009 were organized by the Jewish state to support "their ally" Hizbullah in the parliamentary elections of June 9. The aim was "to help the party in an indirect way to gain more votes" by inciting fear of the Israeli threat in Lebanon. According to the Shaykh, Hizbullah has an interest in maintaining the tensions with Israel in order to portray itself as a pioneer of the resistance, and thereby gain the legitimacy to keep its weapons and increase its political influence. The ultimate aim of this "Zoroastrian-Zionist coalition" is to dominate Lebanon and eliminate the Sunni population by displacing them or converting them to Shi'ism.[37]

In one of his *khutbas*, Shaykh 'Imad Jasim, one of the leading preachers in the Wadi Khalid region in 'Akkar, discussed some remarks made by the Druze politician Wi'am Wahhab, one of the allies of Hizbullah. Wahhab, while criticizing the social norms in Saudi Arabia, called the women in the kingdom "black garbage bags" (referring to their dress).[38] Shaykh 'Imad argues that the politician's aim was to attack the honor of the pious Muslim women who wear the *hijab*. After that, the shaykh turns his attention toward those who are

---

[36] Series of interviews with Shaykh Zakariyya al-Masri and other preachers between 2009 and 2012.

[37] Sermon of Shaykh Zakariyya al-Masri, Hamza Mosque, Tripoli, June 5, 2009.

[38] http://news.nawaret.com/?p=175920 (accessed January 7, 2013).

behind Wahhab with "their dirty media empire and money." The preacher's conclusion is that Hizbullah supports Wahhab and similar figures in order to create *fitna* in the country. By using the strategy of "divide and rule," the party can integrate Lebanon into the future Shi'ite Empire.[39] Salafi shaykhs complement the anti-Shi'a framing described in this section with depicting Lebanese Sunnis as a disenfranchised population. I will discuss this in the following section.

7.1.2 Sunnis as Victims

In the rhetoric of the shaykhs, the oppression of *Ahl al-Sunna* fits into the framework of the cosmic fight between good and evil. The forces of the latter are made up of the Shi'a, Zionism, the United States, China, and Russia.[40] Their aim is to prevent the Sunnis from reestablishing the Islamic Empire "from Indonesia to Andalusia"[41] and to create a Shi'ite state that extends from Yemen through Iran to Lebanon. Together with Israel, this state would secure control of the three great powers (the United States, China, and Russia) over the resources of the Middle East. To realize this plan, Sunnis first have to be oppressed politically, economically, and mentally. Salafi shaykhs situate and frame the current socioeconomic situation within this conspiracy theory.

In many of his *khutbas*, Shaykh Salim al-Rafa'i emphasizes that "Ahl al-Sunna in Lebanon are banned from development."[42] According to him, the conspirators against Islam "determined the Sunnis in Tripoli would live in poverty." Despite the "vast resources" of the northern region, masses of young people are unemployed, the city lacks basic infrastructure, and "drug abuse is omnipresent." In his sermon, Shaykh Salim mentions the case of the airport in Tripoli, which was closed in the 1990s. He stated that a foreign company wanted to renovate and reopen the airport at its own expense. This would have provided 6,000 jobs for the inhabitants of Tripoli. The offer was refused, however, because "Hizbullah forbade its acceptance."[43]

---

[39] *Khutba* of Shaykh 'Imad Jasim, Wadi Khalid, March 18, 2011.
[40] See, for example, *Khutba* of Shaykh Salim al-Rafa'i, Taqwa Mosque, Tripoli, February 10, 2012.
[41] See, for example, *Khutba* of Shaykh Zakariyya al-Masri, Hamza Mosque, Tripoli, October 21, 2005.
[42] *Khutba* of Shaykh Salim al-Rafa'i, Taqwa Mosque, Tripoli, May 11, 2012 or 21 December 2012.
[43] *Khutba* of Shaykh Salim al-Rafa'i, Taqwa Mosque, Tripoli, May 11, 2012.

The shaykh's conclusion as to why the city is economically and socially deprived is that "it is inhabited by committed young men [*shabab multazimin*]. And they [the enemies of Islam] want to depict religious commitment [in the case of Sunnis] as a phenomenon coming together with poverty and chaos." According to him, the following case proves this:

Recently, I was informed by someone about a security meeting between Lebanese state officials. They were debating the alarming situation in the North. I thought they discussed the poverty, the spread of drugs or the lack of order. However, [the person who informed him about the event] told me, No! No! They were inquiring about the fact– and now listen to me well – they were inquiring because the number of the young men who visit the mosques has dramatically increased and they want to devise a plan to strike them!

To prove their argument, Salafi shaykhs often highlight the fact that the situation in other countries is similar. They point out that Sunnis are oppressed and even murdered in Iraq and Iran; that they lack the basic right to practice their religion. According to a common Salafi claim, Sunnis are even forbidden to have a mosque in Iran.

7.1.3   Framing during Media Appearances

Before the ascendance of Salafism in the post–Arab Uprisings period, the only Lebanese Salafi figure who frequently appeared in the media was Shaykh Da'i al-Islam al-Shahhal. This changed when the movement, and especially the *haraki* faction, started to rapidly expand from 2011. *Haraki* shaykhs frequently appeared in various media outlets, such as Lebanese and Pan-Arab Satellite TV channels, newspapers, and online news sites, where they were usually asked for their opinion on the Syrian civil war and its impact on Lebanon.

Shaykh Salim al-Rafa'i, for example, gave numerous interviews to Arab TV channels, such as al-Arabiya, and once even to BBC Arabic. In their media appearances, the shaykh relied on the same frameworks to explain the political situation: In a 2013 interview for Al-Arabiya, he was asked about the conflict between the Sunni militias in al-Tabbana and the Alavites in Jabal Muhsin, and also his role in the Syrian civil war.[44] Shaykh Salim framed these conflicts in a similar way as he did in his Friday sermons. He stressed the oppressed situation of Sunni Muslims in Lebanon. According to the narrative he presented in front of

---

[44] Interview in Al-Arabiya TV channel, December 14, 2013.

the cameras, Hizbullah and certain authorities of the Lebanese state (mostly the military intelligence) are conspiring against Sunni Muslims in Tripoli.

Due to this conspiracy, the "Alavite mafia" led by Rif'at al-'Ayd, the head of the main political organization of Jabal Muhsin, the Arab Democratic Party (*Hizb al-'Arabi al-Dimuqrati* – ADP) can commit crimes against Sunnis unpunished. Furthermore, when the reporter mentioned that unknown individuals shot at Alavites who do not necessarily belong to ADP, Shaykh Salim denied that it would be sectarian violence committed by Sunnis. In his view the shooters were members of Hizbullah, because the party wants to incite intercommunal tensions and war in Tripoli. The shaykh also mentioned that while Sunni Muslims who are accused of committing violent acts are usually arrested and kept in detention for years, this is not the case with members of ADP and Hizbullah.[45] Shaykh Salim implied that if the state fails to protect the Sunnis, they will take the matter into their own hands. He mentioned that if in murder cases the authorities did not arrest the killers who might belong to ADP or Hizbullah, "the offended party (*sahib al-damm*) will seek for justice by themselves." By this, he meant that members of the Sunni community will avenge the death of their fellow Sunnis, as for him *sahib al-damm* is the community itself.

In sum, these appearances on mainstream satellite channels are opportunities for Salafi shaykhs to convey a similar worldview and to underscore the message of their Friday sermons. Yet, unlike Egypt for example, Lebanese Salafis do no possess well known and popular TV channels, where they give advice in matters of daily religious practices.[46] Compared to Egyptian Salafis, the Lebanese Salafis' utilization of the internet is also underdeveloped. Only Shaykh Salim al-Rafa'i Taqwa mosque and CMS possess a YouTube channel, where media appearances and some of the Friday sermons are uploaded. These videos have been viewed a few hundred times in the course of a few years. This is much less than the average number of participants in Shaykh Salim's Friday sermons. The reason for the weak online Salafi presence is the slow internet connection in Lebanon, especially in the northern areas of the country. Due to the short distances and

---

[45] In a BBC Arabic interview on April 10, 2014 Shayk Salim accused the Lebanese state of attacking the followers of Shaykh Ahmad al-Asir (see also Chapter 3) following the "order" of Hizbullah.

[46] In Egypt, after the coup that overthrew president Mursi in July 2013, most of these channels were closed by the new administration.

their generally accessible attitude (see in Chapter 4), it is easy to meet the shaykhs and participate in their *khutbas*, lectures, and lessons in person.

7.1.4   The Arab Uprisings and the Syrian Revolution

As already discussed in Chapter 3, the Arab Uprisings increased the Salafis', and in particular the *harakis* ', standing in the Sunni religious field. Successful framing, just as in the case of the anti-Shi'a discourse, was crucial in this process.

Lebanese *haraki* Salafis emphasize the "Islamic nature" of the uprisings and argue that it is a new phase in the battle between good and evil. According to them, the Sunni masses want to get rid of their oppressors, who are the servants of the *taghut* and implement the orders of Western powers to spread secularism (*'almaniyya*), immoral behavior (*fahsh*), and adultery (*zina'*) among the populations of their countries. In their revolution, however, *Ahl al-Sunna* have to face the opposition of the *taghut* manifested by the secular powers, such as the West, Russia, and China, and the Shi'a and its stronghold, Iran. As a result, the theories of Shi'ite conspiracy and the Sunnis as victims are inherent parts of the framing of the Arab Spring by Salafis.

In a series of *khutbas*, Shaykh Salim al-Rafa'i frames the revolutions as part of one of the last battles between good and evil before the end of the world. He believes that the current events in the Middle East foretell the coming of the age of justice and righteousness and mark the imminent appearance of the (Sunni) *Mahdi*.[47] In his sermons he refers to the three traditions that prove this. The first concerns the types of leadership of the *Umma*:

The Prophetical period among you will be as God wants it to be, then He will end it when he wishes to. Then a Caliphate governing according to the method of the Prophethood [*khilafa 'ala manhaj al-Nubuwwa*] will follow, and it will be as God wants it to be, then He will end it when he wishes to. Then there will be a hereditary kingdom [*milk 'add*], and it will be as God wants it to be, then He will end it when he wishes to. Then there will be a tyrannical kingdom [*milk jabri*], and it will be as God wants it to be, then He will end it when he wishes to. Then there will be a Caliphate governing according to the method of the Prophethood.

---

[47] According to Sunni belief, which is adopted by Salafis, the *Mahdi* will appear at the time when Jesus will return to the Earth. The former will help the latter to kill the Antichrist (al-*Dajjal*) and then they will rule the world together and reestablish justice. "al-Mahdi." In Bossworth, *Encyclopaedia of Islam*.

According to the interpretation of Shaykh Salim, the "hereditary king-dom" means the historical Caliphate that ruled from the Umayyad dynasty until the abolition of the Ottoman state. The "tyrannical king-dom" signifies the contemporary Arab regimes, which are falling one by one due to the uprisings.[48] This *hadith*, according to him, is supported by another one, which foretells the "siege of Iraq" and the "siege of Syria [*al-Sham*]" before the emergence of a caliph. According to the preacher, the first refers to the Iran–Iraq war (1980–1988), because the *hadith* tells us that the siege will be carried out by the Persians (*'ajam*). The second is the ongoing Syrian conflict.

The third *hadith* concerns the appearance of the *Mahdi*. According to this *hadith*, there will be injustice (*zulm*) on Earth to an extent that has not been experienced before. After that, God will send someone from the family of the Prophet who will spread justice on Earth.[49] Shaykh Salim believes that these three *ahadith* indicate that after the Arab Spring, the Caliphate will reemerge and the Caliph will be the *Mahdi* himself.[50]

In the shaykh's rhetoric, the forces of *taghut* are trying to prevent the reestablishment of the "Righteous Caliphate [*khilafa rashida*]."[51] His frame is similar to that used by Shaykh Zakariyya al-Masri. According to him, there are two sides in the battle. The first is the "Camp of Belief [*mu'askar al-iyman*]," where Muslims fight to return to their might (*istirja' al-'izza*). On the other side are all the forces of *kufr* allied to crush the believers and prevent them from establishing an Islamic empire. This camp consists of the West, China, Russia, and the *batiniyyun* (a polemical reference to the Shi'ites).[52] The first two powers forbid military intervention in Syria and try to prolong Assad's rule. Regarding Russia, Shaykh Salim asks why it is support-ing the oppressors when Moscow always used to pose as a supporter of the Arabs against the oppressors. His answer is that if Islam were to become strong in the Middle East, it would spread again in Central Asia and endanger Russia as a Christian empire. This is why all of these powers support the Shi'ite plan to dominate the region, and not the Caliphate.[53] In another *khutba* he mentions that the Syrian revolu-tion is especially important for Lebanese Sunnis, because the Syrian Sunni community, which constitutes the majority of the country, is their "natural extension." If the Assad regime were to fall, Lebanese

[48] *Khutba* of Shaykh Salim al-Rafa'i, April 13, 2012.   [49] Ibid.
[50] Ibid. and *Khutba* of Shaykh Salim al-Rafa'i, April 20, 2012.   [51] See *khutbas*.
[52] Khutba of Shaykh Salim al-Rafa'i, February 10, 2012.   [53] Ibid.

Sunnis would cease to be only one of the communities in the country, but would reunite with the *Umma*.[54]

7.1.5   Solving the Sunni Situation with Pure Islam

For Lebanese *harakis*, the solution to the many ailments and crises that Sunnis face is implementing the uncorrupted form of Islam both in personal and public affairs. They urge their constituency to implement the rulings of Islam and emphasize the importance of solidarity with fellow Sunnis. This serves as the basis of their solution to the "Shi'a problem," the perceived disenfranchisement of their community, or what to do to support the revolutions. This kind of prognostic and motivational framing is attractive to the Salafi constituency, since it does not require a high level of investment and still offers significant rewards.

In one of his sermons, Shaykh Salim al-Rafa'i refers to a *hadith*: "When a servant of God ['abd] commits a sin, a black spot appears on his heart. If he repents, his heart will be cleansed." The preacher explains that the more disobedient (*ma'siya*) the Muslim individual, the blacker his heart becomes. The darker someone's heart is, the more difficult it is for him to distinguish between good and bad, and eventually he falls into the trap of evil. According to his argument, the decadent morality of contemporary Muslims enabled the forces of *taghut* to overwhelm *Ahl al-Sunna*, because they were unable to make the right decision. However, if they obey the *shari'a*, their hearts will be cleansed and God will show them the difference between right and wrong. Here he refers to the following *aya*: "Believers, if you remain mindful of God, He will give you a criterion [*furqan*, to tell right from wrong] and wipe out your bad deeds, and forgive you: God's favour is great indeed."[55] This argument might be similar to that of the purists. However, according to the preacher, Sunnis with dark hearts enable "Iran and its allies in Syria and Lebanon to commit massacres in Syria." If those Muslims knew the truth they would not help the Shi'a to oppress the revolution.[56]

In a different *khutba*, Shaykh Salim argues that success follows if people obey the rules of Islam "beyond prayer and fasting." He gives the example of the *shura* or consultative council. First, he refers to the

---

[54] Khutba of Shaykh Salim al-Rafa'i, February 24, 2012.
[55] Surat al-Anfal 29, Abdel Haleem, *The Qur'an*, p. 112.
[56] Khutba of Shaykh Salim al-Rafa'i, April 13, 2012.

aya, which describes the believers as those who "respond to their Lord; keep up the prayer; conduct their affairs by mutual consultation [*shura*]."[57] According to him, this, along with a range of other citations from the Qur'an and the Hadith, proves that *shura* is obligatory when Muslims take major decisions. As an example, he mentions the consultative council that he organizes every week in the Taqwa mosque (see Chapter 5), which, according to him, has been proven to be effective. In January 2012 the Lebanese authorities arrested one of the famous Salafi shaykhs in Tripoli, 'Abdullah Husayn, because of his fatwa that forbids Muslims to enter the Lebanese army.[58] The participants of the *shura* decided to call for demonstrations until the shaykh was freed. Since 'Abdullah Husayn is very popular even among the *harakis*, despite his purist views, thousands of people responded and blocked major roads of the city. After a few days, the shaykh was released. According to Shaykh Salim's reasoning, they were successful because they had followed the instructions of the *shari'a*.

Less famous *haraki* Salafi shaykhs make similar arguments to that of Shaykh Salim. Shaykh Mahir, a young *'alim* from the Qubba district in his mid-thirties is a good example. He is a graduate of the Islamic University of Medina and a former pupil of Shaykh Zakariyya al-Masri. Shaykh Mahir is not an imam of a mosque, but makes his living from the commissions he receives from the various Salafi colleges, such as Shaykh Da'i al-Islam al-Shahhal's Ma'had al-Hidaya, where he regularly teaches subjects related to *hadith*. He is also often invited to deliver the Friday sermons in Salafi-controlled mosques around Tripoli, and deliver religious lessons and lectures (*mau'iza*).[59]

During one of his lectures in the Qubba district's Hamza mosque, in which I participated, Shaykh Mahir pointed out that "the oppression of *Ahl al-Sunna* by the Shi'a will end if they follow the right *'aqida*." He argued that Hizbullah was able to grow strong in Lebanon due to the support of Sunni Muslims:

These persons [the Sunnis] acted out of ignorance [*jahl*]. If they were firm in their *'aqida* they would know that [the members of Hizbullah] are heretics

---

[57] Surat al-Shura 38, Abdel Haleem, *The Qur'an*, p. 314.

[58] Shaykh 'Abdullah Husayn is an interesting purist. He forbade entering the army because, according to him, there is no *wali amr* in Lebanon who can lead a Muslim army, since the president is Christian. Furthermore, the majority of the officers are Maronites and Shi'ites. According to the shari'a, Muslim soldiers cannot obey the commands of non-Muslims.

[59] These lectures are usually held after the *'asr* or the *maghrib* prayers. During the *mau'iza* the shaykh talks about a Qur'anic verse, a *hadith*, or a socially and politically important topic. These lectures usually last about half an hour.

and *mushrik*s and would not agree to cooperate with them under the banner of "Islamic unity" ... Islamic movements, the Muslim Brothers among them, when Khomeini abolished the rule of the shah they offered *bay'a*[60] to him. If they knew their own *'aqida* they would never do this, helping the *rafida* to implement their conspiracy.[61]

It is worth noting that Salafi framing differs significantly from that of other Islamic movements, such as the Muslim Brotherhood. The latter is far from being a purely messianic or utopian movement. Although its ideology contains such elements, overall, the Ikhwan tends to be rather practical. It also uses conspiracy theories, yet these are much more pragmatic than those of the Salafis. For example, the members of *al-Jama'a al-Islamiyya*, the Lebanese Muslim Brotherhood, also refer to conspiracies linked to Hizbullah and Iran, but they argue that they do not intend to destroy Islam, but simply want to achieve domination in the region.[62] Different proposed solutions also result from this logic. According to the Ikhwan, simply studying the Text and adhering to the rituals are not enough to elevate the Sunnis from their miserable state. Rather, they put emphasis on the importance of education, political consciousness, and building civil society institutions (in the Western sense). In the Muslim Brotherhood's framing, participation in their activities is also crucial. They require their followers to sacrifice some of their time, energy, and, if they can afford it, money for the sake of the movement. Prognostic or motivational framing then is used to urge Sunnis to get back on the right path.

7.2   Why Is the Salafis' Framing Successful?

According to my observations, Salafi frames have strong resonance, especially among the pious middle class and the urban poor (see also Chapter 5).[63] In the case of Tripoli's *haraki* Salafi preachers, the success of their framing has been mostly determined by their own credibility as frame articulators and the empirical credibility of the frames.[64]

---

[60] The Arabic term denotes "the act by which a certain number of persons, acting individually or collectively, recognise the authority of another person." "Bay'a." In Bossworth, *Encyclopaedia of Islam.*

[61] Participation in Shaykh Mahir's lecture, Tripoli, April 19, 2012.

[62] Interview with Fadi Shamiya, a prominent Muslim Brother in Sidon, Sidon, April 15, 2012.

[63] On frame resonance in the SMT literature see Benford and Snow, "Framing Processes and Social Movements: An Overview and Assessment," p. 619.

[64] Ibid., pp. 619–621.

The credibility of Salafi shaykhs as frame articulators is interconnected with their religious authority. A considerable part of the population regards these shaykhs as the most credible source of religious interpretation. At the same time, many see them as the group that is most qualified to lead the Sunni community in Lebanon (at least at the level of city quarters and villages) due to the loss of legitimacy of political leaders such as the Hariri clan or Najib Miqati, and the chronic weakness of Dar al-Fatwa. Unlike these leaders, the actions of Salafis seem to be consistent with their rhetoric. For example, in his prognostic framing, Shaykh Tawfiq, a well-known preacher from the Mina district (see Chapter 4) repeatedly emphasizes the importance of returning to the rulings of the *Shari'a* to solve the problem of poverty in the North.

In one of his *halaqat*, he argues that the Islamic system of *zakat* and *sadaqat* (alms) is in fact a powerful method to establish social justice and can be considered superior to Western social welfare systems. He thinks that poverty is the result of abandoning the rulings of Islam, and the only way to eradicate it is to return to the commandments of the *Shari'a*. The shaykh argues that if the *zakat* and *sadaqat* received from the richer members of the society were handled by faithful '*ulama*' there would be no poor among the Lebanese Sunni community.[65] He then spares no effort in making the "Islamic welfare system" work in reality, at least on the micro-level: He collects *zakat* and alms and distributes them among the poor in his neighborhood. He also has developed a system in which he and other shaykhs can issue vouchers that can be exchanged for medicine and other goods in certain shops. These goods are paid for later from the *zakat* and financial aid from Gulf charities.[66] These practices, in which he invests both religious and economic capital, make the shaykh credible as a frame articulator and, as a result, people tend to accept his arguments about other issues more readily.

In the case of the experimental credibility of the frames, the most important aspect is not the actual validity of its content, but whether the target group perceives it to be credible.[67] Regarding the anti-Shi'a frame, since the Hariri murder (2005) the Sunni population has become increasingly sectarian. Many believe that the Shi'ites aspire to dominate Lebanon and sideline the Sunnis, and that their main tool to achieve this goal is Hizbullah. Hostile rhetoric toward the Shi'a is common, even in secular circles. Sectarianism is present

[65] Dars of Shaykh Tawfiq, 'Uthman bin 'Affan mosque, Tripoli, April 25, 2012.
[66] Interview with Shaykh Tawfiq, Tripoli, April 25, 2012.
[67] Benford and Snow, "Framing Processes and Social Movements," p. 620.

in the discourse of the mainstream Sunni media that is related to the al-Mustaqbal movement and the Hariri clan.[68] The 2006 sit-ins in Riad Al-Sulh Square, the May 2008 occupation of Beirut by Hizbullah and its allies, and Hizbullah's military involvement in the Syrian conflict were perceived as acts launched by the Shi'a, targeting the Sunnis. In Tripoli, frequent clashes between the Sunni militias of al-Tabbana and the Alawite groups in Jabal Muhsin have greatly contributed to the increase in sectarian sentiments. These experiences give even more credibility to the claims of Salafis about the existence of a global Shi'ite conspiracy.

The success of Salafi framing is also a result of the fact that currently, there is no viable counterframing activity.[69] Other Islamic movements or Dar al-Fatwa shaykhs have not come up with a viable approach regarding the Shi'a. The Lebanese Muslim Brotherhood refrains from sectarian rhetoric, and allows only political criticism of Hizbullah. They do so for two reasons. The first is that most ideologists of the Ikhwan[70] reject Salafi-style anti-Shi'ism, which regards the Shi'ite belief system un-Islamic.[71] The second is that al-Jama'a al-Islamiyya has a long history of cooperation with Hizbullah. The group's armed wing, *Quwwat al-Fajr* (Dawn Force) has regularly participated in military actions against Israel in coordination with the Shi'ite militia.[72] Certainly, al-Jama'a al-Islamiyya's intellectual and political approach does not fit with the expectations of the many who resent the Shi'a as a community. The other major Islamic movement in Tripoli, *Harakat al-Tawhid*, is an open ally of Hizbullah. Its credibility has also been undermined because of its implicit alliance with the Assad regime, which crushed the movement in the 1980s.

---

[68] It is easy to discover implicit or explicit sectarian references to the Shi'a in al-Mustaqbal's media, such as the *al-Mustaqbal* newspaper and TV channel.

[69] The literature shows that the absence of successful counterframing greatly boosts the resonance of a given frame. See, for example, Ioana Emy Matesan, "What Makes Negative Frames Resonant? Hamas and the Appeal of Opposition to the Peace Process," *Terrorism and Political Violence*, 24, no. 5 (2012), p. 678.

[70] Israel Altman, "The Brotherhood and the Shiite Question," *Current Trends in Islamist Ideology*, no. 9, November 19, 2009, www.currenttrends.org/research/detail/the-brotherhood-and-the-shiite-question (accessed January 12, 2013).

[71] As I also indicated earlier, it does not mean that all members of the Shi'ite community are regarded as non-Muslims. Salafis, however, consider the totality of the creed and beliefs of the Shi'a as a different religion. Those Shi'ites who do not possess the necessary knowledge to be aware of this still remain within Islam.

[72] "Al-Fajr al-Sunniya Tuqatil fi-l-Janub Wa Tarfud Fatawa al-Firqa," *Ilslamonline.net*, June 6, 2006. http://islamonline.net/ar/news/2006–07/28/06.shtml (accessed April 5, 2010).

The socioeconomic reality of the North as experienced by its ordinary inhabitants also boosts the credibility of the Salafis' "Sunnis as victims" frame, especially if there is no viable alternative. Inequality and a lack of balance are the main characteristics of Lebanon's development. Most economic activity is centered in Beirut and the surrounding area, while the other regions are severely lagging behind in both living standards and human development.[73] A common explanation in the North is that the region is neglected because it is inhabited by Sunnis. Ordinary people often contrast the North with South Lebanon. According to them, the latter is swiftly improving because the Lebanese state is pressed by the Shi'a to inject capital into the region. As a middle-class city dweller explained to me: "There are technical schools everywhere in the South to give a profession to the [Shi'ites'] young generation, while here in the North our daughters are being sent to the Gulf to work as prostitutes and concubines."[74] In saying this, he was referring to some of the newly opened courses for women to train as beauticians, many of whom go on to apply for jobs in the Gulf countries. According to some rumors spreading in the city, these women are in fact supposed to work as prostitutes in the United Arab Emirates and Kuwait. Salafi frames about the deliberate economic oppression of the "Muslims by the heretics and unbelievers" meet with widespread resonance.

The Sunni community's traditional sense of weakness and oppression underscores the experiential credibility of the Salafis' frame of the Arab revolutions further. Considerable segments of society in the North support the Salafi movement because belonging to a strong *Umma* that revolts against and brings down the *taghut* in a cosmic battle elevates them ideologically from belonging to what is perceived as the weakest sect in Lebanon. As I mentioned in Chapter 5, Lebanese Sunnis in the twentieth century inclined toward the concept of Arab Unity rather than accepting multisectarian Lebanon as a final home (*watan niha'i*). Although in the period after the Hariri murder, many observed the "Lebanonization of the Sunnis,"[75] this development seems to have reversed after the breakout of the Syrian civil war. After February 2005, Sunnis started to identify themselves with the state of Lebanon due to their hostile feelings toward Syria, caused by the killing of the former prime minister. However, after the uprisings,

---

[73] www.undp.org.lb/communication/publications/linking/Session4.pdf (accessed January 10, 2013).

[74] Interview, Tripoli, 17 April, 2012.

[75] Rayyan al-Shawaf, "The Transformation of Lebanon's Sunnis," *The Daily Star*, September 21, 2007, www.dailystar.com.lb/Opinion/Commentary/Sep/21/The-transformation-of-Lebanons-Sunnis.ashx#axzz2SmtF3o37 (accessed April 5, 2010).

many members of the community felt that they related once again to their "fellow believers." By revolting against the Assad regime, the masses of Syrians detached themselves from the killers of Hariri and the oppressors of the Sunnis during the Syrian occupation of 1976–2005. This development removed the last barrier that had been preventing the Lebanese Sunnis feeling part of the global *Umma*. The Salafis' frame about equating the revolutions with events predicted in the Scripture fits well with this transformation of a national identity into a Sunni identity.

The nature of the prognostic and motivational framing of Salafis increases the resonance of their frames. Salafis offer easy and rewarding solutions for believers. They do not ask them to make big sacrifices; Lebanese Salafis rarely tell their constituents to go to mass demonstrations and risk their lives by facing the weapons of Hizbullah and their allies. They also do not require ordinary people to invest a lot of time and effort in facilitating the activities of the movement. All they ask is to attend prayer regularly, listen to the Friday prayer, join religious lessons, and perform religious rituals in the right way. In exchange, Salafis offer the strong probability that the individual's life will improve significantly in the near future, since God often rewards those who follow His regulations with mundane success. Furthermore, if more Muslims strengthen their attachment to their religion and correct the way they perform its rulings, this will necessarily lead to the *Umma*'s political and economic success. In short, following the Salafi remedy for the problems identified in the diagnostic framing requires little investment, and at the same time it makes the individual feel morally superior and promises high psychological and material returns.

7.3   Conversion to Salafism

Framing plays the most important role in attracting passive followers to Salafism. However, to gain committed individuals who transform their entire lives in accordance with the movement's principles, these incentives on their own are insufficient. As my data shows, the overwhelming majority of active followers joined the movement for additional reasons.

Those whom I consider committed Salafis have in most cases gone through a radical transformation in their worldview and identity, which can be identified as conversion. Here I have to note that a convert is not necessarily someone who left a certain religious tradition for another.[76]

---

[76] David Snow and Richard Machalek, "The Sociology of Conversion," *Annual Review of Sociology*, 10 (1984), p. 170.

Rather, conversion involves "radical discontinuity in a person's life"[77] and the "reorientation of the soul."[78] That which was previously peripheral in his or her consciousness now becomes central. In other words, the sensory experiences associated with Salafism move to the center of these individuals' consciousness to the extent that this reshapes almost all aspects of their lives.

Frustration, feelings of insecurity, and identity crisis are often described as the main factors that make someone a potential convert.[79] Analyses of affiliation with Salafism in different national contexts suggest the same. De Koning's study shows that young second-generation immigrants in the Netherlands who cannot fully identify with their parents' identity, but who are also unable to adopt that of the host country, are receptive to the message of Salafism.[80] Another account points out that Salafism offers a stable alternative way to Muslim youth in France who fail to identify themselves with the French concept of citizenship based on the notion of Laïcité, and feel excluded and marginalized from the majority of French society.[81] In Indonesia, Salafism is often adopted by young people from rural backgrounds who have been forced by economic circumstances to migrate to the cities. Upward mobility is denied to them, while detachment from their traditional sociocultural context causes feelings of insecurity. Salafism provides them with a space where they can create new bonds of solidarity and an alternative means of social advancement, by reaching a higher level of commitment and piety.[82]

These aspects can also be observed when we examine how someone becomes a committed Salafi in North Lebanon. The majority of "converts" are typically young, in their twenties or early thirties, have middle-class or lower-middle-class backgrounds, and possess a certain level of education. They typically experience the usual frustrations and insecurities of the young generations in the North due to the lack of opportunities for upward mobility. The unemployment rate in the Sunni territories of the North is the highest in the country.[83] Job opportunities

---

[77] Ibid., p. 169.   [78] Ibid.

[79] Anton van Harskamp, "Existential Insecurity and New Religiosity: An Essay on Some Religion-Making Characteristics of Modernity," *Social Compass* 55, no. 1 (2008); John Lofland and Rodney Stark, "Becoming a World-saver: A Theory of Conversion to a Deviant Perspective," *American Sociological Review*, 30, no. 6 (1965).

[80] De Koning, "Changing Worldviews and Friendship."

[81] Adraoui, "Salafism in France."

[82] Noorhaidi Hasan, "The Drama of Jihad: The Emergence of Salafi Youth in Indonesia." In *Being Young and Muslim: New Cultural Politics in the Global South and North*, edited by Asef Bayat and Linda Herrera (Oxford: Oxford University Press, 2010).

[83] Rasha Aboudzaki, "Tripoli, North Lebanon: The Forgotten City," *al-Akhbar*, May 15, 2012, English edition. http://english.al-akhbar.com/node/7367 (accessed May 15,

are meager, even for university graduates. Young people often complain about nepotism and patronage. Without having links to one of the political leaders, it is almost impossible to get a high-level professional position. One often hears comments such as, "if you don't have contacts (preferably to a *za'im*) you won't get a job, whatever diploma you have. If you are well-connected, five classes are enough to be director of a company."[84]

University students in the final years of their education do not see a secure future ahead. Those who have already graduated are often unemployed and rely on support from their families, or have to do low-paying jobs. At the same time, the surrounding society expects them to achieve material stability, establish a family, and pursue a career that is fitting to their level of education, in order to grant the respect and social status to which these young people aspire. In reality, however, they can only dream of becoming a *rabb bayt* (lord of the house); that is, a financially independent married man. The disparity between expectations, ambitions, and opportunities generates a sense of insecurity and frustration. Young men often express that they feel like "nobodies" and "*bala qiyma* [worthless]" in front of elder family members and more successful individuals. They also describe life as boring, as there are no prospects of work, to make an effort and achieve something. Young men try to fill their aimless days by gathering in groups and spending time in cafés, sometimes consuming alcohol and soft drugs. Occasionally, when they have money, they hire prostitutes. Some young men mentioned feelings of guilt, distraction, and emptiness after such activities.

'Adnan, a former soldier and purist Salafi (see Chapter 5), had similar prospects and a similar lifestyle before becoming a committed Salafi. As he recalled, when he was serving in the Lebanese army, he often spent his free time drinking alcohol with his fellow soldiers and "playing with girls" despite his religious upbringing. As he told it, such activities ate considerable chunks of his salary each month. Looking back to his previous life, 'Adnan identifies boredom and aimlessness as the main reason why he lived an "immoral" lifestyle. Yet, drinking and partying provided temporary relief. Most of the time, he had been feeling constant apathy. When trying to expel his feelings of boredom, he often

---

2012); see this UNDP report: www.undp.org.lb/communication/publications/linking/Session4.pdf (accessed May 7, 2016; *Nisbat al-Hurman al-Hadhari: al-Manhajiyya wa Nata'ij al-Dirasa al-Maydaniyya fi Tarablus – Lubnan*, Report, United Nations Economic and Social Commission for Western Asia, 2014, www.unescwa.org/news/poverty-tripoli (accessed May 7, 2016).

[84] Conversation with a group of youths, Tripoli, August 4, 2011.

started to think: "Where I am going, what is the purpose of my life? Why do I exist in the world if my life is not going anywhere?"[85]

Many young Lebanese Sunni men, like 'Adnan, find Salafism and become active followers of the movement. The movement is particularly attractive to them because it provides simple answers to these questions. 'Adnan recalled that after joining the networks of purist Salafis, religious commitment provided structure and meaning to his life. "Now I know, I am in this world to worship God as He wants me to do it. All my acts have to be accomplished in the way God prescribed. If I follow this, everything I do is worship (*'ibada*), i.e. I worship God 24 hours a day."

Another young purist Salafi in his mid-twenties, Nabil, recalled similar experiences to 'Adnan. Just like 'Adnan, he comes from a middle-class family from the Qubba district, and became committed two years before I met him in the summer of 2011. He first encountered Salafism when one of his friends dragged him to visit the religious lessons of Shaykh 'Abdullah al-Husayn, one of the most prominent purists who teaches in the Zahiriyya quarter of Tripoli (see also Chapter 2). Later he joined the network of Safwan al-Za'bi centered on the Abu Samra district's al-Sunna mosque. When I interviewed him, he stressed the all-encompassing nature of Salafism that provides clear instructions to carry out all actions in line with the creator's will. "There is a text for everything, you just need the right *dalil* [proof]. [It is clearly stated] how to interact with others, how to talk with your parents, your fellow Muslims and also with non-Muslims. [There are instructions for] how to consummate your marriage, exactly how to dress and even how to enter the restroom."[86] In Nabil's account, if someone focuses on learning as much as possible about Islam and calibrates their life according to the system that God has codified in the scripture there is no reason to worry about material hardships and unfavorable political developments, as God always rewards those who attend faithfully to His religion.

While young purists most of the time pointed out that Salafism provided them with a structured and predictable life, for *harakis* whom I interviewed, the crisis of Sunni identity in Lebanon also contributed to their conversion. At a time of sectarian polarization, many young men are asking themselves what it means to belong to the Sunni community. Why are Sunnis weak in the face of the Shi'ites and Hizbullah? Many of them perceive that the Future Movement's secular and pro-Western

[85] Interview, Tripoli, April 28, 2012.   [86] Interview, Tripoli, July 29, 2011.

approach will not improve the situation, just as the Arab Nationalist and Leftist movements, to which their fathers used to belong, failed.

I inquired about the process of conversion to *haraki* Salafism when I socialized with a group of young committed Salafis in 2011 and 2012, who were students and associates of Shaykh Salim al-Rafa'i, and were linked to the shaykh's Taqwa mosque. These young people were known as the "youth of the mosque (*shabab al-masjid*)" as they volunteered to fulfill various organizational tasks related to worship and social life in the mosque. For example, they formed an auxiliary police (*indibat*) that helped to instruct the crowds during such events as the Friday prayer, when often thousands participated. Some of these young people fulfilled administrative functions in the mosque and carried out proselytization.

I frequently met with three of these young men, Abu Bakr, Ghassan, and Yahya. All three came from middle-class backgrounds and were relatively well educated.

In Abu Bakr's conversion, political developments after 2005 played an important role. In 2012, when we did most of our interviews, he was thirty years old. Abu Bakr is a graduate of business administration from one of the Lebanese private universities, and he was working in Kuwait in his father's company that sold and installed printers and photocopy machines. Abu Bakr usually spent the summers in Lebanon with his family and socializing among Tripoli's Salafis. As he recalled, before joining Salafism he had not been looking for moral perfection or a predictable life, contrary to many other committed Salafis. Rather, he was enraged by the ostensible attempt of the Shi'ites and Hizbullah to "oppress" Sunnis. As he told me, "after the 2006 [political] crisis and the 2008 occupation of Beirut by the Shi'a I started to think, what does it mean to be Sunni? Before, 'Sunniness' did not mean too much to me, but when the political climate changed and everybody started to speak about Sunna and Shi'a, it made me ask questions."

During one summer he spent in Tripoli, a friend of him introduced Abu Bakr to a number of Salafi shaykhs, including Da'i al-Islam al-Shahhal. According to his account, these shaykhs made it clear to him that being Sunni is equal to adopting all of the rulings of Islam in the form they have been revealed by God. As he put it, "Salafis made me realize that being Sunni means belonging to God's religion and being part of the *Umma*. If we follow God's rulings in full, not as our parents did, Sunnis will change their current miserable situation. Our fathers maybe went to the mosque and prayed, but just as an inherited habit. Otherwise they did not look for God's will. This is why we are weak now." According to him, countless parts of the Text prove this truth.

He quoted the following Qur'an ayah: *In 'idtum 'idna* (If you return [to Me] I return [to you]).[87] Though this part of the scripture has been interpreted in radically different ways, in the common Salafi interpretation, if Muslims return to the true path, God will return his favor to the *Umma*.[88]

For Abu Bakr, this experience did not lead straight to Salafism. Upon his return to the Kuwait, he first sought out other Islamic movements that had a stronger presence among the Lebanese, Syrian, and Palestinian communities of Kuwait, among whom he usually socialized.[89] These were the Muslim Brotherhood and Hizb al-Tahrir. Yet, after spending a few months in both movements, he concluded that neither of them presents strong arguments underpinned by validated proof from the Scripture. As he put it, "both [the Ihkwan and Hizb al-Tahrir] raise slogans about how others oppress Muslims, blame the West and Iran, but do not present how Muslims could improve their own personality to get rid of oppression." Finally, he decided to go with the *haraki* Salafis, and spends summers in Tripoli helping Shaykh Salim al-Rafa'i to manage the affairs of the Taqwa mosque.

7.3.1 Conversion and Social Networks

The widespread presence of Salafism in new media and its networking strategy are the two main reasons why these young individuals come across the movement and later adopt its ideas.[90] In the past decade, Salafism has come to dominate the Islamic content of the internet.[91] In Northern Lebanon, despite the fact that the internet connection is slow, many middle-class youth go online and visit religious websites. They most likely encounter Salafi pages and forums, often even without knowing that those transmit the message of a specific movement. The Egyptian Salafi and Saudi Wisal and Safa' satellite channels, which are popular across the Middle East, also play a very important role. Both the internet and television present an appealing discourse for the youth. Many of my informants encountered Salafism first through new media, which then led them to look for local Salafis to learn more about the movement's ideas. Those who were approached by *da'is* often

---

[87] al-Qur'an, Surat al-Isra' 8.
[88] Interview with Shaykh Salim al-Rafa'i, Tripoli, July 22, 2011.
[89] People from the territory of historical Syria usually socialize together in the Gulf due to the similar culture and dialect, and the frequent cross-border family ties.
[90] De Koning 2009, p. 421.   [91] Ibid.

responded positively to the call due to their previous experiences with websites and TV channels. In other words, the flow of Salafi ideas through the media facilitates the already crucial role of social networks in the recruitment of new active members.

Numerous studies have concluded that in the recruitment processes of various religious and social movements, informal interpersonal contacts play a substantial role.[92] This is particularly true for Salafism. Analyses on the movement frequently emphasize the role of social networks in recruiting new followers. Wiktorowicz, for example, points to the significance of preexisting friendship ties that drag someone to the movement, and the wide availability of Salafi activities, such as *halaqat*, which potential converts can join.[93] My findings in Lebanon confirm the crucial role of informal ties.

Without exception, the active followers whom I interviewed between 2009 and 2012 had chosen to radically change their lifestyles and adopt Salafism after having relatively long interpersonal relationships with Salafi activists. The reason is that Lebanese Salafis, especially those who belong to the *haraki* current, are actively trying to reach out to others. At the same time, probably the majority of the potential converts encountered Salafism prior to contacting the networks of committed individuals, either through the internet or satellite channels, or through the Friday sermon (if the *khatib* of the mosque where they prayed was Salafi). After becoming somewhat familiar with the movement's ideas, these young people usually became more responsive if Salafis approached them, or they even took the initiative to learn more for themselves. In the latter case, they usually started to visit religious lessons, or occasionally participated in informal gatherings as the first step of their socialization in Salafism.

Active followers also look to contact those who can be convinced to refashion their lives in accordance with the movement's standards. Being available to answer questions and assist ordinary believers (*'ammat al-muslimin*) is part of the *hisba* and is therefore considered one of the most important parts of their activism. Active participants frequently approach others in the mosque and their neighborhood to talk about their religious belief. Often these activists provide assistance to young people, such as counseling them if they face mental stress, or

---

[92] Rodney Stark and William Sims Bainbridge, "Networks of Faith: Interpersonal Bonds and Recruitment to Cults and Sects," *The American Journal of Sociology*, 85, no. 6 (1980); James M. Jasper and Jane D. Poulsen, "Recruiting Strangers and Friends: Moral Shocks and Social Networks in Animal Rights and Anti-Nuclear Protests," *Social Problems*, 42, no. 4 (1995).

[93] Wiktorowicz, "The Salafi Movement in Jordan," pp. 233–236.

are socially isolated and alienated. In some cases, Salafi youth try to stop others who "have mixed with bad company" from associating with those who regularly consume alcohol and drugs. Such activities earn them a high reputation and many young people are happy to spend time with them.

One of the most important and interesting methods used by Salafi activists to approach young people is their *da'wa* in popular places where Salafis would otherwise hardly be found, such as cafés and beaches. While other Islamic movements frequently employ these spaces for proselytization, Salafis mostly refuse to go to cafés and beaches because people listen to music, smoke water pipe, or play cards there. According to Salafi views, these activities and the occasional presence of women can awaken temptations in them and turn them away from religion. Some Salafis, however, have abandoned this philosophy. They think that people can be approached where they like to be and where they are relaxed. Here, they refer also to the practices of the Prophet, who did not avoid public places in Mecca or Medina where un-Islamic practices often occurred. The initiative of these Salafis has proven to be very successful and has become one of the most efficient methods of *da'wa* in Tripoli.

Cafés and beaches are important meeting points for middle-class youth in Tripoli and the North. Gathering with friends, drinking coffee, and smoking *argila* creates a kind of "free space" for them, since these places are not under the surveillance of the family and nobody else can hear what they are talking about – unlike when friends gather at one of their homes. The cafés in the Mina district are especially popular, because here the environment is less traditional than, for example, in the Tell district or the Qubba. A group of young people can gain more privacy as it is less likely that they would bump into an older family member or someone from their neighborhood. Indeed, the residents of Tripoli frequently escape from the urban crowds to sit in one of the beachside cafés or restaurants in the Mina district. Gatherings on the beaches close to Tripoli are also popular. In summertime, meetings on the beach consist of swimming, then gathering on the shore and eating dinner. During these occasions, young people often express their concerns about their future and their frustration due to the difficulties of life in the northern part of Lebanon. Salafi *da'is* are able to penetrate these "free spaces" of the Tripolitan youth, and many of these young men are receptive to their ideas.

Ghassan, another member of *shabab al-masjid* in the Taqwa mosque is one of the young Salafi preachers (he is in his mid-twenties) who practice *da'wa* among young Tripolitan middle-class men. When I interviewed him in 2012, he was the secretary and the head of the auxiliary police of the mosque. Ghassan was born into a typical Tripolitan middle-income family in one of the wealthier parts of the Tabbana (which is otherwise known for its deep poverty). He described his family as "non-religious." As he explained, they fast in Ramadan and sometimes read the Qur'an, but, contrary to the parents of Abu Bakr or the purist 'Adnan, they never pray any of the five obligatory prayers and never taught their children anything about Islam.

He told me that his religious turn came after his graduation from high school. Ghassan started working for an electronics company that sells refrigerators. As he recounted, "although I was quite successful in my work, I felt a deep emptiness in my heart and felt as if my life was worthless. Thanks to God it did not last long. I started to pray in the Taqwa mosque and my life quickly changed." Due to the environment in the mosque, Ghassan became one of the prominent young Salafis in the Tabbana. As he recalled, after socializing with youth around Shaykh Salim al-Rafa'i, he managed to talk to the shaykh a few times. The latter convinced Ghassan that such a capable individual as him could utilize his abilities for the sake of fellow Muslims.

Ghassan strongly opposes those (mostly purist) Salafis who, according to him, live between their mosque, work, and family, basically secluded from society. As he explained:

These guys limit their contact with people to avoid temptation and fully focus on religious practice, but they forget that isolation is not the only way of avoiding sin, self-control is also important ... Implementing Islam fully is self-realization, but following only religious practice and ritual is only half of this self-realization. The other half is enlightening others and contributing to the creation of a more Islamic society.[94]

This is why Ghassan thinks that "a wide social network composed of all kind of people is crucial for the *da'wa*. Personal isolation [i.e. meeting only Salafis] leads to the isolation of the *da'wa* as well."

Despite his pious lifestyle, Ghassan appears quite frequently in the cafés that are popular meeting points for young people from his generation. He prefers places without loud music and with few women. Usually, he meets there with young people whom he has met before at work or other places in the city, rather than joining their gatherings. According to Ghassan, he does not start by preaching and convincing these young men to live a more pious life: "This would lead nowhere; they would only escape from me. Rather, I listen to their daily problems and participate in ordinary, worldly conversations. Although in the

---

[94] Interview with Ghassan Hadhuri, Tripoli, July 27, 2011.

time of *salat*, I perform prayer. Most of them follow me at this time even if they would never pray otherwise." Most of the Tripolitans are proud of their Sunni identity, even if they do not pray or do not fast in Ramadan. When somebody proposes that they perform the prayer together, they cannot refuse.[95] According to Ghassan, occasionally praying together creates a sufficiently religious climate to be able to introduce his ideas from a more Islamic viewpoint, or propose an Islamic solution for the socioeconomic problems suffered by these young men. "If I were to try to persuade them to live a more religious life while drinking coffee, it would backfire. They might listen to my arguments politely, but they would not take them seriously." After they have prayed together a few times, Ghassan usually talks about what kind of solutions Islam offers for the social problems of the youth. He tries to convince them that regular prayer, refraining from drinking alcohol, and using their time for something more productive than sitting in cafés all night would improve their life. This might be reading the Qur'an, visiting the mosque, or participating in religious study groups (*halaqat al-durus*). According to Ghassan's account, although most of the youth are partially receptive to his call, some eventually become fully committed.

The 22-year-old Yahya is one of those who became committed Salafis. Ghassan introduced him to me in the Taqwa mosque after the *maghrib* prayer. He is an undergraduate student at the Tripoli branch of the Lebanese University (LU), living in a middle-class family in the Tabbana. He explained his life and worldview before he converted to Salafism:

My parents did not teach me too much about our religion. I knew how to pray, but I did not practice it. Although I used to fast in Ramadan (sometimes not the whole month), I lived Islam only as a tradition and it did not play an important role in my life. My father prays, but my mother and my siblings never do ... I loved music, playing board games or cards. Occasionally I drank beer and almost every night I sat in a café or on the beach with my friends and colleagues at the university, smoking *argila* ... Ghassan sometimes joined us in these meetings. Once I complained to him that I could not really focus on my studies, since we live in a small apartment and therefore there is a lot of distraction. He said that I could go and study in the mosque, since the environment is rather quiet there ... Spending a lot of time in the mosque, the climate somehow catches you. At the time of the prayer I performed the *salat* with the others. Afterwards, I felt that my soul was becoming cleaner. In the mosque, I also got in contact with others who had more knowledge about

---

[95] This is especially the case if somebody cannot claim that they had performed the obligatory prayer before.

the religion, and I joined the study circles as well. Gradually, I found that I hated my former lifestyle and behavior. I threw away my CDs, stopped hanging out at night, and gave up smoking *argila*.

Today, Yahya is one of the most enthusiastic activists at the Taqwa mosque, helping Ghassan to manage the auxiliary police.

Another successful *da'wa* method I encountered in North Lebanon is using the annual Islamic pilgrimage to Mecca (*Hajj*) for proselytization purposes. I discovered that some of my committed Salafi informants got involved in the movement's networks during and after they participated in the *Hajj*. Salafis play quite a large part in organizing trips for Lebanese pilgrims. They operate "*Hajj* travel offices" in Tripoli and Beirut, where people can arrange their documents and travel to Saudi Arabia. When the pilgrims arrive in Mecca, they are divided into groups consisting of fifteen to twenty members. The office appoints a *murshid* (here: spiritual guide) to each group, who is usually a Lebanese Salafi shaykh. The *murshid*'s task is to advise the pilgrims on how to behave and perform the different rituals that are obligatory during the *Hajj*. They also provide religious training, mostly in the form of *halaqat* and personal consultations, while the people are staying in Mecca. Shaykh Ghassan (introduced in Chapter 6) from the Nahr al-Barid camp often served as a *murshid* for Lebanese and Palestinian pilgrims before he moved to Sweden. When I interviewed him, he emphasized how the spiritual guide can play an important role in leading people to "*manhaj* of Ahl al-Sunna wa-l-Jama'a and cleansing them from the *shirkiyyat* [practices and beliefs that contradict *tawhid*]."[96] According to him, during the *Hajj* people find it "easier to accept the truth." In Mecca "there is *baraka* [blessing]" and the "heart of the Muslims opens up to God's message."

Turner and Turner provide a useful analysis to understand the general significance of pilgrimage in a believer's life.[97] In their analysis of Catholic pilgrimage, they argue that pilgrims detach themselves from their social context, and its different social positions, rights and distinctions, and enter into a "liminal" state where these distinctions disappear. During pilgrimage, the individual enters a community of equals where ordinary social structures are temporarily abolished.[98] The authors call this state "communitas," a term which describes "the individual pilgrim's temporary transition away from the mundane structures and social interdependence into a looser commonality of

---

[96] Interview, Orebro, Sweden, June 23, 2012.

[97] Victor Turner and Edith Turner, *Image and Pilgrimage in Christian Culture* (New York, NY: Columbia University Press, 1978).

[98] Ibid., pp. 1–40.

feeling with fellow visitors."[99] During communitas, the individual is subject to serious internal changes or even distortions before reentering his or her ordinary social structure. In the case of the *Hajj*, communitas is symbolized with the *ihram*, the white robe that every pilgrim has to put on before beginning the pilgrimage. The *ihram* strongly resembles the *kafan* (death shroud) and implies that in death, social positions are meaningless.[100] Consequently, during the *Hajj*, the *ihram* is supposed to hide the social background of the believer, detach them from it, and thereby integrate them into the community of equals where only faith has any importance.

In the case of the Islamic pilgrimage, a person's detachment from their local socioeconomic environment is often accompanied by a "re-orientation of the soul" from mundane matters toward God. The *Hajj* is supposed to be a turning point in the individual's life, when he or she gets rid of their sins and mistakes of the past and becomes a better person. Some personal accounts suggest that being in Mecca and the activities and rituals that are performed when there lead to a feeling of continuous closeness to God.[101] In other words, just like daily religious rituals in Humphrey and Laidlaw's analysis, the *Hajj* creates a space for religious experience, albeit a deeper and more persistent one.[102] Salafi *murhsid*s find this "opening-up of the heart" a suitable moment to influence their group members. Besides giving lessons and providing personal consultations during the *Hajj*, Shaykh Ghassan draws on his pre-established transnational contacts. He told me that he frequently travels to Saudi Arabia, where he studied under some renowned *'ulama'* , and maintains cordial relations with others. When these scholars are present during the *Hajj*, he brings his group members to participate in their *halaqat* or just to interact with them on a personal level. Shaykh Ghassan described these *'ulama'* as exceptionally charismatic people who can have a longlasting impact on someone who spends time with them. After the *Hajj*, most people return to their daily lives, but some, especially young people, get involved in Salafi networks and in many cases become active followers.

---

[99] Simon Coleman, "Do You Believe in Pilgrimage? Communitas, Contestation and Beyond," *Anthropological Theory*, 2, no. 3 (2002), p. 356.

[100] F. E. Peters, *The Hajj: The Muslim Pilgrimage to Mecca and the Holy Places* (Princeton, NJ: Princeton University Press, 1994), p. 115.

[101] Conversations with Lebanese individuals who performed the *Hajj* between 2009 and 2012.

[102] Caroline Humphrey and James Laidlaw, *The Archetypal Actions of Ritual: A Theory of Ritual Illustrated by the Jain Rite of Worship* (New York, NY: Oxford University Press, 1994), pp. 78–79.

The latter was true for Shaykh 'Imad, a young (in his twenties) but very popular preacher in Wadi Khalid. As he told me, in his early adulthood, he was a Syrian Ba'th party sympathizer (the ideological backbone of the regime in Damascus). Just like many of the residents in his home region, he was enthusiastic about Hizbullah and the "Axis of Resistance [Mihwar al-Mumani'a]," which consists of the "anti-Imperialist and anti-Zionist" forces such as Iran, Syria, Hizbullah, and Hamas. He was "not really practicing" Islam and led a rather secular lifestyle: He was busy with "worthless" things such as listening to music, smoking, and loitering with other young men. He started studying IT at a college in Tripoli, but did not become a successful student. According to his account, what changed his life was performing the Hajj in 2005. His father sent him to Mecca, hoping that it would precipitate some positive changes in his son's character. He made the journey with a Salafi Hajj office and during the pilgrimage he was deeply influenced by his murhsid. As he explained, the whole experience in Mecca made him realize how meaningless his life was and made him think about finding a goal in life. After returning to Lebanon, he established contacts with Salafi networks and participated in some courses at Da'i al-Islam al-Shahhal's al-Hidaya college. After a couple of months, he concluded that his main task in this life would be to spread the da'wa. A year after the pilgrimage, he adopted the Salafi manhaj and began his studies at Tripoli University in the Shari'a faculty. The political developments and the emerging sectarian tensions also played a role in his turn toward Salafism. When he started to teach and deliver Friday sermons in his home village, he became one of the flag-bearers of anti-Shi'ism in Wadi Khalid.

7.4   Conclusion

Framing is one of the most important tools of Salafis to recruit followers. Successful framing activity appeals to the larger masses, who are seeking a plausible answer to sociopolitical events. Salafi ideology also attracts those young people who feel alienated in contemporary North Lebanon due to the socioeconomic conditions and ongoing identity crisis. They become committed followers of Salafism who seek to adopt its rulings in full by going through conversion. Conversion then is facilitated by the networking strategies of Salafis.

Today, Salafi recruitment strategies in Lebanon have been effective. Large numbers of ordinary believers consider the words of Salafi preachers to be credible, adopt their opinions on current events, and conceive of Islam in accordance with the Salafi concept. Mostly due to the climate of insecurity generated by the Arab Uprisings, there has been a sharp increase in the number of young people becoming active participants.

The interplay of the Sunni–Shiʻi sectarian tensions with the Arab Spring provides fuel for the shaykhs' framing activity. The ongoing Syrian civil war, the decreasing opportunities for the Sunni youth, and the lack of credible alternatives are among the main factors that explain why Salafis are successfully attracting people. However, things might change if stability returns to the neighboring countries and if the economic situation improves in the North. Such developments could favor moderate Islamic movements such as the Muslim Brotherhood. In the case of socioeconomic developments, doors might open for education, and Sunni youth might then see a non-apocalyptic future that leads to economic stability and becoming part of the middle class, rather than to the "Siege of Sham" and the arrival of the *Mahdi*. In this case, the successful movements will be those that can respond to these changes.

Conclusion

Since the 2010–2011 Arab Uprisings, Salafism in Lebanon has become a mainstream movement, with a considerable media presence. Leading figures of the movement, such as Shaykh Salim al-Rafi'i, Ra'id Hulayhil, and Da'i al-Islam al-Shahhal, often appear on local and international TV channels, and write in newspapers and on websites. Unlike a few years ago, the importance of Salafism in Lebanon's current sociopolitical makeup cannot be ignored. Yet, news reports and analyses mostly focus on the movement in this small country mostly in relation to the civil war in neighboring Syria or the series of bombings in Beirut between 2013 and 2015.[1]

This book has shown that Salafism in Lebanon is a proselytization movement whose legitimacy and popularity is rapidly increasing among the members of the Sunni Muslim community. The majority of the country's diverse and fragmented Salafi scene prefers peaceful *da'wa* as their primary means of action. Those, who advocate global jihad are a minority, although a vocal and important one. It is true that there are Salafi Shaykhs, such as Salim al-Rafi'i, who openly call for armed support of the opposition in Syria, and some of their followers ended up fighting alongside the opposition to President Bashar al-Assad. Yet, the same shaykhs are leaders of vast networks of preachers across Northern Lebanon, whose main focus is "purifying" the belief and practices of Sunni Muslims, and not overthrowing the political system by using violence.

The importance of Salafism in Lebanon lies not in its potential to launch armed action, but rather the movement's ability to shape the worldview and religious identity of the regular Sunni believers. In other

---

[1] On November 12, 2015 two suicide bombings occurred in the Shi'a-dominated Burj al-Barajina neighborhood, killing forty-three people. Anne Barnard and Hwaida Saad, "ISIS Claims Responsibility for Blasts That Killed Dozens in Beirut," *International New York Times*, November 12, 2015, www.nytimes.com/2015/11/13/world/middleeast/lebanon-explosions-southern-beirut-hezbollah.html?_r=0 (accessed November 13, 2015).

words, Salafism is accepted as Sunni Islam itself by a growing number of ordinary Muslims, who see the world through the interpretative frames and discourses presented by Salafi preachers. Regular Sunni believers often adopt elements of the Salafis' way of practicing religion, and accept the Salafis' black and white worldview, which depicts the world as a place of struggle between Islam and unbelief. Sunni Muslims belong to the first category, facing the rest of the world who want to corrupt their belief and politically oppress them. This means that Salafism aims to reshape the Sunni religious field by redefining the notion of what a good Muslim is. By this, they challenge other actors on the Sunni religious field, such as Dar al-Fatwa, Lebanon's official religious establishment.

Part of the Salafis' success can be attributed to the effectiveness of their networking strategy. The movement relies more on informal ties than institutional ones, which helps them to survive repression from the Lebanese security services. Furthermore, the interpersonal ties and friendship networks that connect Lebanese Salafis to the Arabian Gulf provide them with important social capital. This facilitates the acquisition of economic capital that manifests in donations from charities and individual donors. Either studying at one of the Islamic universities in Saudi Arabia or informally participating in the religious lessons of renowned Salafi scholars of the country increase the religious capital of Lebanese Salafis. The transnational network of ties between Lebanese Salafis has even helped some of them to establish themselves on the international stage and become influential preachers in Western Europe.

Salafi religious specialists are at the core of the movement's networks. These shaykhs establish their authority by claiming that they represent Islamic orthodoxy, and reinforce this claim by accumulating sufficient religious, social, and economic capital. They successfully craft their image as perfect and pure Muslims and combine it with the ability to access material resources by establishing links to donors in the Arabian Gulf and Lebanon's influential political patrons, and fulfilling the role of mediators in social conflicts. The high degree of religious authority of some of the shaykhs gives credibility to their framing activity, in which they offer explanations of and solutions to the ostensibly oppressed situation of Sunni Muslims.

The structure and strategies of Salafism would not fully explain the movement's success. The historical transformations that affected the Sunni religious field contributed to the Salafis' ability to mobilize various form of capital. The movement gained traction among Lebanon's Sunni community when the Islamic University of Medina provided scholarships for dozens of students who wished to study Islamic religious sciences in the 1980s. Upon return to their home country, the University of Medina alumni created extended proselytization networks across the Sunni-dominated areas of Lebanon. The chronic weakness of the post–civil war Sunni religious establishment, the delegitimization of competitors, such as the Muslim Brotherhood, and the emerging Sunni–Shi'ite tensions created ideal conditions for Salafis to thrive and to become one of the most important sociopolitical players of Lebanon's Sunni community. Lebanese Salafis became part of the diverse networks of transnational Salafism, and benefitted from the available resources in Saudi Arabia, Kuwait, and Qatar. In particular, charities based in Kuwait and Qatar played a deciding role in consolidating the purist and *haraki* factions in Northern Lebanon.

The 2010–2011 Arab Uprisings gave the *haraki* faction an opportunity to dominate Lebanon's Salafi scene. While purists quickly condemned the demonstrations to remove autocratic rulers, *harakis* supported the revolutions in Egypt, Tunisia, and Yemen, and as a result, became active parts of the political landscape. Many Sunni Muslims in Lebanon, inspired by the *harakis'* success elsewhere, saw them as fitter for leading the community than political patrons, who were often considered self-serving and corrupt. The outbreak of the Syrian conflict that significantly deepened the sectarian tensions especially boosted the influence of the *harakis*. Since then, the *harakis'* framing of the current situation of the Middle East as an apocalyptic battle between Muslims and the realm of unbelief (to which also the Shi'a belong) has a growing acceptance among Lebanese Sunnis.

Future developments in currently war-torn Syria might elevate the position of Tripoli to one of the most important regional hubs of Salafism. The movement unquestionably became an important part of Syria's social makeup. Beyond the fact that Salafis constitute important segments of the armed opposition to President Bashar al-Assad's regime, peaceful Salafi *da'wa* is growing in the country as well. Charities from the Gulf countries send preachers along with humanitarian aid to the country's refugee camps. Non-Jihadi Salafi militias, such as *Jaysh al-Islam* (Army of Islam) also provide protection and assistance to preachers who proselytize among the local Sunni population.

In the event of a future settlement of the current conflict, Syrian students of religion who are interested in Salafism might target the Lebanese Salafi religious colleges to pursue their studies, especially before a similar infrastructure builds up in Syria. Since the Lebanese Salafi leaders and their religious institutions are well connected to Gulf countries, Tripoli could be a gateway for students to continue their education at one of the Saudi Islamic Universities. Although Gulf actors today are active in supporting Syrian Salafis materially, in the future the Saudi or Kuwaiti authorities might see the same individuals as security risks and deny them entry visas. However, if Lebanese shaykhs who are already trusted in the Gulf recommend Syrian Salafi students, their chances of securing visas and entry permits would increase.

This indicates that Lebanese Salafis will most likely remain important players in the Middle Eastern region in the foreseeable future. Further studying the transnational linkages of Lebanon's Salafi community to Western Europe and exploring its connections to Australia will provide a fruitful area for future research. Sunni Muslims with Lebanese descent in Australia often turn to Salafis for religious services. Many Australian students, who are now renowned shaykhs in Sidney and Melbourne, have studied in Tripoli's Salafi colleges.

Finally, I consider it important and timely to further study how Salafis influence the structure of the wider Sunni religious field in Lebanon. The currently growing Salafi presence might further alter the already volatile power balance between the different Sunni religious institutions and movements in the country. This might have an impact on the Sunni community's relations to other confessions, and might further increase the sectarian tensions with the Shi'ites. I am making these predictions based on my observations and conclusions; how the future of the region will turn out eventually, only time can tell.

Bibliography

'Abd al-Karim. 'Abd al-Salam bin Barjas bin Naser al. *Mu'amalat al-Hukkam fi Dhu' al Kitab wa-l-Sunna*. Kuwait: Jama'iyyat Ihya' al-Turath al-Islamiyy, 2009.

'Abd al-Khaliq, Abd al-Rahman. *Khutut Ra'isiyya li-Ba'th al-Umma al-Islamiyya* (1987). www.salafi.net (accessed April 10, 2010).

al-Sirat (2000). www.salafi.net (accessed February 7, 2010).

al-Muslimun wa-l-'Amal al-Siyasi. www.salafi.net (accessed February 5, 2010).

bin 'Abd al-Wahhab, Muhammad. *Kitab al-Tawhid*. Riyadh: Maktabat al-Haramayn, 2001.

Al-Radd 'ala al-Rafida (without date). www.tawhed.ws/r?i=1381 (accessed January 10, 2013).

Abdel Haleem, M. A. S. (trans.), *The Qur'an*. Oxford, New York, NY: Oxford University Press, 2005.

Abdel-Latif, Omayma. "Lebanon's Sunni Islamists – A Growing Force," *Carnegie Papers*, January 2008. http://carnegieendowment.org/files/cmec6_abdella tif_lebanon_final.pdf.

Abdelhady, Dalia. "Beyond Home/Host Networks: Forms of Solidarity among Lebanese Immigrants in a Global Era." *Identities* 13, no. 3 (2006): 427–453.

Abdelnasser, Walid M. "Islamic Organizations in Egypt and the Iranian Revolutions of 1979: The Experience of the First Few Years." *Arab Studies Quarterly* 19, no. 2 (1997): 25–39.

Adraoui, Mohamed-Ali. "Salafism in France: Ideology, Practices and Contradictions." In *Global Salafism: Islam's New Religious Movement* edited by Roel Meijer. New York, NY: Columbia University Press, 2009.

Ajami, Fouad. *The Vanished Imam: Musa al Sadr and the Shia of Lebanon*. Ithaca, NY, and London: Cornell University Press, 1986.

Akarli, Engin. *The Long Peace: Ottoman Lebanon 1861–1920*. Berkeley and Los Angeles: University of California Press, 1993.

al-Albani, Nasir al-Din. *"Awda ila al-Sunna."* www.alalbany.net/misc016.php (accessed June 20, 2013).

al-Anani, Khalil and Maszlee Malik. "Pious Way to Politics: The Rise of Political Salafism in Post-Mubarak Egypt." *Digest of Middle East Studies* 22, no. 1 (2013): 57–73.

Altman, Israel. "The Brotherhood and the Shiite Question." *Current Trends in Islamist Ideology*, no. 9, November 19, 2009. www.currenttrends.org/research/detail/thebrotherhood-and-the-shiite-question (accessed January 12, 2013).

Anderson, Benedict. *Imagined Communities Reflections on the Origin and Spread of Nationalism*. London, New York, NY: Verso, 2006.

Antoun, Richard T. "Themes and Symbols in the Religious Lesson: A Jordanian Case Study." *International Journal of Middle East Studies* 25, no. 4 (1993): 607–624.

"Civil Society, Tribal Process, and Change in Jordan." *International Journal of Middle East Studies* 32, no. 4 (2000): 441–463.

Ayubi, Nazih N. *Over-Stating the Arab State: Politics and Society in the Middle East*. London and New York, NY: I. B. Tauris, 2006.

Baumann, Hannes. "The New Contractor Bourgeoisie in Lebanese Politics: Hariri, Mikati and Fares." In *Lebanon after the Cedar Revolution* edited by Are Knudsen and Malcolm Kerr. London: Hurst, 2013.

Baylocq, Cédric and Akila Drici-Bechikh. "The Salafi and the Others: An Ethography of Intracommnal Relations in French Islam." In *Ethnographies of Islam* edited by Badouin Dupret, Thomas Pierret, Paulo G. Pinto, and Kathryn Spellman-Poots. Edinburgh: Edinburgh University Press, 2012.

Beaugrand, Claire. "Framing Nationality in the Migratory Context: The Elusive Category of Biduns in Kuwait." *Middle East Law and Governance*, 6, no. 3 (2014): 173–203.

van Beek, Walter E. A., ed. *The Quest for Purity: Dynamics of Puritan Movements*. The Hague: Mouton de Gruyter, 1988.

Benford, Robert D. and David A. Snow. "Framing Processes and Social Movements: An Overview and Assessment." *Annual Review of Sociology* 26 (2000): 611–639.

Benthall, Jonathan and Jerome Bellion-Jourdan. *The Charitable Crescent: Politics of Aid in the Muslim World*. London, New York, NY: I. B. Tauris, 2003.

Berkey, Jonathan. *The Formation of Islam: Religion and Society in the Near East, 600–1800*. Cambridge: Cambridge University Press, 2003.

Bhaskar, Roy. "Terrorism in Bangladesh: Monster Child of BNP Jamaat." *South Asia Analysis Group*, November 17, 2009. Available from www.southasia analysis.org/%5Cpapers36%5Cpaper3509.html (accessed March 17, 2010).

Bhat, Chandrashekhar and K. Laxmi Narayan. "Indian Diaspora, Globalization and Transnational Networks: The South African Context." *Journal of Social Science* 25, nos. 1–3 (2010): 13–23.

Bian, Yanjie. "Bringing Strong Ties Back In: Indirect Ties, Network Bridges, and Job Searches in China." *American Sociological Review* 62, no. 3 (1997): 366–385.

Bokhari, Yusra, Nasim Chowdhury, and Robert Lacey. "A Good Day to Bury a Bad Charity: The Rise and Fall of the al-Haramain Islamic Foundation." In *Gulf Charities and Islamic Philanthropy: The "Age of Terror and Beyond"* edited by Robert Lacey and Jonathan Benthall. Berlin: Gerlach Press, 2014.

Bonnefoy, Laurent. *Salafism in Yemen: Transnationalism and Religious Identity*. London: Hurst & Company, 2011.

Bori, Caterina and Livnat Holtzman. "Introduction." In *Essays in the Legal and Theological Thought of Ibn Qayyim al-Ǧawziyyah* edited by Caterina Bori and Livnat Holtzman. Rome: Istituto per l'Oriente C.A. Nallino, 2010.

Bosworth, Clifford Edmund, ed. "Ash'ariyya." In *The Encyclopaedia of Islam*, second edn. Leiden: E.J. Brill, 1986.

Böttcher, Annabelle. "Sunni and Shi'i Networking in the Middle East." *Mediterranean Politics* 7, no. 3 (2002): 42–63.

Boubekeur, Amel. "Salafism and Radical Politics in Postconflict Algeria," *Carnegie Papers*, no. 11, September 2008. http://carnegieendowment.org/files/salafism_radical_politics_algeria.pdf (accessed September 10, 2008).

Bourdieu, Pierre. "Genesis and Structure of the Religious Field." *Comparative Social Research* 13, no. 1 (1991): 1–44.

"The Political Field, the Social Science Field, and the Journalistic Field." In *Bourdieu and the Journalistic Field* edited by Rodney Benson and Erik Neveu. Cambridge: Polity Press, 2005.

Bourdieu, Pierre and Loic J. D. Wacqant. *An Invitation to Reflexive Sociology.* Chicago, IL: The University of Chicago Press, 1992.

Broadbent, Jeffrey. "Movement in Context: Thick Networks and Japanese Environmental Protest." In *Social Movements and Networks: Relational Approaches to Collective Action* edited by Mario Diani and Doug McAdam. Oxford: Oxford University Press, 2003.

van Bruinessen, Martin. Agha, Shaikh and State: On the Social and Political Organization of Kurdistan. Utrecht: Ph.D. thesis submitted at Utrecht University, 1978.

"The Origins and Development of Sufi Orders (tarekat) in Southeast Asia." *Studia Islamika* 1, no. 1 (1994): 1–23.

Calder, Norman, ed. *Interpretation and Jurisprudence in Medieval Islam.* Aldershot: Ashgate, 2006.

"The Limits of Islamic Orthodoxy." In *Interpretation and Jurisprudence in Medieval Islam* edited by Norman Calder. Aldershot: Ashgate, 2006.

Cavatorta, Francesco. "Salafism, Liberalism, and Democratic Learning in Tunisia." *The Journal of North African Studies* 20, no. 5 (2015): 770–783.

Cavatorta, Francesco and Fabio Merone. *Salafism after the Arab Awakening: Contending with People's Power.* London: Hurst, 2015.

Chittick, William C. "Sufi Thought and Practice." in *The Oxford Encyclopedia of the Islamic World*, vol. 5., edited by John L. Esposito. Oxford: Oxford University Press, 2009.

Clark, Janine A. "Islamist Women in Yemen: Informal Nodes of Activism." In *Islamic Activism: A Social Movement Theory Approach* edited by Quintan Wiktorowicz. Bloomington: Indiana University Press, 2004.

Coleman, Simon. "Do You Believe in Pilgrimage? Communitas, Contestation and Beyond." *Anthropological Theory* 2, no. 3 (2002): 355–368.

Commins, David. *The Wahhabi Mission and Saudi Arabia.* London: I. B. Tauris & Co Ltd, 2006.

Crystal, Jill. *Oil and Politics in the Gulf: Rulers and Merchants in Kuwait and Qatar.* Cambridge: Cambridge University Press, 1995.

al-Damanhour, Rajab. "al-Tayyarat al-Shi'iyya al-Kuwaytiyya . . . al-Tashakkulat wa-l Masarat." *Islamonline*, November 3, 2009. http://islamoon.islamonline .net/servlet/Satellite?c=ArticleA_C&cid=1235628915074&pagename=Zone-Arabic-Daawa%2FDWALayout (accessed March 5, 2010).

Dawisha, Adeed. *Arab Nationalism in the Twentieth Century.* Princeton, NJ; Oxford: Princeton University Press, 2003.

Deeb, Lara. *An Enchanted Modern: Gender and Public Piety in Shi'i Lebanon.* Princeton, NJ: Princeton University Press, 2006.

Denoux, Guilain. *Urban Unrest in the Middle East: A Comparative Study of Informal Networks in Egypt, Iran and Lebanon.* Albany: State University of New York Press, 1993.

Dessouki, Ali E. Hillal. "Egyptian Foreign Policy since Camp David." In *The Middle East: Ten Years after Camp David* edited by William B. Quandt, pp. 103–104. Washington, DC: The Brookings Institution, 1988.

Diani, Mario. "The Concept of a Social Movement." In *Readings in Contemporary Political Sociology* edited by David A. Snow, Sarah A. Soule and Hanspeter Kriesi. Oxford: Blackwell Publishers, 2000.

"Introduction: Social Movements, Contentious Actions, and Social Networks: From Metaphor to Substance?" In *Social Movements and Networks* edited by Mario Diani and Doug McAdam. Oxford University Press, 2003.

Diani, Mario and Doug McAdam. *Social Movements and Networks.* Oxford: Oxford University Press, 2003.

Dupret, Badouin, Thomas Pierret, Paulo G. Pinto and Kathryn Spellman-Poots *Ethnographies of Islam.* Edinburgh: Edinburgh University Press, 2012.

Eickelman, Dale F., ed. *Muslim Travellers: Pilgrimage, Migration, and the Religious Imagination Comparative Studies on Muslim Societies.* Berkeley and Los Angeles: University of California Press, 1990.

Eickelman, Dale F. and James Piscatori. *Muslim Politics.* Princeton, NJ: Princeton University Press, 1996.

Erdmann, Gero and Ulf Engel, "Neopatrimonialism Reconsidered: Critical Review and Elaboration of an Elusive Concept." *Commonwealth & Comparative Politics* 45, no. 1 (2007): 95–119.

Fandy, Mamoun. *Saudi Arabia and the Politics of Dissent.* New York; Houndmills: Palgrave, 2001).

Farquhar, Michael. *Circuits of Faith: Migration, Education and the Wahhabi Mission.* Stanford, CA: Stanford University Press, 2016.

al-Fauzan, Salih. 'Al-'Aql wa-Mada Hurriyat al-Ra'y', www.sahab.net/home/?p=843 (accessed June 5, 2012).

Gade, Tine. "Sunni Islamists in Tripoli and the Asad regime 1966–2014." *Syria Studies* 7, no. 2 (2015): 20–65.

Gaffney, Patrick. *The Prophet's Pulpit.* Berkeley, Los Angeles, London: University of California Press, 1994.

Gauvain, Richard. *Salafi Ritual Purity: In the Presence of God.* London and New York: Routledge, 2013.

Gellens, Sam I. "The Search for Knowledge in Medieval Muslim Societies: A Comparative Approach." In *Muslim Travellers: Pilgrimage, Migration, and the Religious Imagination Comparative Studies on Muslim Societies* edited by Dale F. Eickelman. Berkeley and Los Angeles: University of California Press, 1990.

Gellner, Ernest. *Muslim Society.* Cambridge: Cambridge University Press, 1983.

Gerlach, Luther P. and Virginia H. Hine. *People, Power, Change: Movements of Social Transformation.* Indianapolis, IN and New York, NY: The Bobbs-Merrill Company, INC, 1970.

al-Ghannam, Ramadan. "Falsafat al-Qatl wa-l-Ightiyal Fi al-Fikr al-Shi'i." *Almoslim.net*, March 22, 2012. www.almoslim.net/node/162346 (accessed January 5, 2013).

al-Ghazali, Muhammad. *al-Sunna al-Nabawiyya Bayn Ahl al-Fiqh wa-Ahl al-Hadith*, 15th edn. Cairo: Dar al-Shuruq, 2007.

Goffman, Erving. *Frame Analysis: An Essay on the Organization of Experience*. Boston, MA: Northeastern University Press, 1974.

Grafton, David. *The Christians of Lebanon: Political Rights in Islamic Law*. London; New York, NY: I. B. Tauris, 2003.

Griffel, Frank. "What Do We Mean by "Salafi"? Connecting Muhammad ʿAbduh with Egypt's Nur Party in Islam's Contemporary Intellectual History." *Die Welt des Islams* 55, no 2 (2015): 186–220.

Habibis, Daphne. "Change and Continuity: A Sufi Order in Contemporary Lebanon." *Social Analysis* 31, no. 2 (1992): 44–78.

Haddad, Fanar. *Sectarianism in Iraq: Antagonistic Visions of Unity*. New York, NY: Oxford University Press, 2011.

Haddad, Yvonne. "Islamists and the Problem of Israel: The 1967 Awakening." *Middle East Journal* 46, no. 2 (1992): 266–285.

Haenfler, Ross et al. "Lifestyle Movements: Exploring the Intersection of Lifestyle and Social Movements." *Social Movement Studies* 11, no. 1 (2012): 1–20.

Haj, Samira. "Reordering Islamic Orthodoxy: Muhammad Ibn 'Abdul Wahhab." *The Muslim World* 92, no. 3, (2002): 333–370.

Halverson, Jeffrey R. *Theology and Creed in Sunni Islam*. New York: Palgrave Macmillan, 2010.

Hamid, Ahmad Fauzi Abdul. "The Impact of Sufism on Muslims in Pre-Colonial Malaysia: An Overview of Interpretations." *Islamic Studies* 41, no. 3 (2002): 467–493.

Hamid, Sadek. "The Attraction of 'Authentic' Islam: Salafism and British Muslim Youth." In *Global Salafism: Islam's New Religious Movement* edited by Roel Meijer. New York: Columbia University Press, 2009.

Hamzeh, A. Nizar. "Clientalism, Lebanon: Roots and Trends." *Middle Eastern Studies* 37, no. 3, (2001): 167–178.

   In the Path of Hizbullah. Syracuse, NY and New York, NY: Syracuse University Press, 2004.

Hamzeh, A. Nizar and R. Hrair Dekmejian. "A Sufi Response to Political Islamism: al Ahbash of Lebanon." *International Journal of Middle East Studies* 28, no. 2 (1996): 217–229.

Harb, Mona. "Deconstructing Hizballah and Its Suburb," *MERIP*, no. 242, (2007): 12–17.

Harris, William. *The New Face of Lebanon: History's Revenge*. Princeton, NJ: Markus Wiener Publishers, 2006.

van Harskamp, Anton. "Existential Insecurity and New Religiosity: An Essay on Some Religion-Making Characteristics of Modernity." *Social Compass* 55, no. 1 (2008).

Hasan, Noorhaidi. *Laskar Jihad: Islam, Militancy and the Quest for Identity in Post–New Order Indonesia*. Ithaca, NY: Cornell Southeast Asia Program, 2006.

"The Drama of Jihad: The Emergence of Salafi Youth in Indonesia." In *Being Young and Muslim: New Cultural Politics in the Global South and North* edited by Asef Bayat and Linda Herrera. Oxford: Oxford University Press, 2010.

Hatina, Meir. *Guardians of Faith in Modern Times: 'Ulama in the Middle East.* Leiden: Brill, 2009.

Haugbolle, Sune. *War and Memory in Lebanon.* New York, NY: Cambridge University Press, 2010.

Haykel, Bernard. *Revival and Reform in Islam: The Legacy of Muhammad al-Shawkani.* Cambridge: Cambridge University Press, 2003.

Haykel, Bernard, Thomas Hegghammer, and Stephane Lacroix, ed. *Saudi Arabia in Transitionl.* New York, NY: Cambridge University Press, 2015.

Hirshkind, Charles. *The Ethical Soundscape: Cassette Sermons and the Islamic Counterpublic.* New York: Columbia University Press, 2006.

"Hizbollah and the Lebanese Crisis." *International Crisis Group,* October 10, 2007. www.crisisgroup.org/~/media/Files/Middle%20East%20North%20Africa/ Ira%20Syria%20Lebanon/Lebanon/69_hizbollah_and_the_lebanese_crisis .pdf (accessed October 3, 2010).

Ho, Engseng. "Empire through Diasporic Eyes: A View from the Other Boat." *Comparative Studies in Society and History* 46, no. 2 (2004).

Hoigilt, Jacob and Frida Nome. "Egyptian Salafism in Revolution." *Journal of Islamic Studies* 25, no. 1 (2015): 33–54.

Holland, Dororthy, Gretchen Fox and Vinci Daro. "Social Movements and Collective Identity: A Decentered, Dialogic View." *Anthropological Quarterly* 81, no. 1 (2008): 95–126.

Humphrey, Caroline and James Laidlaw. *The Archetypal Actions of Ritual: A Theor of Ritual Illustrated by the Jain Rite of Worship.* New York, NY: Oxford University Press,1994.

Imad, Abdul Ghany. "A Topography of Sunni Islamic Organizations and Movements in Lebanon." *Contemporary Arab Affairs* 2, no. 1 (2009): 143–161.

Inge, Anabel. *The Making of a Salafi Muslim Women: Paths to Conversion.* Oxford: Oxford University Press, 2016.

'Itani, Fida'. *al-Jihadiyyun fi-Lubnan: min Quwwat al-Fajr ila Fath al-Islam.* Bayrut: al Saqi, 2008.

Jasper, James M. and Jane D. Poulsen. "Recruiting Strangers and Friends: Moral Shocks and Social Networks in Animal Rights and Anti-Nuclear Protests." 42, no. 4 (1995).

al-Jawziyya, Ibn Qayyim. *Ighathat al-Lahfan Min Masayid al-Shaytan,* http://saaid .net/book/search.php?do=all&u=%C7%C8%E4+%DE%ED%E3 (accessed August 7, 2012).

Johnston, Hank and Bert Klandermans, eds. *Social Movements and Culture.* Minneapolis: University of Minnesota Press, 1995.

Joseph, Suad. "Connectivity and Patriarchy among Urban Working-Class Arab Families in Lebanon." *Ethos* 21, no. 4 (1993): 452–484.

Kaag, Mayke. "Aid, UMMA, and Politics: Transnational Islamic NGOs in Chad." In *Islam and Muslim Politics in Africa* edited by Benjamin F. Soares and René Otayek. New York, NY: Palgrave Macmillan, 2007.

Kamrava, Mehran. 'Royal Factionalism and Political Liberalization in Qatar.' *Middle East Journal* 63, no. 3 (2009): 401–420.

Qatar: *Small State Big Politics*. Ithaca, NY and London: Cornell University Press, 2013.

Kepel, Gilles. *Jihad: The Trail of Political Islam*. London: I. B. Tauris, 2006.

Kabha, Mustafa and Haggai Erlich. "Al-Ahbash and Wahhabiyya: Interpretations of Islam." *International Journal of Middle Eastern Studies* 38, no. 4 (2006): 519–538.

Kerr, Malcolm. *The Arab Cold War: Gamal 'Abd al-Nasir and His Rivals, 1958–1970*, 3rd edn. London and New York, NY: Oxford University Press, 1971.

Khalaf, Samir. *Civil and Uncivil Violence in Lebanon*. New York, NY and Chichester: Columbia University Press, 2002.

Khuri, Fuad I. "The Ulama: A Comparative Study of Sunni and Shi'a Religious Officials." *Middle Eastern Studies* 23, no. 3 (1987): 291–312.

King, Stephen. *The New Authoritarianism in the Middle East and North Africa*. Bloomington: Indiana University Press, 2009.

Klandermans, Bert and Dirk Oegema. "Potentials, Networks, Motivations, and Barriers: Steps towards Participation in Social Movements." *American Sociological Review* 52, no. 4 (1987): 519–531.

Knudsen, Are and Malcolm Kerr, eds. *Lebanon after the Cedar Revolution*. London: Hurst, 2012.

Kohlberg, Etan. "The Term 'Rāfida' in Imāmī Shī'ī Usage." *Journal of the American Oriental Society* 99, no. 4 (1979): 677–679.

de Koning, Martijn. "Changing Worldviews and Friendship: An Exploration of the Life Stories of Two Female Salafis in the Netherlands." In *Global Salafism: Islam's New Religious Movement* edited by Roel Meijer. New York: Columbia University Press, 2009.

"Between the Prophet and Paradise: The Salafi Struggle in the Netherlands." *Canadian Journal of Netherlandic Studies* 33–34, no. 2–1 (2012–2013): 17–34.

Kuran, Timur. "Islamic Economics and the Islamic Subeconomy." *Journal of Economic Perspectives* 9, no. 4 (1995): 155–173.

Lacroix, Stephane. "Al-Albani's Revolutionary Approach to Hadith." *ISIM Review* 21, no. 1 (2008): 6–7.

"Between Revolution and Apoliticism: Nasir al-Din al-Albani and His Impact on the Shaping of Contemporary Salafism." In *Global Salafism: Islam's New Religious Movement* edited by Roel Meijer. New York, NY: Columbia University Press, 2009.

Awakening Islam: The Politics of Religious Dissent in Contemporary Saudi Arabia. Cambridge, MA and London: Harvard University Press, 2011.

Lauziere, Henri. *The Making of Salafism: Islamic Reform in the Twentieth Century*. New York, NY: Columbia University Press, 2015.

Le Gall, Dina. *A Culture of Sufism: Naqshbandīs in the Ottoman World, 1450–1700*. Albany: State University of New York Press, 2005.

"Lebanon: Hizbollah's Weapons Turn Inward." *International Crisis Group Policy Briefing*, May 15, 2008. www.crisisgroup.org/en/regions/middle-east-north-africa/egypt- syria-lebanon/lebanon/b023-lebanon-hizbollahs-weapons-turn-inward.aspx (accessed November 15, 2012).

Leichtman, Mara A. "The Legacy of Transnational Lives: Beyond the First Generation of Lebanese in Senegal." *Ethnic and Racial Studies* 28, no. 4 (2005): 663–686.

Lefevre, Raphael. The "Islamic Emirate" of North Lebanon: The Rise and Fall of the Tawheed Movement in Lebanon, 1982–1985. Cambridge: Unpublished Ph.D. Thesis Submitted at the University of Cambridge, Department of Politics and International Studies, 2016.

"The Roots of Crisis in Northern Lebanon," *Report*, Carnegie Middle East Center, April 2014, http://carnegieendowment.org/files/crisis_northern_lebanon.pdf (accessed January 28, 2017).

Lofland John and Rodney Stark. "Becoming a World-saver: A Theory of Conversion to a Deviant Perspective." *American Sociological Review* 30, no. 6 (1965): 862–875.

al-Madkhali, Rabi' bin Hadi. *Jama'a Wahida La Jama'at Wa Sirat Wahid La 'Asharat: Hiwar Ma' 'Abd al-Rahman 'Abd al-Khaliq* (without date and publisher). www.rabee.net/show_des.aspx?pid=1&id=17&gid= (accessed October 11, 2011).

Mahmood, Saba. *Politics of Piety: The Islamic Revival and the Feminist Subject.* Princeton, NJ: Princeton University Press. 2005.

Makdisi, Ussama. *The Culture of Sectarianism: Community, History, and Violence in Nineteenth-Century Ottoman Lebanon.* Berkeley, Los Angeles, London: University of California Press, 2000.

Marcinkowski, Muhammad Ismail. "Some Reflections on Alleged Twelver Shi'ite Attitudes Toward the Integrity of the Qur'an." *The Muslim World* 91, nos. 1–2 (2001): 137–154.

Martin, Richard C. and Abbas Barzegar. "Formations of Orthodoxy: Authority, Power and Networks in Muslim Societies." In *Rethinking Islamic Studies: From Orientalism to Cosmopolitanism* edited by Carl W. Ernst and Richard C. Martin. Columbia: The University of South Carolina Press, 2010.

al-Masri, Zakariyya. *Dawr al-Imbaraturiyya al-Shi'iyya al-Shuyu'iyya.* Tarablus: Markaz Hamza, 2007.

Istratijiyyat al-Sahwa al-Islamiyya fi-Kayfiyyat al-Ta'amul ma'al-'Almaniyya al-Shariqiyya wa-l-'Almaniyya al-Gharbiyya: Fikra Islamiyya Jami'a (Tarablus: Markaz Hamza, 2009).

Masud, Muhammad Khalid. "Ikhtilaf al-Fuqaha: Diversity in Fiqh as a Social Construction." In *Equality and Justice in the Muslim* Family edited by Zainah Anwar. Petaling Jaya, Malaysia: Musawah, 2009.

Matesan, Ioana Emy. "What Makes Negative Frames Resonant? Hamas and the Appeal of Opposition to the Peace Process." *Terrorism and Political Violence* 24, no. 5 (2012): 671–705.

Meijer, Roel, ed. *Global Salafism: Islam's New Religious Movement.* New York, NY: Columbia University Press, 2009.

"Commanding Right and Forbidding Wrong as a Principle of Social Action: The Case of the Egyptian al-Jama'a al-Islamiyya." In *Global Salafism: Islam's New Religious Movement* edited by Roel Meijer. New York, NY: Columbia University Press, 2009.

Melucci, Alberto. *Nomads of the Present: Social Movements and Individual Needs in Contemporary Society.* Philadelphia, PA: Temple University Press, 1989.

"The Process of Collective Identity." In *Social Movements and Culture* edited by Hank Johnston and Bert Klandermans. Minneapolis: University of Minnesota Press, 1995.

Menza, Mohamed Fahmy. *Patronage Politics in Egypt: The National Democratic Party and Muslim Brotherhood in Cairo.* London and New York, NY: Routledge, 2013.

Merone, Fabio. "Enduring Class Struggle in Tunisia: The Fight for Identity beyond Political Islam." *British Journal of Middle Eastern Studies* 42, no. 1 (2015): 74–87.

Meyer, Birgit. *Aesthetic Formations: Media, Religion, and the Senses.* New York: Palgrave Macmillan, 2009.

Meyer, Birgit, ed. "From Imagined Communities to Aesthetic Formations: Religious Mediations, Sensational Forms, and Styles of Binding." In *Aesthetic Formations: Media, Religion, and the Senses* edited by Birgit Meyer. New York, NY: Palgrave Macmillan, 2009.

Mohamed, Abdul Fatah S. "The Qatar Authority for Charitable Activities (QACA) from Commencement to Dissolution (2004–2009)." In *Gulf Charities and Islamic Philanthropy: The "Age of Terror and Beyond"* edited by Robert Lacey and Jonathan Benthall. Berlin: Gerlach Press, 2014.

Mouline, Nabil. "Enforcing and Reinforcing the State's Islam: The Functioning of the Committee of Senior Scholars." In *Saudi Arabia in Transition* edited by Bernard Haykel, Thomas Hegghammer and Stephane Lacroix. New York, NY: Cambridge University Press, 2015.

al-Mudayris, Falah. *Al-Jama'a al-Salafiya fi-l-Kuwait: al-Nasha't wa-l-Fikr wa-l-Tatawwur 1965–1999.* Kuwait: Dar Qurtas li-l-Nashr, 1999.

Mueller, Carol M. "Conflict Networks and the Origins of Women's Liberation." In *Social Movements: From Ideology to Identity* edited by Enrique Larana, Hank Johnston and Robert R. Gusfield. Philadelphia, PA: Temple University Press, 1994.

Murtada, Radwan. "Marmulak al-Lubnani: Mawlana al-Nassab, Man Yuhasibahu?" *al Akhbar*, September 27, 2011.

al-Mutayri, Hakim. *Al-Hurriyya aw al-Tawfan.* Beirut: Al-Mu'assasa al-'Arabiyya li-l-Dirasat wa-l-Nashr, 2008.

al-Nashif, Nada and Samir El-Khoury. "Palestinian Employment in Lebanon: Facts and Challenges," *International Labour Organization Report*, February 27, 2014.

Nasr, Vali. *The Shia Revival: How Conflicts Within Islam Will Shape the Future.* New York, NY: W. W. Norton, 2006.

Noor, Farish A. *Islam on the Move: The Tablighi Jama'at in Southeast Asia.* Amsterdam: Amsterdam University Press, 2012.

Norton, Augustus R. *AMAL and the Shi'a: Struggle for the Soul of Lebanon.* Austin: University of Texas Press, 1987.

Hezbollah: A Short History. Princeton, NJ: Princeton University Press, 2007.

Opp, Karl-Dieter and Christiane Gern. "Dissident Groups, Personal Networks, and Spontaneous Cooperation: The East German Revolution of 1989." *American Sociological Review* 58, no. 3 (1993): 659–680.

Othman, Aida. "'And Amicable Settlement Is Best': Sulh and Dispute Resolution in Islamic Law." *Arab Law Quarterly* 21 (2007): 64–90.

Otterbeck, Jonas. "Wahhabi Ideology of Social Control versus a New Publicness in Saudi Arabia." *Contemporary Islam* 6, no. 3 (2012): 341–353.

Pall, Zoltan. *Lebanese Salafism between the Gulf and Europe: Development, Fractionalization and Transnational Networks of Salafism in Lebanon.* Amsterdam: Amsterdam University Press, 2013.

"Between Ideology and International Politics: The Dynamics and Transformation of a Transnational Islamic Charity." In *Religion and the Politics of Development: Priests, Potentates, and "Progress"* edited by Philip Michael Fountain, Robin Bush and Michael Feener. London: Palgrave Macmillan, 2015.

"Kuwaiti Salafism and Its Growing Influence in the Levant." *Carnegie Middle East Papers,* May 2014, http://carnegieendowment.org/files/kuwaiti_salafists.pdf (accessed May 28, 2015.

"Kuwaiti Salafism after the Arab Uprisings." In *Salafism after the Arab Awakening* edited by Francesco Cavatorta and Fabio Merone. London: Hurst, 2017.

Pargeter, Alison. *The Muslim Brotherhood: The Burden of Tradition,* Kindle e-book edition. London: SAQI, 2010.

Peters, F. E. *The Hajj: The Muslim Pilgrimage to Mecca and the Holy Places.* Princeton, NJ: Princeton University Press, 1994.

Peters, Rudolf. "From Jurists' Law to Statute Law or What Happens When the Shari'a is Codified." *Mediterranean Politics* 7, no. 3 (2002): 82–95.

Crime and Punishment in Islamic Law. Cambridge and New York, NY: Cambridge University Press, 2005.

Petersen, Marie Juul. "Islamizing Aid: Transnational Muslim NGOs after 9.11." *Voluntas* 23, no. 1 (2012): 126–155.

"Trajectories of Transnational Muslim NGOs." *Development in Practice* 22, no. 5–6 (2012): 763–778.

Peterson, Jennifer. "Going to the Mulid Street-Smart Spirituality in Egypt." In *An Anthropology of Everyday Religion: Ordinary Lives and Grand Schemes* edited by Samuli Schielke and Liza Debevec. New York, NY and London: Berghahn Books, 2012.

Polletta, Francesca. "Free Spaces in Collective Action." *Theory and Society* 28, no. 1 (1999): 1–38.

Portes, Alejandro. "Social Capital: Its Origins and Applications in Modern Sociology." *Annual Review of Sociology* 24 (1998): 1–24.

Price, Charles, Donald Nonini and Erich Fox Tree. "Grounded Utopian Movements: Subjects or Neglect." *Anthropological Quarterly* 81, no. 1 (2008): 127–159.

Rabil, Robert G. *Religion, National Identity, and Confessional Politics in Lebanon: The Challenge of Islamism.* New York, NY: Palgrave Macmillan, 2011.

Salafism in Lebanon: From Apoliticism to Transnational Jihadism. Washington, DC: Georgetown University Press, 2014.

Al-Rasheed, Madawi. *Contesting the Saudi State: Islamic Voices from a New Generation.* Cambridge: Cambridge University Press, 2007.

Robertson, Roland. *Globalization: Social Theory and Global Culture.* London: SAGE Publications, 1992.

Rougier, Bernard. *Everyday Jihad.* Cambridge, MA and London: Harvard University Press, 2007.

al-Sa'idi, Salih Baraka. *Al-Sulta wa-l-Tayyarat al-Siyasiyya fi al-Kuwait: Jadaliyyat al-Ta'awun wa-l-Sira'*. Kuwait: Dar al-Qabas, 2010.

The Sunni Tragedy in the Middle East: Northern Lebanon from al-Qaeda to ISIS. Princeton, NJ: Princeton University Press, 2015.

Saab, Bilal Y. and Magnus Ranstorp. "Securing Lebanon from the Threat of Salafist Jihadism." *Studies in Conflict & Terrorism* 30, no. 10 (2007): 825–855.

Salloukh, Bassel. "Syria and Lebanon: A Brotherhood Transformed." *MERIP* 35, no. 3 (2005), http://ns2.merip.org/mer/mer236/syria-lebanon-brother hood-transformed (accessed May 14, 2013).

"The Limits of Electoral Engineering in Divided Societies: Elections in Postwar Lebanon." *Canadian Journal of Political Science* 39, no. 3 (2006): 635–655.

Schielke, Samuli. "Being Good in Ramadan: Ambivalence, Fragmentation, and the Moral Self in the Lives of Young Egyptians." *Journal of the Royal Anthropological Institute* 15, no. s1 (2009): 24–40.

Egypt in the Future Tense: Hope, Frustration and Ambivalence before and after 2011. Kindle Edition. Bloomington: Indiana University Press, 2015.

Schielke, Samuli and Liza Debevec, eds. *An Anthropology of Everyday Religion: Ordinary Lives and Grand Schemes*. New York, NY and London: Berghahn Books, 2012.

Schwartz, David. "Bridging the Study of Culture and Religion: Pierre Bourdieu's Political Economy of Symbolic Power." *Sociology of Religion* 57, no. 1 (1996): 71–85.

Seal, Patrick. *Asad: The Struggle for the Middle East*. Berkeley and Los Angeles: University of California Press, 1995.

bin Shabib, Daghash al-'Ajmi. *Umara' wa-'Ulama min al-Kuwait 'ala 'Aqidat al-Salaf*. (no publisher): Kuwait, 2008.

Shanahan, Rodger. "Shia Political Development in Iraq: The Case of the Islamic Dawa Party." *Third World Quarterly* 25, no. 5 (2004): 943–954.

Shephard, William E. *Sayyid Qutb and Islamic Activism: A Translation and Critical Analysis of Social Justice in Islam*. Leiden: Brill, 1996.

Sikand, Yoginder. "The Tablighi Jama'at and Politics: A Critical Re-Appraisal." *The Muslim World* 96, no. 1 (2006): 175–195.

Singerman, Diane. "The Networked World of Islamist Social Movements." In *Islamic Activism: A Social Movement Theory Approach* edited by Quintan Wiktorowicz. Indiana: Indiana University Press, 2004.

Skovgaard-Petersen, Jakob. "The Sunni Religious Scene in Beirut." *Mediterranean Politics* 3, no. 1 (1998): 69–90.

Snow, David and Richard Machalek. "The Sociology of Conversion." *Annual Review of Sociology* 10 (1984): 167–190.

Snow, David and Robert D. Benford. "Ideology, Frame Resonance, and Participant Mobilization." *International Social Movement Research* 1, no. 1 (1988): 197–217.

Snow, David, Sarah A. Soule and Hanspeter Kriesi, eds. *Readings in Contemporary Political Sociology*. Oxford: Blackwell Publishers, 2000.

Soage, Ana Belén. "Rashid Rida's Legacy." *The Muslim World* 98, no. 1 (2008): 1–23.

Soares, Benjamin F. and René Otayek, eds. *Islam and Muslim Politics in Africa*. New York, NY: Palgrave Macmillan, 2007.

Stark, Rodney and William Sims Bainbridge. "Networks of Faith: Interpersonal Bonds and Recruitment to Cults and Sects." *The American Journal of Sociology* 85, no. 6 (1980): 1376–1395.

Steinberg, Guido. "Jihadi Salafism and the Shi'is: Remarks about the Intellectual Roots of anti-Shi'ism." In *Global Salafism: Islam's New Religious Movement* edited by Roel Meijer. New York, NY: Columbia University Press, 2009.

"Qatar and the Arab Spring: Support for Islamists and the New Anti-Syrian Policy." Report: German Institute for International and Security Affairs, February 7, 2012. www.swp-berlin.org/en/publications/swp-comments-en/swp-aktuelle-details/article/qatar_and_the_arab_spring.html (accessed June 6, 2013).

al-Sulaymani, Abi Hasan. *al-Tafjirat wa-l-Ightiyalat*. Kuwait: Jama'iyyat SRIH al-Islami, 2008.

Tabar, Paul. Lebanon: A Country of Emigration and Immigration. Report, Center for Migration and Refugee Studies at the American University of Cairo, 2007. http://schools.aucegypt.edu/GAPP/cmrs/reports/Docu ments/Tabar080711.pdf (accessed December 19, 2015).

Tatar-Lahoud, Carine. *Islam et politique au Koweït*. Paris: PUF, 2011.

Taylor, Verta and Nancy Whittier. "Analytical Approaches to Social Movement Culture: The Culture of the Women's Movement." In *Social Movements and Culture* edited by Hank Johnston and Bert Klandermans. Minneapolis: University of Minnesota Press, 1995.

at-Tayebi, Abdul Kader. 'Voluntary Fasting in Islam' www.sahihmuslim .com/sps/sp.cfm?subsecID=IBD09&articleID=IBD090001&articlePages=1, (accessed March 16, 2015).

Telhami, Yvette. "The Syrian Muslim Brothers and the Syrian-Iranian Relationship." *Middle East Journal* 63 no. 4 (2009): 561–580.

Terje Ostebo. *Localising Salafism: Religious Change among the Oromo Muslims in Bale, Ethiopia*. Leiden: Brill, 2011.

Tétreault, Mary Ann. *Stories of Democracy: Politics and Society in Contemporary Kuwait*. New York, NY: Columbia University Press, 2000.

"Bottom-Up Democratization in Kuwait." In *Political Change in the Arab Gulf States: Stuck in Transition* edited by Mary Ann Tétreault, Gwenn Okruhlik and Andrzej Kapiszewski. Boulder, CO: Lynne Rienner Publishers, 2011.

"The New Lebanese Equation: The Christians' Central Role." *International Crisis Group Policy Briefing*, July 15, 2008. www.crisisgroup.org/en/regions/ middle-eastnorth-africa/egypt-syria-lebanon/lebanon/078-the-new-lebanese-equation-the-christians-central-role.aspx (accessed November 15, 2012).

Thompson, Elisabeth. *Colonial Citizens: Republican Rights, Paternal Privilege, and Gender in French Syria and Lebanon*. New York, NY and Chichester: Columbia University Press, 2000.

Thurston, Alexander. *Salafism in Nigeria: Islam, Preaching and Politics*, Kindle Edition. Cambridge: Cambridge University Press, 2016.

Torelli, Stefano M., Fabio Merone and Francesco Cavatorta. "Salafism in Tunisia: Challenges and Opportunities for Democratization." *Middle East Policy* 19, no. 4 (2012): 140–154.

Traboulsi, Fawwaz. *A History of Modern Lebanon*. London: Pluto Press, 2007.

Tucker, Judith E. *Women, Family and Gender in Islamic Law*. Cambridge and New York, NY: Cambridge University Press, 2008.

Turner, Victor and Edith Turner. *Image and Pilgrimage in Christian Culture*. New York, NY: Columbia University Press, 1978.

Ulrichsen, Christian Coates. "Qatar and the Arab Spring: Policy Drivers and Regional Implications." *Carnegie Middle East Papers*, September 24, 2014, http://carnegieendowment.org/2014/09/24/qatar-and-arab-spring-policy-drivers-and regional-implications (accessed May 26, 2015).

Verter, Bradford. "Theorizing Religion with Bourdieu against Bourdieu." *Sociological Theory* 21, no. 2 (2003): 150–174.

Vloeberghs, Waard. "The Hariri Political Dynasty after the Arab Spring." *Mediterranean Politics* 17, no. 2, (2012): 241–248.

Wagemakers, Joas. "The Transformation of a Radical Concept: al-wala' wa-l-bara' in the Ideology of Abu Muhammad al-Maqdisi." In *Global Salafism: Islam's New Religious Movement* edited by Roel Meijer. New York, NY: Columbia University Press, 2009.

A Quietist Jihadi: The Ideology and Influence of Abu Muhammad al Maqdisi. Cambridge: Cambridge University Press, 2012.

"Revisiting Wiktorowicz: Categorising and Defining the Branches of Salafism." In *Salafism after the Arab Awakening* edited by Cavatorta and Merone, New York, NY: Oxford University Press, 2015.

Salafism in Jordan: Political Islam in a Quietist Community. Cambridge: Cambridge University Press, 2016.

Wasti, Tahir. *The Application of Islamic Criminal Law in Pakistan*. Leiden and Boston, MA: Brill, 2009.

Weber, Max. *Economy and Society: An Outline of Interpretive Sociology*. Berkeley, Los Angeles, London: University of California Press, 1978.

Weimann, Gunnar Jochen. *Islamic Criminal Law in Northern Nigeria: Politics, Religion, Judicial Practice*. Amsterdam: Amsterdam University Press, 2010.

Welchman, Lynn. "The Bedouin Judge, the Mufti and the Chief Islamic Justice: Competing Legal Regimes in the Occupied Palestinian Territories." *Journal of Palestine Studies* 38, no. 1 (2008): 6–23.

White, Jenny B. *Civic Culture and Islam in Urban Turkey*. New York: Routledge, 1996.

Whittier, Nancy. *Feminist Generations: The Persistence of the Radical Women's Movement*. Philadelphia, PA: Temple University Press, 1995.

Wiktorowicz, Quintan. "The Salafi Movement in Jordan." *International Journal of Middle Eastern Studies* 32, no. 2 (2000): 219–240.

ed. *Islamic Activism: A Social Movement Theory Approach*. Indiana: Indiana University Press, 2004.

"Anatomy of the Salafi Movement." *Studies in Conflict and Terrorism* 29, no. 2 (2006): 207–239.

Yamani, May. "The Two Faces of Saudi Arabia." *Survival* 50, no. 1 (2008): 143–156.

Zaman, Muhammad Qasim. *The Ulama in Contemporary Islam*. Princeton, NJ: Princeton University Press, 2002.

al-Zumai, Ali Fahed. *The Intellectual and Historical Development of the Islamic Movement in Kuwait*. Exeter: Unpublished Ph.D. Thesis, 1988.

Index

Other Books in the Series